D1546086

Third Edition

Questioning Sociology

Canadian Perspectives

Edited by
Myra J. Hird
George Pavlich

OXFORD
UNIVERSITY PRESS

OXFORD
UNIVERSITY PRESS

Oxford University Press is a department of the University of Oxford.
It furthers the University's objective of excellence in research, scholarship,
and education by publishing worldwide. Oxford is a registered trade mark of
Oxford University Press in the UK and in certain other countries.

Published in Canada by
Oxford University Press
8 Sampson Mews, Suite 204,
Don Mills, Ontario M3C 0H5 Canada

www.oupcanada.com

Copyright © Oxford University Press Canada 2017

The moral rights of the author have been asserted

Database right Oxford University Press (maker)

First Edition published in 2006
Second Edition published in 2012

All rights reserved. No part of this publication may be reproduced, stored in
a retrieval system, or transmitted, in any form or by any means, without the
prior permission in writing of Oxford University Press, or as expressly permitted
by law, by licence, or under terms agreed with the appropriate reprographics
rights organization. Enquiries concerning reproduction outside the scope of the
above should be sent to the Permissions Department at the address above
or through the following url: www.oupcanada.com/permission/permission_request.php

Every effort has been made to determine and contact copyright holders.
In the case of any omissions, the publisher will be pleased to make
suitable acknowledgement in future editions.

Library and Archives Canada Cataloguing in Publication
Questioning sociology : Canadian perspectives / edited
by Myra Hird and George Pavlich. — Third edition.

Includes bibliographical references and index.
ISBN 978-0-19-902010-2 (paperback)

1. Canada—Social conditions—Textbooks. 2. Sociology—
Textbooks. I. Pavlich, George Clifford, editor II. Hird, Myra
J., editor
HN103.5.Q47 2016   301.0971   C2016-905038-6

Cover image: Garry Gay/Getty Images

Oxford University Press is committed to our environment.
This book is printed on Forest Stewardship Council® certified paper
and comes from responsible sources.

Printed and bound in the United States of America
1 2 3 4 — 20 19 18 17

Contents

5 Does "the Family" Exist?
Catherine Krull

Part II · Social Questions 61

6 Is Social Welfare Viable?
Lois Harder

7 What Are the Social Determinants of Health?
Elaine M. Power

8 How Do Immigrants Integrate?
Lori Wilkinson

9 What Are the Challenges of Economic Transition? Exploring the Consequences of Regional Dynamics and Global Shifts
Jennifer Jarman

10 What Is Communication?
Sandra Robinson

11 How Does Media Transform Society?
Daniel Downes

12 Should Policing Be Privatized?
Curtis Clarke

13 What Do Official Statistics Tell Us about Ourselves?
Nob Doran

14 Who Governs Whom in Canada?
Dawn Moore

Part III · Critical Sociological Imaginations 165

15 How Do We Help the Environment?
Myra J. Hird

16 What Is Sovereignty for Indigenous People?
Vanessa Watts

17 What Is Sovereignty in Quebec?
Philippe Couton

18 Is There Justice for Young People?
Bryan Hogeveen

19 Women and Prison: Who and Why?
Kelly Hannah-Moffat

20 How Is Aging a Critical Sociological Problem?
Stephen Katz

21 What Is Global Inequality?
Amy Kaler

22 What Use Is Social Theory?
R.A. Sydie

23 What Questions Has Sociology Deserted?
Lorne Tepperman (with the assistance of Zoe Sebastien)

Acknowledgments

The editors wish to thank all the contributors for their insight and collegiality—the product is a fitting testament to their enormous creativity and talent. We would like to acknowledge the thoughtfulness, support, encouragement, and assistance of Amy Gordon and Colleen Ste. Marie at Oxford University Press. We would also like to thank the reviewers, who provided valuable feedback on this edition:

- Janet Mary Christine Burns, University of New Brunswick
- Deborah Davidson, York University
- Jasmin Hristov, McMaster University
- Riva Lieflander, University of Ottawa
- Sandria Officer, Seneca College
- Curt Pankratz, University of Winnipeg
- Stephanie Skourtes, University of British Columbia

George Pavlich thanks Myra Hird for her friendship of many years. He dedicates his efforts to Carla Spinola, Seth Pavlich, and the memory of Tally Pavlich.

Myra Hird thanks George Pavlich for his enduring friendship and dedicates this book to Eshe, Inis, and Anth.

Contributors

Barry D. Adam
Distinguished Professor, Department of Sociology, Anthropology, and Criminology, University of Windsor, Windsor, ON

Curtis Clarke
Deputy Minister, Alberta Education, Government of Alberta, Edmonton, AB.

Philippe Couton
Associate Professor, Department of Sociology, University of Ottawa, Ottawa, ON

Dawn H. Currie
Professor, Department of Sociology, University of British Columbia, Vancouver, BC

Erin Dej
Postdoctoral Fellow, Canadian Observatory on Homelessness, York University, Toronto, ON

Nob Doran
Professor, Department of Social Sciences, University of New Brunswick (Saint John Campus), Saint John, NB

Daniel Downes
Chair, Department of Social Sciences; Associate Professor, Department of Information and Communications Studies, University of New Brunswick (Saint John Campus), Saint John, NB

Kelly Hannah-Moffat
Professor, Centre for Criminology and Sociolegal Studies, University of Toronto, Toronto, ON

Lois Harder
Professor, Department of Political Science, University of Alberta, Edmonton, AB

Myra J. Hird
Professor, School of Environmental Studies, Queen's University, Kingston, ON

Bryan Hogeveen
Associate Professor, Department of Sociology, University of Alberta, Edmonton, AB

Jennifer Jarman
Associate Professor, Interdisciplinary Studies and Sociology, Lakehead University, Orillia, ON

Amy Kaler
Professor, Department of Sociology, University of Alberta, Edmonton, AB

Stephen Katz
Professor, Department of Sociology, Trent University, Peterborough, ON

Deirdre M. Kelly
Professor, Department of Educational Studies, University of British Columbia, Vancouver, BC

Catherine Krull
Professor of Sociology, Dean of Social Sciences, University of Victoria, Victoria, BC

Dawn Moore
Associate Professor of Legal Studies, Department of Law, Carleton University, Ottawa, ON

George Pavlich
Canada Research Chair in Social Theory, Culture and Law, Professor of Law and Sociology, University of Alberta, Edmonton, AB

Elaine M. Power
Associate Professor, School of Kinesiology and Health Studies, Queen's University, Kingston, ON

Sandra Robinson
Instructor II, Communication and Media Studies, School of Journalism and Communication, Carleton University, Ottawa, ON

R.A. Sydie
Professor Emerita, Department of Sociology, University of Alberta, Edmonton, AB

Lorne Tepperman
Professor, Department of Sociology, University of Toronto, Toronto, ON

Vanessa Watts
Director, Indigenous Studies Program, McMaster University, Hamilton, ON

Lori Wilkinson
Professor, Department of Sociology, University of Manitoba, Winnipeg, MB

Introduction: Sociological Questions

George Pavlich and Myra J. Hird

What Is Sociology?

As with other disciplines, this question attracts almost as many responses as the number of texts in which it is raised. Not wishing to add a static response to that dubious record, we will avoid describing sociology as a field definable by a fixed object of study, a core set of theoretical texts, a required theoretical approach, or even as a discipline held together by the use of one (scientific?) method.[1] Instead, this book identifies sociology as a discipline that resists integration; it is an ever-evolving craft, a process of systematically understanding, conceptualizing, and engaging our historically specific relations with others and the wider consequences of these relations. Framed thus, sociology emerges as a changing but systematic attempt to create, assemble, or reassemble concepts to examine the assumptions that shape our relations with others as historical forms of social being.

Such a view echoes the work of an influential sociologist, C. Wright Mills (1916–62), who viewed sociology as providing spaces to create a uniquely sociological imagination. For Mills (1959), the sociological imagination may be described as a "quality of mind" that seeks to "achieve lucid summations of what is going on in the world" (5). As the basis of sociology, this frame of mind promises "an understanding of the intimate realities of ourselves in connection with larger social realities" (15). Sociologists, for Mills, develop this quality of mind by making imaginative leaps to connect the most intimate of personal "troubles" (experienced by particular individuals) to a history of the most general structures that shape a given society. Such leaps enable us to develop broader understandings of ourselves by connecting our current self-identities and wider socio-historical formations. The understandings help us to address the social patterns "of which we are at once creatures and creators" (164).

The sociological imagination forms one part of the history of sociology—a history that reaches back beyond Mills's writings to the work of nineteenth- and early-twentieth-century theorists such as August Comte, Karl Marx, Max Weber,

Émile Durkheim, and Herbert Spencer. These theorists' influential thinking permeates the ideas and research found in this book. For instance, Auguste Comte (1798–1857) is credited with coining the term *sociology* in the early nineteenth century; he outlined a positivist sociology that was meant scientifically to explain the morality shaping our relations with others and, thus, to provide a way to secure social progress. In the late nineteenth century, Karl Marx (1818–83) developed a comprehensive critique of capitalist society based upon the unequal relations individuals have with modes of production, labour, and property, a critique that continues to inspire radical sociological analyses of societies and their political economies today. Also writing in the late nineteenth and early twentieth centuries, Max Weber (1864–1920) provided a theory of how a kind of rational (means–ends) way of thinking had radically transformed most areas of society, creating distinctively modern political, economic, legal, cultural, and social institutions. A good example of this rationalization process occurred in the administration of modern societies, which increasingly relied on formal bureaucracies that operate with great efficiency but come at the cost of ridding the world of magical enchantment and diminishing life to a cold "iron cage" of rationality. Weber's analysis of bureaucracy still inspires many critical sociological analyses, including studies of organizations, rationalization, and authority. Émile Durkheim (1858–1917) focused his attention on understanding both how individuals are shaped by independent "social facts" and how the structures of given societies are shaped by basic underlying factors, such as the changing divisions of labour within a group. Nineteenth-century theorist Herbert Spencer (1820–1903) was keenly interested in applying Darwinian evolutionary theory to society, and he coined the phrase "survival of the fittest" to describe how individuals interact with one other in society.

Although quite different in their various ideas and theories, what each of these founding sociological theorists shared was a commitment to situating individual beliefs, values, and actions within a wider group and societal context. Put another way, each of these founding theorists argued both that individuals cannot be understood outside of their societal milieu and that sociology offers a unique way of analyzing this social context.

In keeping with this fundamental starting point, and working within Mills's sociological imagination as a helpful and accessible way of thinking about the relationships between individuals and society, this introduction explores different facets of the sociological imagination in four related sections. The first section uses hypothetical examples to describe basic characteristics of the sociological imagination, while the second situates sociological thinking against other disciplines. The third section outlines three influential theoretical approaches in sociology often used to help create sociological imaginations. In the fourth section, we discuss the basic role that questions play in formulating a sociological imagination. Reflecting a central theme of this book, this section shows how fundamental questions can arrest everyday views of the world and open us up to a reflexive sociological imagination.

Sociologists and the Sociological Imagination

What sort of thinking is distinctive, although not necessarily exclusive, to sociology? In responding to this question, and to elaborate upon Mills's previously noted "quality of mind," it is important to differentiate between two of many possible ways of thinking about the world—namely, the *everyday* approach and the *sociological* approach.[2] Typically, we rely on everyday, taken-for-granted assumptions to help us negotiate our lives. I may, for instance, know that I am in a hurry because I am late for an appointment. This perception encourages me to drive faster or speed up my walking pace. In such circumstances, we seldom stop to consider the underlying assumptions of time or the actions that follow from our common impressions of time. We do not ordinarily question what is assumed when claiming to "be in a hurry" or trying to "keep an appointment." For instance, we seldom reflect on how the idea of "hurry" relates to socially established conventions of time or how these ideas are ingrained in the sorts of individuals that we are. The common-sense meaning maps that we use to guide us through life, once learned through socialization, become taken-for-granted frameworks that condition our everyday thinking and actions.

To take a related example, you might ask someone, "Excuse me, what is the time?" Ordinarily, you would not expect that person to engage me in a philosophical discussion of time or a history of how global time standards came to be established, and so on. In our everyday thinking, when we ask someone what the time is, we expect an answer like, "Oh! It is a quarter past five." In turn, you are likely to thank the person; through the interaction, both questioner and respondent embrace a shared common-sense view of time.

However, suppose the respondent happens to be a sociology major conducting fieldwork and responds thus: "What do you mean 'Do I have the time?' What is time? In what sense can one have it? Do you mean to imply that I, as a human being, can own the time?" This response is likely to strike you as facetious, if not downright rude. But it would also disturb the everyday, common-sense meanings that we ascribe to the term *time*. Through this unusual interaction, the sociology major may prompt you to consider alternative possibilities. You may, for instance, think differently when understanding and responding to your world. Were this to happen, the questions would have encouraged you to examine assumptions grounding your common-sense ways of acting around time. In the process, you might begin to experience a quality of mind that is akin to Mills's sociological imagination.

The point could also be made through an even simpler example. Let's say that I wish to hang a picture on the wall and so reach for my hammer. In this situation, I typically do not raise questions about the nature of the hammer's existence (Is it real? What is the true nature of a hammer? Who defines what a hammer is?). I simply want to use it to drive a nail into the wall. However, there are situations that propel me to reflect on the being of the hammer. Let us suppose that after repeated and accurate swings of the hammer, the nail simply does not budge. I might hold the hammer up to scrutiny, asking, "What is this confounded thing, and what is wrong with it?" These sorts of questions explicitly focus our thoughts on the hammer's existence, and prompt us to adopt an attitude beyond ordinary ways of existing. Again, events interrupt everyday patterns of thought to provoke fundamental questions, paving the way for reflective frames of mind to surface.

These examples suggest that we often harbour several different qualities of mind. On the one hand, there are our ordinary, everyday and immediately familiar patterns of thought (for example, asking the time to make a meeting or thinking about how to place the nail in the wall to hang the picture). They make up the usual, familiar attitudes through which we approach our worlds. On the other hand, there are moments where we arrest these everyday, common-sense ways of thinking and acting. A sociology major's challenging response, or my reaction to the hammer's failure, provoke more reflective thinking about the usual assumptions of time, or about the hammer's existence.

As noted, the second mode of thinking encapsulates a quality of mind akin to a sociological imagination. This sort of thinking requires a leap in which we, as participants in given social contexts, suspend our comfortable, everyday understandings of things. We do so in order to think differently about how we interact with others, and through this process we encounter the basis of sociological ways of thinking, speaking, and writing. This process moves beyond the everyday languages that make up our common-sense understandings, and appeals to theoretical languages that allow us to have a different take on similar events.

In this sense, it is not too much of a push to suggest that becoming a sociologist is akin to learning a new (analytic) language, which requires a specific kind of preparation. To think sociologically, we remain participants of ordinary life. We do our shopping, check social media, play sports, visit with friends, go to work, etc. But, in addition, we must learn to pore over particular aspects of that life from different perspectives (e.g., collective, socio-historical, critical), using the concepts derived from a dynamic, systematic, theoretical, critical, and empirically informed language. Doing so involves processes of learning how to think about collective life differently from the ways provided by everyday social meanings. A basic tool for negotiating the passage from everyday to reflexive sociological thinking is none other than the difficult, the arresting, the provocative—even if always elusive—*question*.

In this sense, as discussed later in this introduction, sociological thinking most often starts at moments of astute questioning. Such questioning challenges the limits of ordinary, common-sense frames of meaning and may lead us beyond the vocabulary and grammar of everyday thinking to sociology's conceptual languages. But how does sociological thinking relate to other academic disciplines?

The Sociological Imagination and Other Disciplines

Suppose you are drinking coffee on the deck of your friend's small urban back garden. Dew glistens on the green leaves of a maple tree, reflecting the bright morning sunlight. This tree is undoubtedly the outstanding feature of an otherwise bleak garden. Your friend's mood is glum as she tells you that she cannot pay mounting bills and debts. As a single parent, she supports a child and, when not trying to make ends meet, spends time trying to find a job that will accommodate her child-care responsibilities.

She tells of being unable to buy the basics, including groceries, water, and electricity. Your friend has fallen on hard times of late, and she talks now of knowing what the term *poverty* really means. She even confesses to thinking about pilfering some "good food" and has entertained ways of committing benefit fraud. Each time, however, she has thought better of resorting to fraud and has let her life take its increasingly strained course. She has become frazzled by her predicament, however, and blames the changing times; more specifically, she points to increasing calls for the erosion of social welfare and the increased costs of heating, water, and electricity. Unable to find a job that will allow her to tend to her child, she has become dependent upon social services and is perturbed by the identity this has foisted upon her. She stares meaningfully into her cup and sighs deeply. You place your hand, reassuringly, on her shoulder.

There are many ways to analyze this snippet of life. In academic life, different approaches are often used to distinguish between specific disciplines (e.g., engineering, anthropology, medicine, history, chemistry). However, the boundaries both within and between disciplines are never clearly defined; their borders are usually contested, they change over time, new disciplines are created, others are merged, and there are often explicit calls for interdisciplinary work. But universities still distinguish between disciplines, even if in different ways. They usually isolate social sciences and humanities from the natural sciences, medicine, etc., viewing the former as focusing on the human dimensions of a situation.

Referring to the previous example of your friend's situation, a so-called natural science such as plant biology might refer to the species of maple tree in question, enlightening us on how energy from the sun helps to sustain, through photosynthesis, the life of the tree with its bright colours. A physicist could examine the properties of the sun's refracted light through the prism-like bubbles of liquid, while a chemist might seek to establish whether the liquid in view is water or some other translucent substance secreted by the tree. The physiologist might collaborate with medical colleagues, indeed, with our noted chemist, to study the potential effects of coffee on the human body.

Within the social sciences, however, the economist might describe redistributions of money flow in free market contexts, explaining your friend's current plight as a result of basic adjustments to markets. Psychologists, by contrast, might discuss the elements of the mind that explain your friend's depressed mood and might prescribe possible treatments for her "frazzled" state. Those of a more psychoanalytic bent may interpret what lies buried in your friend's expressive sigh or in your comforting gesture. Feminist psychologists, on the other hand, might locate the effects of patriarchal power relations that sustain disproportionate gender relations and that disadvantage women. Political scientists would likely point to underlying changes to previous welfare state formations, to the ways in which the state is nowadays pressured by neo-liberal calls to surrender (i.e., sell off) many public services to private enterprise (e.g., water facilities, electricity). Classical criminologists might point to the supposed cost–benefit, rational, calculations that your friend makes before thinking about stealing. They would undoubtedly note her free choice to obey the law rather than face the punishments dealt to those who fall foul of it.

Sociologists, in comparison, are likely to approach the setting in the back garden through a rather different set of perspectives. The use of the plural form of *perspective* is deliberate, for there is little consensus on the exact ways in which sociology ought to proceed. However, there are distinguishing approaches and practices of those who aim to develop specifically *sociological* (rather than, say, economic, political, etc.) approaches. Without suggesting that there are absolute distinctions, one might say that sociology tends to be involved with naming, understanding, and critically evaluating collective patterns through which people live out their lives. These are often referred to as the *societal* aspects of contexts.

Yet, as noted, sociological imaginations are generated from many different theoretical approaches and license diverse practices, from participant observations, interviews, theorizing, critical analysis, interpretation, and political engagement to surveys, laboratory experiments, and statistical analyses. The sociological imaginations of this book's chapters, however, tend to draw on three main traditions, asking questions involving sociological traditions that themselves highlight different aspects of our relations with others as the social: subjective interaction, social structures, and social transformation. Most of the chapters draw simultaneously—in some measure at least—on aspects of all of these traditions and in various ways. Several also draw on other theoretical orientations, but to address all of these would take the present discussion too far away from its introductory aims.

Three Sociological Approaches

Subjections

First, some sociologists develop a sociological imagination from theoretical traditions centred on how we interact with other subjects. These interactions create meanings that shape our views of the world and so affect how we act. The sociological traditions are concerned with interpreting and explaining social relationships—they deal with the meanings and actions that these relationships generate. Max Weber, a key figure in developing this approach, defines social relationships thus: "The term 'social relationship' will be used to designate the situation where two or more persons are engaged in conduct wherein each takes account of the behavior of the other in a meaningful way and is therefore oriented in these terms" (1980, 63). He distinguishes between behaviour (say, a random movement of your hand) and socially meaningful behaviour (say, a wave). He calls the latter "social action." For Weber, sociology is concerned only with *social* actions and relationships.

Weberian-inspired sociological imaginations therefore focus on social actions, shared meanings, and relationships between subjects. They focus on *inter-subjectively* created meanings that guide people's actions.[3] With reference to the example in the previous section, these sociological imaginations might emphasize how you and your friend interact using meanings that both of you understand. Weberian-inspired sociological imaginations would examine how these meanings allow you to interact with one another and with the object world. They may also ask how processes of socialization (that is, how you are taught to embrace the meanings of a given society) have helped to create you and your friend as particular kinds of individuals (subjects) capable of functioning in *this* society.

Within this approach, sociologists are likely to ask the following sorts of questions: Why do you behave and think in the ways you do? How do social interactions shape people's world views, and how does the latter affect the ways people subsequently behave? How do the meanings by which you make sense of the world lead you to act more or less predictably? What wider social history makes possible the thoughts and actions that colour your friend's and your social worlds? How do you come to interpret images, actions, gestures, and words in particular ways?

To be sure, over time, people have identified themselves and each other as subjects in many different ways. For example, imagine a thirteenth-century serf is transmuted to a conversation you are having with a friend today. This serf, who hails from a radically different social context, would likely not understand the meanings you and your friend use to communicate effortlessly with one another. The serf may not even see him- or herself as an individual subject, as someone with private thoughts, capable of free ownership, and so on. An unfree peasant (serf) is a creature of a very different social world, belonging to a way of being with others that was shaped by an entirely different social context. Consequently, a peasant's view of the world (and understanding of his or her location within that world) would be very different from the beliefs of a person today.

The serf example challenges the idea that individual subjects are essentially and universally the same. At the very least, this example indicates that subjects assume very different forms, and their understandings of themselves and their worlds vary greatly—depending upon the social contexts from which they emerge. Thus, Weberian-inspired sociological approaches require us to shelve the everyday view that "I" am essentially (i.e., at my core) a constant, unchangeable, and absolute individual. These approaches draw on a theoretical tradition that views subjects as malleable creators (agents) and creatures (products, effects) of a given social history and context. Moreover, such approaches give rise to specific questions, such as those in the first part of this book, directed toward the possibility that various images of the self (as a free agent with a particular sexual orientation and ethnicity) are produced out of social interactions within a socio-historical context.

This idea—that perceptions of the self are a product of social interactions within a socio-historical context—is associated with what is known in some quarters as structuralism and post-structuralism. While these are complex ways of understanding the world, structuralism, briefly, refers to the idea that cultural products such as language and texts have an underlying structure. In other words, structuralism provides a way of understanding objects in any given society as having a fundamental structure. Noam Chomsky, for instance, argued that all languages share a "universal grammar"; children learn the individual language of the society into which they are born, but every language is similarly structured by a set of rules. In sociology, structuralism takes various forms but clings to the idea that systematic enquiry can discover regular, recurring, and ordered patterns of social behaviour (e.g., from the micro-rituals of crossing streets at traffic lights or the way students file into lecture halls, to the regular ways that the education system feeds into economic and political systems). Structuralists describe these patterns as *social structures*, which are thought to create individual human subjects. For structuralist thinkers, if individual subjects appear to have a stable nature—a core—then this is precisely because of the relative stability of primary social structures.

The essays in Part I, and in other chapters of the book as well, draw on what may be loosely termed "post-structuralist" approaches.[4] This set of approaches expands upon and responds to the structuralist view. Post-structuralists agree that subjects (e.g., *people, I, you, he, she*) are created identities, but they challenge the view that social structures exist in any absolute way. For them, subjects are always products of unpredictable and changing (thus not regular) historical contexts. From this perspective, any attempt to discover regular social patterns is not possible—such claims are always beliefs, artificial impositions. All things (including language, knowledge, images of truth, the sociologists, the subject, etc.) are located within ongoing and unnecessary flows of history. Two key French theorists often associated with post-structuralism, but who do not identify themselves as such, are Jacques Derrida and Michel Foucault. Derrida's work in part indicates that language is assembled and used in very different ways—in current practices in our contexts, language is used in such a way as to create particular images of the subject (see Derrida 1976). For example, the use of the first person as the subject of language often imparts the impression that individuals are absolute beings with a core essence. (For example, the statements "I am rational," "I am happy," etc., use language in such a way as to suggest a unified or fixed "I.")

Foucault also rejects the idea of a stable subject, but he emphasizes power relations as the key to understanding how particular images of individuals and selves are created (Foucault 1980a). In addition, both Foucault and Derrida challenge the idea that there are universal truths to discover; for them, truths (say, about subjects and social structures) are always achievements of hard truth-producing "work" in particular contexts. Some feminist writers modify this approach to accommodate distinctive ways to redress the plight of women in contemporary societies (Weedon 1997). The sociological imaginations of Part I tap post-structuralist traditions to question various everyday senses that people have of themselves as "selves," as free beings, as "girls," as sexual beings, as family members, and as political agents.

Some might ponder how Mills's sociological imagination, which grows out of classical sociological thinking, could relate to a post-structural challenge to hierarchies of such classical thinking. Our response is simply this: diverse post-structuralist orientations do not eschew the classics but rather read them through different interpretative lenses to expose classical sociological thinking to marginalized "others" (e.g., women, people of colour, Indigenous people) who are excluded by particular theories of society. In so opening up classical sociology to its others, post-structuralist thought renders the questioning posture championed by Mills's sociological imagination in new ways, and so enables a revitalized way of imagining how to be with others. To be sure, as we shall see later in this introduction, this approach suggests a rather different version of critical thinking. The approach to critique does not follow the usual attempt to secure absolute judgments of existing societies—judgments that claim to be able to show society how it might achieve progressive change. Instead, post-structuralist thinking is more concerned with relentlessly opening existing social contexts to what they might become (see Pavlich 2000; 2005). Post-structuralism does so, in large measure, through the art of continuous and never-ending questioning—the very heart of any sociological imagination.

Framing the Social

Another tradition used to generate sociological imaginations views collective life as a distinct object in its own right. Imagine the idea this way: While walking home from university, you happen to glimpse a fair-sized flock of Canada geese flying overhead. You are struck by the overall patterns created as the geese dart and fly in their various courses. Interestingly, one can focus attention on the antics of a particular goose, the interactions of a smaller grouping, or indeed on the changing shapes of the whole flock. The sociological tradition referenced in Part II of this book tends to focus on collective groupings, or the whole flock. These sociological approaches typically explain wide social structures by referring to other social structures, rather than to individual characteristics. In these approaches, the collective whole is explained through the component (social) groupings, and such groupings, in turn, serve to explain why individual geese act as they do.

As a forerunner of this approach, Émile Durkheim observed that society should be seen as an entity in and of itself, made up of social facts. For him, sociology ought to explain any society by focusing explicitly on its underlying "social facts."[5] Durkheim (1938) regarded sociology as a unique science that would take "social facts" (not individuals) as its basic object of study. From this perspective, sociologists might explain why an individual acts in a particular way by turning not to psychological or even economic factors but specifically to *social* facts. These social facts may be actualized through individuals and even through the interactions between individuals. But, for Durkheim, they exist independently of any one individual; that is, they are detached from, and then serve as a constraining force over, a particular individual's actions. A Durkheimian sociological approach might tend to use scientific methods to explain human behaviour by studying how social facts are related to one another. Thus, to explain why an individual committed a criminal act, a Durkheimian sociologist would not look to, say, the psychological (or genetic) makeup of the offender. Instead, he or she might look to explain the social facts of crime in relation to other social facts (for example, by describing general crime rates and then relating them to corresponding poverty rates, or economic growth rates, to explain the emergence of particular, individual crimes).

Developing this sort of imagination, Durkheimian-inspired sociologists might ask the following questions of our example of your friend's situation: Can the social fact of increasing impoverishment be explained by wider economic (e.g., free market) and political (e.g., the decline of the welfare state) changes? How can qualitative, quantitative, or theoretical analysis be employed to study the social facts of this situation? For instance, in your friend's case, what social facts lie behind her particular reliance on social welfare? Is the fact of growing social inequality in Canadian society related to the facts of free market economic arrangements, or to class, gender, and ethnicity? What scientifically based policy recommendations and interventions might help to change society for the better?

The chapters of Part II develop various sociological imaginations around the theme of the "social." Though diverse, many of these essays also implicitly embrace the post-structural idea that the social does not exist absolutely; if it exists at all, this is so because of given "systems of truth" located within a given history. These essays suggest an imagination directed toward showing how the social, as a concept, could generate more fair, public-spirited, compassionate, gender-equal, non-imperialist, and just ways of associating with others.

Critical Sociology and Social Transformation

In our third approach, a well-established critical sociological tradition nurtures various critical imaginations. These imaginations seek to understand the injustices of given contexts, with an underlying objective of finding effective ways to bring about incremental, or indeed revolutionary, social change. Many budding sociologists may have direct experience with what it means to be poor, to witness the destruction of beautiful environments for short-term pecuniary gain, to bear the brunt of coercive control, or to be on the receiving end of prejudicial discriminations based on ascribed gender, ethnicity, sexual identity, youth, old age, deviance, eccentricities, and so on. Glimpsing the harsh effects of unequal chances to live a preferred life, being touched by the glint in the eye of the downtrodden child, seeing the ruthless effects of social exclusion, bearing the brunt of cold discriminations, or experiencing the horrors of intolerance, some seize upon sociology to make sense of—in order to fight against—social injustice. Sociology, in such quarters, serves as a theoretical awakening, a means of discursively explaining experiences of injustice and directing political action in search of social change.

There are many different sociological imaginations of this ilk, but most tend to assume a macro (wide) focus and might approach our example of your friend's situation through questions such as the following:

- What social patterns and structures have created the conditions in which your friend must now negotiate who she is and what to do in her day-to-day life?
- How is her individual situation a product of wider power formations that advantage some people (e.g., the wealthy) and disadvantage other groups (e.g., the lower class, women, the young, the elderly, ethnic minorities) within Canada?
- What collectively shaped ideas, decisions, and actions make it possible for some people to own property and permit others to rent from them (e.g., a capitalist society based on private property ownership)?
- What socio-political decisions create conditions for, and frame, the type of life your friend now lives?
- How are these decisions made, who makes them, and what sorts of effects do they have?
- How have the economic arrangements of the day favoured the wealthy or powerful at the expense of the poor or oppressed?
- In whose interest is it to continue the free-market policies that entrench a particular brand of capitalism?
- What sorts of institutions are created to develop, enforce, and monitor wider decisions as policies?
- What can be done to change the present society to bring about a different (fairer, more just, equal) society (see Marx and Engels 1948, 1970)?

The chapters of Part III mobilize aspects of this tradition—but with the aim of developing a sociological imagination that deliberately examines the ways in which sociological knowledge can speak to power relations by naming and indicating the effects of particular "truths" in everyday life. Again, post-structuralist themes are implicitly tapped in this part's chapters that consider power and knowledge to emerge as closely connected processes (that is, truth is created through power relations, just as knowledge helps to set up particular power relations—see Foucault 1977, 1980a, 1980b). What is taken to be true in any social context is a socio-political achievement, not an independent discovery. As such, critical sociological imaginations are particularly concerned to ensure that knowledge that challenges current social forms be given a legitimate voice.

Without critical analyses, there is little to challenge current social forms with all their injustices, inequalities, and so on (Pavlich 2000). The dangers of tyranny are never far away when critique is disallowed, and this is precisely why the authors of the chapters in Part III call for new knowledge-producing environments—ones that encourage, rather than stifle and silence, critical imaginations.

No doubt, over the past four decades critical sociologists have confronted the validity of modes of critique embraced by their analyses (Pavlich, 2005). For example, many social critics have rejected the view that critique or critical thinking necessarily involves judgments of given societies based on absolute, universal, or known criteria deemed capable of defining progressive social change. If nothing else, postmodern analyses of the 1980s and 1990s forcefully challenged the idea that universally agreed-upon criteria could be achieved (is this idea not simply an illusion, a myth, of modern thinking?), or that such criteria might guide universal social progress. Indeed, one might ponder whether modern versions of foundational criteria can be made to apply to all societies without replicating an imperial approach that most critical theorists question (recall that "others" are always created by universal declarations). As well, writers such as Jean-François Lyotard (1984) noted how modern critical forms, based mostly on founded judgment, were facing an increasing crisis of legitimacy in social contexts where belief in absolute conceptions of knowledge had been seriously challenged by surrounding events (world wars, apartheid, the Holocaust, etc.). Such events were not prevented by, and in some cases actually derived support from, modernity's rationally inspired quest for universal criteria as the basis for judging how to "advance" society. In the wake of these events, an uncertainty contoured many societies as more people questioned the view that absolute, universal criteria could serve as a basis for pointing to social progress. One response to this situation has been the quest to not abandon critical thinking, and commentators have sought new "grammars of critique" appropriate to current socio-historical horizons (see Pavlich 2000, 2005). Such grammars are increasingly less attached to founded judgment as a way of practising critical thinking, and more concerned with attempts to permanently open social beings to imagine what they might become. Fundamental questioning and the resultant sociological imaginations, we argue, are central to grammars of critique that downplay the role of universally founded judgment.

Why the Questions?

To sum up, we have noted several approaches that inform the sociological imaginations of this text. In general, one might say that most sociologists are involved with naming, understanding, critically questioning, and/or seeking to change the collective patterns and groupings in which people live out their lives collectively—these are often referred to as the *societal or social* aspects of life. Is there one sure way to develop this imagination? As Mills makes clear, there is no hard and fast blueprint, but we have already noted a basic tool for that task: an ability to raise fundamental questions about our collective being.

Even a cursory glance at the present text reveals its emphasis on questions. The title *Questioning Sociology* conveys the message from the outset. The introduction has itself tried to communicate a sense of sociological thinking by posing questions. In addition, every contributing chapter is developed out of a specific question. Despite the chapters' differences, all adopt an interrogative stance. In each case, various examples of the sociological imagination emerge as a result of responses to questions that require analysts to *reflect* on collective issues.

The practice of *asking questions* that lead beyond the limits of everyday common sense is thus a basic methodological resource for sociological thinking. That is, to repeat the logic adopted, sociological thinking occurs at moments when we suspend our participation in everyday, common-sense ways of understanding and acting in the world. Sociological thinking starts by reflecting on those understandings and actions. Instead of using familiar meanings to negotiate being with others, sociologists look to other (sociological) meaning horizons. Developing a sociological imagination is very much like learning a different language or a new vocabulary, syntax, grammar, diction, style of expression, and so on. This language may be related to everyday life, but it involves a specifically reflective, *questioning* orientation that leads us beyond the limits of familiar common-sense understandings.

Yet sociology explores ideas and actions in a language that is neither homogeneous nor complete—it is always evolving and changing. Since sociological thinking reflects on moments in history, and since these moments are constantly changing and never beyond question, sociology itself must remain open to new ways of exploring social life. In particular, sociological qualities of mind require us to go beyond the limits of given (everyday) ways of communicating. These qualities of mind require us to question the objects, concepts, and images that are simply assumed in ordinary life.

Learning to think sociologically is, thus, without end, because there is no final or finite language to learn. Sociology does not have one canon or doctrine that all sociologists must observe. Instead, the languages of sociology are multiple, dynamic, and forever developing through new ideas, texts, presentations, and so on. These languages continuously conceptualize how we might become social subjects, how we might associate with others though our passing histories.

However, sociology's methodological reliance on questions is even more basic. That is, underlying all versions of the sociological imagination are questions that many sociologists must face:

- What methods are appropriate to address the collective aspects of our lives?
- Can the scientific methods of the natural sciences (physics, chemistry, etc.) be transposed to a different context to explain social facts?[6]
- Or is the subject matter of sociology so different that it requires its own unique methods of analysis?
- If so, in what ways are the objects of sociology different from those of the natural sciences (say, sexuality versus gravity)?

- What methods can best address such objects?
- Is sociology a discipline that must remain committed to studying its objects using scientific methods (Durkheim 1938)?
- Should it interpret social meanings with the greatest possible conceptual precision in order to understand social being (Weber 1968)?
- Should sociology aim to describe a "taken-for-granted" reality, or critically assess how that reality is created in context?
- Should it, by contrast, analyze a given society against a justified image of an ideal, advanced, equal, or rational society?
- Should sociology, for instance, not only name the social structures responsible for your friend's poverty but also suggest ways in which those structures can be changed to bring about a better society (Marx 1970)?

This last question implies that societies are able to change. It also supposes that sociological analysis can help point both to appropriate directions for change and to the mechanisms for achieving such changes (e.g., through revolution—see Marx and Engels 1948, 1970).

At the same time, we emphasize that such questioning applies not only to social challenges but also to the very discipline of sociology, as is addressed in the final chapter. If any systematic pattern of thinking (a discipline?) is to grow and remain nourished, it must permanently remain open to new ideas, to new theories, and to new approaches. As such, sociological questions may just as importantly and valuably question the historical practices and thinking of sociology. The very practice of questioning sociology should therefore be treated not as a threat but as the lifeblood to secure vibrant, open, and always responsive approaches to how we might become with others. Overall, the basic point is this: while sociologists use particular kinds of questions to arouse the sociological imagination, they also make abundant use of questions to reflect on their own practices. The reign of the question is therefore basic to developing a sociological imagination. Were sociology to have a motto, it would, no doubt, look something like this: "Question, Question, and Question Again!"

Notes

1. Indeed, as Anthony Giddens (1987) puts it, "Like all other social sciences . . . sociology is an inherently controversial endeavour. That is to say, it is characterised by continuing disputes about its very nature" (2–3).
2. Like the topics of earnest dinner conversations with good friends, where people argue over the world's plight and try to solve its most intractable problems, sociology often does examine pressing issues. However, unlike spontaneous meal-based musings, sociologists have—perhaps even before August Comte's *Cours de Philosophie Positive* (1975 [1838]) put the term *sociology* into wider circulation—historically positioned their discussions as systematic analysis. Indeed, Comte claimed sociology as the royal science—the queen of all sciences—because, unlike others (physics, chemistry, etc.), sociology dealt with the basis of collective being: human morality. This made it logically prior to all other sciences because without stable social

moorings, without peaceful social arrangements, all else becomes impossible. Could sophisticated computers be invented, understood, developed, and deployed if a society were incapable of preventing its members from annihilating one other? First things first, according to Comte, and sociology's promise to explain peaceful, rational coexistence is among the first of sciences.

3. See Weber (1968) and Berger (1963).

4. For a more detailed discussion of post-structuralism, see Seidman (2013) and Calhoun (1995, 113–16).

5. For Durkheim (1938), "A social fact is a way of acting, fixed or not, capable of exercising on the individual an external constraint; [or again] every way of acting which is general throughout a given society, while at the same time existing in its own right independent of individual interpretations" (13, emphasis in the original).

6. Some say this question betrays a deep-seated insecurity about the relative status of *social*—as opposed to say *natural*—sciences. Disturbed by the charge that sociology is not a "real" science or that it is always a depraved cousin to its natural ("hard science") counterparts, many sociologists respond by clinging inveterately to "science" like nobody else. They try to be more scientific than any other scientist. No doubt this unfertile obsession has its own sociological pedigree, and its legacy *has* yielded many taxonomies, classifications, and descriptions of the seemingly obvious. For example, visit the far reaches of an older library and locate yourself at the spot where sociology texts are filed. Look for the dusty tomes of yore that—if ever pried from the unsullied comfort of long-forgotten shelves—herald the functions of this or that social system or that, more ambitiously, posit the absolute nature of all social existence. This "science" falls prey to the ravages of time, and its claims to final truth are exposed as rooted in a given time and place.

PART I

Subjections

The first part of this book tackles questions regarding how we identify our-selves as particular individuals or small groupings of people. It wrestles with matters of the self—the "I," our emotions, our families—which seem so immedi-ate to us. In different ways, the chapters in Part I challenge the view that "I" (our sense of self) is a primitive, fixed, primary being that exists in advance of any so-cial interactions. Each chapter points to different means through which broader social relations create this self.

George Pavlich's chapter—"Am I Free?"—begins by challenging everyday views that selves are naturally free. (That is, I am different from a stone or a flower because my nature as a human being is not fully determined—I am free to choose, within wide limits, how to act.) Pavlich taps into this view by noting the extent to which Canadian society is based on images of individual freedom. Its founding liberal philosophy assumes that individuals are by nature free and that state or other powers curb that freedom. Against this familiar view, Pavlich explores the possibility that neither the so-called "individual" (the "I") nor the supposed freedom often attached to such individuals actually exists before inter-actions with others. Rather, both our conceptions of "individuals" and "freedom" are products of social interactions at given moments in history. If this is so, then, drawing on the work of Michel Foucault, one might argue that historical power relations and freedom are not necessarily opposite ideas, as is often thought. This leads Foucault to imagine a rather counterintuitive idea: namely, that power is sometimes exercised precisely by imposing "free" individual identities. This is es-pecially the case for liberal democracies in which governments claim the right to govern in part because they guarantee individual freedoms (freedom of speech, assembly, religion, and so on). However, if power is exercised by requiring each "I" to be free in specified ways, then we are forced to reconsider what we mean when we say "I am free." In seeking to be free, individuals can end up endorsing a freedom that effectively allows them a narrow choice—namely, that of choosing their own chains.

Chapter 2 examines how identity is socially fashioned by invoking a particular sociological imagination directed at these questions: "Who Am I? Who Can I Become?" Dawn Currie and Deirdre Kelly refer to empirical research to reveal girls' experiences of how peer relations help to shape their sense of self. This research explores how an individual's image of self is sustained by complex interactions among social, political, economic, and cultural structures that surround the individual. Currie and Kelly show how adolescent girls are actively involved in developing identity projects in social contexts that enable particular quests for selfhood. Through these projects they develop notions of selfhood and work out who they take themselves to be (the "I") and who they might become. Based on 28 interviews with girls between the ages of 12 and 16, the research challenges two divergent strands of thinking: (1) mainstream sociology's failure to investigate identity projects of non-dominant groups (mistaking dominant identities as the norm); and (2) also the view that girls are simply passive victims of "adolescent femininity." Currie and Kelly instead analyze the words of adolescent girls that describe numerous pressures to "fit in" (conform) with conservative and traditional notions about how girls should dress, talk, act, and relate to others. Although these pressures are both intense and relentless, the researchers are clear that adolescent girls are active agents, too. They make use of opportunities to resist wider relational structures and pressures. While those girls who do resist do not necessarily create entirely "free" subjectivities, they are at least able to construct alternative, and sometimes oppositional, understandings of themselves.

The following chapter by Barry Adam explores another dimension of the self, by responding to this question: "Why Be Queer?" In his formulation of a sociological imagination, Adam details the complex mechanisms through which social relations within western society define, manage, and regulate sexuality. He outlines a complex history of social processes that led to the "invention of homosexuality as a juridical and medical category." These social processes also generated a negative bias—a *homophobia*—against those selves who identify as lesbian, gay, bisexual, and transgendered people. Dominant institutional structures within society, such as the law, medicine (especially psychiatry and psychology), education, and public policy arenas, encourage us to identify as selves who align with prevailing gendering practices. Despite the noted costs of defining oneself as queer, Adam convincingly challenges "the ugly taskmaster of homophobia." He argues against oppressive social censures that fail to comprehend benefits to be gained from diversity in all its forms. He concludes by noting that were all selves to reject homophobia, those selves' personal horizons would be greatly expanded, enhanced, which, in turn, could potentially help many more people to be at "peace with themselves."

In responding to the question "How Do We Think about Mental Illness?" Erin Dej explores different ways that selected subjects have been understood and targeted as requiring the attention of mental-health systems. Noting how the populations of these systems are disproportionately shaped by gender, poverty, and race categories, this chapter questions the so-called scientific objectivity of the "medical model" behind the nineteenth-century creation of modern psychiatry. She asks readers to rethink and explore the social bases of mental phenomena referred to as "mental illness" and to challenge this response: ". . . when we hear the words 'mental illness' we think of someone who is very sick; who behaves strangely; who makes us uncomfortable; who maybe even scares us; and who does not fit in with everyday society." Her chapter questions such understandings by examining how the history of scientifically orientated psychiatric institutions, diagnostic practices, and officially sanctioned treatments has shaped our beliefs about mental illness and has done so through the distorted lens of a dominant medical model. Dej outlines how, in the 1960s, this model was challenged by a growing deinstitutionalization movement, which called for the abolition of mental hospitals and for appropriately humane community-based services. Even if that movement failed to live up to its ideals, it did spawn a social approach to mental phenomena that took root in anti-psychiatry (Cooper, 2013) and later "mad movements." Whatever their shortfalls, these approaches have broadened our perspective and potentially provided a different "paradigm" for approaching mental illness in ways that maximize the rights, freedoms, and privileges of all people.

In the concluding chapter of Part I, Catherine Krull questions another frequently taken-for-granted idea whose existence many accept without question—the family. She notes that despite an enormously growing diversity of what we consider to be family in Canada, images of a "traditional" nuclear family (with a male breadwinner/female caregiver binary) often "remains firmly fixed in our collective imagination as the most recognizable and most desired family form." For her, this a mistaken view; it is better to recognize the diversity of what today is known as the family in Canada. Her point here is that while families do exist and do matter, we should recognize that family diversity is the norm. Consequently, sociology should acknowledge that a common definition of the family will always prove elusive because "how we understand the family is how we experience it." Since there are many different such experiences, it does not make sense to define the family (as has often been the case in the sociology of the family) by who belongs to it—rather, the family needs to be approached by "what it does." And in this lies Krull's call for an understanding of different forms of families, recognizing that each form is directly generated out of specific social conditions. Families then may be conceived as "varied social units" that generate experiences conditioned by various socio-economic processes, including those of gender, class, ethnicity, workplace, and exclusionary relations.

1 Am I Free?

George Pavlich

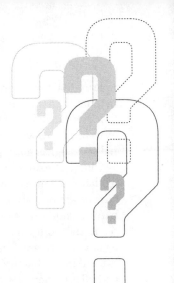

Introduction

Some bandy the term *free* around as though its meaning were so obvious as to merit little further attention. After all, we who inhabit a country like Canada live in a "free society" that allows us to carry on with our everyday lives without undue interference from the powers that be. We exercise all kinds of free choices in the course of each day: whether or not to eat breakfast, which clothing fashions to follow, whether to attend classes or work, which mode of transport to use, and whether to join a protest against a ruling government on a given issue. No matter their different potential effects, we certainly make many choices on a daily basis.

Over and above personal choices, free societies provide formal legal assurances for specified freedoms. The Canadian Charter of Rights and Freedoms, for instance, is designed to protect "fundamental freedoms," including the freedom of religion, conscience, expression, peaceful assembly, and association. Privacy laws claim to safeguard individuals from unfair intrusions into their private lives by state or other agencies. Laws relating to elections require that we are free to cast votes for leaders or parties that we feel will do the best job, without being pressured by coercion or force. Capitalist economic systems support unfettered free markets as a foundation for wealth creation. Culturally, artists, writers, musicians, and dramatists often champion individual freedoms. These various hallmarks of liberal democratic societies indicate just how prominently images of individual freedom feature in the everyday political, legal, social, economic, and cultural spheres of our lives.

It is hard, then, to deny that we do exercise free choice, but in what sense does this mean that I am free? It certainly does not mean that I may do exactly as

I please under any circumstances.[1] So perhaps we need to rephrase the question in more precise terms: in what way am I free when I exercise the choices available to me as a member of this society? The present chapter explores this question by examining two ways of approaching the title question that have inspired influential sociological approaches.

First, it examines a popular liberal view that individuals are "born free," or that freedom is a natural part of all individuals. From this viewpoint, individuals are by nature free and society should as far as possible encourage that natural condition to thrive. Individual freedom is pictured as the opposite of restrictive political and social powers; it can only thrive where the state's force or power is reigned in. Thus, sociology—as a science of society—should try to expand individual freedoms by discovering the basic workings of free societies, and offer recommendations on how to achieve these in particular contexts.

Against this position, we will consider a second viewpoint, espoused by influential French thinker Michel Foucault. He challenges the main assumptions of modern liberal ideas. For Foucault, individuals are not born free; instead, **power relations** are responsible for creating "individuals" as well as the particular freedoms ascribed to them. From this vantage point, what we are as individuals— our pleasures, our desires, likes, and freedoms—is produced by power. Foucault's alternative view of freedom, individuals, power, and society has important implications for the role of sociology, especially for a critical sociology that tries to expose the dangers of given power formations. His view also offers a unique response to the question "Am I free?"

Sociology and Liberal Images of Freedom

"Man is born free; and everywhere he is in chains." (Rousseau 1983, 165)

In this brilliantly condensed quote, the first line of Rousseau's famous work *The Social Contract*, lies the founding assumption of modern liberal sociology's approach to freedom. Freedom is taken to be a basic natural attribute of human beings.[2] As an illustration, one could think of individuals born on a desert island. Left to their own nature in an ideal society, without being coerced by formal powers, people would—according to one reading of Rousseau—grow up and live as natural, free, and sociable beings. They would freely and naturally choose social rules under which they would be prepared to live. However, for Rousseau, modern industrial societies constrain people rather than free them from the shackles of past societies. (Hence he finds people "everywhere in chains.") As such, modern individuals, who are by nature free and sociable beings, find themselves in societies that restrain their natural inclinations.

Rousseau's liberal view prefaces several influential sociologists—including Marx, Durkheim, and Weber—to the extent that all sought tolerant, free societies. Let us explore this wider liberal backdrop to the concept of freedom in greater detail, before turning to Foucault's alternative view.

Freedom and Responsibility

Following from the above, a liberal response to the question "Am I free?" would be this: yes, as a human being you are born (i.e., your makeup) a free being. A stone does not have the ability to choose how to act—its presence is predetermined by its surroundings. Equally, a lion is born with instincts that generally dictate how it lives out its life. It may learn hunting skills, and it could be a better or worse hunter; but instincts require it to hunt for survival. Lions cannot be held responsible for their actions, for they do not make free moral or political choices. If a lion eats a zebra, we do not say that it is immoral (implying that it can be held responsible for its actions), for it is following instincts. Similarly, an acorn does not decide whether or not to grow into an oak tree. None makes strictly moral choices; none has the capacity to rationally choose how to exist or to decide on the most ethical ways to behave.

From this perspective, human beings are distinct because they possess a **free will**; they are able to make rational decisions on how best to live their lives. They are not completely controlled by basic instincts, or environments, but can choose life courses from a range of possibilities. Such choices include physical things, such as how to grow (through diet, exercise, etc.) or whether or not to reproduce, but also extend to questions about the sorts of people they want to be (reliable, compassionate, selfish, courageous, etc.), which careers to pursue, and so on. As such, within certain biological constraints, people are born with an ability to choose particular life paths. Freedom is therefore part of our special makeup—it is a distinguishing essence.

Before and after World War II, a group of influential philosophers associated with so-called **existentialist** ideas expanded upon this view. Most notably, the work of Jean-Paul Sartre (1964 [1938], 1970) and Albert Camus (1991 [1947]) described the cold, harsh realities that face us because of our unique makeup. Their work insists that no matter what situations we find ourselves in, no matter how constrained or seemingly hopeless, we are always doomed to be free.[3]

Consider the case of a downtrodden person who is horribly exploited by a master. One could think of past times where "masters" who "owned" "slaves" felt entitled to treat them harshly. Let us say further that one unfortunate case involves a person of bondage (a "slave") who is tied up and about to receive another lashing from her or his master. Even when so restrained, the person on the receiving end is free to respond in different ways, or to imagine the situation in different ways—as a painful example of injustice, as a good reason for plotting revenge on a master, as part of the inevitable fate of a "slave"—or perhaps to let the mind wander in a dream world of sumptuous feasting, etc. Any number of possibilities could be entertained. For existentialists, this provides evidence that human beings are inescapably condemned to be free. Our lives are always undetermined and, hence, free. Therefore, foreshadowing existential thought, Rousseau argues that "to renounce liberty is to renounce being a man, to surrender the rights of humanity and even its duties" (1983 [1762], 170).

The idea of being condemned to freedom is beautifully characterized by Jean-Paul Sartre's philosophical novel *Nausea* (1964 [1938]). This book chronicles the life of an ordinary man who is forced to confront a life of freedom. As the story unfolds, Sartre shows how being condemned to freedom comes with awe-inspiring responsibilities. We may choose freely, but we are also responsible for our choices. Sartre describes the sheer burden of choice and responsibility in a world that is ultimately meaningless. Because we are free, we are free to make meaning; but—and here is the catch—we can never be certain that the choices we make are the best, right, just, fair, or correct ones. That casts the shadow of unease that defines how we live; we make choices never quite knowing whether they are ethical or not. And then we are held accountable for those choices. As we recognize this grave situation, this terrible fate, we are struck with what may be called anxiety of a fundamental, existential kind, a pitiful nausea. We try to overcome that nausea by doing everything in our power to deny our freedom, by trying to hide behind the semblance of doing things out of necessity (i.e., not having any choice).

This thinking has been incorporated into sociology in various ways, including in the 1970s through an existential sociology (see Douglas 1970a; Douglas and Johnson 1977). This approach worked out of the assumption that we are free to choose the social meanings that we do. It focused attention on the social effects of individuals being condemned to freedom. Closely related to this approach was a so-called **ethnomethodological** approach to sociology, which analyzed the logic of the "methods" (methodology) that people (ethno) use to create meaning in the ever-changing social horizons in which they find themselves (Garfinkel 1967, 1986; Hilbert 1992).[4]

Despite their differences, these various sociological approaches assume that individuals are fundamentally free and note that such freedom includes an ability to create meaning.

Power and Freedom

> "Being free stands opposed, classically, to being in someone else's power, being subject to the will of another." (Ivison 1997, 1)

As noted before, Rousseau's critique observes that in modern society people are "everywhere in chains." He worries that individuals have been trapped in power networks that restrict their innate capacity to live as free beings. In a characteristically liberal move, power is described as the opposite of freedom: where there is freedom, power is absent. Conversely, where power works unhindered, where it compels completely, freedom is no more.[5] No doubt, this formulation implies a specific conception of power; namely, power is identified with political institutions that inhibit or constrain individual freedom.

This image of power finds clear expression in Thomas Hobbes's (1989 [1651]) famous work *The Leviathan*. Hobbes accepts that individuals are born free and are at least potentially able to do anything within their grasp. With such absolute freedom, they can choose to help each other, but they can just as easily decide to kill one another to maximize their self-interests. In a "state of nature," in a natural condition where individuals are absolutely free to do whatever they please, Hobbes describes a horrific "war of each against all" so that life is "nasty, brutish and short." However, because individuals are egoistic and rational beings who pursue pleasure and turn away from pain, they also recognize that it is in their self-interest to band together to form a "social contract." Through this contract, they promise to forgo specific freedoms and yield them to one sovereign power (the state). In turn, they receive the sovereign's protection and the security to live life without the constant threat of death, terror, theft, and so on. With such amassed powers, this sovereign can enforce the social contract as enshrined in formal rules, called laws.

This intriguing and important analysis presents a view of power as a way of restricting, limiting, constraining, and checking individual freedom. Power is a top-down affair; it is possessed by a sovereign (state, parliament, king, queen, etc.), and it is exercised over subjects. In this framework, power limits, stops, prevents, or coerces (Wrong 1988). The implication is that where power operates, natural freedom is limited; power and freedom are thereby inversely related.

What does this mean for the question "Am I free?" Clearly, if we hold to this view of power, then I am only ever free when power is held in check, where a sovereign power does not interfere with basic choices. In contexts where a sovereign does exert power, even if this is considered legitimate (e.g., through a democratic rule of law), my freedoms are constrained by the exercise of power, where some or other power forces me to act in specific ways. So, we are never quite free in the presence of a power over us. We need, according to this view, domains of freedom in which sovereign power is disallowed. Liberal thinkers have long pondered and tried to develop such domains, from the early images of "public life" (Sennett 1992), to "civil society," to images of the "social" or "community" as domains free from state power (Habermas 1971).

Free Individuals in Society

Various forms of liberal sociology have pursued ways to develop free societies that maintain individual liberties beyond the coercive intervention of sovereign powers. The current dream here has been to sustain free individuals through appropriate social groupings; or, to put it differently, sociologists aimed to discover a free society that would support equal and free individuals within it. Despite significant differences, liberal sociologies suggest a slightly moderated version of the chapter's overarching question: what sorts of societies nurture and protect free individuals beyond state coercions? Let us take Durkheim's (1989 [1893]) specific suggestions in his famous text *The Division of Labour in Society* as a case in point.

Durkheim (1964 [1895]) arguably does not deny that there may be a biological (natural) component to "individuals." However, he insists that sociology is concerned only with that part of individuals affected by society. This part is important because the type of society into which humans are "socialized" largely decides whether they will live as free individuals or not (1989 [1893], 238–9). Just as societies evolve into different types, so the subjects that make them up assume different forms: people only come to view themselves as "individuals," and more-over as "free individuals," in modern societies. The "type of society" is in turn determined by the way it organizes labour to secure its members' survival (i.e., how tasks are divvied up—how food is collected, how children are tended, how people are educated, how decisions are made, etc.). Thus, for Durkheim, pre-modern societies are typically held together by "mechanical solidarity" (1989 [1893], book 1, ch. 2). Here necessary tasks are strictly regulated and sparsely divided (often between men and women, between tribal elders and others). These societies do not separate individuals, apart from the roles they play as members of clans or tribes. Group members are not, that is, identified beyond social functions, duties, and roles defined by customs, rituals, etc. Here, it makes little sense to talk of naturally free individuals, since members are not so differentiated.

By contrast, Durkheim argues that modern capitalism—with expanding populations and industrialized forms of production—produces a type of society that divides its labour functions in new and complex ways. In particular, tasks are broken down into specialized workings and require many different individuals working in concert to get the overall job done (e.g., to get an orange onto my plate involves many people who expend labour on assorted tasks, including developing seeds, growing plants, transporting fruit to supermarkets, selling, etc.). This type of society is, for Durkheim, glued together by an interdependence of functions called "organic solidarity."[6] Members of this society perform specialized labour tasks, making them highly dependent upon one another for survival (e.g., a housekeeper may place his money in the bank, but the manager of that bank might depend on the housekeeper to prepare food; both rely on others to produce food, etc.). This mutual reliance on complex labour functions makes it possible for modern societies to develop what Durkheim calls a "cult of the individual," where members regard themselves (or identify) as "individuals"—as free beings, who collectively make up society. It is only in modern types of society that it becomes possible for an "individual" to respond affirmatively to the question "am I free?"

An Alternative View of Individual Freedom

We have so far examined liberal views on freedom and society. We saw how some social thinkers regarded freedom as somehow (naturally or through social evolution) located within individuals but limited by coercive power. Although deeply influential in sociological thinking, there are certain problems with this approach. For example, if modern society and its unique power structures shape individuals, then does modern society also create the freedoms ascribed to its members? Is power really then the opposite of freedom, or do liberal forms of society or government actually help to create a specific kind of freedom? Raising these questions has encouraged thinkers like Foucault to develop alternate understandings of freedom, power, the individual, and society. This alternative framework also suggests a different way to understand the role of sociology.

For Foucault, freedom is never the same, regardless of where it is found. The statement "I am free" is always uttered in a specific historical context. It is not independent of, outside, or impervious to a given social history. That is, all versions of freedom, including those that are held so dear in Canada today, are born to a specific history. Just as it may be possible to trace your family tree, so it is possible to trace the family of ideas associated with our images of "freedom." Following this logic, one may use the term *freedom* to describe our ability to shop "freely" within the limits of a budget when visiting a local mall. But we would surely be using the term very differently from those wanting to revolutionize societies for greater individual freedom. Quite literally, the meaning of *freedom* is dependent on the context in which it is used (see Bauman 1987, 1988). Freedom is not then a universal concept with one meaning across different times and places; rather, it is very much the product of different historical horizons.

Two further questions arise from this idea. First, if individuals and their freedom are dependent on context, then is individual freedom ever universal? Second, is the freedom that we hold dear in Canadian society the opposite of power, or does, say, the state—and law—help to shape the sort of freedom available to us as members of this society?

Power's Products

Turning to the first question, Marx and Engels (1976, 20) challenge the view that individual freedom is universal. But more than this, for them, not only is freedom located in history, but so too are Hobbes's seemingly naturally free individuals. I am not then naturally, and for all time, an individual—let alone a free one—as common sense might dictate. Rather, social relations at a given moment in history create the very idea that we are "individuals." As Marx puts it, "The human being is . . . an animal which can individuate only in the midst of society" (1973 [1939], 84). This is a profound statement: it means that all of us, with our different identities—from the clothes we wear to our images of self, from the pleasures we enjoy to the dislikes we avoid, from our most intimate thoughts to our most public expressions—are creations of a given social context. And so too is the image of freedom that we associate with our individuality.

But what specific mechanisms create "free individuals"? For Foucault (1977, 1978, 1980a), the answer is clear: power relations. While this is not the place to detail his intricate and complex images of power,[7] it is nevertheless important to note that Foucault understands power as a relation—not as something that is possessed by an entity (e.g., an individual, a king, a corporate tycoon, a prime minister, a parliament, etc.), and not as simply a top-down, constraining force. If anything, power relations are exercised through techniques used by historically placed subjects as they relate to one another. Such relations involve actions directed at shaping other actions through local "clashes of will." Power is therefore not simply repressive and constraining—it is a creative force that shapes actions through local, interactive contests. In concert, such local power relations sometimes link up to form overarching historical and social structures. Yet, power shapes all social relations; it also creates us as historically specific subjects (peasants, vassals, free individuals), defines who are "other" (e.g., friends, enemies, etc.), and produces the meanings through which we understand the world around us (see Foucault 1978, 92–8).

In this sense, power does not so much restrain, constrain, and limit what individuals can do—it actually creates individuals. Foucault's deeply influential book *Discipline and Punish: The Birth of the Prison* (1977) is about many things, but it also describes how a new technique of power—discipline—emerged with the advent of modern societies to create specific kinds of "normal" individuals. Discipline effectively shaped "normal" individuals, separated them from the so-called abnormal, and located them as the "docile bodies" of modern society (135ff). Foucault saw disciplines such as sociology, psychology, criminology, and education as types of knowledge that formed an important part of modern society's attempts to create normal individuals. But his basic point is this:

> The individual is not to be conceived as a sort of elementary nucleus, a primitive atom, a multiple and inert material upon which power comes to fasten, or against which it happens to strike. . . . In fact, it is already one of the prime effects of the power that certain bodies, certain gestures, certain discourses, certain desires, come to be identified and constituted as individuals. The individual, that is, is not the vis-à-vis of power; it is . . . one of its prime effects. (1980a, 98)

As products of power relations, the normal individuals of modern society also came to be defined as free (i.e., liberated from the yokes of past societies). But such individuals were not free by nature; rather, liberal power relations created individuals who were "obliged to be free" if they were to become the "normal" people of modern societies (Rose 1994). In this way, modern power relations created rather limited images of "free individuals."

However, Foucault goes further. He argues that at a deeper level, power and a more basic sense of freedom imply one another directly. There is no power relation without this kind of freedom—it is not possible for a subject to try to shape another subject's actions (i.e., exercise power) without the subjected having a basic measure of freedom. By definition, therefore, power must involve a degree of resistance, which implies freedom (Foucault 1982). For power relations to exist, subjects must be free at least to resist: "Where there is power, there is resistance" (1978, 95).

Given Foucault's alternate formulation, in what sense might one claim to be free? Clearly, we may deem ourselves to be free, but individuals are not born naturally free, nor do free individuals exist outside power relations. Rather, the very claim "I am free" must always be understood from within given historical contexts. The "I" is a historical product of power relations in a given society, and the freedom ascribed to that "I" is similarly created.

This approach suggests at least two issues. First, the obligation to be "free" in a "normal" way is required of us as subjects living in a "free society." But such freedom is limited. Marx and Engels (1976, 301) note of nineteenth-century individuals that they may have been free to choose which religion to belong to, but they were not free choose whether to be religious or not. In our times, we may choose to own various sorts of property (land, cars, iPads, etc.), but this society does not allow us to choose not to accept private property relations. I cannot—without facing significant sanction—take another individual's car on the grounds that I choose not to believe in private property! Canada requires its subjects to be free in circumscribed ways, to perform rituals and engage the world as very specifically defined free individuals. To do otherwise is to risk sanctions imposed on those deemed incapable of making "rational" or "proper" free choices (e.g., children, the insane, the dangerous, etc.—see Rose 1994). Freedom in this sense is an important mechanism through which given power relations operate. Power is exercised through our claims to be free; saying "I am free" is to endorse the "free society" that has created both the "I" and the "freedoms" that "I" hold so dear.

A second element of the limited freedoms espoused by a free society is this: there is always the possibility of resisting, of standing up to, the freedoms of a given society. The point is not that it is possible to arrive at a "natural" state of freedom that escapes all power. However, we can use our current freedoms to imagine and work toward other sorts of freedom. But the latter freedoms will always themselves be relative to specific power relations and social formations. This is inescapable. Yet, we can escape the limits of given power formations and the types of societies they structure. If one sort of freedom supports existing social patterns, there is another liberty that conjures different and alternate social relations, subjects, and freedoms. In this sense we might want to say that a "free society" is never a static entity; on the contrary, a free collective entity is always open-ended, always open to imagining and practising freedom in new ways. Sociology can provide an important vehicle for reflecting on current forms and imagining new types of freedom. It also actively expresses freedom by questioning (rather than blindly accepting) past notions of what is necessary to be a free individual.

Conclusion: Am I Free?

This chapter has outlined influential liberal responses within sociology. Its reply is clear: yes, we may all be born free, but there are social and political conditions that constrain us and stifle our freedom. From this vantage point, we should try to ensure that we protect as many basic freedoms as we can from being taken over and destroyed by central powers. Sociology emerges in this story as a science seeking the true nature of a free society, recommending ways to achieve this ideal.

From an alternative, Foucauldian-inspired viewpoint, our question is rather more difficult to answer. Yes, in one sense I am free, but I am free in ways that are defined within a socio-political history. That is, "I" am a creation of power relations that have fashioned me as an individual in a particular society, and the freedoms that are granted to me are neither universal nor natural. When I claim to be free I do not so much assert my freedom from power as accept a given form of power. In other words, individual freedom is not outside of power but rather one of its products. Freedom is always relative to context, and a free society inevitably embraces finite possibilities of what it is to be free. One may here glimpse a different vision of freedom not defined through the individual or a free society. Though somewhat abstract, one might say that freedom could also be located in our ability always to imagine new ways of thinking (indeed even about freedom!) and new ways of acting as free subjects in specific contexts.

But, in short, "Am I free?" The preceding discussion has surveyed various approaches, leaving you free to decide which of these, if any, best answers the question. The point to underscore here is that in challenging everyday common sense about the issues at hand, you begin to glimpse a practice of thinking sociologically. This text explicitly encourages you to think through questions for yourself, and this involves a freedom that should be cherished. By engaging sociology, you may not be able to say with absolute conviction whether you are free or not, but you will be able to say that you have exercised a freedom to think otherwise than is normally the case. The challenge is to keep that spirit alive, and never to allow thought to close itself off as something that cannot be questioned.

Review/Summary Questions

1. What do you understand by this statement: "I am naturally free"? Would this mean that you as a "free individual" necessarily create society? Can your response explain why some societies place us, as Rousseau suggests, "in chains"?

2. Does the Canadian state (1) limit, or (2) create individual freedoms, or (3) do both of these? What does your answer say about the link between the Canadian state and a "free" society?

3. Are state power and freedom opposing concepts?

4. Is the very idea of individual freedom, as Durkheim suggests, relative to a given (modern) form of society?

5. If, as Foucault suggests, we are partially governed through the freedoms we hold so dear, can we rely on our freedom to challenge government decisions?

Notes

1. This statement echoes Miller's common view that freedom "is a claim to throw off the chains that enslave us, to live our lives as we ourselves decide, and not as some external agency decides for us" (1991, 2).

2. Rousseau uses the exclusionary term "man," and at the time of his writing he does not appear to mean to include women under the rubric. As well, it would seem that men of peasant backgrounds, those who were not church nobles, aristocrats, or commoners, are similarly excluded. However, subsequent liberal theorists, especially through the work of later feminist writers and socialist thinkers, broadened the term to include all human beings. (See Weedon 1996.)

3. As Sartre notes, for human beings, "to be is to *choose oneself*... freedom is not a being; it is the being of man" (1970, 151).

4. These approaches grew out of a phenomenology that tried to understand society by understanding the meanings generated by individual actors and the choices they make (Schutz 1962; Berger 1963; Berger and Luckmann 1967).

5. Elsewhere, he states that "the larger the state, the less the liberty" (Rousseau 1983, book 3, ch. 1, 210).

6. Durkheim uses the term *organic* to suggest that these societies are held together by their functional interdependence in much the same way as an organism, say the human body. Think of it this way: your heart has various functions (pumping blood through the body via a systems of valves) to perform, just as the lungs oxygenate the blood, the brain sends signals to vital muscles, etc. The heart, lungs, and brain all perform identifiable functions, but the entire body requires that all of these functions be coordinated to exist in a healthy state. In an analogous way, society (the whole body) is made up of many different interdependent functions (the banking system, commercial systems, education systems, etc.). These functions must be integrated and coordinated for society to exist in a healthy state. Social solidarity is assured here because many functions must be coordinated for people to survive.

7. The interested reader might consult any one of many secondary sources, including Pavlich (2013 2000), Smart (1985), and McNay (1993, 1994).

2 Who Am I? Who Can I Become?[1]

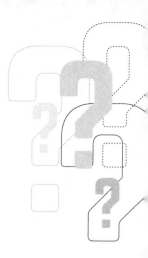

Dawn H. Currie and Deirdre M. Kelly

Introduction

Historically, sociologists have not studied "who I am" (my **identity**) as a social project. This neglect reflects the fact that socially dominant groups tend to (mis)take their own identities for naturally occurring norms. Thus it primarily has been those designated as "other"—women, people of colour, sexual "deviants"—who have questioned how we become "who we are." Women were among the first to ask "Who am I?" and "What can I become?" Our need to do so reflects how the social definition of what it means "to be a woman" historically has been authored by male "experts" (Bartky 1997). Women have been denied the exercise of what constitutes us as social subjects in liberal democracies: self-determination. Thus, the movement by women to claim selfhood challenged not simply femininity as a seemingly naturally occurring identity but also the patriarchal status quo.

In this chapter, *selfhood* refers to a specific form of identity: our sense of what we "are" and therefore what it is possible for us to "do" and to "become." *Selfhood* captures the meaning that our social presence has for us and thus sustains a degree of predictability in our encounters with others. For adults, much of the routine work entailed in reconstituting "self" occurs at a level below ordinary consciousness. During adolescence, however, figuring out who we are and who we want to be becomes an urgent task. As a time of physiological maturing, adolescence coincides with heightened awareness of the gendered and sexualized nature of our social identities. This awareness is not limited to youth, but much public concern surrounds especially the sexualized self-expression of teens. In reaction to what is seen as the overtly sexual dress of schoolgirls, for example, there is much discussion about dress codes for public schools. Frequently lost in this debate is what the often extravagant displays of selfhood mean to the youth themselves. In this chapter, recognizing this gap, we draw on interviews with 28 girls between the ages of 12 and 16. We explore how girls talk about their social presence at school, referring to their identity projects as "doing girlhood."

Academic interest in youth culture has a long history in sociology (see, for example, Hollingshead 1949; Coleman 1961; Hebdige 1979; Shanahan 2007). For the most part, however, everyday understandings of adolescent selfhood have been influenced by developmental psychologists, many of whom view adolescence as a time of "stress and storm" (Erikson 1968). This view emphasizes adolescence as a time of "risk," especially for girls: what girls risk is a lowering of their self-esteem, setting the stage for such problems as disordered eating, hatred of the female body, depression, and self-inflicted harm. Feminists[2] link this process to recognition on the part of girls that femininity requires adopting a subordinate identity valued for passivity and compliance. (See, for example, Pipher 1994; Brown 1998; and Brumberg 1997.)

While we do not dismiss the importance of research on these kinds of issues, we challenge the view of girls as victims of **adolescent femininity** through an exploration of their **agency**. By acting within constraints that shape their daily existence, girls negotiate their identities while making decisions about how to interact with others. In analyzing this negotiation, we distinguish between "agency" as what girls say and do, and "power" as processes that make some ways of being sayable and doable, and others not. While girls play an active role in defining who they are and whom they want to become, "doing gender" engages us with forces that do not simply shape "who we are" but also limit our capacity to "be otherwise." Understanding what girls say and do requires recognition of both the pressures on youth to take up conventional ways of being and their ability to resist processes that reconstitute girls' subordination to boys. In the latter, we see possibilities for social transformation.

In order to understand the individual agency of girls sociologically, our work explores the ways that girls' subjectivities are constituted through **discourse**, which refers to ways of thinking and talking that bring social reality into existence. Discourse coordinates girls' talk with "ways of acting, interacting, valuing, believing, feeling with bodies, clothes, non-linguistic symbols, objects, tools, technologies, times and places" (Gee 2002, 25). In our work, the cliques that characterize school cultures operate as semi-autonomous spheres of cultural production that sustain particular discourses about girlhood. These cliques, and not individual girls, are thus our unit of analysis. We begin by discussing a clique that enacted and reinforced conformity to conventional femininity—"popular" girls.

Policing Conventional Girlhood

As explained by 15-year-old Emily,[3] "Most people don't define us for who we are but for who we hang out with." Within this context, being identified as a member of the "popular" crowd was desirable; the popular crowd were the "cool kids" who "go out and do stuff" (13-year-old Vikki). Because popularity is being known or recognized by classmates, and being sought after as a friend, popularity is a source of personal power. Membership in the popular clique thus could be a source of conflict among girls in our study. As 16-year-olds Christine and

Kate explained, "There's so much gossiping and like backstabbing, whatever. You know, [some] people don't like [other] people." Although many girls did not like this type of behaviour, especially when they were the target, most, like 14-year-old Riva, accepted the dynamics surrounding popularity as simply "the way it is."

Even though the girls in our study were drawn from a broad range of schools, their explanations for popularity were consistent: "You have to be cool . . . like wear the right clothes and talk the right way" (13-year-old Liv). "You know, they're all like 'Oh, I'm so fat,' and they diet and stuff like that. And then they just get more skinny. . . . I guess that's their whole image" (13-year-old Vanessa). According to 14-year-old Anna, to be popular "you have to hang out with the right crowd every day, even though you want to hang out with somebody else." And you have to "keep up" your reputation because "if you do even one little thing wrong, it gets talked about everywhere" (14-year-old Vera). What do these kinds of "rules" tell us about girls' agency as a social and not simply personal phenomenon?

As mentioned, in our study *agency* refers to what girls say and what girls do. Girls' self-expressions cannot be read as simply "choices" about "who I am," however; rather, girls must navigate between being deemed "okay" or "normal" by their peers rather than "weird" or "different" (Jones 1993, 5). For many girls, fitting in at school was a source of constant stress, not simply in terms of avoiding negative peer labels but also in terms of the need to keep up with the trends that made girls popular. The problem was that "styles change all the time. Like now there is flares and then there was capris and then no tank tops and that went away and platforms was the big thing one year" (12-year-olds Sally and Marie).

Christine Langer-Pueschel/Shutterstock.com

Girls' self-expressions cannot be read as simply "choices" about "who I am"; rather, girls must navigate between being deemed "okay" or "normal" by their peers.

Given the pressures for conformity, it interested us that some girls actively embraced identities that aspiring "populars" like Sally and Marie worked hard to avoid. During exploratory focus groups with young university women,[4] we were encouraged when 18-year-old Stephanie exclaimed that, during high school, "We called ourselves 'geeks' and we thought it was good." Excited by this "confession," 19-year-old Myra added, "My friends and I, like we called each other geeks. . . . We even got our physics teacher to make buttons that said 'The geeks shall inherit the earth!'" In the past, the identity as a "geek" would have marginalized young people among their peers (Milner 2004). Willingness to embrace "geekiness" challenges the image of girls as lacking self-esteem and turning negative judgments inwards. For us, it signalled girls' ability to escape conventional identity norms and suggested that girlhood can be self-consciously rewritten. Consequently we were drawn to interviews with high school girls who deliberately constructed identities that made them distinct from rather than similar to the popular crowd at their school. While not intending to create a dichotomy of "regular" (read: conforming) and "alternative" (read: emerging feminist) girls, in the discussion below we refer to these participants as "alternative" girls (see Driscoll 2002; Brown and Thomas 2014).

Being "Who You Are": Challenging Convention

Popular girls were not well liked by the girls we designated as "alternative":

> Sandy: They wear these really tight tank tops. And they all look the same. . . . I mean it's also the way they act too. It's not just how they dress. They all act like "Aaahhh." Ditzy like. (14 years old)

Sandy complained, "They act stupid when they're really smart or something." For 15-year-old Zoe, "They're always the same. Like they talk the same, they always dress the same. And it gets annoying after a while." Agreeing, Pete (also 15) claimed, "Their main goal in life—at least it looks like to me—is to be 'cute.'" Pete directed annoyance toward "the way they live their lives through an image that kind of pisses me off. The whole 'girl thing' . . . being skinny, pretty, makeup. Uhmm. Lots of money. . . . Kind of living their life for a guy. . . . I think it's just totally wrong to live your life like that."

Among other things, these kinds of comments illustrate how dress is one of the most visible, hence culturally encoded, representations of gender. It is also one of the most "policed" aspects of girls' self-representations. While the "ordinary" practices of looking pretty and attracting boys were accepted, signalling "excessive" sexual agency earned disapproval. Errors could be costly: if labelled "slut," a girl faced rumours that could be difficult if not impossible to counteract (White 2002).

Despite the stress associated with the "right" styles, for alternative girls the fluidity of meaning surrounding dress opened possibilities for oppositional self-presentation (Gleeson and Frith 2004). According to 14-year-old Gauge, "They're [popular girls are] sheep and we're like penguins. Sheep [pause] all do the same things, and penguins are cooler." However, being "penguins" earned Gauge and her interview partner Spunk the label "weird" among their peers. At the time of their interview, Gauge was wearing a skater T-shirt and baggy pants, while 14-year-old Spunk was dressed in black and sported a shaggy haircut: "I wear a lot of black and I have a lot of chains and I have a dog collar and—I don't know. I just like that kind of stuff." Significantly, Gauge and Spunk were among the girls in our study who had taken up skateboarding, a physical activity that until recently has been dominated by boy skaters. Their case illustrates that dress does not simply signal "girlhood" as an identity label but shapes what it is possible for girls to "do" (Pomerantz, Currie, and Kelly 2004; Kelly, Pomerantz, and Currie 2005). For these girls, dress was an expression of resistance to the pressure for conformity and an opportunity to "play" with gendered norms. What made their transgression possible?

In our study, the designation of "popular" was associated with what Connell (1987) calls an "emphasized femininity": a form of femininity, defined at "the level of mass social relations," that is based on women's compliance with their subordination to men and "oriented to accommodating the interests and desires of men" (1987, 183). Emphasized femininity is the most culturally valued form of femininity, reflected in the prevailing beauty standard for womanhood.[5] We connect emphasized femininity to Butler's notion of a **heterosexual matrix**: "a hegemonic discursive/epistemic model of gender intelligibility that assumes that for bodies to cohere and make sense there must be a stable sex expressed through stable gender . . . that is oppositionally and hierarchically defined through the compulsory practice of heterosexuality" (Butler 1990, 151, note 6; also see Youdell 2005 and Ringrose 2008).

While girls repeatedly claimed that popular kids had money—to buy the right clothes and do cool things—popular girls were also described as pretty, thin, and attractive to boys. For them, emphasized femininity was a route to social approval; hence their avenue to power. As feminist researchers, we were aware of how the pressure to conform to emphasized femininity is implicated in the lowered self-esteem of many girls. Given the potential risks of transgressing the norms that regulate status in peer cultures, what gave the girls we designated as "alternative" their power to be otherwise?

Admittedly, it was our hope that participants would cite feminism as an influence for their resistance to emphasized femininity. For the most part, however, our desire was not fulfilled. While 15-year-old Gracie expressed pride in exclaiming, "I am a feminist," it was far more common for girls to distance themselves from feminism, as did Sandy: "I wouldn't say I was a feminist. I mean, I am for it." Whether embracing or actively resisting the conventions of emphasized femininity, the most forceful discourse we heard in girls' talk was that of an individualism that allowed girls to claim to be "unique." By **individualism** we refer to the way that alternative girls talked about "being yourself," employed to signal authenticity of self-representation. It allowed girls to claim what Gee (2000–1, 111) calls a "core identity" that constitutes a sense of what we call "selfhood" (albeit never fully formed or always potentially changing). As a taken-for-granted category, "being myself" foreclosed discussion that might otherwise draw attention to the instabilities and inconsistencies that typify any individual's self-construction. For example, 14-year-old Beverly emphasized, "I want to be known as, like, who I am." Like other alternative girls, Onyx (also 14) reasoned, "Everyone's unique, and if you change that you wouldn't be unique any more. You'd just be like wanting to be something else. And that's not you."

This ability to be "unique" rather than "feminist" was not entirely disappointing to us. Individualism enabled some girls in our study to resist the social pressures that were so stressful for Sally and Marie. Onyx argued that "if you keep adjusting yourself to fit in," you could lose yourself, a problem that she saw as "the centre of teenage problems":

> Not finding yourself again. Not knowing what you're worth. Thinking that you are only good if someone else finds you to be who they think you should be. And I think this is a big time for kids our age to either go one direction or the other.

Grover's self-confidence was also expressed through a discourse of "being yourself":

> I know who I am and I am confident with who I am. . . . I think you should just let someone, you know, express themselves the way they want to be expressed. And I am against people, you know, saying, "You shouldn't look a certain way" like that because, you know, "it's not pleasing," "it's degrading," or something like that.

This search for authentic selfhood was an important theme in interviews with girls who rejected the emphasized femininity that made girls popular. In contrast to the fakery exemplified by popular girls, claiming a "real" selfhood enabled Grover and Onyx to position themselves outside the male-centred culture at their school. It enabled girls to claim identities that are devalued within practices of emphasized femininity. To be sure, we are not claiming that popular girls would not use a similar vocabulary. However, as practised by the alternative girls in our study, a discourse of authentic selfhood signals possible awareness of the socially constructed nature of femininity and thus opens up the search for selfhood to critical introspection:

> Sandy: Yeah. You're more like—I think it's more like you're independent, especially from your parents. I think you become more like—like you think the way you want to more and like, you know, you're more social. And I don't know. You just kind of know yourself better than

when you were younger. . . . You know yourself and you've been around longer, so like you just make better decisions and—

Onyx: It's like between wanting to be a woman and realizing that you are one. Maybe that's what this age is all about.

This ability to reflect on "realizing you are a woman" is important: like other girls, Sandy described 15 as "the 'breaking age,' where you are trying to figure out who you are. And what you want to do. And stuff like that." It encouraged us that despite their descriptions of life at school as complex and stressful, Sandy and Gracie celebrated girlhood as giving them freedom to explore "who you really are" with girlfriends:

I think probably it's better being a girl because you can be like more "who you are" because the guy—you can't really talk about things that much. And with girls, like your friends are usually really important to you. You can always talk to your friends if you want to. And I don't think that it is the same for guys. I mean, they have friends, but they can't, like call their guy friend up and be like "Oh, I have a problem." (Gracie)

Given that both these participants claimed that "girls have a lot more stuff to deal with" than boys, the freedom they associate with being able to be "yourself" is significant. In this context "authenticity" opened up ways for girls to think about new possibilities for "doing girlhood." It thus gave individual girls the power to "do" girlhood in new ways. Does it also signal the power for girls to rewrite girl-hood as a social rather than a personal identity, an act we would associate with transformative agency?

"Playing with Gender" Online: The Limits of Individual Resistance

How individual actions can effect social change has been a central question in sociology since its inception. Historically, sociologists framed their answers through debates over the relationship between agency and structure. In large part, debates revolved around how structures—operating through the social in-stitutions that are the focus of sociological inquiry—determine what individuals do, how institutions are created and maintained, and what limits, if any, struc-tural constraints have on individuals' capacity to act independently. Beginning with Durkheim, a long-standing argument has been that sociology should be concerned only with social structures as the enduring, ordered, and patterned social relationships into which individuals are born. Because these social struc-tures predate any individual (and continue after she or he is gone), they determine the life paths of individuals—whose personal desires and actions are insignificant, sociologically speaking. One problem is that this reasoning considers social structures, not people, as sites for agency. Its critics reject a sociology within which people disappear, arguing that sociology should study the way by which individuals create the world around them (Abercrombie, Hill, and Turner 1984).

Sociologists have tended to emphasize either social structures or the agency of human actors in their explanation of social change. More recently, sociologists have attempted to offer a "third" way of thinking about these issues. Giddens (1984) employs the concept of **structuration** to signal the mutual dependency rather than opposition of human agency and social structure. He maintains that social structures should not be seen as barriers to individual action but, rather, as being implicated in an individual's ability to act: the structural properties of social systems provide the means by which people act, but they are also the outcome of those actions. He uses the term *reflexivity* to refer to the way in which individuals monitor their aspirations and behaviour in response to the ongoing flow of social life (3).

Following Giddens's view, the notion of "reflexive modernization" has become one of the most influential ideas in contemporary sociology. While the term **reflexivity** has been taken up in various ways, writers agree that there is something distinctly new about the contemporary period of modernization that has enhanced the reflexive nature of social life through the proliferation of communication technology and easier access to knowledge. These developments enlarge our agency by expanding individuals' capacity to orient themselves in the social world: today we have the ability to reflect on and monitor our social presence to a degree not possible in previous societies. As a consequence, we no longer passively accept our destiny as prescribed by the traditional patterns into which we were born but instead construct our own ways of being in the world. Thus our personal histories are not predetermined because our biographies are characterized by mobility and flexibility as we continually reinvent ourselves. People in post-industrialized nations are free to choose much more about their lives than was even thinkable in the past—for example, they actively choose their occupations, whether to marry and have children, to alter their sexed and racialized bodies, and so on. By claiming that gender, class, and family "roles" no longer have a determining influence on individuals, these writers describe Western societies as "detraditionalized" (Adkins 2002).

At first glance, these kinds of arguments may have intuitive appeal: our contemporary culture is characterized by a rhetoric of free choice embracing everything we do, from participating in democratic elections to reshaping our bodies. Within this context, a subset of girls in our study—whom we called "computer" girls—expressed pleasure in bending gender online and rebelling against both emphasized femininity and hegemonic masculinity. Many of these girls reported that online activities allowed them to rehearse different ways of being before trying them out in offline situations, where they might have been (or were) reined in or shut down for going against perceived expectations of their gender. Some experimented with playing the "bad girl" or taking on masculine and/or gay personas. For example, Shale, age 14, often wore a baggy plaid shirt, baggy jeans, and no makeup—a style meant to convey a lack of concern for mainstream fashion. By her own description, Shale was bisexual, an enthusiast for anime (a style of Japanese animation) and online gaming. In an online role-playing game, Shale described entering the Vampire Desecrated Cathedral as a "normal girl"; her profile featured the picture of a "cool looking chick" she had found on a website. Shale discovered the hard way, however, that "if your picture doesn't show some scantily clad woman, they kick you out":

> I walk into this one place, and nobody talks to me. And I'm like, "Why are you all ignoring me?" . . . Then you look at, like, the other pictures, and they're [showing] really, really, really revealing clothing, and you're just, like, "Hmm." And then you go and change your picture, and you come back, and they all start talking to you, and you're like, "Wow! You're shallow!"

In this way, through "experimentation," Shale learned that garnering attention online as a girl or woman was bound up with sexual objectification and that gendered boundaries, online, are more heavily policed than she had anticipated. Her experience parallels the serious and sustained online threats to feminist critics of sexism in videogames (we have in mind the "GamerGate" campaign[6]). It also confirmed that her experiences were not unusual; in a recent US survey of adults, young women (aged 18 to 24) reported experiencing particularly severe forms of online harassment (i.e., sexual harassment and stalking) (Duggan et al. 2014; also see Mantilla 2013; Steeves 2014). For this reason, we question the extent to which "gender nonconformity," despite its recent appearance, signals freedom in choosing "who we are" and "who we can be." As boyd (2008, 137) argues, "putting aside the question of risk, what teens are doing with this networked public is akin to what they have done in every other type of public they have access to: they hang out, jockey for social status, work through how to present themselves, and take risks that will help them to assess the boundaries of the social world. They do so because they seek access to adult society."

As Adkins (2002) notes, while theoretically emphasizing individual agency and power, proponents of the notion of reflexive modernization fail to illustrate empirically how and whether individuals are truly free from the constraints that accompany being socially designated as "women." Nor do they consider the social distribution of the resources that make the notion of personal "choice" meaningful (Hennessy 1995). The thesis is itself gendered because men, more than women (and then only some men), have benefited from the kinds of "freedoms" posited by reflexive modernization writers. Notably, women have not been "freed" from having to subordinate their individual aspirations and biographies to the needs (and desires) of others. The skeptics of the notion of reflexive modernization question whether femininity has in fact been freed from traditional constraints. With them we ask whether stories from the girls in our study illustrate how young women today reflexively control notions of "who we are" and "who we can become."

Conclusion

To recognize limitations on social change is not to argue that change is impossible; to do so would be to deny the agency of people and the efficacy of feminism as a collective movement for social change. The question for sociologists is how individual resistance can foster such a collective. As we have seen, most of the girls in our study would agree with 14-year-old Grenn's experience: "Being a girl" means that "You're supposed to be a certain way. The other girls expect you to be that way. You go against them, then they hate you." What has interested us is how girls can "go against" conventional notions of girlhood. To be sure, girls' search for selfhood entails many factors that go beyond school culture and thus are invisible in our interviews. Mothers, fathers, sisters, brothers, teachers, and numerous other people play an important role in the identity projects of young girls; this role, however, is not heard in our text. What can be heard in girls' refusal of conventional girlhood is a **neo-liberal** discourse of selfhood, a discourse that rhetorically values autonomy and self-determination. This discourse, more than the discourse of feminism, enables girls to position themselves against conventional femininity. This positioning is accomplished by taking up "me, myself, and I," an empty signifier in everyday discourse: "I'm me, and if they [other kids] don't like me, then they can kiss my ass" (13-year-old Sara). This is not to claim that the girls who strive to win approval by remaining within the confines of emphasized femininity do not espouse selfhood through this way of talking. Rather, we hear "me, myself, and I" as part of a struggle for girls to gain a voice independent of definitions espoused by others. In this chapter, we have seen the personal gains, but also the social limitations, of their struggle.

Sociologically speaking, the seemingly obvious "self" evoked by these girls is not an essential and transcendent form of social being but, rather, a historically specific and culturally limited practice of self-production (Nelson 1999). What remains hidden in girls' talk of authenticity, but nevertheless gives shape to projects of self-construction, are "larger" economic, political, and institutional processes (Byrne 2003; Connell 2004). Once we recognize selfhood as a culturally specific way of achieving and maintaining a social presence, we can link it to the competitive individualism of contemporary consumer culture. Within this context, we should not be surprised that socially approved identity projects require the display of the "right" symbolic capital, such as clothes, makeup, and attitude. While dress and self-presentation were also important to the girls we designated as alternative, their identity projects were characterized by self-conscious rejection of symbols associated with both consumption and conventional girlhood. This rejection was no minor accomplishment: the pressures on girls to conform are considerable, as testified by the experiences of computer girls.

The question that remains—and will be answered in the future—is whether these kinds of transgressions signal the transformation of girlhood as a social (and potentially feminist) project rather than a personal project. For the moment, talk about "self" as an "object" of introspection reminds us that, potentially, girls are able to reflect on and actively negotiate the (immediate) conditions of their gendered performances, as claimed by reflexive sociologists. The problem remains, however, that although identifying as specific kinds of individuals fostered some reflexive thinking about selfhood, it also limited the transformative potential of girls' agency. After all, the ability to "speak" oneself into an "alternative" existence requires the speaker's belief in that ability; belief in gender equality is a condition for girls' self-mastery. Such a belief might render the kinds of social change advocated by feminism redundant in their eyes:

> We're equal, as equal as we're going to get. . . . they feel that they don't have that much power and that's why they think they should be feminist, because they feel that men have more power. I don't feel that men have more power, and so I don't think I should have to be a feminist. (Sara)

Despite these claims, the girls easily provided examples when asked about sexism at school. Sexism was just as easily dismissed, however: "It bothers me a little bit, but I think they're [the guys are] being jackasses. And it has nothing to do with the truth" (Sara). This kind of thinking allowed many girls in our study to claim that while feminism might have been necessary "in the past" when women faced barriers in the workplace as a site of self-determination, it is no longer needed. In this way, just as academic claims of **detraditionalization** render invisible the kinds of pressures girls described toward conventional femininity, "individualism" in girls' talk mystifies the operation of power in their everyday lives. Such mystification can prevent us from seeing, in the words of Marx (1975 [1852], 103) that while we make our own worlds, we do so under conditions that we have not chosen. In our (limited) study, there is little evidence that the contemporary culture promoting conventional gendered norms that sustain inequality no longer influences girls' thinking about "who they can be" and "who they can become." Clearly, only a sociology that challenges such a culture can contribute to positive social change.

Review/Summary Questions

1. In this chapter we explored the importance of dress at school for the girls in our study. To what extent are the girls correct in claiming that the pressure to "look" a certain way makes life at school harder for girls than for boys? Do boys experience similar pressures? Why is self-presentation so important to youth? Does this kind of pressure resonate with your experiences of high school?

2.   Thinking about your experience of high school, can you remember any situations when different standards were used to assess the performance or behaviour of girls versus boys? If so, how were these different standards justified? At the time, did you agree with the practice? Has your thinking been challenged since you became a sociology student?

3.   In this chapter we discussed "emphasized femininity" as a form of femininity associated with popularity for girls. Is there an "emphasized masculinity" that is similarly valued for boys? What performances of masculinity make boys popular among their peers?

4.   Thinking about your own experience of high school, do you think that gendered expectations are changing among students? Among teachers? Among parents? Give concrete examples to justify your answers.

5.   Adults often explain what they find puzzling or difficult about teenage behaviour as a consequence of peer pressure. How might a sociologist discuss these concerns with interested parents/adults?

Notes

1.   The research for this chapter was supported by funding from the Social Science and Humanities Research Council of Canada.

2.   *Feminism* defies a succinct definition. In this chapter, *feminism* signals commitment to the accomplishment of gender equity, despite theoretical and political disagreements over how to accomplish this goal. For an overview of the schools of feminist thought, see Jaggar and Rothenberg (1993), Beasley (1999), Lorber (2005), and Mandell (2005).

3.   All names used in this chapter are pseudonyms chosen by the girls.

4.   In order for us as adult researchers to better understand young women's experiences of public school, we conducted focus group discussions with young female university students before we began our fieldwork with younger girls.

5.   "Emphasized femininity" corresponds to what others might call "conventional" or "traditional" femininity. We point out that what Connell describes as emphasized femininity is based on white, middle-class expectations for "good girls."

6.   GamerGate refers to a campaign of online sexual harassment largely organized through a Twitter hashtag, #Gamergate, and aimed at silencing feminist video-game developers (e.g., Zoe Quinn and Brianna Wu) and cultural critics (e.g., Anita Sarkeesian). "GamerGaters" initially targeted individual women, revealing their personal information to the wider public and inciting violence against them, including death and rape threats. These violent acts led some women to flee their homes and cancel speaking engagements. GamerGaters then moved on to successfully pressure big-name advertisers into pulling ads from online gaming and news websites (e.g., Gamasutra, Gawker) featuring feminist commentary. Although the campaign began in 2014, the term *GamerGate* has come to signify online harassment of women and cyber misogyny.

3 Why Be Queer?

Barry D. Adam

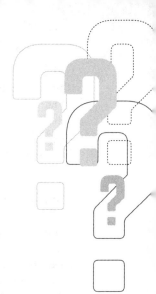

Introduction

Is the question "why be queer?" yet another claim for tolerance or multicultural-ism? Is it about me, a heterosexually identified person sitting back and deciding whether I will let them, the queer people, do their own thing? Or about me, a gay, bisexual, lesbian, or transgender person pleading once again to be left alone to conduct my own life? Is it yet another affirmation of the individualist ethic that stands in for a morality of advanced capitalist societies like our own—I do my thing, you do your thing, we won't bother each other, and thus we realize society as we know it?

In this chapter, I would like to push against this conventional understand-ing in Canadian society—which is, perhaps, not so bad a convention given the alternatives that prescribe censorship, suppression, persecution, or worse. The argument I will advance is that queerness cannot so easily be assigned as a trait of "other" people and that looking at the world through a queer optic tells us a lot about how that world is organized and affects everyone. In short, we are all impli-cated in the queering of some people and not others, and queer dynamics circle back to shape who we all think we are and the spaces we accord to ourselves and others for self-expression. Queerness is in some sense inescapable: it inhabits so-called alpha males (perhaps especially alpha males) as much as it does lesbians. Why be queer? It is not so much a question of being queer or not but a story of resisting, denying, and externalizing—or allowing and embracing—things queer and all of the implications that follow.

Minoritizing, Universalizing

So are homosexual people a minority, or is erotic and affectionate feeling for other men and women within all of us, whether a little or a lot? In this insoluble dilemma rests a large story about how people make the worlds they live in, divide them into basic categories, draw distinctions between self and other, and conflict over who gets to wrap themselves in the flag of the right and the good and who is exiled from this charmed circle (Sedgwick 1990). It is not difficult to see how all this works in societies like our own: there is a divide—on one side heterosexuals; on the other, lesbians and gay men. But what interests both sociology and **queer theory** is this: Why do we think that? How did it get that way? Is it true?

On one hand, the answer to the latter question is clearly affirmative. Lesbian, gay, bisexual, and transgender (LGBT) people have come to be identified as a people not unlike such familiar ethnicities as Italian-Canadians or African-Canadians (presuming that LGBT people are allowed to play a part in the national imaginary at all). They are, in sum, a part of the whole yet separate. They have an identity marked out from the rest, a geography with neighbourhoods and venues of their own, cultural artifacts such as festivals and magazines, and a history. And there are good socio-historical reasons why Western societies have arrived at this point. LGBT identities have been forged over centuries of change.

The shift away from agrarian production to wage labour in Western capitalist societies reorganized traditional kin relationships, diminished parental supervision of their children's choices in partners, and concentrated large numbers of people in urban environments (Adam 1996). These changes have been profound for everyone regardless of sexual orientation and have created the conditions for greater faith in romance as a determinant of partner selection, an enhanced ability to create households on one's own volition (rather than living with families of origin), and greater possibilities for meeting new people in the expanding cities. These changes were grounded in opportunities afforded by wage labour with its (limited) financial autonomy, at first mainly for men and subsequently for women as they too entered wage labour. In addition to these socio-economic preconditions in Western societies, overt persecution by Judeo-Christian authorities against "sodomy" pressed those whose emotional lives were with people of their own sex into a camp of the sexually "other" and invented, then sharpened, a boundary that reinforces that "otherness."

On the other hand, the answer to the question as to whether homosexual people are a distinct minority is clearly negative. The historical and anthropological record shows that the foregoing brief history of the West was not inevitable but, rather, just one of several possibilities. For example, the anthropological record reveals that at least some Indigenous societies on every inhabited continent include socially valued relationships with a homosexual aspect. These relationships fall into a few major patterns typically defined by life stage, gender, status, and/or kinship (Adam 1985; Greenberg 1988; Murray 2000).

One major pattern, well documented in the Americas and Polynesia, is the "berdache," "two spirit," or transgendered form in which gender fluidity, gender mixing, or gender migration appears to be possible for some men and a few women. In these societies, homosexual relations are part of a larger pattern in which men and women take up some or most of the social roles and symbols typical of the other gender and enter into marital relations with other people who have conventional gender attributes (Jacobs et al. 1997; Lang 1998).

A second major pattern takes the form of hierarchical, military, age-graded, and mentor/acolyte relationships in which adult men who marry women also take a romantic and nurturing role with younger, subordinate males (Dover 1978; Herdt 1984; Adam 1985; Halperin 1990). Examples of this pattern have been documented in ancient Greece, medieval Japan, pre-colonial Africa, and Melanesia.

A third pattern, sometimes overlapping with the first two, orders homosexual relationships along the same kinship lines as heterosexuality. Thus, if members of a particular clan are considered appropriate marital partners (and others are deemed inappropriate), both males and females of the appropriate clan may be considered attractive and acceptable partners. There are Australian and Melanesian cultures in which, for example, one's mother's brother was considered both an appropriate marital partner for girls and an appropriate mentor (including a sexual aspect) for boys (Adam 1985). Similarly, in some societies where the accumulation of bride price is the prerequisite to attracting a wife, occasionally women with wealth can avail themselves of this system to acquire wives (Amadiume 1980), and men can provide a corresponding gift to the families of youths whom they take into apprenticeship. These kin-governed bonds have been documented in some societies of Australia, Africa, and Amazonia. These major patterns point to the fact that there is no unitary idea of homosexuality in different societies, no single role or attitude toward same-sex sexuality, and no predominant conception of social approval or disapproval.

Historical research shows that same-sex eroticism and affection tend to coalesce around four major themes in Western societies (Halperin 2002): (1) effeminacy, (2) pederasty or "active" sodomy, (3) friendship or male love, and (4) passivity or inversion. Martha Vicinus (1992) identifies the social scripts of the "passing woman," the "mannish woman," the "libertine," and the "romantic friend" as sites in which female bonding is most often found. All of this is to say that sex between men or between women has often not been the primary defining identity but, rather, a practice or trait that gained visibility as part of these social forms. Same-sex attraction and bonding, then, appears to arise more often in a few major patterns and social sites, entering at times into the lives of majorities or minorities of the inhabitants of a society. Conversely, homoeroticism may be shaped by these patterns or driven underground according to the precepts and prejudices of these societies.

The political and philosophical traditions of the West are rooted in a society that has endorsed homosexual relations of the mentor/acolyte model. Indeed, most of the heroes of ancient Greek mythology had male lovers; the founding of democracy is attributed to the male couple Harmodias and Aristogeiton, who slew the brother of the tyrant Hippias in 514 BCE (Halperin 1990; Foucault 1978). In unexpurgated translations of Plato's *The Symposium*, Socrates rhapsodizes about how the love of youths leads to the love of beauty and thus to the love of wisdom. Yet modern Western tradition has suppressed, denied, and appropriated this homoerotic heritage, consigning it to sin, sickness, or crime. The gradual shaping and consolidation of Christian doctrines into the orthodox canon law and the propagation and enforcement of these views by the Roman Catholic Church from the twelfth century onwards replaced the heroic friendships valued by the ancients with the idea of the sodomite (Jordan 1997).

Like the traditions it suppressed, the concept of the sodomite cannot simply be equated with modern ideas of the homosexual. In ecclesiastical law, sodomy typically referred to a vague, comprehensive category of sexual practices that lack pro-natalist objectives, including non-reproductive heterosexual acts and bestiality as well as homosexual practices. The consolidation of church power through the first millennium of the Christian era included the gradual eradication of indigenous European forms of sexual friendship (Boswell 1994). By the fifteenth and sixteenth centuries, sodomy became a charge pursued by the Inquisition, with varying degrees of rigour in different countries, along with its campaign to suppress Jews, witches, and others who did not conform to religious norms. In the sixteenth through twentieth centuries, Christian orthodoxies imposed by military conquest on Indigenous populations of the Americas, Africa, and Asia actively extinguished local forms of same-sex bonding as part of larger campaigns of cultural colonialism or forced these local forms underground. The conceptualization of homosexuality as a sinful, non-reproductive sexual act then became widely established as governments and empires acted in concert with established churches to enforce cultural and juridical dominion over much of the world's population in the Christian realm.

As **nation-states** emerged from empires in the eighteenth through twentieth centuries, many of them organized their criminal codes out of the legacy of canon law, depending on the social ingredients that went into state formation and their relation to church control. With the rise of nation-states in the context of a Eurocentric, Christian, modern world system, the modern conception of homosexuality emerged as a sexual act attributed to a class of people subject to social sanction and criminal penalty (Adam 1995; Stychin 1998). As the world economy mobilized masses of people in cities, and as states devised more efficient systems of supervising, regulating, and policing their populations, homosexual men (and later women) began to fall into the criminal justice systems of Europe. From the early example of the fifteenth-century Venetian republic to eighteenth-century campaigns to catch and suppress organized sodomy (that is, the nascent gay world) in Britain, the Netherlands, and Switzerland, state agencies (and, at least in Britain, societies for the reformation of morals as well) swept up hundreds of men and some women in its punitive nets. The legacy of this nexus of church and state-building has been the disciplining of same-sex eroticism, the categorization of its adherents as a people apart, and the invention of homosexuality as a juridical and medical category.

By the nineteenth century, gay and lesbian venues had been firmly established in the major cities of Europe and North America and became subject to occasional exposés by police, physicians, and moralists, who have bequeathed us often shocked descriptions of "colonies of perverts." In Western societies such as our own, then, people with homoerotic interests and gender dissidents have been forged into peoples with LGBT identities—or perhaps better said, LGBT identities have arisen among those willing to stand up for the right to love and live with the person(s) of one's choice. Why be queer? It is less a question about a "fact" than a defence of a larger world of choice, an aspiration to find a way to what feels right in relating to other people, and a discovery of innovative ways to connect erotically and emotionally.

In Canada, LGBT communities and movements have often sought to realize these aims by availing themselves of and working with the avenues afforded to citizens in a liberal democratic society. These avenues and rights have been not so much preordained as struggled for, contested in court, and demanded of recalcitrant governments (Adam 1995; Kinsman 1996). In the 1950s and 1960s, when public debates centred on whether homosexuals were criminals or mentally ill, the struggle was to gain freedom from police harassment and psychiatry (Kinsman and Gentile 2010). Canada decriminalized homosexuality in 1969 (for two consenting adults in private), and psychiatry began to de-pathologize it, beginning in the early 1970s. In the last decades of the twentieth century, a long struggle in provincial legislatures, courts, and finally the federal government succeeded in including "sexual orientation" in human rights law, a symbolic affirmation of the full citizenship rights of lesbian, gay, and bisexual people (but less clearly transgender people, a struggle that continues). At the turn of the twenty-first century, relationship recognition, for example, in the form of same-sex common-law relationships in Ontario or civil unions in Quebec, had been affirmed by the courts. In 2005, the Canadian Parliament extended marriage to everyone regardless of gender such that any two persons (of age) could assume the legal rights and responsibilities of marriage.

So are we not back to minority rights, some version of multiculturalism, or the concerns of a minority that by definition need not occupy the energy and attention of the majority? Sometimes it may seem so, but more often the implications are much more far-reaching.

Disciplining Gender and Affection

Homophobia (that is, anti-LGBT sentiment and practice) is scarcely a thing of the past. Indeed, it is alive and well in many places, most notably schools, conservative religious institutions, some arenas of government, and certain regions and populations. An obvious answer to "Why be queer?" might be "No way. I don't want to be derided, despised, even attacked"—which leads in turn to these questions: Why are so many resources put into keeping homophobia active? What are the many popes, politicians, preachers, mullahs, and schoolyard bullies gaining from the volley of hate that they actively lob in the direction of anyone they can label, whether they have any idea of their actual sexual orientation or not? Homophobia is more than prejudice that will simply wilt in the face of reason (Adam 1998). Consider this finding from a study of 10- to 14-year-old schoolboys:

In many countries it is now commonplace for researchers and media commentators to voice particular concern about two features of masculinity: young men's worsening record of academic attainment in comparison with girls and their propensity for violence. . . . [V]arious studies have identified the forms of masculinity that gain most respect as involving hierarchies based on toughness, threat of (or actual) violence, casualness about schoolwork, "compulsory heterosexuality" and a concomitant homophobia. . . . As a result, boys and young men are forced to position themselves in relation to these issues, whether or not they wish actually to be violent or disengaged from schoolwork. (Phoenix, Ann, Stephen Frosh, and Rob Pattman. 2003. 'Producing contradictory masculine subject positions.' *Journal of Social Issues* 59 (1): pp. 179-95)

Homophobia is not just anti-LGBT activity, then; it functions as a whip to keep everyone toeing a particular gender line. Homophobia operates particularly forcefully among men and boys, demanding a strict conformity that few can ever believe they have finally and comfortably attained. It works as a policing mechanism, both among males policing each other and as vigilance over oneself. Homophobia is comprehensive and demanding; it disciplines presentations of self, manners, and gestures. It prescribes the things in which one can legitimately take an interest, forcing other interests into the closet. If doing well in school becomes one of those supposedly insufficiently masculine things to do, then there are many boys convinced that they must sacrifice their own potential on the altar of toughness. Of course, homophobia also regulates relationships among males, limiting warmth, affection, and mutual support. It even prescribes what one can wear, eat, drink, say, or dream of lest one fall vulnerable to the charge of being a "sissy." Moreover, homophobia is ubiquitous and relentless: the epithet "that's so gay" has become one of the most widespread insults in Canadian schoolyards today despite the fact that it almost never refers to anything that is characteristic of gay worlds or sensibilities.

So is homophobia an essentially male dynamic? Traditionally, masculinity and femininity have not been simple mirror images of each other. Girls and women have usually been afforded more leeway in gender in that many accomplishments and activities associated with men can also be done by women without impugning one's integrity as female. Feminism as well has developed and consolidated a strong critique of the disadvantages of strict conformity to feminine gender requirements, defined them as a form of oppression, and pointed out how they have inordinately limited women's access to employment and opportunity. Nevertheless, women are far from immune to homophobia. Opponents of the women's movement were quick to try to paralyze it by charging that feminists were "just a bunch of lesbians," and the movement did some soul-searching before deciding that it was the gender whip of homophobia that was the problem, not lesbians in the women's movement. Anti-lesbian ideologies and practices typically aim to thwart women from making their own choices and asserting their independence (Rich 1989). Today, the heightened visibility of things gay and lesbian has amplified anti-lesbian homophobia in everyday life. As Taylor and Peter (2011) found in their survey of schools, girls also increasingly suffer the verbal and physical violence of homophobic bullying.

By now it should be evident that homophobia does not act alone; it operates like, and often together with, a number of other "isms," including sexism, racism, and able-ism, as well as prejudice based on social class. All of these practices share similar tactics through which people perceived to be vulnerable are picked out for special persecution. It is not surprising, then, to see that studies of prejudice find that those who rank highest in measures of homophobia are precisely the same people who are more likely to score highest for racism and sexism (MacDonald et al. 1973; Henley and Pincus 1978; Morin and Garfinkle 1978, 31; Adam 1978, 42–51; Larsen et al. 1983; Bierly 1985; Herek 1988; Britton 1990; Seltzer 1992).

Indeed, the link between homophobia and sexism is strong. How can males revile all things feminine in themselves and other men without it affecting their valuation of women as a whole? These "othering" dynamics of homophobia can mesh with racism and able-ism in that schoolchildren of colour or different abledness can be particularly vulnerable to being labelled and minoritized (Taylor and Peter 2011). What is striking from a national survey of bullying in Canadian schools is the sizable proportion of students suffering gender-related and homophobic harassment who are not in fact lesbian, gay, bisexual, or transgender themselves (Taylor and Peter 2011). For example, that neither Hamed Nastoh nor Azmi Jubran were gay in sexual orientation did not stop them from being gay-baited and gay-bashed throughout high school (Teeter 2005; Ramsay and Tremblay 2005). As a result, Nastoh committed suicide at the age of 14 in 2000. The Surrey school board, responsible for the school that he attended, responded by refusing to permit any anti-homophobia curricula in Surrey schools. A ruling in Jubran's case by the British Columbia court of appeal in 2005 upheld the finding of a human rights tribunal that school boards cannot shirk their responsibility to make schools a safe place for students.

Schoolyards are just microcosms of larger social forces. Conservative religious organizations have frozen homophobia into religious doctrine and do not hesitate to avail themselves of human rights legislation guaranteeing religious freedom in order to promote homophobia at the same time that they actively seek to deny the same human rights protection to LGBT people. The Canadian samesex marriage debate drew together the conservative and **fundamentalist** wings of a wide range of religions from fundamentalist Protestants to the Roman Catholic hierarchy, along with conservative Jews, Muslims, and Sikhs. At the same time, some adherents of all these faiths organized to oppose conservative leaders because they understand all too well how the dynamics of "othering" can and do hurt them as well and that the prerequisite for a peaceable society with social justice is an end to the politics of exclusion. At the United Nations, the recognition of basic human rights for LGBT people was long held hostage by a powerful bloc composed of the United States (as successive Republican governments remained

Material republished with the express permission of: Edmonton Sun, a division of Postmedia Network Inc.

In some places in Canada, the protection of LGBT children is still contentious. In 2015, Alberta passed Bill 10, mandating that all schools must allow their students to form a Gay–Straight Alliance (GSA)—a support group for LGBT students that has been shown to improve student quality of life and reduce bullying and suicides—if they want one. This was a reversal of original Bill 10, which required students who wanted to form a GSA to petition the courts.

captive to the Christian right), the Vatican, a set of Islamic states, and assorted dictatorships (Barris 2005; Rahman 2014). This same bloc stands in the way of the advancement of women in wresting control of their own reproductive potential from patriarchs and governments.

There are homophobia hot spots associated with governments as well. As the United States became affirmative of LGBT rights under the Obama administration, Russia passed a law revoking freedom of speech and assembly from LGBT people, resulting in police and gang persecution (Wilkinson 2014). British colonialism left a legacy of anti-sodomy laws stretching from south Asia to sub-Saharan Africa to the Caribbean. In the 2010s, a wave of anti-gay legislation in Uganda, Nigeria, Cameroon, and the Gambia (often aided and abetted by the Christian right in North America) led to beatings, discrimination, and an increase in LGBT refugees from those countries (Ireland 2013). In Canada, it is censorship imposed by several layers of official regulation—from Canada Customs and Revenue regulations to obscenity law, bawdy-house law, and provincial film classification—that falls heavily on the small cultural institutions of the LGBT community (Cossman et al. 1997; Weissman 2002).

There are as well more subtle forms of homophobia—as when LGBT lives are closely policed and thrust into a "closet" because everything LGBT people do is supposedly about "sex" and therefore must be kept hidden. Same-sex courtship, romance, partnership, home-building, mutual support, and communication through the arts are not always allowed the same public manifestation accorded to others but, rather, are often subject to warning labels and restrictions.

Conclusion: Queer = Freedom

So why be queer? By now it must seem as though there are rather a good many reasons not to be queer, but I would argue that most of us have a great deal to gain by throwing off the ugly taskmaster of homophobia that dictates who we must be and dare to want to be.

Is there something about a queer viewpoint on the world that is interesting, insightful, and beneficial to all? If there is a "gay sensibility," it is not shared by all LGBT people, and it may be appreciated by many who are not gay. If it does exist, it is not easy to define since LGBT people have at least as many viewpoints and disagree with each other as much as anybody else. Even so, there is in the arts and literature of LGBT communities something of a tradition of critical awareness, irony, and "camp" that understands the pomposity and dead weight of the moralists and bullies who take themselves too seriously and seem to have nothing better to do than try to run other people's lives. There is a long tradition of laughter that extends from gay bars to philosophical texts in response to a machismo that believes in itself, to dogmatic righteousness, and to gunslinger swagger. After a century, the plays of Oscar Wilde and Noel Coward still delight as they slyly send up the pretentiousness and absurd officiousness of social worlds trying to act the way they are "supposed" to. Philosophers such as Wittgenstein, Barthes, and Foucault have stood out in their interrogation of the hidden assumptions and power dynamics of Western modernism. While their stances might not be linked to their homosexuality, one still might argue that their experiences gave them a vantage point on the world from which these underpinnings became more visible (Halperin 1995). Some of the most fundamental texts that puncture the ostensible "naturalness" of gender also benefit from the queer optic (Rubin 1975; Butler 1990; Butler 1993), as do some of the humorous texts that deflate puffed-up gender defenders (Simpson 1994).

So why be queer? Or, more precisely, why tolerate the tyranny of homophobia? One can only wonder at the deformation of male character caused by the taboo on all things "feminine." Gentleness, style, aesthetics, dance, even intellect fall under the searchlight of homophobia as it casts its chill over ever wider territory. The emotionally crippled male has become a virtual icon of women's literature and psychology as women try to cope with the "stiff" consequence of male gender disciplining (Faludi 1999). At one time, Englishmen could kiss each other with impunity; then sometime around the sixteenth century, this act too began to fall under "suspicion" (Bray 1982). Fortunately, there remains considerable cross-cultural variation in inter-male gestures of casual affection: men from Morocco to China can walk arm-in-arm or hold hands in public without fear of reproach. But will Western gender panic contaminate their relaxed approach to affection, or will we in the West begin to learn something from them?

Homophobia also places women on a gender tightrope when they dare to enter traditionally masculine realms. The high rate of expulsion of women from the US Armed Forces was a case in point: the image of women carrying out the demands of military service soon attracted the homophobic gaze, since the gender whip requires that military women act both as "women" and as "men" simultaneously (Scott and Stanley 1994). That raises the question as to whether increasing equality for women disrupts gender or stimulates a wave of **gender policing** (or both). As long as the entry of women into more and more male-identified fields makes the male pretense that men alone are capable of doing these jobs appear increasingly ridiculous, there is hope that gender discipline will collapse of its own absurdity. But at the same time, there are signs that the easy expression of intimacy among girls and women is falling under "suspicion," pressing them toward homophobic male standards of coldness.

The truth is that there have never been firm boundaries dividing sexual orientations in the lived experiences of most people. Studies of sexuality repeatedly reveal considerable behavioural bisexuality, experimentation, fluidity, and change over the life course. Some of these ambiguities have been recognized in schools in the form of gay–straight alliances that challenge homophobia without requiring members to declare an identity allegiance. But we are still left with these questions: Why is so much energy put into labelling other people "gay" and drawing the boundaries that enforce a dictatorship of gender conformity? Why be queer? Challenging homophobia has the potential to make everyone much more at peace with themselves—even lesbians and gay men who themselves are hardly immune to the demands of gender. Still, LGBT people are necessarily on the front lines of resistance to homophobia, often the pioneers who innovate new kinds of relationships (Weeks et al. 2001; Adam 2004; Adam 2006) and challenge the boundaries that reserve jobs for one gender or the other. A little more queerness in a lot more people might expand everyone's horizon of personal expression and opportunities.

Review/Summary Questions

1. What social and historical conditions led to the formation of groups of people identified as gay, lesbian, bisexual, or transgendered?
2. What forms do same-sex bonds take in different societies around the world? What does this say about common notions of homosexuality?
3. How does homophobia affect nearly everyone regardless of sexual orientation?
4. Has the fear of things queer stunted the growth and expression of men and women?

4 How Do We Think about Mental Illness?

Erin Dej

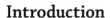

Introduction

The concept *mental illness* conjures up many different images. Maybe it reminds us of the self-help section of our local bookstore and its promises to solve our relationship problems or to help us self-actualize. Perhaps we think of mental-health initiatives at school or work that offer counselling services and seminars on how to find balance in our lives. Or the concept might evoke images of a close relative diagnosed with depression. Often, though, when we hear the words *mental illness* we think of someone who is very sick, who behaves strangely, who makes us uncomfortable, who maybe even scares us, and who does not fit in with everyday society.

In this chapter we rethink what we know about mental illness. We consider where our modern notions of mental illness come from, as well as the techniques and practices used to promote a specific way of thinking. Finally, we explore the anti-psychiatry and mad movements, both of which offer alternative perspectives on mental illness.

How Do We "Know" Mental Illness?

The Medical Model

Scientific psychiatry developed in the nineteenth century as a medical approach to understanding madness. It concentrated on the body as the site of mental distress. Two people, Tuke and Pinel, are often credited with developing the modern-day asylum and its scientific methods of treatment (Cockerham 2003; Everett 1994). Renowned philosopher and historian Michel Foucault (1988 [1964]) questions whether Tuke and Pinel's developments were scientific, arguing instead that they provided a moral approach to mental illness. Foucault notes that, beginning in the nineteenth century, psychiatrists became experts on mental illness and used this authority to impose moral judgments on others. According to Foucault (1988 [1964]), many of the techniques placed responsibility on individuals for their distress. As psychiatry grew more powerful, "psy"-experts emerged. "Psy" refers to psychiatry but also to psychology and other disciplines related to these areas. The links that psy-experts made with medicine allowed the discipline to gain credibility and to use neutral and objective language (such as *etiology, symptoms, treatment*), regardless of its moral basis.

The use of psychiatry to explain differences in behaviour informs the broader literature on deviance. When we decide that certain attitudes, behaviours, or actions are "normal," this means that others are "abnormal" (Downes, Rock, and McCormick 2009). When we use psychiatry to classify some people as sick and/ or bad, we are making claims about what we consider "normal." Using this classification also assumes that anyone who acts outside this continuum of normality is not only abnormal but is biologically different from everyone else (Pfohl 1994).

Psychiatry is now part of the medical model. Mental distress is regarded as an illness—that is, a problem arising from a biochemical disorder, genetic predisposition, or a virus (Tew 2005). Psychiatrists study the brain, where chemical changes are thought to create syndromes. The medical model looks for a single, technical explanation for a problem and often ignores the social circumstances that bring about distress or a crisis (Goffman 1961). As Laing (1971, 24), a founder of the **anti-psychiatry movement**, claims, "This [medical] model, when applied to a social situation, helps us to see what is going on about as much as do dark glasses in an already darkened room." That is not to say that those who subscribe to the medical model do not consider external circumstances; but in order to maintain the model's connection to physical medicine, environmental factors are often thought of as simply triggers to biochemical changes in the body. Even in cases where there is little physical evidence to support a purely biological connection, a medical approach prevails (Cockerham 2003; Rogers and Pilgrim 2010). For example, although post-traumatic stress disorder (PTSD) is considered one of the few mental illnesses grounded in the social/interpersonal context (Becker 2004), the psychiatric literature suggests that there is a psychological and biological predisposition to PTSD that is triggered by a traumatic event (Keane, Silberbogen, and Weirerich 2008).

Psychiatry's connection to the medical model is evident in the *Diagnostic and Statistical Manual* (DSM). The DSM was created in 1952 and is used to classify the various mental disorders for the purposes of diagnosis. The aim of the DSM is to provide stability and consistency to psychiatry; however, critics suggest that the DSM is used to gain influence over the public, the media, and the government by presenting psychiatric diagnoses as scientific and research-driven (Caplan 1995; Kutchins and Kirk 1997) and by hiding the moral and political influences involved. Claims of deviancy are necessarily caught up with issues of power and politics (Greenberg 2013; Pfohl 1994).

The addition, and later removal, of homosexuality from the DSM is an example of the manual's value judgments that hide behind the claim of scientific rigour. Homosexuality was listed as a mental disorder in the first DSM, but was removed in the early 1970s, a move that Kutchins and Kirk (1997) note involved little scientific discussion. Beginning in the 1960s, meetings of the American Psychiatric Association (APA), which produces the DSM, were inundated with protests about the validity of categorizing homosexuality as a mental illness. In 1974, members of the APA voted to remove homosexuality from the DSM. Afterwards, a new diagnosis, gender identity disorder, was added to the DSM, which some argue is a way to maintain homosexual behaviour as an illness (Conrad 2007; Zucker and Spitzer 2005).

The Targets of Mental Illness Diagnosis

Despite these criticisms, the medical model prevails—partly because psychiatry does not attempt to cure mental distress and so cannot fail. Unlike physical medicine, psy-experts only claim to manage symptoms (Rogers and Pilgrim 2010; Russell 1995). As Bean (2008, 8) argues, "Its acceptance has also been assisted by the law of repetition: if assertions are made with sufficient regularity, and by people of high status, eventually they will become accepted." The medical model survives in psychiatry not because it is necessarily useful but because of its coupling with key players in the medical and pharmacological fields. One of the most compelling critiques of the psy-discipline is the evidence suggesting that some groups are more likely to be diagnosed with mental illness than others. Among these groups are women, the poor, and racial minorities.

Critical scholars widely acknowledge the overrepresentation of women in the mental-health system. Women are more likely than men to be diagnosed with personality disorders, such as eating disorders, generalized anxiety disorder, obsessive compulsive disorder, or borderline and dependent personality disorder (Holmshaw and Hillier 2000; Russell 1995). Women are also more likely to be prescribed psychotropic medication (which acts on the mind) and to be given electroconvulsive therapy (ECT) (Brommelhoff et al. 2004; Holmshaw and Hillier 2000).

There are a number of hypotheses about why women are diagnosed with mental illnesses more often than men. Women who do not conform to traditional notions of femininity—what it means to be a woman—are more likely to be diagnosed with a mental illness. For example, women who are competitive, aggressive, or independent may be labelled with any number of personality disorders because these traits are devalued in women, although they are considered acceptable among men (Meyer et al. 2011; Russell 1995). Even when women conform to stereotypical notions of "womanhood," they may become involved in the mental-health system for being overly sad, fearful, or dependent. As Holmshaw and Hillier (2000) note, women are caught in a Catch-22 situation in which either adopting the ideals of femininity or resisting them can lead to a mental illness diagnosis. Finally, there are some broad diagnoses that are gender specific to women and that may be applicable to any number of women. For example, premenstrual dysphoric disorder (PMDD) was added to the DSM in 1993. PMDD is described as a severe form of premenstrual syndrome. Critics of PMDD suggest that the diagnosis can be used on any number of women to discredit them and that describing it as a mental rather than physical illness reveals a moral judgment (Browne 2014; Caplan 1995).

Psy-experts rarely recognize poverty as the cause of distress. Approximately one in three homeless people in Canada are labelled mentally ill (Davis 2006); however, we have to question the connection between homelessness and mental illness. Just as the psy-literature depicts women as more fragile than men, Bresson (2003, 312) argues that it is politically beneficial to equate mental illness and homelessness because it holds individuals responsible for being "fragile" and "vulnerable" rather than the social environment in which they are situated. Similarly, others suggest that the very nature of homelessness, living in public spaces, and the most common responses to being homeless (inappropriate dress/ appearance, depression, agitation, unresponsiveness, etc.) are considered symptoms of a mental illness (Marcus 2003; Snow et al. 1986). Although it is important to recognize the distress many individuals living in poverty experience, the mental-health system may not be the most adequate or helpful response to the problems they face.

People of colour are also overrepresented in the mental-health system. Research from the United States shows that white people are significantly more likely to perceive African Americans as aggressive, unintelligent, and lazy. Given that psy-experts are predominately white, these assumptions may lead to **institutional racism**, characterized by a collective failure to provide the same type of care to people based on their race (McKenzie and Bhui 2007) and to explain the disproportionate number of mental-illness diagnoses for certain racial groups. Constatine (2006) finds that people of colour who experience racism on a daily basis may develop coping mechanisms, such as becoming suspicious of others or feeling a sense of persecution. These characteristics can be considered symptoms of paranoid personality disorder or schizophrenia. Moreover, members of a racial minority experiencing distress are also less likely to receive support and counselling than are white people (Constatine 2006). As we can see, the complex connection between gender, class, race, and mental illness helps us to think critically about who is diagnosed with a mental illness and how the mental-health system may be perpetuating stereotypes and how it may be used as a method of managing certain populations.

What Happens to People Labelled Mentally Ill?

Several strategies informed by the medical model are used to treat, manage, and control individuals diagnosed with a mental illness. We will review the most popular techniques: hospitalization and psychotropic medication.

Once referred to as asylums, institutions for individuals diagnosed with a mental illness are generally accepted as a way to control individuals deemed to be a danger to themselves or others. Goffman (1961) referred to these as **total institutions** because people's daily lives are completely controlled; these actions were considered justified in the name of science. Faith in hospitals as institutions of care has, in some cases, led to an abuse of power—for example, using patients as uninformed research participants for medical experiments, especially for new forms of psychotropic medication (Stenfert Kroese and Holmes 2001). Although deinstitutionalization (discussed below) reduced the number of people incapacitated in mental hospitals, involuntary commitment continues as a technique for managing the mentally distressed, especially for individuals linked to the criminal justice system and those designated as the "most dangerous" (Cockerham 2003).

The most common form of treatment is the use of psychotropic medication, referring to medication designed to have an effect on the mind (Davis 2006). Chlorpromazine was introduced in the 1950s as a medication to reduce hallucinations among individuals diagnosed with schizophrenia. It continues to be used today for a variety of diagnoses (Cockerham 2003). Since that time, many new types of psychotropic medications have been prescribed to individuals diagnosed with a mental illness, often as the only form of treatment. The widespread use of medication has had a dramatic effect on how individuals diagnosed as mentally ill are managed. Relying primarily on psychotropic medication leads to a depersonalization of treatment, in that there is significantly less contact between doctor and patient, and there is less interest in dealing with the nature of the distress itself (Rosenhan 1973, Whitaker 2010). Pfohl (1994) suggests that psychotropic medication is a method used to chemically control individuals who have an abundance of deviant thoughts or who have acted deviantly and has led to the development of **Big Pharma**. "Big Pharma" refers to large pharmaceutical companies that yield a great deal of economic and political power. The overreliance on psychopharmaceuticals for everything from anxiety to shyness and sadness (Conrad 2007) has reinforced the notion that distress is a biological problem; this overreliance misrepresents medication as a cure rather than as a way to manage symptoms (Cockerham 2003; Rogers and Pilgrim 2010). In fact, the overwhelming use of medication is often cited as one of the most significant catalysts to deinstitutionalization.

Deinstitutionalization: Ideas and Reality

The 1960s witnessed increased criticism of how all sorts of social institutions, including mental hospitals, were run. People became skeptical of experts and called for less structure and less state intervention. The policy of **deinstitutionalization** was the most dramatic shift of all the changes (Cohen 1985).

The central tenet of deinstitutionalization was a call for people in distress to receive assistance in the community rather than be locked up, often involuntarily, in a hospital. Deinstitutionalization "involved a shift of the sites and responsibility for treatment and support from institutional to community set-tings, and has been associated with a fragmentation of mental health service delivery" (Wilson 1996, 71). The community was seen as a humane alternative to mental hospitals, and the diversion of individuals who would otherwise be institutionalized was based on the idea that people diagnosed with a mental illness should have their basic rights protected, whenever possible (Davis 2006; Stroman 2003).

What Went Wrong?

Although the decision to deinstitutionalize individuals diagnosed with a mental illness occurred in the 1960s, the impact of the movement was not felt until later. In Canada, for example, although the capacity of mental hospitals was reduced by 70.6 per cent between 1965 and 1981, the number of beds in the psychiatric ward of general hospitals increased dramatically. It was not until the 1990s that this number decreased as well (Sealy and Whitehead 2004).

The promise of deinstitutionalization was that people in distress would re-ceive supports in the community (Wilson 1996, 73). These goals, however, were not achieved. The resources meant to bring about a smooth transition from the mental hospital to community integration were either not present or inadequate. Davis (2006) suggests two reasons for this. First, there was a lack of coordination between care providers and individuals seeking services. Many individuals com-ing out of the hospital ended up on the streets, but the supports were often not located in the same areas as the people who needed them, were only open during the day and not at night, or did not have the staff consistency necessary to build relationships in the community.

Second, different service providers did not communicate with one another and therefore could not coordinate the types of services offered. Service organ-izations had trouble getting started or maintaining their position. Although generally members of the community agreed with the idea of moving toward community support, they campaigned against having mental-health services in their neighbourhoods. This is an example of the **not in my back yard** (NIMBY) syndrome. In turn, many individuals released from the mental hospital into the community felt abandoned by the communities that were meant to be there for them. Many also felt as though they were taking a passive role in their recovery and that they were being managed rather than treated. As Rogers and Pilgrim (2010, 198) claim, "The inhumanity of the asylum has simply been replaced by the negligence of the community." This statement exemplifies one of the most negative effects of deinstitutionalization: **transcarceration**, which refers to the move from one institution to another (Arrigo 2001; Lowman, Menzies, and Palys 1987). People previously placed in asylums are now being housed in prisons, nursing homes, general hospitals, homeless shelters, etc. (Stroman 2003). Al-though deinstitutionalization did not unfold as planned, it does represent a more social way of thinking about mental illness.

The Development of the Mad Movement

Anti-Psychiatry

Among those most vocal about deinstitutionalization in the 1960s were those identified as anti-psychiatrists. The anti-psychiatry movement was largely made up of psychiatrists who were critical of their own discipline. Doctors such as Szasz, Laing, and Cooper questioned the moral judgments that they saw as the real basis of mental illness diagnoses. The anti-psychiatrists studied mental illness as a social construction; they recognized how individuals' personal and social circumstances affected their behaviour and focused on how that behaviour is understood by others. For example, Szasz (1989, 16) coined the term *problems in living* to describe the personal difficulties that interest the psy-disciplines. He added that mental illness is in fact an individual's "struggle with the problem of *how* he should live (emphasis in original)." Szasz's assessment of problems in living is consistent with our example of homosexuality being labelled a mental illness until the 1970s. Until that time, many considered homosexuality a problematic way to live.

Although the anti-psychiatry movement lost momentum by the 1980s, some psychiatrists, scholars, and others still identify as anti-psychiatrists. This movement challenges us to reconsider how mental illness is understood. Anti-psychiatrists ask how we know what we know about mental illness. They use intellectual critiques of mental illness (Ussher 1991), and many call for the abolition of the mental-health system as we know it. Anti-psychiatrists are critical of forced treatment and the institutionalization of individuals identified as mentally ill. The anti-psychiatry movement built a foundation for the mad movement, and its proponents often work with contemporary anti-psychiatrists (Burstow 2004).

The Mad Movement

Mad activists began to organize collectively in the 1980s throughout North America and Europe (Rogers and Pilgrim 2010). As people labelled mentally ill began to move out of hospitals and into the community, they were able to talk openly about their experiences of the mental-health system, organize collectively, and stop relying on critical psychiatrists to speak on their behalf. Since that time, the movement has had varying platforms and priorities. The **mad movement** moves beyond the intellectual debates of the anti-psychiatrists (Dain 1989; Rogers and Pilgrim 2010) and is committed to direct action, including protests against laws allowing involuntary commitment, ECT, and forced treatment (Beresford 2005; Stroman 2003). As the movement developed, activists began running community-based mental-health services, such as outreach programs and crisis intervention services (Rissmiller and Rissmiller 2006; Stroman 2003). The mad movement takes up the challenge presented by the failure of deinstitutionalization to establish resources in the community and help people in distress.

Table 4.1 A comparison of the medical model and mad movement paradigms

	Medical Model	Mad Movement
Cause of distress	Individual pathology, genetics	Social factors, inequality
Common treatments	Medication, hospitalization	Self-help and peer support, building a supportive network
Goal	Manage symptoms	Recovery, feeling better
Site of treatment	Mental hospitals, doctor's offices	Community-based mental-health services
Experts	Psychiatrists	Individuals
Role of the individual in distress	Passive	Active
Notable scholars	Tuke and Pinel	Szasz, Laing, Burstow

Although activists define themselves in different ways, the mad movement can be loosely divided between survivors and consumers. Survivors (otherwise known as ex-patients) reject the medical model (sometimes this means rejecting psychotropic medication) and focus on user-controlled alternatives. Consumers (otherwise known as clients) find fault with, but generally accept, the medical model and try to reform the system and to include consumers in mental-health decision making[1] (Burstow 2004). Although these differences may cause tension among some activists, the mad movement has a number of common goals that reflect the views of both consumers and survivors: self-determination, empowerment, the use of narratives, and recovery.

Self-determination entails promoting the dignity of those labelled mentally ill. Cook and Jonikas (2002, 91) define *self-determination* as "clients' rights to be free from all involuntary treatment; to direct their own services; to be involved in all decisions concerning their health and well-being; and to have meaningful leadership roles in the design, delivery, and evaluation of services and supports." For mad activists, self-determination is a human right, not a privilege; it allows people to manage their own lives and well-being (Chamberlin 1990).

Empowerment is closely related to self-determination. McLean (1995) defines *empowerment* as connecting the personal and the political by refusing to place responsibility on the individual for the social conditions that lead to a mental illness diagnosis. Empowerment can mean taking power over one's life through assertiveness, gaining self-esteem, taking an activist role, etc. (Cohen 2005). For consumers, empowerment can also mean being knowledgeable about all treatment options and making informed choices about the types of mental-health services one receives (Chamberlin 1990).

Rather than relying on what psy-experts say about mental illness, the mad movement uses the narratives of individuals who are diagnosed with a mental illness to inform what they know about mental distress and to resist the dominant view of the medical model (Crossley and Crossley 2001). Using narratives allows mad activists to "re-story" (Pollack 2005) the collective experience of the mental-health system and of individuals' personal understanding of their history and self-identification by validating their experiences and finding others with similar stories. Burstow and Weitz's (1988) book uses poetry, essays, and journals from psychiatric survivors/consumers to showcase the experiences of individuals in the mental-health system and to fight the oppression of people labelled mentally ill.

Finally, recovery is the ultimate goal for people in the mad movement. Recovery encompasses individual success from the personal, social, and structural impediments to mental wellness. For the mad movement, recovery may be anything from someone's changing attitudes or feelings, developing a social network, finding employment, contributing to the community, etc. (Cohen 2005). Recovery is not synonymous with a "cure"; instead, mad activists focus on coping strategies, individual satisfaction and dignity, being functional, and having self-determination (Cook and Jonikas 2002). With these goals in mind, the mad movement adopts strategies to achieve recovery, such as receiving social support, participating in social activism, undergoing hypnotherapy, participating in self-help groups, and having good physical health (taking vitamins, eating properly, exercising, etc.). These tactics may be used on their own or in conjunction with psychotropic medication.

Conclusion

In this chapter, we considered some of the different ways we can think about mental illness. First, we studied the creation of modern psychiatry and its links with the medical model, beginning in the nineteenth century. The medical model is built upon the principles of objectivity and scientificity, but the definition of mental illness is fraught with moral and subjective judgments, as seen through an analysis of the DSM. Moreover, we looked at how the categories of gender, poverty, and race are disproportionately represented in the mental-health system.

When someone is diagnosed with a mental illness, the medical model endorses various treatments, including hospitalization and the most popular form of treatment, psychotropic medication. The use of medication is so prolific that large pharmaceutical companies, known as Big Pharma, have a strong presence in economic and political issues.

The mental-health system underwent an enormous transformation in the 1960s as deinstitutionalization took effect. The goal of deinstitutionalization was to provide treatment in the community so that individuals diagnosed with a mental illness could retain as many human rights and privileges as possible. In reality, however, not enough resources were relocated to the community, and many former patients were left without support, sometimes leading to homelessness or involvement with the criminal justice system.

The call for rights was central to the anti-psychiatry and mad movements. The former was popularized in the 1960s by psychiatrists who were critical of their own discipline. The contemporary movement is made up of consumers and survivors who are also critical of the mental-health system and seek alternative ways of thinking about mental illness and providing relief from distress.

From this analysis, we can reconsider the assumptions that come with the medical understanding of mental distress. Kuhn (1970) notes that there are different paradigms that inform how we come to know something. When we learn new information or look at what we know from a different perspective, we may realize that a new paradigm is necessary to make sense of what we see. There is always potential to see something differently, and we have to be critical about how we have come to know mental illness. The medical model is not the only way to explain and support people in distress. Indeed, if we are open to new ways of thinking about distress, we are likely to empower people and help those in need without using oppressive tactics.

Review/Summary Questions

1. How does psy's use of the medical model affect the way we think about mental illness?
2. What is the most popular form of treatment for mental illness today? What are some of the problems with relying on this form of treatment?
3. What were some of the challenges facing the deinstitutionalization of the mentally ill? How did this affect those seeking care?
4. What are the main tenets of the mad movement? How do they differ from the medical model?

Note

1. There is much disagreement about the meaning of the term *consumer*, as it suggests a sense of choice in a private system, which is not an accurate representation of the public mental-health system (Diamond 2013; Rogers and Pilgrim 2010).

5 Does "the Family" Exist?[1]

Catherine Krull

Introduction

To address the question of whether the family exists, we first need to understand what we mean by the word *family*. The image that first springs to mind for many people is that of a legally married heterosexual male/female couple and their biological children. Despite growing family diversity in Canada, this nuclear family structure, centring on the male breadwinner/female caregiver binary, remains firmly fixed in our collective imagination as the most recognizable and most desired family form (Nelson 2006; Bibby 2004).

The assumption that the nuclear family structure is both ideal and representative of Canadian family life has been incredibly powerful. Public policies, laws, government benefits and pensions, national censuses, access to contraception and reproductive technologies, and the structuring of employment and schools have all been shaped and impacted by this **hegemonic** idea. As a **normative** rule, non-nuclear family forms become viewed as subordinate, deficient, or even flawed—terms like "broken families," "adoptive families," "stepfamilies," "single-parent families," "lesbian, gay, bisexual, transgendered [LGBT] families," "voluntary non-kin families," "childless families," and "other-mother families" make sense only if understood in reference to the normative, nuclear ideal (Krull 2011, 11). As such, Canadian family diversity is often read as a criterion of family decline and the deterioration of marriage as an institution—an interpretation often used to justify and necessitate public scrutiny and surveillance. Any assessment of the condition of Canadian families requires an understanding of the underlying assumptions and complex legacy of the "traditional" nuclear family.

Situating the "Traditional" Family

Although the "traditional" nuclear family form is often mistakenly considered to be both timeless and universal, its pervasiveness as an ideal form is much more recent. And the idea that families have only lately undergone change is also inaccurate—"many of Canada's 'new' family forms have always existed but some have done so in the margins, in the shadows, or during specific historical and economic contexts" (Albanese 2010, 5). Changes that produced the North American nuclear family began "at different times in different classes, meant different things to families occupying different positions in the industrial order, and did not proceed in a straight line" (Coontz 2010, 39–40). Some changes—like the development of the male breadwinner model, which separated home and work along gender lines, and a restructuring of many households to include only the husband, wife, and their biological children—coincided with industrialization. And it was not until the 1930s that nuclear family relationships were considered the centre of emotional bonds; before this time, emotional bonding between kin members (siblings, cousins, parents, uncles, aunts, etc.) and close same-sex friends was considered equally important.

Family change has never occurred without public reaction: "Commentators in the 1920s hearkened back to the 'good old days,' bemoaning the sexual revolution, the fragility of nuclear family ties, women's 'selfish' use of contraception, decline of respect for elders, the loss of extended kin ties, and the threat of the 'Emancipated Woman'" (Coontz 2010, 42). "Safeguarding the family" was among the top post-war priorities of the federal government, leading to the establishment of the Canadian Council on Child and Family Welfare (later the National Welfare Council) in 1932, an organization committed to research on families and related policy initiatives (Comacchio 2014). And although the moral panic over "family decline" subsided during the Depression and the Second World War, it re-emerged with a vengeance after 1945. Of primary concern were rising divorce rates, falling fertility rates due to delayed births, and the aggregate number of middle-class women in the paid workforce (Milan 2000; Saccoccio 2007). Post–Second World War government efforts, the media, and professionals did much to reinforce the idea that women's proper place was in the home as wives and mothers. The Family Allowances Act of 1944, for example, mandated that the federal government pay mothers five to eight dollars per month for each child 16 years and younger (Marshall 2006, in Comacchio 2014). In the late 1940s and throughout the 1950s, women's average annual income was 50 per cent less than that of men, despite women's higher education levels (Lowe 2006, 12). For those women who had a choice about whether to engage in paid work, low wages reinforced the idea that women's proper place was in the home. Academics were also guilty of exalting the nuclear family structure and the gendered division of labour as progressive, inevitable, and ideal (Krull 2011; Bradbury 2000, 2005). As renowned sociologists Parsons and Bales argued, "the importance of the family and its function for society constitutes the primary set of reasons why there is a social as distinguished from purely reproductive differentiation of sex roles . . . the male adult will play the role of instrumental leader and the female adult will play the role of expressive leader" (1955, 315–41).

Canada's media frequently offered advice columns and radio talk shows instructing women how to be "good" mothers and wives. Women could pursue their own interests, according to *Chatelaine* magazine, as long as they did so in the name of motherhood: "[T]he accomplished woman should also know a little about everything, since her destiny and that of her children are tied to the fate of the world" (quoted in the Clio Collective 1987, 303; see also Spencer 2006). Television shows, such as *Leave It to Beaver* and *Father Knows Best*, also reinforced the idea of the happy well-adjusted 1950s nuclear family; in these shows, fathers were exalted as successful breadwinners and mothers applauded for having embraced their self-sacrificing role as family care-workers (Krull 2011).

Government and employment policies, influenced by the media, academics, and other professionals, were incredibly successful. The die had been cast in the public imaginary: adult men were natural breadwinners, while the modern woman was fundamentally a wife and mother (Spencer 2006, 226; Baker 2001, 92). Within a few years, fewer than 5 per cent of Canadians believed it acceptable for mothers to be employed outside the home. Accordingly, the percentage of women remaining single dropped significantly, marriage rates soared, and the average age of marriage decreased by two years so that more than 40 per cent of women were married by their twenty-second birthday (ibid.). An unprecedented Baby Boom ensued and, by 1959, women were having an average of 3.9 children (Ambert 2006, 9). Not surprisingly, the education gap between men and women dramatically increased and divorce rates plummeted to only one in twenty marriages (Milan 2000; Owram 1999). As domesticity and consumerism skyrocketed, there was for many a sense of stability and a renewed faith in family life, all of which diminished the earlier perceived threats of family decline (Lowe 2006). Approximately 100 years after the "cult of domesticity," more Canadians than in any other era were finally able to approximate the Victorian ideal of the male breadwinner family (Comacchio 2014, 34).

The relative stability and optimism of this decade, however, was anomalous, aggrandized over the ensuing years, and certainly not experienced by all Canadian families; gross inequities existed across racial, class, religious, age, sexuality, (dis)ability, and gender lines. The adversity suffered by many families often occurred in silence, which only marginalized them further (Luxton and Corman 2001, 40). Knowledge or suspicion of an individual's being gay were grounds for firing, many public schools segregated African-Canadians, and concerted government efforts were aimed at rupturing Aboriginal families. Families headed by unskilled or non-unionized workers, women, recently arrived immigrants, and the families of unilingual Francophones in Quebec failed to "share in the bounty" in an era of widespread economic prosperity (Comacchio 2014, 33). But marginalized groups were not alone in being negatively affected by the privileging of the nuclear family model. Difficulties experienced within many middle-class nuclear families were obscured because it was simply not conceivable that ideal families could suffer from "alcoholism, substance abuse, spousal abuse, child abuse, poverty, mental illness, stress and marital problems . . . But, at the time . . . airing dirty laundry was considered shameful" (Lowe 2006, 12). And since family matters were private, many struggled with problems in silence. This was particularly true for women who, because of their subordinate status within families, their restricted access to resources, and their isolation in their homes, were cut off from any potential support from friends and the community.

Legacy of Privileging the Nuclear Family

Despite evidence to the contrary, the 1950s are still referred to as the "golden age" of the family. **Neo-conservative** narratives bemoaning family decline and advocating a return to traditional family values have infused Canadian politics for some time. Proponents of this view argue that the rise in divorce, single parenthood, cohabitation, same-sex marriage, and feminism, coupled with rising individualism and weakening religiosity, are responsible for eroding family values and placing children at risk (Walker 2003, 407). The rhetoric of strengthening nuclear families and the traditional values of marriage was the foundation of the Family Coalition Party's platform in the 2007 Ontario provincial election, which ran a record number of candidates in 83 electoral districts and won more than 35,000 votes. Likewise, Ted Morton, Alberta's former minister of finance and enterprise and a former political science professor, tried but failed to pass Bill 208, which sought to prevent human rights complaints against teachers and marriage commissioners who do not accept gay marriage (McLean 2010, 2006). Morton also maintains that "social scientists are finally recognizing the social and economic value of the traditional family and the moral infrastructure that it helps to sustain" (Morton 1998).

Idealizing the traditional nuclear family in this way reinforces the fallacy that families operate as independent, self-contained units that satisfy the needs of their members and that the family is ideally suited for raising children. The evidence, however, is to the contrary. Paid work by both parents is a necessity and not a choice for most two-parent families. As such, the majority (85 per cent) of parents are employed, and non-family members are often involved in child care (Vanier Institute of the Family 2010a; Hansen 2005; Iacovetta 2006). Furthermore, marriage does not guarantee stability, as evidenced by high Canadian divorce rates (Le Bourdais and Lapierre-Adamcyk 2004, 937–8), and healthy, adjusted children are just as likely to be found in non-nuclear families (Walker 2008; Strohschein 2007; Smart and Neale 1999). Privileging the nuclear family also places a higher value on children who are genetically related to their parents, which explains a booming reproductive services industry despite numerous Canadian children waiting to be adopted; adoption is clearly viewed as an "inferior way of forming a family" (Satz 2007, 525). The persistence of the nuclear family form "continues to haunt the interpretation of relationships and the assignment of responsibilities" in the collective Canadian imagination (Harder 2011, 10).

Contrary to research demonstrating that marriage, mothering, and fathering have dissimilar meanings for different communities and, as such, are highly contested categories (Baines 2004a; Baines and Freeman 2011; Das Gupta 2000; Collins 2000, 1990; Nelson 2006; Smith 1987), non-normative Canadian families continue to be scrutinized and even penalized. The history of residential schools, the "sixties scoop,"[2] and existing child-welfare practices are but three examples of colonial and paternalistic government initiatives that intended to force conformity but that resulted in ravaging Aboriginal families, communities, and cultures (Krull 2006; Das Gupta 2000; Baines and Freeman 2011). Recently, the federal government admitted its culpability:

> We now recognize that, in separating children from their families, we undermined the ability of many to adequately parent their own children and sowed the seeds for generations to follow. . . . The government of Canada sincerely apologizes and asks the forgiveness of aboriginal peoples for failing them so badly. (Former prime minister Stephen Harper, quoted in Curry and Galloway 2008, A1)

Despite such apologies, federal policies undermining Aboriginal families continue, evidenced by a child-welfare system in which almost half (48.1 per cent) of foster children are Aboriginal (Statistics Canada, 2011)—more than 8000 Aboriginal children (about 5 per cent of all Aboriginal children) have been removed from their homes across Canada (Canadian Press 2008; Krull 2010). And the state not only interferes with how certain parents care, teach, and safeguard their children; it also determines who legitimately belongs to a family. Even after liberal changes to Canada's immigration policies, the nuclear family model continues to be used as a standard in deciding which family members can immigrate to Canada. The dominant immigration discourse connotes that Canada's family reunification program "needs to be based on the Canadian nuclear family, not the extended Asian or African family" (Neborak 2013, 11).

Although Ottawa has been involved in family life for more than a century, only a fragmentary set of programs and policies exists, rather than a comprehensive national family policy. The state has tended to limit its involvement primarily to situations of child abuse, child neglect, and limited family financial resources; and even in these situations, intervention has varied by gender and across different income and cultural/ethnic groups (Baker 2010). The constitutional impediment to developing a cohesive national family policy is that different levels of government—federal, provincial, and territorial—have assumed different responsibilities. Ottawa focuses primarily on income support, while provincial and territorial governments primarily concentrate on welfare assistance, child protection, and other services, all resulting in significant regional variations (Krull 2014; O'Hara 1998). Embracing a neo-liberal agenda that individualizes family/work pressures and difficulties, the different levels of government have typically relied on surveillance techniques to identify those who are deserving of state support. Child-welfare and child-care benefits are cases in point. Little (2011, 203–4) argues that the available evidence notwithstanding, in blaming adults for poverty and unemployment, the neo-liberal state has "embraced a discourse calling for the alleviation of the child poverty and promoting social policy that separates children's needs from [those] of their parents. . . . Poor mothers are

raising poor children, and it is the mothers' poverty that must first be addressed
. . . not increased surveillance mechanisms for poor mothers." It is not surprising
that poverty rates remain high despite an aggressive national campaign to eradicate child poverty (Krull 2014). Recently, the federal government introduced the
"Family Tax Cut," a new non-refundable tax credit for eligible couples with min-
or children. The tax cut is based on the net reduction of federal tax that would be
realized if up to $50,000 of an individual's taxable income was transferred to the
individual's eligible spouse or common-law partner (Canada Revenue Agency,
2014). Research from the Howe Institute, however, suggests that income splitting
is primarily beneficial for families earning more than $125,000 a year (Laurin
and Kesselman 2011). Clearly, neo-liberal agendas tend to privilege nuclear families, particularly white, middle-class, two-parent ones, while targeting and even
penalizing non-normative families.

Canada's Family Diversity

The ideal nuclear family form not only has had dire consequences for many Canadians; it also does not reflect how most Canadians live as families. Just about a
quarter of all census families[3] were classified as nuclear families in 2011 (Statistics
Canada 2012a), which corroborates observations from the Vanier Institute of the
Family (2011):

> The most significant change affecting definitions of families over the
> last fifty years has been the gradual uncoupling of socially acceptable
> sexuality, marriage, parenting and cohabitation. Regulations and ex-
> pectations about mutual economic support have also changed . . . It has
> become easier for more people to engage in different practices and as a
> result, families have changed dramatically.

The institution of marriage has also become less prevalent. Whereas married-
couple families comprised 80 per cent of all family forms 20 years ago, they account for only 67 per cent today; similarly, the percentage of common-law couple
families has increased from 7 per cent to over 16 per cent, surpassing the number of lone-parent families for the first time in 2011 (Statistics Canada 2012a).
And even when the 2005 Civil Marriage Act (Bill C-38) was first passed, legal-
izing same-sex marriage, only 17 per cent of same-sex Canadian couples opted
to marry (Statistics Canada 2007). Today, only a third of same-sex couples have
married (Statistics Canada 2012a). Not only are there fewer marriages, particularly in Quebec[4]—marriages no longer endure as they once did. Approximately
41 per cent of marriages are terminated by the thirtieth wedding anniversary,
while the percentage of repeat divorces—people divorcing two or more times—
has tripled in the past three decades (Statistics Canada 2012a).

Given the waning popularity of marriage and the wider acceptance of divorce,
the percentage of children living with married parents in the same household has

significantly decreased over 20 years—from about 81 per cent to 66 per cent—and the number of lone-parent households, especially female-headed ones, has been steadily rising. Indeed, in 2011 approximately 8 in 10 lone-parent families were female lone-parent families (Statistics Canada 2012a). The 2011 Census also counted stepfamilies for the first time. In the past, stepfamilies typically resulted when one spouse died and the other remarried; today, stepfamilies generally result from remarriage following a divorce or the dissolution of a common-law union (Vanier Institute of the Family 2010b). In Canada, stepfamilies account for approximately 13 per cent of all couple families with children, out of which 7 per cent of couples with children are simple stepfamilies while 5 per cent are blended families. Most complex stepfamilies include at least one child of both parents as well as at least one child of one parent only (approximately 4 per cent of all couples with children) (Statistics Canada, 2012a.).

Adding to family diversity is the significant increase in education levels: approximately 64 per cent of Canadians between 25 and 64 years have either college or university education (Statistics Canada, 2013a). As such, young adults leave home, marry, or cohabit and have children at a later age. Increased education levels have also altered gender roles in both the home and the workplace (Vanier Institute of the Family, 2010c). The financial constraints associated with post-secondary education, the high costs of housing, and difficulty finding jobs in the same area as one's partner have resulted in the creation of a new family form—LAT or **living apart together couples** who are in a stable relationship but do not live together (Turcotte 2013). In 2011, approximately 7 per cent of Canadians aged 20 years and over were in an LAT relationship (ibid.).

Concurrently, the birth rate has decreased by more than 50 per cent, and the average number of children per woman has dropped to well below the requisite 2.2 for population replacement (Milan 2013). In Canada, more families are composed of couples without children than those with children—45 per cent and 39 per cent, respectively (Statistics Canada 2012a). Paradoxically, children live with their parent(s) much longer, often into their twenties (Turcotte 2006), and the transition to adulthood is taking longer to complete (Clark 2007). According to the Vanier Institute of the Family (2013), "the proportion of young adults aged 20 to 29 living in the parental home has increased from 27 per cent in 1981 to 42 per cent in 2011."

And it is not just that Canadians are opting to have fewer or no children. How they can become parents has also radically changed as surrogacy, sperm banks, in vitro fertilization, transnational and transracial adoption, and the implanting of frozen embryos have become more commonplace.[5] Moreover, how Canadians parent is also changing. According to the Vanier Institute of the Family (2010d, 8), "[T]he division of labour in parenting has become a more complex process with more role ambiguity, more emphasis on negotiation of roles, and more fluidity in the way that parents respond to the demands of everyday life." Fathers have become much more involved in doing care-work for their children (Doucet 2014, 2011, 2006b, 2004). The most recent statistics from Statistics Canada (2008) suggest that the percentage of stay-at-home fathers has increased by 25 per cent since 1976, while the proportion of stay-at-home mothers has decreased by approximately the same figure (Doucet 2014). In Canada (excluding Quebec), 13 per cent of eligible fathers claimed parental benefits in 2009 (Statistics Canada 2009). As a testimony to Quebec's generous family policy, approximately 79 per cent of eligible fathers took parental leave in 2009 (ibid.).

Age-related provisions were identified as the single most common form of care provision in 2012 (Sinha 2013). Thirty-nine per cent of the 8 million family caregivers in Canada provide care to an aging parent (Turcotte 2013). Given that disability has been increasing, related to an aging population, the number of Canadians doing elder care is expected to rise. But younger family members caring for senior family members remains less prevalent than the reverse situation (McDaniel 1997, 2003; Rozanova, Northcott, and McDaniel 2006; Mandell and Wilson 2011). Multi-generational bonds have become an increasingly important resource to many Canadian families, perhaps "more important than nuclear family ties for well-being and support" (Bengtson 2001, 5; see also Collins 2005; McDaniel 2001, 2002, 2008; Pahl and Spencer 2004; Roseneil and Budgeon 2004; Stacey 1996, 2004). Approximately 6.3 million grandparents reside in Canada. Of these, almost one-half are under the age of 65, and many are still employed; the majority provide valuable assistance—both financial and care-work—to their families (Vanier Institute of the Family 2013). Skip-generation households are also becoming commonplace: according to the 2011 census, among children aged 14 and under, close to 5 per cent lived in households that contained at least one grandparent. Of these children, 30,005 (0.5 per cent) lived in skip-generation families, that is, with grandparents and not with their parents (Statistics Canada 2012a). Approximately 44 per cent of Aboriginal grandparents are involved in raising grandchildren (Baines and Freeman 2011). Ethnicity and immigration status are also associated with multigenerational living in Western countries such as Canada (Chappell, McDonald, and Stones 2008). Families of Asian origins, particularly immigrant families, are most likely to live in multigenerational households (Gee 1997). In one study, for example, the authors found that among South Asian older adults living in Edmonton, Alberta, those who immigrated later in life were less likely than those who had immigrated earlier to live alone or only with a spouse, resulting in an increase in the number of multigenerational households (Ng, Northcott, and Abu-Laban 2007). Clearly, "the traditional nuclear family is a social institution facing stiff competition" (Krull 2014, 293).

Created families or **fictive kin relationships** are also becoming important as families are progressively separated by geographic distance. Created families function in ways similar to many other families in terms of caring and supporting one another. The major difference is that fictive kin are chosen: "[T]hey are free of many of the more formal role prescriptions which govern families' relations" (de Vries 2010; cf. Maupin 2007, 3, who distinguishes between "logical families" and "biological procreative families"). Although more Canadians are choosing to live within created families, family sociologists warn that using the language of "family" to define and legitimize these alternative social units might obscure their uniqueness and importance (ibid.).

The more than 200 ethnic groups in Canada have also contributed to the multitude of ways in which we live as families. Approximately one in five Canadians is foreign born, the highest proportion among the G8 countries (Statistics Canada 2012b). As the permeability of national boundaries has increased due to globalization and transnationalism, families divided by borders have become common, although their transnational experiences vary by gender, age, ethnicity, country of origin, and occupational class (Dreby 2006; Krull 2011). For instance, one study found that transnational Chinese families in Vancouver exemplified how "social relationships can operate over significant distance, spanning national borders, and reducing the importance of face-to-face context in personal interaction" (Waters 2002, 118). In a testimony to persistent transnational ties, a recent report suggests that Canadians, mostly foreign-born, remit close to $24 billion overseas in one fiscal year (Maclean's 2013). However, this is not the case for all **transnational families**. In comparison to non-immigrants, immigrants are more likely to earn significantly lower incomes and have difficulty finding employment and housing (Lowe 2006, 6). In responding to global market demands for low-wage female domestic and service labour, numerous women from developing countries have left their families to take on low-paying domestic work abroad. The consequence has been new forms of marginality (Dreby 2006, Krull 2006, Lan 2003, Young 2001), an international division of gendered reproductive labour (Salazar Parreñas 2008, 2005), and new mothering arrangements as these workers try to care for their own families from a distance (Mandell and Wilson 2011; Hondagneu-Sotelo 2007). Clearly, care-work remains "gendered, raced, and classed in its norms and expectations, in its involvement and intensity, in the relationship of caregivers to care recipients, and in its effects on individuals and social arrangements" (Mandell and Wilson 2011, 30).

Modifications in market work have affected Canadians differently. The male breadwinner–family wage model of 48 hours for 48 weeks for 48 years, often associated with the ideal nuclear family, no longer reflects the majority of paid-market work (Siltanen and Doucet 2008, 98). Whereas 67 per cent of 1950s family households had a single earner, only 14.4 per cent have one today (Lowe 2006; Vanier Institute of the Family 2010a: 5). Globalization has changed the kinds of jobs and sectors in which Canadians work. A growing number of Canadians are also working in part-time, temporary, or self-employed jobs that offer low pay, little or no job security, and few benefits. Intensifying pre-existing employment inequalities, most of these jobs are held by women, who make up almost 75 per cent of the part-time workforce: more than 60 per cent in part-time or part-time self-employment and approximately 70 per cent in part-time shift work (Siltanen and Doucet 2008, 98; Vanier Institute of the Family 2010b, 1). Shift workers also "report lower levels of satisfaction with their work–life balance than regular nine-to-five day workers and are more likely to report role over-load—that is, having too much to do and not enough time to do it" (Vanier Institute 2010d, 1). Women remain overrepresented in certain occupations, have fewer opportunities but more workforce constraints, receive less pay than men in all occupations, and remain responsible for the majority of unpaid household and family care-work (ibid.; Siltanen and Doucet 2008, 105; Mandell and Wilson 2011; Baker 2010; Bezanson 2010).

The "great recession" of 2008 has further entrenched inequalities and family conflict by differentially impacting families as well as individual family members (Bezanson 2010; Duffy and Pupo 2011). One-half of the alarming 486,000 job losses between October 2008 and July 2009 were suffered by young people be-tween the ages of 15 and 24; men aged 25–54 lost twice as many jobs as women in this age group (Tipper and Sauvé 2010, 2), primarily because of a marked decline in demand for manufactured and industrial products, particularly in the auto-mobile-related sectors (Bezanson 2010, 9). Many of these jobs have been replaced by "jobs with poor characteristics," precarious part-time and temporary work filled mostly by women (Duffy and Pupo 2011, 101). By the end of the third quar-ter in 2009, average household debt to income ratio increased to an unpreced-ented 145 per cent, and the average household debt reached $96,100 (Tipper and Sauvé 2010, 2). Of course, some families are experiencing these burdens more intensely than others: 59 per cent of employed Canadians would have trouble making ends meet if their paycheque were delayed even one week (ibid, 4). Cri-tiquing **neo-liberalism**—Canada's economic response to this crisis—the argu-ment is that

> the great recession, then, creates a crisis in social reproduction for fam-ilies who must find new ways to respond at the household level to the varied needs of members, often without adequate resources. . . . These crises—which ultimately affect our collective social and human cap-acities and capabilities . . . have left families increasingly vulnerable. (Bezanson 2010, 6–7)

Neo-liberalism has, moreover, disproportionately affected women, especial-ly those marginalized and/or most dependent on the state, such as low-income mothers (Little 2011, 199). The great recession has substantially exacerbated the disparity between families in poverty and those with resources; indeed, the rich-est 20 per cent of Canadians took home 44.2 per cent of total after-tax income, whereas the poorest 20 per cent's share was only 4.9 per cent (Canadian Centre for Policy Alternatives 2011; cf. Vanier Institute of the Family 2011). Also telling is the number of people using food bank services. According to a recent report by Food Banks Canada (2014), an alarming 850,000 people ask for help from a food bank each and every month.

More positively, the new economy is facilitating a trend "toward gender con-vergence" in both paid work and care-work. As already noted, women have for some time taken on greater economic responsibilities and, more recently, men are becoming more involved in domestic and care-work. The "traditional patriarchal male—the boss, breadwinner, and head of the household—will likely find difficulty in fitting into either the new economy or emergent families and communities" (Duffy and Pupo 2011, 112). Some scholars predict that young adult men may even become more involved in their families and communities and less committed to their employment given this climate of employment insecurity (Rubin and Brody 2005; Duffy and Pupo 2011).

Conclusion: Families Exist and They Still Matter

Families exist and they matter; and, importantly, there is not just one kind of family—that is, one that reflects the supposed golden ideal of the 1950s. If Canadians today were asked what "the family" is, there would be as many responses as people asked. The reason is simple: how we understand *family* is how we experience it. While agreeing that a typical family is mythical, the majority of Canadians also maintain that family is the most important thing in their lives; moreover, they prefer to live as families. What has changed in the past half-century is the multitude of ways that Canadians understand the meaning of this institution. However, there tends to be an incongruity between personal experiential understandings and the ideal traditional nuclear family so deeply rooted in culture and memory. In the end, *family* cannot be defined by who belongs to it but, rather, by what it does.

Family diversity does not necessarily imply choice. One does not choose to be an impoverished single mother or to traverse the obstacles that immigrant families often experience. Of course, choices about how we live as families do exist; many people can choose with whom to cohabit or marry, whether to have a child as a married or single parent, whether to move to a different country, and more. Class, ethnicity, age, education, gender, sexuality, support networks, geographic region, access to resources, and other factors determine and shape our choices. While the nuclear family still prevails in the public imaginary as the ideal form—despite growing diversity in how Canadians choose to live as families—the concomitant deinstitutionalization of marriage and the tendency of Canadians to move in and out of different family forms throughout their lifetime indicate that the links between traditional and non-traditional families are fluid, not closed.

Moreover, the perception that work and family are incompatible spheres that need to be reconciled or balanced is premised on the male breadwinner/female homemaker traditional family model (Krull 2011). Opting for one or the other part of the equation speaks to the dilemma of "choice" between professional employment and family; a long-familiar frustration is that both cannot be done well or can only be accomplished with the most skilful of balancing acts. Many conceptions within family and work literature—reconciliation, balance, conflict, integration—begin with the notion of a division in need of reconciliation. Despite the multiplicity of family types, workplaces, and political institutions today, the traditional family model persists, reinforcing the widely accepted conception of separate family and work spheres. Not surprisingly, for some time the household work/paid work dichotomy has produced feminist critiques centring on the dearth of effectual government policies facilitating family care-work within the economy of employment.

Thus, families need better government support; but Canadian family policies have not only been in short supply, they also have not adapted to the changes that have taken place over the past few decades. Parents, especially women, do not need direction on how to balance work and family; they need options that increase their choices so they do not have to choose between family care-work and paid work. Policies that aid all parents in incorporating family and work are essential. Alternatively, we can continue denying, resisting, displacing, and holding to a singular ideology of the family by not providing social and economic conditions that make life for diverse contemporary families viable, let alone dignified and secure. It is evident that "families constitute the basis of Canadian society and government policy must account for these changes, particularly as they pertain to families raising children" (Krull 2014, 293). The rest of Canada can learn from Quebec, which has taken the lead by implementing comprehensive family policies geared toward assisting parents in balancing paid work and family responsibilities, promoting parental employability, and reducing poverty—such as its universal, inexpensive 24/7 child-care program, and the 2004 Act to Combat Poverty and Social Exclusion. As a result, Quebec's child poverty has decreased by 50 per cent, children's test scores have improved, and the province now boasts the highest percentage of mothers who are in the workforce (Canadian Council on Social Development 2008; CUPE Ontario 2008; Krull 2010). A recent study by the Canadian Centre for Policy Alternatives (CCPA) reports that Quebec's provincial policies, particularly low daily fees, have made it "dramatically cheaper for parents to place children in child care" (CCPA 2014). While Quebec's family policies remain the most innovative and ambitious in the country and provide North America's only example of an integrated approach to family policy, the rest of Canada has yet to even develop a comprehensive poverty reduction plan.

We need to accept that families are crucially important to Canadians, but also that families are varied as social units and that their survival is connected intimately to the economy and workplace. How Canadian society understands this situation and responds to the dissimilar needs, strengths, opportunities, and challenges confronting families must be at the forefront as we move through the twenty-first century.

Review/Summary Questions

1. What are the underlying assumptions and pervasive legacy of the "tradition-al" nuclear family?
2. The 1950s have been discursively constructed as the "golden era" of the trad-itional nuclear family. Discuss the role of the media, government policies, and academics in perpetuating this ideal.
3. What are some of the "new" family forms in Canada? What value lies in having a variety and diversity of families in Canada?
4. What are some of the challenges faced by immigrant families in Canada?
5. How has neo-liberalism affected women? How does it impact family–work balance?

Notes

1. I would like to acknowledge the excellent research assistance of Mushira Khan, who is com-pleting her PhD in Sociology at the University of Victoria.
2. The "sixties scoop" was a government initiative that involved child-welfare authorities taking Aboriginal children from their homes, communities, and cultures—without permission and often forcibly—and adopting or fostering them out to primarily non-Aboriginal families.
3. A census family is composed of "a married couple or a common-law couple, with or without children, or of a lone parent living with at least one child in the same dwelling. A couple can be of the opposite sex or of the same sex" (Statistics Canada 2007, 10).
4. Quebec also has the highest cohabitation rates in the country: approximately 31.5 per cent of all couples live common-law compared to 12 per cent in the rest of Canada (Statistics Canada 2012a).
5. Access to the array of reproductive choices differs across gender, class, sexuality, age, and race (Roberts 2005; Fogg-Davis 2005; Bartholet 2005; Davis 2001; see also the edited volume by Haslanger and Witt 2005). Moreover, reproductive technologies have been used primarily to reproduce normative understandings of family rather than to radicalize them (Baker 2005; Satz 2007; Spar 2006; Cornell 2005; Haslanger 2005; Throsby and Gill 2004).

PART II

Social Questions

Part II shifts the focus of our discussion from self-identity to explicit concerns with the concept of the "social." Recall that the "social" refers to a subject terrain that emerges when we focus directly on collective relations in and of themselves—without reducing this terrain to individual or psychological matters. More specifically, the essays in this part explore forms of the social in different contexts, showing how to address it (as well as why it is important to do so), and examining the concept's contemporary relevance.

In the opening chapter, Lois Harder argues that most Canadians expect publicly funded social programs and even assess governments on their ability to provide effective social services. In effect, Canadians have responded in the affirmative to Harder's question, "Is Social Welfare Viable?" However, this endorsement, Harder argues, does not capture several important changes to the very idea and provision of social welfare. Harder outlines the unique history of social welfare in Canada before highlighting an influential attack on (Keynesian) social welfare precepts that emerged in the 1980s (especially in the area of social assistance), launched by people aligned with broadly based "neo-liberal" frameworks. They did so from within a rapidly changing socio-economic context and alongside a protracted constitutional crisis. Despite internal differences, advocates of neo-liberal thinking sought to reduce the state's role in regulating markets, families, and communities, calling for increasing "private spheres." When directed to social welfare, this approach called for a system overhaul, emphasizing private (consumer) "choice" and "responsibility." Harder highlights how such thinking helped to bring about significant changes to social welfare, such as with the National Child Benefit. Examples of this order show the extent to which social welfare is directly involved in shaping individual and social identities, "integrating citizens into the prevailing mode of economic production," and legitimating particular forms of government. The examples indicate that the viability of any vision of social welfare (such as Keynesian or neo-liberal) is dependent on how it reinforces social relations between individuals, families, markets, and the state. Harder concludes by considering whether the time has now arrived to ask whether neo-liberal approaches to social welfare are themselves viable.

In Chapter 7, Elaine Power imagines the idea of the social from a different vantage as she asks, "What Are Social Determinants of Health?" Rather than understanding health as a purely individual matter dependent on advanced clinical intervention, she adopts a broader view that recognizes health as socially generated. For example, certain social groups—such as people who live in poverty, Indigenous people, and racialized minorities—are more prone to disease and death than other ("richer, more powerful") groups. It is striking that such configurations of health, death, and disease tend to operate within and across countries. Furthermore, they may be understood by referring not so much to individual factors but to "social determinants of health"; that is, the "social, political, economic and cultural conditions, forces and factors that influence how health is distributed among groups and populations." Exploring how such social determinants shape the distribution of health, death, and disease in populations, Power argues that the pursuit of social justice can liberate societies from inequality, racism, sexism, and the negative effects of colonialism—thereby improving overall population health.

In responding to the question "How Do Immigrants Integrate?" Lori Wilkinson's chapter provides an overview of migration to Canada, exploring why people come here, where they tend to settle (and how this changes over time), and the extent to which different immigrants participate in Canadian society. Tapping various sociological imaginations on the question of immigration and settlement, Wilkinson explores how sociologists understand economic, social, and cultural integration into society. She notes, too, that excluding people for participation can lead to dissent and disruption. Wilkinson concludes the chapter by showing how different sociological traditions explain "how immigrants can succeed or fail in various aspects of the integration process." The outcome of the latter, no doubt, will have important effects on the overall shape of future society.

Chapter 9 offers a sociological analysis of the Maritime region's economy in response to the question, "What Are the Challenges of Economic Transition?" Specifically, Jennifer Jarman explores changes to the ways that livelihoods are produced in Canada's Atlantic region. Evoking a sociological imagination that draws on Marx and Weber, Jarman references some key economic changes that have affected the social orders of people living in the region. She does so by first outlining the region's historical reliance on a natural resource–based economy. Jarman then outlines more recent economic changes that have produced high rates of unemployment and an "out-migration of young Atlantic Canadians" with various consequences. In efforts to stem such outflows, various economic initiatives—such as call centre work—try to create sustained employment. On the basis of field research into the call centre industry, Jarman outlines and assesses the contours of such work. Despite several perceived problems with the industry—its transience, its image problem (e.g., unsolicited phone calls), the fact that it involves close employee surveillance, and so on—she notes that it does provide entry-level jobs at the lower end of the service economy. As such, this industry "goes some way toward replacing the lost resource-based jobs in industries such as coal mining, fishing, and agriculture." Jarman concludes by indicating that the Atlantic region case shows how changes to livelihoods have consequential effects on a society.

Chapter 10 addresses another essential element of the fabric of the social by posing this question: "What Is Communication?" The word *communication* stems from its Latin root, *communicare*, which means "to share" and involves "the imparting, conveying, or exchange of ideas, knowledge, information, etc." There are thus many ways of communicating and indeed ways to understand communication—for example, through sociological and other (communication studies) imaginations. Sandra Robinson provides a summary of different models and approaches that explore various elements of communication as "a technology, social process, practice, and cultural phenomenon central to human experience." These theories enable us to understand how communication changes over time. They also allow us to see that what is pictured as communicating in context is intricately involved with, and shaped by, changing social and technological forms. Robinson shows that studying communication today "requires us to think not simply of the effects of the meaning of a message symbolically coded for transmission as communication"; rather we should understand that the very codes, technologies, and software program fuelling contemporary digital communications are multidirectional and help to shape messages in our society. For example, Robinson tells us that "[i]n this moment of communication-by-Twitter, in short 140 character bursts, McLuhan's ideas seem very relevant: the medium of Twitter indeed shapes the message."

Continuing along these lines of communication, Chapter 11 asks an important question about media technologies in Canada and beyond: "How Does Media Transform Society?" Reflecting on the social significance of a changing media landscape, Daniel Downes describes a shift in the past 25 years from old to new media. Old media are characterized as having emerged from a single source (a newspaper company, for instance), and as delivering a single content with the aim of creating a common experience among the audience. One of the main features of old media is that the direction of communication moved from media outlets (governments and corporations) to a mass audience. Mass audiences, in other words, did not interact with or control the media's content or form. Moreover, old media was most often concerned with communicating middle-class values to its audience. As technology, industry (for instance, phone and television cabling), and regulations developed and converged, the old shifted to new digital and interactive media. With the invention of the Internet, Facebook, Twitter, Tumblr, Instagram, and so on, media "users"—that is, members of the social—are able to take a much more active role in shaping media's content and form. As a result, as Downes notes, new media target a much more diverse and fragmented global audience. And precisely because many different people post new media content, the sources are less professional. Whether old or new, concerns about the negative influence of the media on attitudes and behaviours continue to be voiced and debated. Whereas 1930s society once worried about young people sitting with strangers in a darkened movie theatre, people today are concerned with (say) young people's access to uncensored material on the Internet. Sociologists are interested in the dramatic shift from old to new media and in its implications for social structures and relations. Downes indicates the depth of the change in these words: "Audiences have fragmented and migrated to new sources of information, but have also become 'users' and content providers in the new media environment, requiring of us new skills and awareness of the importance of mediated communication."

Chapter 12 tackles a rather different social question: "Should Policing Be Privatized?" Curtis Clarke starts by indicating that such a question is perhaps inadequate when dealing with a context where policing has already, in many areas, been privatized. In fact, he argues that Canadian policing has for some time been privatized, to a greater or lesser degree. This has generated a "plural policing environment" that has radically altered how we might approach concepts about the provision, accountability, and public good of policing services. The privatizing of policing has also problematized the role of the state in each of these domains. As Clarke points out, the idea of policing as a public good has faced considerable challenges in this ethos, fuelled as it is by a neo-liberal ideology that calls for the privatization of previous state-run services; this privatizing process blurs the lines between private and public spheres. As a result, policing provides a useful site in which to examine the complex relationships among the state, ideology, and its citizens, suggesting new possibilities for understanding the very idea of a public good (for example, through civic coordination). Such issues raise important questions about the role of the state in providing "equitable policing" that holds key stakeholders responsible for public safety. Perhaps a more apposite question in the context of Canadian society would be this: "How will new forms of policing challenge the role of the state in providing equitable policing, and how might state regulation ensure that all providers are held accountable and responsible for public security and safety?"

In Chapter 13, Nob Doran responds to the question "What Do Official Statistics Tell Us about Ourselves?" He does so by narrating a personal intellectual journey through various social theories dealing with the status of official statistics. Doran expressly challenges the common-sense view that official statistics provide an objective, impartial representation of different aspects of society. He outlines two levels of critique directed at this view. On a local level, Doran describes how ethnomethodological approaches in sociology alerted him to the subjective, everyday decisions that statistical researchers must inevitably make when creating statistics, especially the founding categories (e.g., suicides, homicides) that purportedly impartial statistical methods are directed at. Rather than leading sociologists to accept social statistics as neutral knowledge, critical approaches encourage sociologists to examine the everyday social relations that produce particular statistics. Doran argues that Dorothy Smith's feminist and Marxist-inspired formulations help further by focusing explicitly on how power creates official social statistics. He also endorses Foucault's claim that power and knowledge are inseparably connected—this opens the way for sociologists to examine types of power that create statistical knowledge. Doran then outlines various debates on the precise form of that power, before urging readers to reflect on how their age, class, gender, ethnicity, etc. affect their interpretations of specific claims and texts.

The final chapter of Part II—"Who Governs Whom in Canada?"—begins by recalling one of the book's recurring themes: governance, or the ways in which people's thoughts and actions are part and parcel of the ways they are controlled and ruled. Author Dawn Moore recognizes that we in Canada are governed by a complex interface of formal, informal, local, and general control techniques and in a situation where there are multiple forms of government and jurisdictions (the criminal code, national defence, treaties with First Nations, Aboriginal governance, etc.). As well, "the formal right to govern is assigned through legislation to various levels and forms of government." Different theorists—Durkheim, Marx, Gramsci, and Foucault—have understood the complexities of such governance through various concepts of morality, social inequality, ideological domination, or micro forms of power (e.g., discipline) and normalization. Having outlined these various approaches to the question of governance, Moore outlines various checks and balances designed to ensure that rulers do not go beyond authorized powers. In this respect, her analysis shows how the Charter of Rights and Freedoms is "the most important law in the country" when it comes to ruling the rulers, to keeping governors in check. It is also one that is continuously interpreted and so is shaped by, and yet also shapes, a changing Canadian society.

6 Is Social Welfare Viable?

Lois Harder

Introduction

The question of social welfare's viability is, at its heart, a question of how we think about the relationships among citizens and between citizens and the state. Why is the state interested in social well-being? What responsibilities should the state have for the well-being of the people it governs? And if well-being matters to the state, should the state attend to people's needs through public services, or should it encourage the market, charities, families, or individuals to ensure that people are adequately educated; cared for when ill, young, or elderly; and have adequate income to sustain themselves? Finally what are the consequences of how we choose to define and address issues of social need?

In Canada, only a few voices advocate for complete individual responsibility for citizen well-being. Most of the discussion focuses on the purposes and means of providing welfare and the correct proportions of a welfare mix—that is, what the optimum division of responsibility should be among the state, market, community, family, and individual in providing for people's needs. Canadians, then, have decided that social welfare is viable and should survive. We continue to demand publicly provided social programs, assess the quality of our governments at least partly in terms of the services they provide, and expect that legislation and state action will reflect and enforce the (contested) social norms that shape our interactions. But the statement that welfare is viable obscures some profound changes in social welfare provision. It is these changes and the shifting political and social context in which they emerged that is the focus of this chapter.

Although state-provided social services have existed in Canada since the nineteenth century, the heyday of social welfare came in the years following the Second World War. The war was a watershed moment. It followed a decade of severe economic depression in which many people who wanted to work simply could not find jobs. In turn they had no wages to spend in the market and thus there was no demand for goods. The war effort put an end to these difficulties, but politicians and policy-makers feared that post-war military demobilization might bring about a return to the pre-war economic scenario. Some political leaders also worried that a failure to provide for their citizenry might intensify worker unrest and increase the appeal of a communist alternative. This prospect needed to be avoided not only because of the potential economic effects, but also because of the political and social consequences that were likely to arise if the heavy sacrifices of soldiers and their families were not acknowledged and rewarded. Immediately following the war, there was also a social climate of solidarity. People had worked together in pursuit of a common cause and thus the idea that the people—through the agencies of the state—were responsible for protecting each other from a variety of social, economic, and political risks had an intuitive logic.

This general social tenor provided fertile ground for the ideas of John Maynard Keynes, the architect of post-war economic management in industrialized countries. Keynes asserted that in times of economic downturn, national governments should establish social programs to ensure that people would still have enough money to purchase goods, thus sustaining individuals and families and keeping economies functioning. In the **Keynesian welfare state**, governments were to finance this intervention by increasing taxes in times of economic growth and by deficit spending during economic slowdowns.

Flash forward to the present and we find a more unsettled approach to the governance of economies and social life. Beginning in the late 1960s, globalizing economies, transformations in labour markets, and changing family formations disrupted the basic assumptions on which the Keynesian social welfare structure was built. Since 1980, Canada, like its Western counterparts, fully embraced a new approach to governing, known in academic contexts as neo-liberalism. Neo-liberalism was a response to the perceived failures of Keynesianism, particularly high levels of public debt, declining economic competitiveness, and a "culture of entitlement," through which an overly generous **welfare state** was said to have created a passive, dependent citizenry with a weak work ethic. Adopting this perspective, governments reformed or simply terminated the social programs of the Keynesian welfare state and **deregulated** (to varying degrees) the exchange of goods and financial transactions. The idea of solidarity or collective responsibility was replaced with an emphasis on the competitive individual, who was to address his or her needs in the market. The 2008 financial crisis did not shake this emphasis on individual responsibility, but it did undermine, at least temporarily, the belief that markets could reliably ensure the health of national economies. The financial collapse of many of the world's large banks, investment firms, and some national treasuries indicated that regulation was necessary and that the state did have a role to play to ensure some stability in the financial system. The leaders of the world's major economies agreed that the Keynesian prescription of financial stimulus provided the means to recovery. But the financial crisis was not neo-liberalism's "Berlin wall moment," as some commentators had predicted. Instead, rising debt in European economies prompted a return to austerity, achieved through deeper cuts to social programs (Brodie 2014, 259–60). And while this response was more muted in Canada—and the crisis less deep here—the volatility of commodity prices, which are so important to Canada's economy, may yet incite a similar set of policy prescriptions.

Defining Social Welfare

Before we interrogate these shifts in greater detail, and thus provide a context for the issue of social welfare's viability, we need to understand what is meant by our central term. *Social welfare* describes programs that fall into three major categories: (1) education (primary, secondary, and post-secondary), (2) health (hospital care, doctor visits), and (3) income supports (old age and disability pensions, unemployment insurance, and social assistance). Indeed, we are familiar with social welfare in a variety of guises—for example, student loans, minimum wage laws, and health insurance.

Some social welfare programs are delivered as direct services. For example, children attend primary and secondary school; sick or injured people go to clinics and hospitals. Other programs are provided indirectly—that is, through the tax system. The tuition and textbook tax credit and registered retirement savings plans operate on this basis. Rather than governments setting up a program or a bricks-and-mortar institution, recipients are reimbursed or credited for purchasing a service in the marketplace. Indirectly provided social programs may reduce the tax owed by eligible citizens or provide funds to people who meet relevant criteria. A low income, for example, entitles people to the Goods and Services Tax Credit, paid quarterly, and low-income families with children receive the Canada Child Tax Benefit every month.

Our eligibility for social welfare is also determined on a variety of bases, generally categorized as universal, contributory, and means-tested. Access to health care in Canada, for example, is a universal entitlement available to all Canadian citizens and permanent residents regardless of income. Employment Insurance (EI) and the Canada/Quebec Pension Plan (CPP/QPP) are contributory social programs in that all workers and employers pay a portion of their earnings into these schemes. However, due to eligibility criteria, contributions do not guarantee access to benefits when people need them. Finally, means-tested programs are provided to people who can demonstrate that they lack sufficient economic resources to meet their basic needs. Perhaps the most notorious means-tested program is social assistance, commonly known as "welfare." Indeed, social assistance was a key site of neo-liberal policy reform in most Canadian provinces. That said, arguments concerning the state's role in providing for citizen well-being have taken place in a number of policy areas.

The Keynesian Welfare State

Keynes's ideas were adopted in Canada but had to be modified to the country's unique circumstances. Keynes's programs relied on relatively closed national economies that would enable national governments to heat up or cool down levels of demand in order to mediate market fluctuations. Since the arrival of European settlers, however, Canada's economy has been open and export-driven and, thus, particularly susceptible to demand from international markets. The second difficulty was Canada's highly decentralized federal system of government—particularly the fact that constitutional jurisdiction over one of the most important tools for implementing Keynesian prescriptions—social policy—lies with the provinces. This is not to say that the federal government has no role in social policy. For example, a constitutional amendment enabled the federal government to administer unemployment insurance and pensions, and the federal government makes regular use of the tax system to provide indirect social programs. Ottawa has also regularly used its spending power to encourage provinces to adopt particular programs and standards. Nonetheless, provincial agreement is a prerequisite for federal social policy initiatives.[1]

The tension surrounding jurisdictional control over social policy points to one of the key rationales for social welfare's survival: the role of social programs in demonstrating to voters that their governments are actually doing something for them. Citizens want to see what their tax dollars are buying, and social programs fill this role. Moreover, in providing for the well-being of citizens, governments articulate a sense of "we-ness" that builds solidarity among citizens and can help to shore up support for a particular provincial (or federal) administration. The capacity of social programs to perform this role is powerfully demonstrated in Quebec, where a succession of provincial leaders, both federalist and sovereignist, have staunchly defended that province's **constitutional autonomy** in this domain. They insist that social programs are integral to the articulation and protection of Quebec's distinctiveness within Canada.

If Keynes's economic management ideas required adaptation to the Canadian context, his assumptions about an appropriate family form were more easily applied. Grounded in the prevailing belief that men and women had distinct roles, part of Keynesian policy included the payment of a family wage to workers. Men's salaries were to be relatively high in order to enable them to provide for their wives and children. In turn, women would attend to the caring needs of the family, with some support through social programs. Critics have pointed out that recent immigrant and racial minority families were often excluded from this vision due to wage discrimination (O'Connor, Orloff, and Shaver 1999, 111). Further, the apparently natural two-parent, single-earner family had to be reinforced through law. For example, women's participation in the labour market had been actively encouraged during the war years when the call to arms drained industrial and agricultural workforces of their male employees. After the war, in an effort to free up industrial jobs for returning veterans, new tax measures were implemented that severely penalized two-earner families (Prentice et al. 1988). As well, employers were allowed to refuse to hire married women, and women did not have the right to demand the same wage as men when they performed the same work. Divorces were difficult to obtain; women could not establish bank accounts or acquire credit without their husbands' permission; and sexual assault laws did not recognize rape within the context of marriage as a crime.

The Crisis of the Welfare State

The Keynesian model of social welfare was always subject to debate and contestation, but its viability was not seriously doubted until the 1980s. By this time, globalization had challenged the capacity and desire of governments to protect national economies, while pressures to reduce public spending and to encourage citizens' involvement in their own governance had increased the appeal of **decentralization**. Further, the political urgency of shielding people from social risk had diminished as memories of the Depression and the Second World War grew hazy and the triumph of capitalist economies over their communist alternatives became ever more certain. Instead, the pressing issues were what to do about government deficits, stagnating economies, rising unemployment and inflation, and (depending on one's political bent) moral decay.

With regard to social welfare, Anglo-American governments and their supporters focused on the expense and the consequences of social programs. This focus was maintained regardless of the ideology of the governing party. Although social welfare was originally envisioned as a means to offset social risks, detractors argued that it had engendered grave misuses of programs, undermined people's willingness to work, and created a dependent citizenry. As well, a number of societal shifts and legislative reforms spurred on by feminists as well as by anti-racism and anti-poverty advocates sparked a policy backlash. Initiatives such as pay equity (equal pay for work of equal value) and employment equity laws (which sought to improve the representation of women, disabled people, racialized minorities, and Aboriginal peoples in large government and corporate workplaces) were resisted or withdrawn on the grounds that their implementation was too expensive and (erroneously) that they valued quota fulfillment more than merit.[2]

The most vicious rebuttal of Keynesian social welfare was reserved for the terrain of social assistance. Citing an upward trend in the number of benefit claimants, a number that did not diminish substantially during the economic recovery of the late 1980s, and borrowing from the anti-welfare rhetoric of the United States, Canadian governments implemented a series of measures to reduce benefits, tighten eligibility criteria, and detect fraud. Governments evaluated their success on the basis of caseload reductions—the number of people removed from the welfare rolls—but invested little energy in determining what became of people who, already in dire financial straits, could no longer count on public assistance. The Alberta government's (short-lived) policy of giving social assistance recipients bus tickets to British Columbia, for example, was indicative of this lack of concern (Peck 2001, 218).

After the Welfare State

Although vigorously resisted, the resolution of the "crisis of the welfare state" was ultimately determined to lie in the neo-liberal strategies of privatization, marketization, decentralization, individualization, and **familialization** (Brodie

1997). The **neo-liberal welfare state** sought to reduce the role of the state in the private sphere—the market, the community, and the home—and, where necessary, to resituate responsibility for public services to the level of government that would be most responsive to the needs of specific communities. Neo-liberals argued that a reinvigoration of the private sphere in all of its dimensions would create a "virtuous circle." They believed that less regulation of markets and increased emphasis on the provision of social services through the market rather than through the state would encourage greater responsiveness to people's needs. Competition would keep costs low while encouraging innovation. A revitalized market would generate jobs, in this view, resulting in less need for social programs (although it was also important to reduce the generosity of income support programs to ensure that workers would be available and willing to work, thus driving down wages through competition in the labour market). Fewer social programs would reduce the costs of governing, thereby contributing to more robust national accounts, reduced taxes, and an enhanced climate for investment. People would be required to live by their wits, thus further stimulating innovation and competitiveness and encouraging the most talented and hard-working people to reach their potential rather than being held back by cumbersome and stifling state regulation and demotivating levels of taxation.

The growing popularity of this set of ideas formed the context in which the question of social welfare's survival was raised. Reconfigured social programs would require a rethinking of the relationship between citizen and state, a rethinking that is illustrated in the shift in terminology—a shift from "security" to "choice" and "responsibility."[3] Neo-liberals (and indeed progressive reformers) asserted that people should be free to select services that best suited their needs and to pursue interests that would contribute to self-development. The possibility of making poor choices was central to this freedom, as neo-liberals believed that the prospect of negative consequences would inspire people to make prudent decisions. When neo-liberal reformers turned their gaze on the family and its role in assuming formerly state-provided services, responsibility emphatically trumped choice. Feminist critics of neo-liberalism have been particularly attentive to this development (Lewis 2001; Jenson and Sineau 2001). They observed the degree to which reduced hospital and long-term-care budgets rely on the labour of family members. Work that had been performed by medical professionals became the duty of a wife, mother, or daughter, whether or not she had the skill, time, or desire to assume these caring tasks. This assumption effectively fell back on "traditional" as well as Keynesian ideas about the gendered **division of labour** despite the fact that wage rates and social policies no longer supported the male-breadwinner family model.

The New Social Welfare

Persuading voters to support a neo-liberal reconfiguration of Canada's social policy regime required a careful plan of attack. While many people were displeased with elements of the Keynesian welfare state, they did not necessarily see greater reliance on the private sphere as the resolution to their concerns. Moreover, the neo-liberal reform effort also had to proceed carefully around programs that had most successfully articulated a collective Canadian identity. For example, the ideas that ill health can befall anyone and that a robust public health-care system is the most important defining feature of the Canadian identity (true in both Quebec and the rest of Canada) suggest that the old notions of collective identity and mutual obligation remain resilient in the face of neo-liberal alternatives (Brodie 2002, 69; Soroka 2007). Still, the neo-liberal marketing plan has had some notable successes. Canadians have generally accepted the characterization of post-war social programs—particularly income support programs—as passive, overly generous handouts that provide too soft a cushion. Canadians have been persuaded by proposals for the creation of an active citizenry that would provide a springboard into the job market and a hand up in times of need. The language of activity, encouragement, and expectations feeds into a sense that citizens need to become more responsible for their own well-being rather than blaming "the system" for their troubles.

In the 2000s, the original slash-and-burn approach of neo-liberal social policy reform took on a slightly gentler tone. European governments as well as the Organisation for Economic Co-operation and Development (OECD) raised concerns regarding the negative social consequences of strict neo-liberal policies. The language of social cohesion, social exclusion, and social investment began to emerge. And while this language was not as prevalent in Canada, Canadian policy-makers did shift their energies from cutbacks to policies that focused on strategic investment. As Denis Saint-Martin explains, the new social policy language emphasized opportunity and the future (2007, 284–5). The emerging regime was dubbed the **social investment state**, and its key figure was the child (Jenson and Saint-Martin 2003; Wiegers 2007). The innocence of children and their obvious dependency made them a suitable object for governments needing to demonstrate their commitment to citizens while embracing neo-liberal individualism. But, even more importantly, children represented the promise of the future, providing a useful distraction from the discomfort of the present.

In this spirit, the federal Liberal government implemented the National Children's Agenda. One of its key programs was the income-tested National Child Benefit (NCB), which had already been introduced in 1997. Provided to families with children, the benefit is offered on a sliding scale—the more income you earn, the lower the benefit. The program also includes a supplement (and, potentially, provincial programs) for families with very low incomes that is designed to encourage them to remain off social assistance. As well, the Liberals also began to invest in early childhood education and embarked on a series of negotiations with the provinces to increase access to child care. But in a fascinating example of the continued resiliency of ideological debate, once the Conservative party was elected in 2006, it promptly cancelled these agreements (but maintained the NCB) and implemented the Universal Child Care Benefit (UCCB). In its universality, this program appears to swim against the tide of neo-liberal reform. On the

Table 6.1 Summary of Keynesian State and Neo-Liberal State

	Economy	State	Family
Keynesian welfare state	• Regulated • National	• Save in good times • Spend in bad times	• Heterosexual, nuclear family with male breadwinner, female caregiver
Neo-liberal state	• Deregulated • Competitive • Globalized	• Policies enabling competition • Reduced protections for workers (Employment Insurance, minimum wage, pensions) • "hand up, not a handout" • Emphasis on children (at least in Canada)	• Family diversity, but two incomes generally necessary • Care purchased in the market or provided by extended kin networks

other hand, it did replace a more expensive child care initiative, and the benefit it delivers is so small that parents must continue to rely on their own resources to meet their children's care needs. Moreover, the UCCB and the announcement, in 2014, of an income-splitting proposal for two-parent families with children under 18 also provide a strong indication of the Conservative government's preferred family form and the party's effort to negotiate between neo-liberalism and moral conservatism. As these programs are most generous to families in which one parent remains out of the workforce to care for children, it provides a larger benefit to two-parent, single-earner families that are sufficiently wealthy to enable one adult to withdraw from paid work. Since the value of these programs is relatively low, again, the benefits cannot reasonably be claimed to meet the purported objective of "providing choice in child care" (Torjman 2015). (The UCCB provides $160 per month, per child under age six, and $60 per child age six to eighteen—which is taxable and thus reduced for income earners, and the maximum available benefit from income-splitting is $2000.) These programs do, however, represent a modest investment in the future while also tipping the hat to the family values of the past.

Conclusion

In this discussion of social welfare, I have argued that the question of its ongoing viability is a product of a particular historical moment in which the fiscal crisis of the state became the focus of public policy. However tempting the elimination of public responsibility for personal well-being might have been to some neo-liberal ideologues, a full-scale public withdrawal from the care of citizens was never really in the cards. The role of social policy in legitimating governments, in integrating citizens into the prevailing mode of economic production, and even in articulating a national identity has made social welfare a key instrument of governance.

These general claims about the significance of social welfare should not, however, blind us to the very significant differences in the way that social welfare is conceived and the dynamism in its purposes. The Keynesian social welfare system, as we have seen, established social programs that buttressed the specific workings of Canada's post-war economy, reinforcing the single-breadwinner, two-parent nuclear family with its gendered division of labour and building a sense of national identity. However, as political struggles were undertaken and economic structures shifted, this arrangement began to weaken, creating a crisis and subsequently a new neo-liberal attempt to articulate the relationships among citizens (as individuals and in families), the market, and the state. Under neo-liberal social welfare prescriptions, a globalized economy is supported by active labour market policies, including a more competitive labour market, enhanced choices for service provision, and increased personal responsibility for forming and maintaining the ties that bind—whether these be at the level of the family, the community, or the nation. What these changes demonstrate is that the viability of any specific social welfare order, whether envisioned by post-war Keynesians or contemporary neo-liberals, rests on whether it establishes a mutually reinforcing and supportive relationship among the individual/family, the market, and the state. It seems to me that some attempt to articulate a more or less coherent framework for these relationships will continue to be a feature of governance for the foreseeable future.

Signs of stress are apparent in the neo-liberal social welfare regime. Concerns about the adequacy of private service provision, the inability of low-wage work to provide an adequate income and the income disparities that it produces, the inattention to work/family balance, and the consequences of budget reductions on public services are matters of growing public concern. How these concerns will be addressed is, again, an open question. Perhaps we will soon find ourselves asking, though this time in a new context, whether neo-liberal social welfare is itself viable and can survive.

Review/Summary Questions

1. What was the social and political context in which the question of social welfare's survival emerged?
2. How has Canadian social policy changed from the Keynesian welfare state to the neo-liberal era? And how does the social investment state fit in?
3. The chapter argues that during the Keynesian welfare state period, social policy was important in articulating a Canadian national identity. Is this still true? Why or why not?
4. Why were social assistance programs singled out as the area of social policy most in need of reform?
5. Why are children so important to the social investment state?

Notes

1. The federal government's Apprenticeship Incentive Grant (AIG), announced in 2014, is an exception to this rule. Whereas other social programs have permitted provinces to opt out of the federal initiative and be compensated to run their own provincial program, this option is not automatically available under the AIG (Usher 2015).

2. For a discussion of the federal government's unwillingness to abide by the terms of its own pay equity laws, see Fudge (2002, especially 115–24). Regarding employment equity, see Bakan and Kobayashi (2000). Employment equity laws in Canada required employers to hire job candidates from the four identified groups when there was no demonstrable difference between the equity candidate and the person from the non-targeted group. Quotas were not part of this system, although it was expected that the representation of women, members of visible minorities, disabled people, and Aboriginal peoples would increase.

3. The terminology gets a bit complicated here. *Neo-liberal* refers to a person or policy that advocates private over public provision. The term invokes the idea of "liberal" in its original eighteenth-century form, which promoted the individual over the collective and the institution of rights to protect individuals from the incursions of the state. Both Conservative and Liberal governments in Canada have been characterized as "neo-liberal" since the 1980s. The term *neo-conservative* adds further complexity to the mix. Neo-conservatives are distinguished from neo-liberals at the level of morality. Whereas neo-conservatives and neo-liberals generally agree on issues surrounding the freeing up of markets from state control, they part company when it comes to the state's role in legislating morality. Neo-conservatives, for example, tend to support restrictions on abortion, resist legalization of recreational drug use, and uphold traditional notions of the nuclear family, preferably with a stay-at-home mother. To the extent that neo-liberals weigh in on these debates, they generally tend to advance the opposing position.

7 What Are the Social Determinants of Health?

Elaine M. Power

Introduction

Over 2000 years ago, the founders of the Western medical tradition, Hippocrates and Galen, observed inequalities in health related to social circumstances. They noticed that some groups of people in ancient Greece had higher rates of sickness and died earlier than other groups. We can make similar observations about Canada today. For example, Indigenous people, who tend to be poorer and have less education than non-Indigenous people in Canada, have much higher rates of almost all diseases and a significantly shorter lifespan than those who are not Indigenous. We see this relationship regardless of income or level of education, suggesting that other factors, such as racism, are at play. Whether the main causes of disease are infectious (such as HIV/AIDS and tuberculosis) or related to lifestyle (such as diabetes and heart disease), some groups of people, including people who live in poverty and racialized minorities, develop these diseases more often and die of them sooner than richer, more powerful groups. We see a similar pattern in premature or early deaths related to accidents and violence. This general pattern holds true within countries and among countries of the world, and throughout history. These patterns of death and disease can be explained by what we now call the social determinants of health.

The social determinants of health (SDOH) are social, political, economic, and cultural conditions, forces, and factors that influence how health is distributed among groups and populations. Overall, there is general agreement about specific social determinants of health, including the following (see, for example, Davidson 2015; Mikkonen and Raphael 2010; Raphael 2009; Wilkinson and Marmot 2003; World Health Organization Commission on the Social Determinants of Health 2008):

- Income
- Education
- Racialization

- Employment
- The work environment
- Early child development
- Food security
- Housing and neighbourhoods
- Social support, social inclusion, and social cohesion
- Gender

While public health statisticians and epidemiologists tend to examine these determinants individually, sociologists understand that they interact and intersect, with multiple effects on health. Generally, in the social determinants of health literature, health is measured narrowly, by its opposites: rates of disease (**morbidity**) and death (**mortality**). These end points are specific, concrete, relatively easy to measure, and readily available for population health studies, even though they actually measure the *absence* of health.

Underlying forces, such as **globalization** (Labonté 2015), **capitalism** (Coburn 2004), **patriarchy** (Bird and Lang 2014), and **colonialism** (Czyzewski 2011), are increasingly being recognized as "broader" determinants of health or determinants of the social determinants of health. The literature on the social determinants of health demonstrates clearly that the distribution of power in society together with issues of **social justice** are the most important factors influencing overall **population health** and the health of groups of people in society.

Understanding how social factors influence health is rarely discussed in the popular discourse on health, which overwhelmingly blames individuals when they get sick, especially with a chronic disease. The dominant understanding of health is that individuals have control over and are responsible for their lifestyle habits, such as diet, exercise, alcohol consumption, and smoking, which promote either health or disease. While lifestyle habits are important determinants of health at the individual level, these lifestyle habits are also socially patterned. When examining *groups* of people at a population level (rather than individuals), the social determinants of health are more important contributors to patterns of disease and early death than individual lifestyle habits. This means that health and **longevity** (or lack thereof) are products of social, political, and economic forces. It also means that if we want to improve population health (for example, increase the average lifespan of people in a country or narrow the gap between those who have the shortest and the longest lifespans) we need strong, interventionist governments that will develop social policies and take action across government ministries and programs (e.g., health, education, income security, employment, Aboriginal affairs). However, in our current **neo-liberal** era, this style of government has been attacked as inefficient and wasteful of taxpayers' dollars. In such a political climate, it is easier to blame individuals for their poor health and attribute health and longevity to the disciplined efforts of responsible citizens to manage their lifestyle habits and maximize their health. In the longer term, we can expect that government inattention to social determinants of health will gradually erode the gains made in health and life expectancy over the twentieth century and widen **health inequities** within countries.

Situating the Social Determinants of Health

We have known for centuries that the factors and forces that structure people's living and working conditions affect their health. For example, in his classic study *Conditions of the Working Class in England, 1844*, German philosopher Friedrich Engels (who co-authored *The Communist Manifesto* and other publications with Karl Marx) connected the exploitation of the workers under capitalism to their appalling living and working-conditions, high rates of disease, and shortened lifespans. Working-class people in the mid-nineteenth-century industrial cities of England lived in overcrowded housing in poor condition; ate inadequate diets and adulterated food; drank alcohol instead of contaminated water; lacked sanitation; worked long hours, six to seven days per week, in dangerous factories; and had no medical care and no access to education. It is not surprising, then, that infectious diseases—including cholera, typhus, and tuberculosis—were rampant; infant and maternal death rates were astronomical; and industrial accidents and tenement fires regularly killed working-class people. As a result, the average lifespan of a member of the working class was only 15 years, less than half that of members of the upper class, who lived on average to 35 years of age. Engels thought that the rich and powerful were guilty of "social murder" for ignoring the dangerous and unhealthy conditions in which the working class lived and worked, even though they knew that people suffered terribly and died young as a result. Engels believed that the only solution was for the working class to unite, overthrow the capitalist class, and institute communism.

A German contemporary of Engels was pathologist and biologist Rudolf Virchow. Considered to be the father of "social medicine," Virchow came to understand how the overall material conditions of life created the opportunities for health or illness. After analyzing a typhus epidemic in Upper Silesia (now Poland), where thousands died in 1847, he concluded that disease and early death were caused by poverty and **political disenfranchisement**. Less radical than Engels, Virchow believed that increased employment, better wages, local autonomy in government, agricultural co-operatives, and more progressive taxation would lead to fewer epidemics, better overall health, and increased longevity.

Lifespans in industrialized countries have improved dramatically since the nineteenth century as a result of government policies and programs, such as banning child labour and instituting mandatory primary and secondary education, workplace health and safety regulations, and public health measures—such as sewer systems, clean drinking water, food safety regulations, and vaccinations (Szreter 1988). For much of the twentieth century, we took these advances for granted and paid little attention to how the social organization of society affects our health. With the rise of modern Western medicine during the twentieth century and the increased power and status of medical doctors, medicine was given credit for the increase in lifespans, and access to health care came to be seen as the most important determinant of health. This fallacy was recognized in Canada after Medicare was implemented, when health inequities did not disappear even after all Canadians gained free access to health care (Hancock 1986). It started to become apparent (once again) that factors other than access to health care were at play.

Interest in the **public health** field that is now known as the social determinants of health began to grow in the 1980s and 1990s. By 2005, there was enough research evidence about the social determinants of health that the World Health Organization (WHO) struck a special international study group, The Commission on the Social Determinants of Health, to examine global health inequities and make recommendations to improve them. The Commission concluded that "social injustice is killing people on a grand scale" and that "bad policies, economics and politics" are responsible for global health inequities. The social determinants of health, not biology, are responsible for children who are born in the poorest part of Glasgow, Scotland living on average 28 years less than those living only 13 kilometres away; for girls born in Lesotho living, on average, 42 years less than those born in Japan; and for women in Afghanistan having a 1 in 8 chance of dying in childbirth compared to a 1 in 17,400 chance in Sweden. The Commission hoped that societies and governments around the world would understand the evidence that supported its three main recommendations and act to improve the health of all. The three recommendations are as follows:

1. Improve daily living conditions, including the circumstances in which people are born, grow, live, work, and age.
2. Tackle the inequitable distribution of power, money, and resources—the structural drivers of those conditions—globally, nationally, and locally.
3. Measure and understand the problem and assess the impact of action.

To date, there is little evidence that Canadian governments have taken the report seriously. Instead, one in five Canadian children and four in ten Indigenous children live in poverty, despite a 1989 all-party resolution in the House of Commons to end child poverty by the year 2000 (Campaign 2000, 2014). Four million Canadians, including over a million children, live in households where there is not enough money for food (Tarasuk et al. 2015). And life expectancy for people with Aboriginal ancestry is three to fifteen years shorter than the Canadian average, with the Inuit having the biggest gap (Statistics Canada 2010). Furthermore, suicide rates for Inuit are six to eleven times the Canadian average; indeed, Nunavut, a territory that is 85 per cent Inuit, has one of the highest youth suicide rates in the world (Young et al. 2015).

Paul Watson/Toronto Star/Getty Images

Four in ten Indigenous children in Canada still live in poverty. In this photo, Neeveacheak, with her one-year-old niece, Nancy, withdraws cash in Taloyoak, Nunavut. She spends two-thirds of her monthly income on food.

How the Social Determinants of Health Get under Our Skin

The social, political, and economic forces of the determinants of health "get under our skin" and affect our health through physiological reactions to the worry and stress of living in poverty and through food insecurity, income insecurity, poor housing, racism, lack of social support, social exclusion, and so on. Moreover, living and working in hierarchal and competitive environments appears to create stress that adversely affects health for everyone, not just those at the bottom of the hierarchy. Evidence from long-term studies of British civil servants, the Whitehall Studies, shows a gradient in health that corresponds with occupational status in the civil service. Those with the lowest occupational status have more disease and die earlier than the group with the next lowest occupational status, and so on. This gradient is clear and strong, despite the fact that none of these civil servants lives in poverty. The relationship holds for a variety of diseases and causes of death. For a disease such as coronary heart disease, which has specific and well-known risk factors—including smoking, hypertension, and high cholesterol—the known risk factors can account for only one-quarter to one-third of the difference in longevity between the highest and lowest occupational categories. Indeed, in the original study, those at the top of the hierarchy who smoked had less coronary heart disease than those at the bottom who were non-smokers. Overall, those at the top were twice as likely to be healthy as those at the bottom. The principal investigator of the Whitehall Studies, Sir Michael Marmot, proposes that the amount of control that people have over their work may help explain the relationship between occupational status and health. Similar gradients in health associated with social position (whether measured by income, education, class, or occupational status) have been shown to exist in all wealthy countries. Marmot calls this "the status syndrome," which is the widely observed phenomenon that higher social status and better health go hand-in-hand. Other research on the status syndrome has shown, for example, that Nobel Prize nominees do not live as long as Nobel Prize winners, even though the identity of nominees is hidden for 50 years.

Similar mechanisms may be at work with the controversial proposed relationship between income inequality and health. Two British epidemiologists, Richard Wilkinson and Kate Pickett, have shown that once a basic standard of living has been established in a country, higher levels of income equality (a measure of hierarchy) better explain long life expectancy than total wealth (Wilkinson and Pickett 2009). For example, even though the United States is the richest country in the world, it has high levels of income inequality and the average life expectancy is lower than many other countries, including some that are much poorer. Wilkinson and Pickett's work suggests that as income inequality rises, which has happened in many countries since the end of the twentieth century, eventually, we should expect to see longevity start to decline. Other research suggests that welfare state programs may counteract the negative effects of growing income inequality.

Whether people experience stress from poverty, from racism, from being low in the status hierarchy, or from other causes, stress activates biological systems, including autonomic, neuroendocrine, immune, and inflammatory responses in our bodies. For example, stress produces the physiological "fight or flight" reaction through the autonomic nervous system, releasing hormones, such as adrenaline, that increase heart rate, breathing, and blood pressure, and tense the muscles for flight. The stress response can be life-saving when one is responding to an acute stress; however, chronic stress, such as that caused by living in poverty or in a racist environment, takes a significant toll on physical and psychological health. Chronic stress can impair the immune system, accelerate aging, cause structural changes in the brain and impair metabolism, and lead to higher rates of high blood pressure, heart disease, diabetes, headaches, and abdominal obesity. Moreover, children who have chronically stressed parents have higher rates of some diseases, such as asthma (Sapolsky 2004).

Stress also has psychological effects, including anxiety, depression, insomnia, and impaired concentration. Stress even appears to affect our genes. Researchers have found associations between chronic stress and the protective casing at the end of a strand of DNA, called a telomere (Epel et al. 2004). People, such as those who grew up in poverty, who are experiencing or have experienced chronic stress have been found to have shorter telomeres than control groups. Shortened telomeres disrupt the cells' ability to divide properly and are associated with cell death, inflammatory responses, and numerous chronic diseases, including dementia, depression, heart disease, diabetes, and cancer. Moreover, the new science of **epigenetics** has shown that stress changes the expression of genes, turning genetic switches off and on, and that these changes can be passed on to children. Thus, we are beginning to understand the biological mechanisms by which social, political, and economic forces impact our health.

A Life Course Approach to the Social Determinants of Health

A life course approach to the social determinants of health helps us to understand that social determinants interact and intersect, with immediate, cumulative, latent, and pathway effects. One fascinating study of babies born during the Dutch famine shows the latent effects of poor fetal nutrition on adult health and, again, how political conditions get "under the skin." In 1944, near the end of the Second World War, millions of people in the Netherlands ran out of food because of a German blockade. The famine was so severe that people resorted to eating tulip bulbs to try to quell their hunger. Researchers in the Dutch Famine Birth Cohort Study examined the health records of babies born to mothers who were malnourished during the famine. Not surprisingly, they found that those babies were smaller than normal at birth. Low birth weight appears to be a key marker for later health effects. As the researchers tracked the health records of children born of famine-affected mothers, they found that many years later rates of obesity, hypertension, diabetes, heart disease, kidney disease, and other chronic diseases were much higher. Children whose mothers were affected by the famine in the second trimester of pregnancy also had higher rates of mental illness as adults. In addition, researchers found that the children of women born during the famine were also more likely to suffer ill health, suggesting epigenetic effects.

Other research studies also support what is called "the Barker hypothesis" (named after epidemiologist David Barker), which states that poor nutritional status in girls and women, before and during pregnancy, is the cause of chronic disease in adults of the subsequent generation. This expanding field of research, which examines the effects of parents' and grandparents' circumstances on their descendants' health, is known as "the developmental origins of health and disease," or DOHaD. DOHaD research shows that the broad conditions in which we are conceived, born, and live for the first two or three years of life affect adult health and how we die.

When seen through the lens of the dominant discourse on health, which holds individuals responsible for health, such evidence can be used to perpetuate **mother-blaming**. However, many of the stressors that have intergenerational health effects are associated with social determinants of health, such as class and racialization. This suggests that progressive societal changes (for example, to reduce and eliminate racism) and improved social policies to support health and well-being (such as reducing and eliminating poverty) will have profound and far-reaching effects on health in the future. Unfortunately, the health effects of such changes may take many years to fully manifest, requiring expensive and complicated longitudinal research to provide supportive evidence. Moreover, voters and governments may be reluctant to make investments whose payoffs will be realized so far in the future.

Many social determinants researchers have begun to focus attention on early childhood because of the growing evidence of the extraordinary effects of childhood experiences on adult health and because of the evidence that these effects may be then reproduced in the next generation. Growing up in poverty is especially damaging to health. As Dennis Raphael puts it, childhood poverty is a "launch pad for a lifetime of health problems" (Raphael 2011). Babies born to mothers who are poor have already experienced nine months of a less than ideal environment. Mothers living in poverty often suffer from poor nutrition (as they cannot afford healthy food), stress, relationship difficulties, and mental health problems.

As we have seen, the latent effects of these conditions show up many years later in higher rates of adult chronic disease. But some effects of poverty are more immediate. Children living in poverty are more likely to suffer a range of diseases, from asthma to iron-deficiency anemia. The longer children live in poverty, the more that disadvantage accumulates and the worse the health effects become (Brooks-Gunn and Duncan 1997; Raphael 2011). These are known as cumulative effects.

There are also pathway effects. This means that early life experiences affect later life experiences. One crucial pathway operates through educational attainment, which is related to childhood socio-economic position and a predictor of future socio-economic position. Educational attainment is also an independent predictor of longevity. This means that, as a group, those who have higher levels of education tend to live longer than those who have lower levels of education (Wilkinson and Marmot 2003). Children who live in poverty are also more likely to struggle in school (Brooks-Gunn and Duncan 1997). For example, they more often develop cognitive and behavioural problems, such as learning disabilities, that make school more difficult. Other factors associated with poverty, including lower parental vocabulary and less likelihood of parents reading aloud to children, also affect children's performance in school. Getting sick more often means lower school attendance, which then compounds difficulties in school achievement as children miss out on class lessons. In addition, the level of educational attainment affects the type of employment that adults are able to obtain (another social determinant of health) and the level of income that they are able to make.

Children who live in poor families also tend to have adverse experiences of other social determinants of health, such as food insecurity, poor housing, and unsafe neighbourhoods. Moreover, the health effects of poverty may also be compounded by racism. There is incontrovertible evidence that racism independently affects health. For example, in the United States, black women with a university degree are two-and-a-half times more likely to have low-birth-weight babies than university-educated white women (Collins and Butler 1997). Moreover, racialized groups, such as blacks in the United States and Indigenous people, also tend to have higher rates of poverty.

Overall, children who live in poor families have worse health and tend to die more often than children who live in richer families. Childhood poverty sets a life-course trajectory of cumulative disadvantage that impacts adult health, along with latent health effects that independently affect adult health (Raphael 2011). There are also indirect effects, for example, operating through personality development, such as having less sense of control over the circumstances of one's life. Children who grow up in low-income households may also be more likely to adopt unhealthy, addictive habits, perhaps as a way of coping with stress, such as smoking and alcohol consumption (Davidson 2015). The evidence is clear that growing up in poverty has devastating effects on health in multiple ways, resulting in unnecessary human suffering, lost human potential, reduced economic activity, and higher health care expenditures.

Conclusion: What to Do?

In its population health approach, developed in the 1990s, the Canadian government recognized the importance of improving the general living and working conditions of all Canadians as well as the importance of social justice strategies to reduce health inequities among population groups. The population health approach requires strong government intervention and adequate taxation revenues to develop welfare-state programs that provide the following:

- Income security
- High-quality and accessible primary, secondary, and post-secondary education
- Universal health care
- Affordable housing and child care
- Public transportation and other such programs that have direct and indirect effects on the quality of our lives and our health

Despite official government recognition of the importance of the social determinants of health for population health, Canada has been moving in a direction that undermines our fiscal ability and political willingness to tackle the social determinants of health (Bryant, Raphael, Schrecker, and Labonte 2011). Almost 40 years of living in a neo-liberal political climate in Canada has produced growing income inequality; increased income insecurity and precarious employment; high levels of poverty, food insecurity, and homelessness; deteriorating access to post-secondary education; and an increasing sense of isolation and competitive individualism that undermines social cohesion, social solidarity, collective action, and democracy itself. Shifting this ideological climate will not be easy, despite the evidence of its profoundly detrimental effects on health.

One strategy that shows some promise in breaking neo-liberalism's ideological stranglehold on our collective imagination is a guaranteed annual income (GAI) or basic income guarantee (BIG) (Klein 2014). A basic income guarantee, available to all who need it and allowing individuals and households to meet basic needs for food, clothing, shelter, and other essential goods, would go a long way toward addressing poverty and income insecurity and their adverse health effects. There is a strong economic case for a BIG/GAI, with estimates that for every dollar invested, eventually we could save at least two dollars in reduced costs for health care, education, and the justice system. However, perhaps the most important effect of a universally available BIG/GAI would be to promote a sense of social solidarity and social caring, knowing that there is a social safety net that will support us and help us live full, meaningful lives. As Naomi Klein (2014, 461) claims, in the context of addressing global climate change, "arguing for a universal safety net opens up a space for a full-throated debate about values—about what we owe to one another based on our shared humanity, and what it is that we collectively value." Canada had a successful BIG/GAI pilot project in the 1970s called "Mincome," which eliminated poverty in the town of Dauphin, Manitoba for four years (Lum 2014). Other countries are experimenting with providing cash transfers to low-income households and seeing impressive results on health and well-being (Standing 2008).

If we could implement a BIG/GAI to address poverty and income insecurity, the resulting enhancement of social solidarity and democracy may also open up the space to discuss and address deeper social determinants of health. For example, Canadians urgently need to confront the ongoing effects of colonialism on the health of Indigenous people and to implement meaningful interventions, especially self-determination in social, political, and economic decision-making (Reading and Wien 2009). We also need to tackle pervasive racism and sexism. These will be difficult and potentially slow processes of social justice, but the eventual payoffs in improved population health will be enormous.

Review/Summary Questions

1. What can we learn from the history of what is now called the social determinants of health?
2. What is the impact of neo-liberalism on health?
3. How do experiences of childhood poverty affect adult health?
4. Why are governments reluctant to act on the evidence about the social determinants of health?
5. How would the implementation of a basic income guarantee (BIG)/guaranteed annual income (GAI) improve population health?

8 How Do Immigrants Integrate?

Lori Wilkinson

Introduction

At the outset, we should identify and define what is meant by *immigrants* and *integration*. Who is an **immigrant**? In its broadest sense, an immigrant is someone who is living, either temporarily or permanently, in a country other than the one in which he or she was born. Take a minute to think about this definition. What is missing? What is limiting about it? From a practical standpoint, we would need to define a time limit for an immigrant. Is a tourist an immigrant? No, because the tourist and visitor intend to leave the country after a certain period of time. Is a **temporary worker** an immigrant? Legally no; the temporary worker is bound by law to return to his or her country of origin at the termination of the work visa. However, Canada has some programs that allow certain select temporary workers to convert their status into permanent residency as long as they fulfill certain requirements. How about the other end of the spectrum? If I have lived in Canada for 10 years or more, am I still an immigrant? If I came to Canada when I was two years old and my parents subsequently become citizens, do I automatically become a citizen? If I was adopted at birth and brought to Canada as an infant, am I still an immigrant? The answers to those questions vary. From a legal standpoint, one remains an immigrant until citizenship has been granted. Many immigrants will have obtained citizenship long before 10 years have passed. In Canada, immigrants can apply to become a citizen after three years as long as they pass a citizenship test, pass a language test, complete required paperwork, and fulfill certain legal requirements and obligations. Children under the age of 10 automatically become citizens when their parents accept citizenship. Although impossible to summarize immigration and citizenship rules in a single paragraph, we can say that the definitions of *immigrant* and *citizen* are complicated, based on complex legal issues that are beyond the scope of this chapter. We can also say that the social demarcations of just who is and is not an immigrant and identifying when someone stops being an immigrant are equally complex but are the focus of this chapter.

Linked to the definition of an immigrant is the issue of **integration**, which is a multi-step, though not necessarily linear, process by which newcomers become part of their new society. Integration involves more than the host society's making economic, social, and cultural space for newcomers, however. Several researchers describe integration as a two-way process where newcomers also adapt and change some of their habits, lifestyles, and perceptions to become part of the host society. Newcomer adaptation must be accompanied by changes on the part of members of the host society, who also experience cultural, lifestyle, and perceptual changes—although not on the same scale as those experienced by newcomers. This two-way process is what separates integration from other forms of immigrant adaptation, such as assimilation, the melting pot, and other processes evident in other countries. Integration is what separates Canada from countries that only claim to practise multiculturalism, and this suggests a reason why governments look to this country for advice about settlement and adaptation for their newcomers. Studies of immigrant integration have been around for a long time; the term can even be traced back to the works of Auguste Comte, Émile Durkheim, and Talcott Parsons (Bolaffi 2003).

This chapter, as much as this space allows, reviews some of the major themes, theories, and concepts involved in immigration and settlement. Along the way, it addresses two questions:

1. How do immigrants become active and participating members of society?
2. How do sociologists understand integration?

We begin with a short description of the demographic characteristics of immigrants to Canada and then examine how immigrants enter the country. The next two sections describe the sociological understanding of economic, social, and cultural integration. The chapter ends by asking some pertinent questions about the future of sociology and immigration studies in Canada.

Some Important Demographics of Immigration in Canada

Canada has, rather incorrectly,[1] been called a nation of immigrants. Today, one in five people living here were not born in the country (Statistics Canada 2013c), leaving Canada with the highest proportion of foreign-born nationals among the G-8 countries and one of the largest permanent populations of immigrants in the world. Between 2006 and 2011, 1.3 million newcomers arrived to our country (Statistics Canada 2013c), adding to the already nearly 5.4 million immigrants already settled here. The challenge to policy-makers, settlement organizations, and other institutions that help people is to provide the services newcomers need to successfully settle and integrate, which can be a challenge given the diversity of this country's immigrant population.

For the past 30 years, three countries have contributed the largest number of newcomers to Canada:

1. *The Philippines*, which sent over 152,000 people between 2006 and 2011 (13.1 per cent)
2. *China*, which sent over 122,000 during that time (10.5 per cent)
3. *India*, at 121,000 (10.4 per cent) (Statistics Canada 2013b)[2]

There is a reason behind this mass migration of people from these three countries. India, China, and the Philippines are countries of emigration, where over 10 per cent of their people live abroad. More importantly, on Canada's side, is the removal of the last racist restrictions from Canadian immigration law, which did not occur until 1976. Prior to that time, immigration officers could use race or ethnicity as conditions for barring entry, usually using the euphemism "not suited to the climate," which meant that significantly fewer **racialized minorities** were granted permission to enter the country at that time.

Where do immigrants tend to live? Until recently, the cities of Montreal, Toronto, and Vancouver attracted over 75 per cent of all newcomers. Today, less than 60 per cent of all immigrants live in these cities—with newcomers increasingly likely to locate to second-tier cities, such as Edmonton, Winnipeg, and Saskatoon, or to even smaller, more remote areas, such as Fort McMurray, Alberta; Thompson, Manitoba; or Whitehorse, Yukon (Statistics Canada 2013c). The wealth of jobs and investment opportunities is what draws newcomers to these more remote and less populated areas and has opened up new opportunities for settlement agencies, which traditionally had not operated in these areas.

What Do Immigrants Do in Canada?

People migrate for a variety of reasons. Some move to be closer to their family and friends. Some are forced to leave their country of origin because of religious, sexual, political, gender, or other forms of persecution. Others leave for better job, investment, and educational prospects, either for themselves or for their children. The Canadian government has created over 330 different classifications of immigrants—describing all the ways that people can legally enter the country. For our purposes, we can group immigrants into three categories:

1. **Family class immigrants**: These immigrants are admitted on the basis of a very close personal relationship with someone already living in the country. They would include children under age 19 years, fathers and mothers, and young siblings. They cannot be aunts, uncles, cousins, or other relatives, which causes significant problems due to the cultural differences in the definition of *family*.

2. **Refugees**: These are people fleeing persecution from their country of origin. There are refugees who are identified by the United Nations High Commission for Refugees (UNHCR) as bona fide persons in need of protection, while the Canadian government also has a class of persons that the country deems to be in need of protection.[3]

3. **Economic class immigrants**: These are people arriving for economic reasons. Family class immigrants make up approximately 25 per cent of the newcomers to Canada, while refugees make up about 12 per cent; the remainder are those arriving for economic reasons.

Economic Immigrants: A Reserve Army of Labour

The largest proportion of immigrants arriving today (nearly two-thirds) come to Canada for economic reasons and can be considered the *economic class*.[4] Members of the economic class come to Canada to work, to invest in a new or existing business, or to create their own business. In the neo-liberal government, it is this class that is considered most valuable. Although there are many people already living in Canada who are unemployed, newcomers tend to create more jobs than they take and they tend to pay more taxes than they ever use in terms of social welfare and health care (Javdani and Pendakur 2014; Baker and Benjamin 1995; Akbari, 1991).[5] In a neo-liberal welfare state, this is one of the reasons why immigrants are so valuable. Another reason they are valuable lies here: many newcomers will do jobs that Canadians can't or won't do. On the upper end of the job spectrum, Canada has long had a shortage of skilled professionals in many industries, including health, engineering, and applied sciences. On the lower end, shortages in low-skilled work in the construction and service industries fuel growth among those with less than high school education (Government of Canada 2015). It is estimated that by 2022, two-thirds of all job vacancies will require workers with a college diploma or university degree; the remaining one-third will require those with high school diplomas or less (Employment and Social Development Canada 2013). The population of workers born in Canada cannot fill all of the job vacancies, so immigrants are expected to take 1.063 million of these jobs (Employment and Social Development Canada 2014), accounting for 16.5 per cent of all the jobs created in that 10-year period (calculations by author).

The problem that many immigrants face, regardless of entrance class, is finding a job that appropriately uses their skills, education, and previous work experience. Most immigrants discover that it is not so easy to have their foreign-attained credentials recognized in the Canadian labour market. This is euphemistically known as the physician-driving-a-taxi phenomenon. It has been estimated that among recently arrived immigrants, over 50 per cent have jobs for which they are significantly over qualified. (Wilkinson et al. 2015). This problem is more pronounced among refugees, where upwards of 70 per cent are working in jobs that do not recognize their skills and education (Wilkinson et al. 2015).

Refugees have more difficulty translating their work and educational experiences into equivalent jobs in Canada because it is often difficult for them to provide job references (former employers may also be dislocated due to war or might be dead) and to provide proof of educational credentials (a popular tactic among invading armies is to destroy the educational records of major post-secondary educational institutions). Without references and proof of education, many refugees find it difficult to find good work in their new home. Even those in the economic class have difficulty finding work that matches their job experience and educational credentials, although the rate is closer to 50 per cent.

Why do immigrants have difficulty finding work in Canada that matches their educational and skill levels? Karl Marx wrote about the reserve army of labour over a century ago. The concept is still relevant today when we think of how the government values the role of immigrants in Canadian society. Immigrants and other marginalized groups form a reserve army of labour in that they are generally willing to work for lower wages than those born in Canada, and they may be more apt than workers born in Canada to endure working in jobs for which they are overqualified. They are eager to work because settlement costs money: one cannot live in Canada without shelter, clothing, or food. More often than not, immigrants come as families, so many have dependent children who also require food, shelter, and education.

Newcomers are often unaware of the regulations and rules around work, allowing unscrupulous employers to take advantage by paying them less or making them work more hours—often without overtime pay—and some may perform work in unsafe environments. For example, several high-profile complaints involved Tim Hortons and the conditions under which their immigrant employees work. In one case, immigrant employees were forced to return the money they were paid in overtime to the owner of a food outlet. The owner threatened to send the foreign workers back to their home countries if they did not comply (Carmen and Meissner 2014). In other cases, unscrupulous employers try to take advantage of the fact that immigrant workers do not know Canadian labour laws and standards and thus try to exploit them by making them work more hours for less pay. But only a small minority of employers take advantage of newcomers. Moreover, it is not just fast food franchises that depend on the work done by immigrants. Banks, universities, hospitals, police services, and scientific labs are among those who routinely hire immigrants to do the work that other Canadians won't or can't do (Mehler Paperney and Bourbeaut 2014).

Economic integration is an important aspect of settlement and one that has attracted the attention of many researchers in the field. Successful economic integration often takes years, and it takes more recently arrived immigrants even longer to achieve income and job parity with those born in Canada. Elements of successful economic integration involve finding a job that fits immigrants' skills, education, and previous work experience. It also includes obtaining a decent, living wage as well as more personal and psychological conditions, such as job satisfaction and feelings of fulfilment. Many immigrants do achieve economic integration in their lifetimes. Others do not but hope that their children will benefit as they grow up.

Social and Cultural Integration

The economy is not the only sector in which integration takes place. Newcomers need social, cultural, and religious spaces to make Canada their home. In many ways, social and cultural integration, though distinct, are just as important as successful economic integration. An immigrant may feel a part of the neighbourhood, may feel like a "real" Canadian, and may become fluent in English or French, while at the same time working at an unfulfilling job. Conversely, even the most economically integrated newcomers may lack a sense of social or cultural integration, feeling isolated, victimized by discrimination, or like they don't belong.

How does an immigrant integrate both socially and culturally? This is where the notion of the two-way process of integration is important. People will not feel at home when a majority of their neighbours and acquaintances make them feel unwelcome. So how do Canadians measure up? There is some good news to report. A recent poll conducted by CBC News (2014a) reveals that 75 per cent of Canadians feel that we are a welcoming society for all ethnic groups; and in a separate poll, 79 per cent of Canadians feel comfortable hiring someone of a different ethnic origin (CBC 2014b). Sadly, there are other, more disturbing measures of social and cultural dissonance in Canada. Over half of all Quebeckers, for example, feel that religious diversity is more of a liability than an asset for Canada and that most Canadians have no friends from minority groups (CRRF and ACS 2014). Among immigrants, research that I and my colleagues have conducted has found that among recently arrived immigrants, 25 per cent of males and 24 per cent of females experience racism or discrimination always or sometimes. Another one-quarter feel as though they are not a part of Canadian society (Wilkinson et al. 2015). Taken together, these findings are disconcerting. If we recall, 6.3 million people living in Canada were not born here—meaning that one-quarter of all immigrants experience discrimination and don't feel a part of Canadian society. This is no small number.

Societies that fail to make large parts of their population feel welcomed are in danger of disintegrating. Marginalized persons who live in such societies will feel threatened, depressed, unhappy, and unhealthy. Constructivists will argue that when large sectors of society are marginalized or unhealthy, then the community, economy, and other social institutions suffer as well. Conditions in France, for example, could lead to widespread social unrest. Even before the terrorist attacks at the *Charlie Hebdo* magazine in January 2015, large numbers of French-born persons had experienced severe social marginalization. Poor, disenfranchised, and young French people, mainly young men from the former French colonies of Libya, Morocco, and Algeria, have long been under- or unemployed, under-educated, and relegated to the far-flung suburbs of French society. As a result, they have not integrated into French society in large numbers, and as academic M.G. Oprea (2015) describes the situation,

> low-income housing was constructed after more families arrived and the immigrant population swelled. Tenements were built far outside downtown areas and always at the end of public transportation lines. These "suburbs," the *banlieues*, are much more like (the) inner cities in the United States. Unemployment is high, the standard of living is low, and police checks are frequent. Immigrants are geographically separated from mainstream France—out of sight, out of mind.

Physically separating the newcomers in France has greatly enhanced their perception of being marginalized. From the host society perspective, geographically isolating an already marginalized group has only enhanced social, cultural, and economic divisions. In 2006, after months of rioting and violence in Paris suburbs, American economist Bernard Salanié (2006) described the "obscenely low employment rate" (40 per cent) of second- and third-generation African young men who were and continue to be described by French media as "foreigners" despite being born and raised in France. To the media, the government, and the general public, the riots and discontent were the result of racism and Islamophobia, but a closer look reveals that the staggering unemployment in these areas is a major contributor not only to economic but to social and cultural exclusion. This is one example where the intersection between economic, social, cultural, and religious integration can be a lesson for Canada. Excluding people by any means can lead to cultural and social unrest.

A balance between economic, social, and cultural integration is key to the successful welcoming of newcomers and the development of social cohesion. The way the government and host society view immigrants can cause difficulties in long-term social and cultural inclusion. One of the biggest challenges is the identification and labelling of immigrants. On one hand, Canada has a system for legally admitting immigrants, helping them to settle and become citizens. It is based on a system of integration, where the newcomer and the host societies adapt to one another so that we can live together in relative harmony. How can integration occur if there isn't a known process for shedding the label of "immigrant" and truly becoming a Canadian? This is one of the contradictions in Canadian law, society, and research on immigration. We expect as a country to integrate all newcomers and we expect them to want to integrate. On the other hand, the government, the public, and researchers tend to assume the notion "once an immigrant, always an immigrant." For example, in cases where even a naturalized citizen becomes involved in criminal activities, the tendency is to refer to that individual as an immigrant first.

We can think of the example of Ben Johnson, the disgraced Olympic 100-metre runner, who won and subsequently lost the gold medal in 1988 for the

New citizens are sworn in during a Canada Day ceremony in Milton, Ontario. Does Canada do a good job balancing social, economic, and cultural integration?

© Stacey Newman/iStock Photo

illegal use of steroids. Almost all media outlets described Johnson as a Jamaican immigrant, despite his having lived in and been a citizen of Canada for over half his life (Marsh 2008). In other, even more tragic examples, naturalized citizens who have committed crimes despite living their entire lives in Canada have been deported to their countries of birth, where they have subsequently been murdered, in contravention of United Nations regulations.[6] In a recent case, Hussein Jilaow, a Somali-born Canadian living in Winnipeg, was deported to Somalia in 2007 after serving time for drug- and gang-related offenses. Three months after returning to Somalia, a country he had not visited since he was 13 years old, he was brutally murdered (McIntyre 2009), one of several cases of young men murdered after deportation. In sum, although integration is supposed to imply settlement and inclusion on the part of both newcomers and the host society, in practice, the adage "once an immigrant, always an immigrant" seems to stick.

Another problem with Canadian attitudes toward immigrants is the expectation that most of the changing and adaptation is placed upon the immigrant and very little responsibility is placed on the host society. The ideal form of integration is to involve change and adaptation on both parts. The reality, however, is that the expectations are high that immigrants will change. Most have to learn a new language; all will have to adapt to a new culture and way of life. The host society, on the other hand, simply absorbs the immigrant with little change expected on society's part.

Sociology's Contribution to Understanding Immigrant Integration

As this chapter has explained, integration—on the part of both the immigrant and the host society—plays a central role in determining successful settlement among newcomers. Integration is also key to producing a cohesive, welcoming society. Canada has a long way to go to become a fully welcoming place for everyone; indeed, there is much work to do. Sociologists can help with this type of work. We have already identified and researched key concepts, such as integration, multiculturalism, marginalization, and discrimination, which will help governments, organizations, and social institutions restructure themselves into a more welcoming community. But many questions and problems remain.

How can a sociological perspective help us to understand Canada's successes and failures in welcoming newcomers? We have already indicated that sociologists, including Compte, Marx, Durkheim, Parsons, and others, have asked these questions early in the development of our discipline. Each of the theoretical traditions in sociology have variously explained how immigrants either succeed or fail at integration. For Talcott Parsons, following a Durkheimian structural functionalist perspective, successful integration involves the ability of newcomers to accept a new way of life and potentially leave their old traditions, language, and culture behind in a process called **assimilation**. In this model, complete and successful assimilation can occur only when the newcomer fully embraces the new culture. In more contemporary post-structuralist versions of this theory, we speak of **segmented assimilation**, where the failure of institutions to accommodate newcomers has meant the development of a contemporary underclass of immigrants who do not fit in economically, socially, or culturally (Zhou and Bankston 1998).

In the Marxist tradition, a contemporary theory of immigrant integration is called the **ethnic enclave perspective**. This theory suggests that there are two competing economies in Canadian society. There is the mainstream economy, which contains the popular, Western-backed businesses we are familiar with; this economy serves the largest market, that of the host society. Alongside the mainstream market is the ethnic enclave, designed specifically to employ and to provide specialized services for marginalized ethnic groups (Li 2003). An example of an ethnic enclave would be the Chinatowns that exist in nearly every major Canadian city. Here, services may be provided in a Chinese language, and shops may sell imported goods that appeal to the Chinese expat community. The ethnic enclave even employs a large number of Chinese migrants and Chinese-speaking persons; in many places, one can receive tax preparations, legal services, restaurant and some health-care services in Cantonese or Mandarin. What further separates the ethnic enclave from the mainstream economy are the wages that employees are paid. Accountants, for example, make significantly more working for an accounting firm located in the mainstream economy than they would make working for a company servicing the ethnic enclave. In this way, the wages for those in the enclave are lower than those working in the mainstream. Evidence to suggest the ethnic enclave exists in Canada is strong (Kazemipur and Halli, 2009).

Conclusion

It would take an entire textbook to outline all the theories of immigrant integration, but for our purposes, we note that each of the sociological traditions has contributed significantly to the development of many theories regarding how immigrants can succeed or fail in various aspects of the integration process. Our understanding of immigrant integration is more complicated and nuanced than can be presented in this chapter. There are many research questions that remained unanswered, and there are a wealth of opportunities for students and new researchers to become involved in what is one of the most active areas of sociological studies in Canada today.

Review/Summary Questions

1. What happens when immigrants are not fully integrated into a society?
2. Explain why the term *immigrant* is problematic. Give examples.
3. Compare and contrast the post-structuralist and Marxist theories of integration. Which one, in your opinion, best describes the situation faced by immigrants in Canada today?
4. Explain how sociological perspectives help us to understand the integration process of immigrants in Canada.
5. What are some of the challenges immigrants face in integrating?

Notes

1. In reality, the founding peoples of Canada are our Indigenous peoples. In popular and historical parlance, however, the French, English, and Indigenous peoples are all deemed to be Canadian founders.
2. The other seven countries making up the top ten immigrant-sending countries in the past five years include the United States, Pakistan, United Kingdom, Iran, South Korea, Colombia, and Mexico.
3. These persons are called "designated class refugees" and are those from countries that are not UN-specified refugee-sending countries. They include those fleeing gender-based, sexual-based, and religious-based persecution.
4. Economic class immigrants include the principal investigator—the person looking for work or investing the money to start or support an existing business. Dependents are the close relatives (spouse and children) who accompany the principal applicant.
5. This research is highly contested, with conservative economists arguing that it costs more to host immigrants and that they are a drain on the social welfare net. Their methodologies have been greatly disputed. More recently, however, researchers have found that the net economic benefits brought by recent immigrants are significantly less than earlier-arriving cohorts (Javdani and Pendakur 2014).
6. It is unlawful for any country to deport even the most dangerous of criminals to countries where there is a high degree of certainty that torture or death will occur upon extradition. The example of the extradition of dual Syrian-Canadian Maher Arar to Syria and his subsequent imprisonment and torture is a case in point. Arar was subsequently exonerated and granted $12.5 million by the Canadian government in compensation (CBC 2007).

9 What Are the Challenges of Economic Transition?

Exploring the Consequences of Regional Dynamics and Global Shifts

Jennifer Jarman

Introduction

This chapter works within a tradition of sociology that views the economic aspects of life as important for understanding any **society**. The classical sociologist, Karl Marx, argues this most forcefully. The type of thought that stems from such an approach has been labelled "economic determinism." A Marxist thinks that many of a society's key structures and, most importantly, its system of social hierarchy or class structure are fundamentally determined by the type of economic production dominant in a society (Marx 1998 [1848]). Thus a feudal society, in which wealth is created through the agricultural production from large land holdings, creates a system of **social hierarchy** of lords and peasants. This is very different from a modern capitalist society in which wealth is created largely through the operation of factories producing manufactured goods, and in which the main social division occurs between those who own the means to produce manufactured goods and those who must sell their labour power and work as employees for someone else. In both of these societies, the most powerful are those who own a resource and the weakest are those who do not. The difference is that in the feudal society the most empowering resource is land, whereas in a capitalist society the resource that empowers is capital. In a feudal society the land-holding nobility based in rural areas are the most powerful people, whereas in a capitalist society the capital-owning financiers based in urban centres are the most powerful.

Marx's explanation of the nature of society has been very influential, but it has also been challenged by other sociological thinkers. Max Weber, another major German contributor to the development of the discipline of sociology, produced a fundamental critique of Marx's approach. Weber wrote an important book, *The Protestant Ethic and the Spirit of Capitalism*, in which he argues that other factors, such as the religious life and beliefs of society's members, might be just as important and might indeed be considered more significant influences on a society than its economy. His arguments emphasize that changes in religious beliefs and values occurred first, and then had the consequence of changing the way society's economy is organized.

Much twentieth- and twenty-first-century sociology has been written starting from one of these viewpoints. Whether one ultimately argues that the economic base determines all other aspects of social life—as did Marx—or that there are complex interactions between economic and other areas of social life such as the spiritual—as did Weber—much of economic and industrial sociology shares a common perspective: that the question of understanding how a society produces livelihood for its members is an important part of understanding its essential character and major challenges.

This chapter explores what happens when Canada's Atlantic region experiences change in the way livelihoods are produced. It explores the nature of the economic changes underway in Atlantic Canada and asks the key question: "How does economic change affect the lives and social hierarchies of the people who live in this region?"

Unemployment and Underemployment in Atlantic Canada

Atlantic Canada is home to some of the oldest communities in North America. The economic underpinnings of these communities have been the resources—fish, timber, coal—and commerce arising from the use of these resources, as well as other maritime activities, such as ports, the navy, a coast guard, and mercantile fleets. Over the past 20 years, however, the fishing industry has been plagued by problems because of a combination of over-fishing and **climate change**. The shrinking of Canada's rail system, moreover, ended the need for the coal and steel industries that had provided its rails. As well, trade and commerce have continued shifting westward over the past 100 years as the rest of the North American continent has developed; this has also had the consequence of jobs shifting westward.

The Atlantic region now has some of the highest rates of unemployment in Canada. While the unemployment rate for the whole of Canada is 6.6 per cent, unemployment rates across the four Atlantic provinces range from a low of 8.3 per cent in Nova Scotia to a high of 11.3 per cent in Newfoundland (Statistics Canada 2015), meaning that every Atlantic province has a higher rate of unemployment than the national average. Making things even more difficult for those living in Atlantic Canada, many of the remaining jobs are seasonal—those related to the fishing industry, to agriculture, and to the tourism industry, for example.

The consequence is that many opportunities for employment alternate between high-intensity work and long periods of unemployment. Indeed, this pattern was noted over 30 years ago (Butler and Smith 1983).

Today's young Atlantic Canadians do not aspire to agricultural, resource-based, or manufacturing careers. An analysis of the aspirations of young people in urban Hamilton, Ontario and in rural and urban Nova Scotia shows that youth—those in rural areas and those in urban areas, those whose parents were professional workers, and those whose parents were working class—are "remarkably homogeneous" in their aspirations to "middle-class male" careers—in other words, to service sector work (Thiessen and Blasius 2002). This explains the turn to higher education: faced with uncertain futures in the occupations their parents chose, young people are pursuing formal education instead.

Out-Migration and Atlantic Communities

One of the long-standing problems in the region has been the failure to retain its own **human capital**. *Human capital* refers to the investments, such as education, training, and health care, that have been made to make people more able to participate in the economy (Becker 1993). Provincial governments invest in the region's people throughout their lifetime by funding schools, colleges, and universities as well as health clinics, medical offices, and hospitals. When migration out of the region is large, the ability to continue to support investment becomes increasingly problematic. As a result, the "brain drain," or **out-migration** of workers, especially those who are skilled and educated, has been a subject of both public discussion and policy analysis. Ross Finnie (2000), for example, has shown that high provincial unemployment rates, high rates of collection of employment insurance benefits, and the absence of employment income induce people to migrate to provinces where opportunities are better. Further, he shows that young people with higher educational qualifications are more likely to move than older people with weaker qualification profiles. Michael Corbett adds to our understanding of who leaves and who stays. He finds that women are more likely than men to leave rural communities, but again he finds that both educated women and men who leave "have acquired considerably more high school and higher education credentials than their stayer counterparts" (Corbett 2007, 434). Maurice Beaudin and Sébastien Breau (2001) report that data for 1995 showed New Brunswick and Prince Edward Island losing large numbers of their new graduates; Nova Scotia actually increased its number of new graduates but not enough to compensate for the overall loss of human capital. More recent analysis, by the Atlantic Provinces Economic Council, shows that the trend continues, with the consequence that fully 14 per cent (340,000) of the region's population has migrated out to other provinces. Of these, 70,000 were in the age group 15 to 24 (Beale 2008, 1–2).[1] Projecting the trend forward, the Conference Board of Canada suggests that Atlantic Canada will lose 73,600 more people by 2031, with declines ranging from 3 per cent to 13 per cent across the four provinces. As in Finnie's earlier work, the most significant trend continues to be the loss of the younger, working-age population to other regions (Akbari 2014). At the same time, while the size of the population that is aged 65+ increases across the whole country, this out-migration of young Atlantic Canadians means that the proportion of the population that is senior in Atlantic Canada is projected to be over 30 per cent in Nova Scotia and New Brunswick, and between 32 per cent and 36 per cent in Newfoundland (Statistics Canada 2014). Atlantic Canada will be an even "greyer" population in the near future unless the region starts to retain its younger population.

For provincial governments, the continued departure of young educated people poses a problem. Education budgets are one of the largest categories of expenditure for provincial governments. How do provincial governments legitimize continued expenditure for students who leave the province as soon as they graduate when the same governments must fund other areas of need, such as health care, for those who remain? If these provincial governments do not invest in education, on the other hand, they do not build the type of labour force capable of supporting higher-level industries. But if they do invest in higher education without any way of retaining labour, then the investment in higher education is a loss to the region.

The departure of young people also creates problems for the reproduction of stable communities. When young people move thousands of miles away in search of jobs, who looks after the older people? Even with extensive air transport networks, electronic communication, and cheap telephone rates, family support of elderly people becomes very difficult when people live a great distance away. Human capital retention, particularly of young educated people, becomes a priority for both communities and governments.

Will a "New Economy" Keep Young People in the Region?

The experts discussed previously (e.g., Finnie 2000, Beaudin and Breau 2001, and Chaundy et al. 2012) agree that young people leave Atlantic Canada due to the shortage of jobs for them. But what is the effect of the arrival of new industries in the region? For there are indeed some new areas of economic activity producing new types of jobs.

One new type of economic activity is **call centre**, or contact centre, work: the region now has a reasonably large share of the Canadian call centre industry. Estimates of the size of this new industry vary—one report published in 2010 suggests that the size of the call centre sector is disproportionally larger than other sectors in Ontario and in some of the Eastern provinces (Vincent and McKeown 2008), while another report suggests that 25 per cent of the Canadian "business services" industry is located in the Maritimes (Akyeampong 2005, 6). By 2006, the contact centre industry accounted for almost 10 per cent of employment across the Atlantic Canadian region (Contact Centre Canada 2009, 26), making it a major employer. From the perspective of stemming the out-migration of young people, this new industry employs young people: "The greater reliance on the youth labour force is evident in all regions, but is especially marked in Atlantic Canada and in Manitoba" (Contact Centre Canada 2009, 22).

Call centres began to arrive in Atlantic Canada in the early 1990s as a result of the global expansion of the American economy at a time when the American economy was growing. The call centre industry had begun in the US in the 1980s and expanded within the US until approximately 3–4 per cent of the American labour force worked in a call centre. Then the industry began its global expansion. Its first move was north into Canada, a country fairly similar in cultural terms, where there were large pools of unemployed people who spoke a type of English that could be easily understood by American listeners. At the same time as there was a demand from the industry for new locations outside the United States, the province of New Brunswick started an aggressive campaign to recruit new businesses to come to the region. Former premier Frank McKenna's much-heralded and much-criticized strategy of making New Brunswick "open for business" involved identifying the strengths of the New Brunswick labour force and attempting to develop an industrial mix that would capitalize on these strengths. Because of the heritage of both the Acadian French and the English, one of the strengths identified was a labour force containing many bilingual people. Call centres, relying heavily as they do on communication and language skills, were identified as an appropriate industry for the province. New Brunswick sent a team of recruiters into the United States to inform US firms of the opportunities available in New Brunswick and to help facilitate the location of operations to New Brunswick. The province thus had an "active" campaign of recruitment. The result was the creation of some 6000 new jobs by 1997 (Buchanan 2000).

The region's three other provinces—Nova Scotia, Prince Edward Island, and Newfoundland and Labrador—developed their call centre strategies somewhat later. By 1998, at least 41 firms had set up operations in Nova Scotia. As of July 2005, there were at least 65 centres in the province with a total labour force of approximately 15,000. Existing operations, such as Convergys, have expanded their operations, growing from 800 employees in one centre to multiple centres with a total workforce of over 2600. Tiny Prince Edward Island has adopted a similar passive strategy regarding call centre recruitment. Nonetheless, at least 11 call centres had opened their doors there, with a total workforce of 1192 in 2003 (MRSB Consulting Services 2003). Newfoundland and Labrador also had an actively growing industry: by the year 2000, the province had 15 call centres (Newfoundland and Labrador Government 2001), including at least one large call centre with more than 1000 seats.

Service Sector Employment versus Work in Traditional Industries

The new job growth is in the service sector. These new jobs do not draw on the natural resources available, nor is the region's geographical location particularly important. These call centres could be located anywhere else in the world, given the possibilities that new telecommunications infrastructures create for firms, allowing them to connect instantly and cheaply to diverse locations around the globe.

The new job growth draws on a very different kind of skills and training than those required in the old economy. Although a small number of workers have made the transition from the old to the new economy, those in the industry are generally not people displaced from older industries. The fishers, foresters, farmers, miners, and steelworkers tend to be older males, with lower levels of formal education and based in rural areas (Jarman, Butler, and Clairmont 1997).

The new industry also has a different profile. Some of the call centre workers are indeed the children of the fishers and foresters, but they have had to make a significant transition in terms of upgrading their education from elementary to at least high school certification, and many centres require a university degree. While some call centres are in rural areas, the largest call centre concentrations are in cities, which means that some workers have had to leave their rural communities to find work. Despite a popular image of call centre work as "low-end" jobs, they demand higher educational levels than did the jobs of previous generations. Providing information, problem solving, or selling in an environment that is strictly "voice-to-voice" is a complicated social process. Workers have none of the usual visual cues that have governed human interactions since our species first began to walk upright. The industry thus puts a premium on people with well-developed social skills. Most of the better call centres train people how to use their voices and improve their phone-handling skills as well as how to use computer databases quickly in order to obtain information pertinent to the inquiry. Literacy is also important in the call centre because the teleservice representative must access and record information accurately. Thus social skills, literacy skills, communication skills—such as speech and listening and computer competency—are all essential in a call centre.

Another element of the contemporary call centre workplace that sets it apart from other types of workplace is that many centres, especially those that serve multiple clients, operate in highly competitive environments. Most managers report that expectations for both the quality and the speed of service delivery have been rising steadily since the mid-1990s. Customers expect their calls to be answered quickly; they hate to be placed in queues listening to music even for a minute; and they want their questions answered efficiently without a second or third call-back. Increasingly, customers expect the service to be available 24 hours a day, 7 days a week.

Constant employee surveillance has become a feature of most call centre workplaces. The centres usually contain large databases of valuable information, ranging from business information to information governed by privacy and data protection and security laws. The call centre industry has responded with a range of measures to protect this data, including careful selection of employees, installation of security cameras, recording of all interactions, and regular "listening in" on employee conversations. Many industries have been forced to create tighter and tighter surveillance and security procedures in recent years— and the call centre industry is certainly one of them, creating new challenges and strains for workers and managers alike.

The Call Centre Industry in Atlantic Canada

Most of the jobs created by the call centre industry are full-time permanent jobs—year-round rather than seasonal in nature as so many other Maritime jobs have been. According to Statistics Canada, 83.5 per cent of the jobs in the industry are full-time, with the remaining 16.5 per cent being part-time jobs. This is a higher ratio than that in the rest of the service sector (77.3 per cent full-time and 22.7 per cent part-time) (Akyeampong 2005).

Full-time year-round employment is precisely the kind of employment that the region needs if it is to break out of its reliance on the employment insurance system. Furthermore, year-round "shore-based" work provides a steady income over other types of work in the region, such as that provided by the region's fishing vessels, oil platforms, navy, coast guard, or merchant fleets, all of which often require people to be away for weeks or months at a time. Sociologists and anthropologists have amply documented the difficulties this creates for family life, both because of worries about dangerous work at sea and because of the difficulty of managing the intermittent presence of partners in the family environment (Binkley 1994, Harrison and Laliberte 1994).

Although the industry seems to have a clear preference for urban areas, job growth has also occurred in rural areas where communities have been suffering badly from high unemployment levels. While call centres developed first in urban centres, as urban labour markets reached saturation, call centres opened in smaller towns and rural locations, giving new hope to those who want to stay in the region and find jobs. The number of jobs being created has been significant. According to Statistics Canada, the "technology-driven fast employment growth in business support services" has benefited Atlantic Canada more than any other Canadian region (Akyeampong 2005). Figures drawn from the diverse sources cited earlier in this chapter suggest that there are now tens of thousands of workers employed in the industry on the East Coast, which is important given its high unemployment levels compared to those of the rest of Canada.

While these jobs are not the highest-wage jobs in the economy, call centres do tend to pay above the minimum wage. Akyeampong reports that in Canada as a whole, the average hourly wage rate for call centre employees in 2004 was $12.45 and average hours of work amounted to 35.2 per week (Akyeampong 2005, 3). This works out to an average yearly income of $22,788 for Canadian call centre workers. The average hourly wage for a person in the group aged 15 to 24, for example, was $10.81 in April 2005 (Statistics Canada 2006a). Additionally, many of the call centres provide significant benefit packages, with medical, dental, educational leave, and pension plans.

These jobs help retain human capital in the region, and furthermore they employ a group that has typically been footloose—young workers. The industry trains its employees constantly and thus plays a role in human capital development. One of the groups least likely to engage in lifelong learning or, in other words, to update their own skill sets is the group with the lowest educational qualifications. Thus on-the-job training, as opposed to periods of credential upgrading outside the workplace available to those with some high school education, is likely one of the best ways for an individual to achieve improvements in skill and capability. Indeed, the industry's norms for training (optimum class size of 10 to 12 employees and one-on-one coaching) compare favourably with publicly funded institutions of higher education, where staff–student ratios are much higher.

Despite concerns about the "flighty" nature of the industry, the call centres have so far been fairly stable in the region. There have been some failures, but on the whole the companies that arrived have stayed in the region. Indeed, some have opened multiple centres, including Sykes (formerly ICT Group) and Atelka (which has gone through multiple ownerships and reorganizations and was formerly Davis and Henderson, Resolve, and prior to that Watts Communications). While some people have predicted that the advent of self-serve web portals would eliminate the need for call centres, the centres have so far simply added web support to their service provision. Far from disappearing, calls from people who fail to navigate websites successfully have become longer and more complex.

Two problems, however, have emerged in recent years. The first problem relates to the portion of the industry that relied on out-sourced American contracts. This part of the industry grew during the 1990s and continued to do so up until the beginning of the twenty-first century. During this period, the Canadian dollar declined against the American dollar, making Canadian labour relatively cheap as well as available. However, as the Canadian dollar began to rise from January 2003 onwards to July 2011, Canadian labour became more expensive, with the consequence that there were job cuts and some closures in the Atlantic region. These changes in the Canadian dollar also coincided with the emergence on the global scene of other competitors working to attract industry to their own regions. In particular, India and the Philippines became important global players from the early 2000s. As a result, at least one company, Convergys, closed some of its operations in Atlantic Canada in the twenty-first century, while at the same time started up large operations in the Philippines, performing the same work of serving English-language North American markets.

The second problem is more specifically local in nature. It relates to the life cycle of employment in a call centre. Although the industry hires a lot of young workers, these workers typically have higher expectations and requirements for income as they move through their own life cycles. This life cycle perspective includes the issue of how many people want to continue to work in this industry for their whole lives, and also the issue of whether the industry itself can afford to employ people as they become more expensive, given that older employees' salaries usually increase over time.

Conclusion

This chapter asks what happens to a society when there is substantial change in the ways in which people make their living. It uses the example of industrial change in Atlantic Canada. In past centuries, Atlantic Canada's economy was built around the region's natural resources, principally fish, lumber, coal, and agriculture, as well as its strategic position for international trade and commerce between America's east coast and the European markets. Over the past 50 years, these industries have fallen on hard times, leaving the region with high levels of unemployment. To use Nova Scotia as an example, by 2012, agriculture, forestry, fishing and hunting, mining and oil and gas, utilities, construction, and manufacturing had declined to the point that they accounted for only 18.7 per cent of jobs. Their annual growth rate was projected to be a mere 0.1 per cent over the 2013–15 period (Service Canada 2014, 18). Service industries—such as trade, finance, insurance, professional, scientific and technical services, education, health services, and so forth—on the other hand, constituted 81.3 per cent of the employment and were projected to have a small increase of 0.4 per cent over 2013–15. This service economy of white-collar workers differs greatly from the resource-based economy of the past few centuries. This means that young people are now forced to consider new types of occupations and careers very different from those that employed their parents. Many young people are relocating to other areas of the country to find work. Their parents, on the other hand, are living their senior years without the close support of the younger generation. This situation creates challenges in terms of support both for the younger generation and for the older generation. Provincial governments continue to struggle to support the old industries, find ways to attract new industries in order to stem the out-migration, and generate a new economy capable of employing those who want to live in the region.

The chapter also discussed the case of one new industry, the call centre industry, which provides employment to significant numbers of people in the Atlantic region. This industry arrived in the 1990s. It has sometimes been characterized as flighty and exploitative and so not a good solution to a region with economic development problems. Despite some of the industry's problems, however, it provides many entry-level jobs with pay levels ranging from minimum wage to rates at least double that, with benefits including medical, dental, and pension plans. The jobs are at the lower end of the service economy, however. But unlike some other industries in the region, jobs are available year-round. The track record of this industry so far indicates that it has created tens of thousands of jobs for people with high school and bachelor's degrees. This goes some way toward replacing the lost resource-based jobs in industries such as coal mining, fishing, and agriculture.

What can we conclude with regard to the question of how a society changes when the nature of people's livelihoods changes? When jobs are simply lost, young people are the first to depart for better prospects, creating a skewed age structure with communities composed principally of older people. For both the young and the old, family life is made more difficult due to long-distance separations. As a result, retention strategies that focus particularly on youth jobs become very important. A shift from a resource-based economy to a service economy also requires a more educated population. Such shifts change the life chances of those living within communities—those who are more easily able to acquire new skills, certifications, diplomas, and degrees have more options whether they choose to stay or go. There is some evidence that women in the region seem more able to educate themselves, suggesting that women are becoming somewhat more empowered in the process. Those who are unable to acquire new skills, certificates, diplomas, and degrees face the loss of their ability to earn a living and a loss of social power.

Both of the sociologists—Marx and Weber—mentioned at the outset of this chapter were concerned to understand how social divisions and social hierarchies within a society change as its economy changes. In the case of Atlantic Canada, we can see that the changes discussed in this chapter enhance the position of some and weaken the position of others. In particular, the position of those young people who are able to successfully achieve high levels of formal education is strengthened, whereas the position of those unable to gain qualifications—along with that of the older generation, whose skills and experience are based in a declining economy—is weakened. Furthermore, those living in urban areas have benefited from the arrival of new types of industry. In rural areas, the older industries have declined and the new industries have only slowly moved into the rural areas when available urban labour was exhausted, with the result that some rural areas are losing population and supporting infrastructure. Finally, the departure of so many young people searching for work in other regions creates increased pressure, particularly for elderly people left behind to face the challenges of their old age by themselves. In conclusion, we can indeed see that the structure of social equality and inequality within Atlantic Canada alters as the livelihood structures change, with new possibilities available to some but not to all.

Review/Summary Questions

1. What is human capital?
2. What is "out-migration"?
3. What are the consequences of economic change for young people in the Atlantic region? For old people in the Atlantic region?
4. The chapter mentions that some researchers think that young people's career aspirations centre on service sector work to a greater degree than was true in the past. Reflecting on the aspirations of members of your own high school graduating class, would you say that this description fits their aspirations?
5. When you consider the economy of the place in which you grew up, do you think its characteristics are similar to or different from those described in this chapter?

Note

1. Atlantic Canada includes Newfoundland and Labrador, along with the three Maritime provinces of Nova Scotia, New Brunswick, and Prince Edward Island.

10 What Is Communication?

Sandra Robinson

Introduction

As human beings, we communicate in all kinds of ways: through speech, gesture, and other nonverbal physical cues, as well as through text, image, clothing, brands and logos, sound, hairstyles, and even architecture. We communicate with each other as individual members of society, with family and workmates, whether face-to-face or, increasingly, through short text messages from our smart phones. Nowadays we can communicate with a potentially global audience and with our extended circle of friends, acquaintances, and professional contacts through social media, such as Facebook, Instagram, Twitter, or LinkedIn. Communication is now global and instantaneous, enabled by advanced digital technologies that not only structure our personal and professional online social networks but also organize networked communication for business and government.

Communication of some kind or order permeates every aspect of society, but what is communication? Why, as sociologists, might we be interested in thinking about, and studying, communication? The introduction to this book talks about the way "we rely on everyday, taken-for-granted assumptions to help us negotiate our lives" without questioning the underlying assumptions about how and why we do the things we do. Communication is one of the things we rarely consider beyond our own common-sense understanding or feeling for what it means to communicate with other people, whether face-to-face or through our communication devices, such as smart phones, laptops, and applications.

Setting aside mass media, mass communication, and new media, which are covered in Chapter 11, this chapter explores what communication is. At the outset, it examines how we define and comprehend communication through particular models and approaches. For example, influential models include the transmission view and ritual view, the bias of communication model, medium theory, and **cultural studies** has affected our understanding of the media of communication. All these models or approaches help to explain the complex parameters of communication as a technology, a social process, a practice, and a cultural phenomenon central to human experience. The last section of this chapter reviews how communication studies is approached and reveals the diversity of the communication field. In particular, cultural studies, critical theory, and feminist and queer analyses each offer a critical approach for communication studies. They set out different frameworks to explore the relationship between communication and social power. Taken together these models of communication and approaches to the study of communication can help us engage critically with communication as an object through which to think about broader socio-historical processes and to think beyond our everyday experience.

Understanding Communication

The word *communication* comes from the Latin word *communicare*, meaning "to share," and is defined as "the imparting, conveying, or exchange of ideas, knowledge, information, etc." ("Communication" 1961, p. 240). Communication can also be considered an expressive act that occurs between individuals, as well as within communities, institutions, and broadly across populations, whereby ideas, meaning, attitude, argument, and understanding significant to human social and cultural life are conveyed (Peters 1999).

If we stop to think about it, communication happens constantly around us. As individuals, we engage in, or produce, communication in many ways: from ordering a coffee to waving to our neighbour. At the same time communication comes "at" us, or we receive it, from all directions and in different forms, including such diverse media as TV shows, streaming content via our phone "apps," satellite radio, billboards, and personalized ads on our Facebook page. Our government and political parties communicate to us through political advertisements, propaganda, legislation, speeches, and announcements. The structure of our built environments (the houses, buildings, and roadways of our cities, towns, and rural areas) represents something about their function, meaning, and place in our society. A mosque, church, or synagogue communicates its function as a place and space for spiritual worship, whereas an imposing government building such as the Parliament of Canada symbolizes democracy, communicating a sense of authority and legislative power.

Communication and its expression through words, writing, print, broadcast, performance, or Internet streaming is clearly important to many societies and certainly in Canada. In Canada, we have a well-established legislative framework that governs spheres of communication. Canada protects the right to communicate as a fundamental freedom set out in the Charter of Rights and Freedoms, in section 2(b), guaranteeing the "freedom of thought, belief, opinion and expression, including freedom of the press and other media of communication." While Canadians have a right to communicate, other limits also constrain that right, including our privacy laws and sections of the Criminal Code of Canada dealing with criminalized expression, such as hate speech. There are two principal legislative acts that govern communications in Canada: the Telecommunications Act (transmission or carriage) and the Broadcasting Act (content), overseen by the Canadian Radio-television and Telecommunication Commission (CRTC). Canada's regulation of communication is influenced by "cultural nationalism," to ensure the protection and production of cultural content in Canada (Canadian content or "CanCon") and to limit foreign ownership of Canada's media and communication industry. There are historic reasons for this approach, namely our close proximity to the United States and its well-developed creative and media industries, and the objectives of nation building, given the vast territory and diversity of the Canadian population, to ensure a coherent national identity through cultural expression (Hamilton 2009).

There are, then, many ways of communicating and, accordingly, different ways of understanding what communication is. As James Carey reminds us, "communication, through language and other symbolic forms, comprises the ambience of human existence" (2009, 19). It is so much a part of our everyday lives that we sometimes fail to intellectually engage with it as an object of critical inquiry.

Models of Communication

At the present time communication that does not occur face-to-face is bound up with information technology. We communicate through network-enabled transactions and transfers using debit and credit cards as we shop or when we use smart phones to do our banking, email a message, or book a train ticket. In these instances, communication messages are sent between people, processes (point of sale systems), and things, such as a bank or credit card or phone, enabled by some form of electronic system. These electronic communication systems require computers, software, and networks to process the communication sent between the sender and the receiver. The idea of communication as transmission between a sender and a receiver was influenced by the twentieth-century expansion of communications technology and was the dominant paradigm in communication studies for decades. The development of the telegraph, telephone, and wireless radio as the means to transport information between two different points has influenced our contemporary understanding of, and feeling for, communication. Communication was associated with a bridging effect; it was understood as a way to connect or transact across a distance, overcoming geography and time.

This idea—that distance, geography, and time are important to how we understand communication and culture—was addressed by Harold Innis, a founding figure in Canadian communication studies associated with what became known as the Toronto School. The Toronto School formed around Innis and Marshall McLuhan, another key Canadian communication scholar, and focused on the structure of those media that were used to communicate (de Kerckhove 1989). The Toronto School had an important role to play in focusing interest on the materiality of communication, often from a political economy perspective. This perspective grounds communication in specific material processes enabling communication—such as paper, wires, and electronic infrastructure, including the Internet—and in the material forces of profit, power, and control of media industries (Flew and Smith 2011). Taken together, this material focus considers the broader media and communications environment or ecology that includes people, processes of communication, technology, and outcomes that combine to produce our sphere of communication. For Innis, this meant paying close attention to the link between transportation and communication while emphasizing that matter-in-transmission "matters"; the content (the message or information being communicated) is as important as the process of communication.

The idea of communication linked to the transportation or transmission of a message is ancient. Traditional knowledge and oral history as communication precede writing. By the time of the Greek philosophers, oral speech and the ability to persuade an audience to adopt a particular meaning in the message conveyed was a valued means of disseminating knowledge, so much so that Plato feared writing as a threat to memory (Hansen 2010). The printing press, when it came into widespread use after the late fifteenth century, introduced a new means of reproducing messages and circulating knowledge by book, pamphlet, or map, which subsequently moved along established networks of transportation (Eisenstein 1979). Innis had a unique way of understanding different types of communication and media that he explained as the **bias of communication**, and explicitly linked modes of transmission to particular media forms (1951). For Innis, these two different types of communication, oral and print, suggested that communication held a bias toward either time or space. **Time-biased media**, such as stone and clay, are durable and long lasting, which encourages the extension of stable empires over time, as in ancient Egypt. These physically substantive media of communication were heavy and could not easily be reproduced, moved, or widely circulated. Oral communication, or speech, is also considered time-biased because Innis felt it required a stable, well-developed social community to enable face-to-face communication. **Space-biased media**, on the other hand, are considered light and portable. These media of communication, such as paper, could be transported over large distances to facilitate the expansion of empire across space. The transmission of messages across a territory could happen more frequently and quickly because the media were easily reproduced and transported. Broadcast media can be considered space-biased media because of their extensive reach and because messages, or content, can change frequently. Ultimately, Innis believed that stable societies achieved a balance between time- and space-biased media of communication.

When Prime Minister Justin Trudeau gives a speech at a community event, is it time-based or space-based, according to Harold Innis? Why?

Understanding communication as messages and information that are sent between two different points or poles is known as the **transmission model of communication**. Its technological roots can be found in the scientific study of information and communication that began in the first half of the twentieth century (Carey 2009; van Loon 2008). Research into the science of communication and information theory was concentrated at Bell Laboratories in the United States as well as at several universities. This research focused on how to transmit electronic messages between a sender and a receiver over a distance. In 1948, Claude Shannon and Warren Weaver published *The Mathematical Theory of Communication*, explaining communication as a mathematical and statistical quantity, or signal, transmitted electronically (1949; Johnston 2008). While this theory explained how information could be sent as an electronic message, it viewed information as straightforwardly technical or as an "encoded" signal from the sender that would be "decoded" by the receiver. The main interest was in the technical means of transmission and control over the process of transmission from end to end. The transmission view, therefore, is more concerned with the transport of messages as information for the purposes of control and in particular "communication [as] a process whereby messages are transmitted and distributed in space for the control of distance and people" (Carey 2009, 13). Or, as Robert Craig explains, the transmission model is "conceptualized as a process in which meanings, packaged in symbolic messages like bananas in crates, are transported from sender to receiver" with little thought as to how we use and consume the "bananas" (2001, 125).

The transmission model evolved to become part of other, more complex models of communication that incorporated cultural analysis. Raymond Williams, the British cultural theorist, worked from the transmission model of communication to develop a rich cultural critique of television in which he considered its form (the technology of TV and broadcasting), use, and effects (1990 [1974]). His work also included a critique of medium theory directed at its principal theorist, Marshall McLuhan. **Medium theory** took the view that cultural content was intertwined with specific media forms (TV, film, radio, and so on) and influenced what and how people think (Flew and Smith 2011; and see McPhail and McPhail 1990). This means that for media theorists, such as McLuhan, studying the media, technology, and form is important because they can amplify aspects of culture and reshape society. For Williams, this media theoretical model of communication reflected a version of technological determinism, which suggests that social change is determined by technology alone (1990). Williams was interested in how technology (and in particular the technology of television) was socially created: social forces, power relations, and competing interests combined to produce new technology and steer its development (Flew and Smith 2011; Mackenzie and Wajcman 1999). McLuhan stressed that the media of communication affect the modern human world and in particular add to, or extend, our human "senses." This extension operates much like a prosthetic or addition to our bodies and minds in that "the personal and social consequences of every medium—that is of the extension of ourselves—result from the new scale that is introduced into our affairs by each extension of ourselves, or by any new technology" (McLuhan 1994, 7). McLuhan's focus on the media as prosthetic suggested that culture could not be understood separately from the media of communication; culture, in this view, is always in mediation through the technological forms of media. These competing views—Williams's cultural critique and McLuhan's media theoretical approach—continue to distinguish approaches to the study of communication.

Another way to understand communication is through what Carey characterized as the **ritual model of communication**. This view understands communication as a social and cultural creation. Carey thus does not link it to the technology of communication or simply to the extension of information across space, but to the representation of shared beliefs constituted by communication as a symbolic process "whereby reality is produced, maintained, repaired, and transformed" (2009, 19). For Carey, the idea of ritual communication is grounded in the idea that communication is profoundly social and at the same time recalls the historical and linguistic roots of the word itself, such as *community* or *commonness*. Ritual communication is also understood as a constructive process in the making of culture as a sphere of human action. In many ways, the ritual view is a much richer and nuanced model of communication that can contribute to our sociological imagination, but it does not foreclose on the transmission view or deny the role it plays in understanding communication. Communication as culture means we cannot simply study individual aspects of communication, such as the sending and receiving of messages, as separate from other areas of life but ought to approach its study through a cultural analysis that considers the meaning, reception, use, and means of communication.

Doing Communication Studies

Communication studies is an interdisciplinary field drawing on a wide range of disciplines, including sociology, psychology, economics, philosophy, computer science, media studies, and political economy. It can sometimes be difficult to distinguish communication from media or communication studies from media studies. Communication has a technical aspect—the sending and receiving of messages—and media has a technological component as the medium or substrate of communication. Bruce Clarke argues that communication itself does not store messages but that media does so because it mediates, contains, and archives the information or content of the communication (2012). For example, print media fix communication in words on paper. The newer, digital media transmit or stream content (information) and store it simultaneously. It's not surprising, then, that communication studies often engage with both communication and media.

In Canada there has been a focus on critical communication studies that "both advances criticism of the existing world system and promotes the 'critical state' that would transform it" (Mosco 1983, 246). The critical approach is often opposed to the administrative approach that took hold in the United States in the 1940s alongside the expansion of media industries—such as radio, television, and film—and was shaped to a large extent through the work of sociologist Paul Lazarsfeld. Lazersfeld deployed statistical methods in his studies of media effects on individual behaviour, focusing on **quantitative studies** and large-scale surveys (Hamilton 2014). In the 1940s, the critical sociologist C. Wright Mills, so instrumental to the development of twentieth-century critical sociology (as discussed in the introduction), went to work for Lazarsfeld. He researched, among other things, mass communication and public opinion (Sterne 2005). Mills often made use of studies originating in administrative research and its methodology. At the same time, he began to develop his critique against the institution of professional sociology. From the perspective of researchers who adopted a more critical stance following Mills's later work, the administrative approach did not adequately engage with the role of power within corporate media systems. This split, between critical and administrative approaches, was crucial to the development of the Canadian field of critical communication studies (Hamilton 2014).

Critical communication studies, in Canada and elsewhere, is best thought of as a critical project rather than a unified approach within the field. There are some important theoretical influences that come from European critical theory, known as the **Frankfurt School**, as well as from feminist, queer, and post-colonial theory, that encourage a critical approach to issues of power and social change, identity, gender, race, and sexuality.

The Frankfurt School—most notably including Theodor Adorno, Max Horkheimer, Herbert Marcuse, and, later, Jürgen Habermas—was known for its critical sociology through Marxist critiques of capitalism, commodity culture, media industries, and communication and social power (Wiggershaus and Robertson 1995). Studies in the political economy of communication often draw on aspects of this critical tradition to study the media and communication industries, hierarchical power relations between media consumers and mainstream corporate media producers, and the implications of cross-media ownership on our public sphere and democratic life (Mosco 2009; Shade and Lithgow 2014; Winseck 2008). Feminist approaches often combine aspects of critical theory with a gender-based analysis to reveal how communication subjects are always already constituted by a sex-gender system within media by examining gender stereotyping, the representation of women in media, and intersectional studies of gender, race, and sexuality (Byerly 2012; Sawchuk 2014). Queer theorists explore how different queer communities use the Internet to build spaces of connection and communication (Bryson 2004) or examine representations of homosexuality in mainstream media (Padva 2008). Gender, race, and sexuality also are explored in relation to online virtual games in terms of game characters, narratives, and gender parity and through video game culture online. These studies reveal a gamer culture complicated by issues of identity, difference, and sexuality, often exposing deeply sexist, racist, and homophobic expression in both game play and associated discussion forums (Brookey and Cannon 2009, Nakamura 2009, Shaw 2009).

Conclusion

This chapter explored some of the theories and models of communication and different approaches in communication studies. The transmission of messages as communication occurs across all facets of society, yet, as Carey stresses, communication does not occur only in transmission but is constituted by social processes as part of culture. For McLuhan, the transmission of communication required media as the mode of conveyance, and this meant that "each form of transport not only carries, but translates and transforms, the sender, the receiver, and the message" (1994, 90). This work points toward the idea that the media of communication—whether radio, television, or the Internet—make a difference in how we interpret, understand, or make sense of the message or communication; in short, "the medium is the message" (McLuhan 1994, 7). In this moment of communication-by-Twitter, in short, 140-character bursts, McLuhan's ideas seem very relevant: the medium of Twitter indeed shapes the message.

Contemporary scholarship on communication, as a study apart from the media of communication and media studies specifically, tries in many ways to set a path away from the dominance of the transmission model. On the one hand the transmission model was set out in the pre-digital era, dominated by orality, literacy (writing and print), and wire-bound electronic communication (such as the telegraph and telephone, and later by wireless radio and broadcasting technology). Yet, on the other hand, the transmission view persists although the mode of communication has shifted from electronic to digital. A mix of physical infrastructure, such as cables, computers, wireless cellular networks, and satellites, now connects communication systems composed of digital "bits" or digital code. So the idea of transmission is not dead, but contemporary digital systems have revolutionized the means of communicating. The study of communication today requires us to think not simply about the effects of the meaning of a message symbolically coded for transmission as communication but also about how code itself—the software programming that sits behind our contemporary digital communications, encompassing content, control, and coordination—shapes our communicative milieu. Communication today is not linear. It is not organized between two poles or points set up to send and receive messages. Communication, rather, is multidirectional—a dimension in which the form of content and the form of expression cannot be separated into two discrete modes—transmission or ritual—for the sake of analysis (Slack 2012). More than ever, we may need to think about the media of communication, from social networks to satellite radio, and the statements, acts, and expression that ground us in fundamentally material practices of communication connecting bodies to networks, to computers, and to each other.

Review/Summary Questions

1. How would you define *communication*?
2. How would you explain the bias of communication?
3. What distinguishes the ritual model of communication from the transmission model?
4. What would Harold Innis think of the Internet: does it exhibit a bias in communication?

11 How Does Media Transform Society?

Daniel Downes

Introduction

This chapter explores the significance of media technologies and media institutions in contemporary Canadian society. The chapter will describe the characteristics and transformation of what I shall refer to as the "old" media. Several frameworks for thinking about the media will be presented and a number of questions raised about the content, operation, and structure of the media. Finally, we will examine changes in the media landscape following the widespread adoption of the Internet and mobile communication and ask to what extent the concerns of the old media remain pertinent today.

The Context of Mass Communication

Most of the technological innovations we live with today have been developed in the last century and a half. That's an extremely short period of time when measured against the history of human civilizations and culture. Many of the communication devices we use and the interactions we engage in did not exist even a decade ago. For example, each of the following is a relic of the years since 2000: YouTube, Facebook, Twitter, Google Earth, Tumblr, Instagram. Along with new forms and channels of communication, today we have access to the historical archive of media content. In principle, much of the texts of sound recording, radio broadcast and television broadcast, cinema, and publishing are available through digitization in ways that were precluded by earlier technologies and patterns of information dissemination. This situation both deepens and flattens our experience of mediated culture. What are some of the consequences of a media environment that has grown so vast and so quickly?

Mass communication describes the process of creating shared meaning between mass media and their audiences. Mass communication refers to the process by which a complex organization of professional communicators, using varied and expensive technological infrastructure, produce and distribute standardized, public messages aimed at a large, scattered, and heterogeneous audience. In addition, mass communication involves hundreds or thousands of people, and there is no immediate feedback between receivers and the source of a message. Newspapers, magazines, radio, television, and film are all examples of mass media.

In general, the old media are mass media. They presume a single content distributed to a large audience at the same time. The goal of mass communication is to create a common experience, thereby fostering homogeneity in its audience. In Canada, we have a long history of thinking about physical transportation networks, information technologies, and communication institutions. This interest has appeared in a set of recurring and related questions about the roles and responsibilities of the media, including how new technologies (from the Canadian Pacific Railroad to the information technologies of radio, television, and the Internet) can be used for the project of nation-building and fostering a sense of national community. With regard to the content in the Canadian media, the recurring question is whether media content reflects us. Indeed, debate is often centred on what we can or should do about the abundance of US content carried by Canadian media outlets. As media companies are social institutions, how should the balance between freedom of expression and the rights of such companies to pursue their own interests be weighed against the perceived power of media to exert political, social, or economic influence? Finally, these issues raise the question of the role of government: what, if any, role should government play in regulating the operation or structure of the media?

Mass communication in Canada helped to create a national consciousness by creating shared experiences for readers, listeners, and viewers. But increasingly mass communication has become a force of economic growth and competitiveness. Vipond (1992) argues that by the end of the nineteenth century, mass media played a mediating role as one of the principal institutions by which individuals were brought into the transition from traditional to modern forms of society. She suggests that the media played an important role in educating rural migrants who were by then living and working in cities, as well as immigrants to Canada who were encouraged, through the media, to adopt a set of middle-class values that seemed natural through their repetition in the media (Vipond 1992, 10). The saturation of Canadian-owned media with US content is the result of tensions between two Canadian idea systems. On the one hand, Canadians have fostered a myth of communications promising that a new technological system will bind us together. Charland (1986) argues that the very idea of an English Canadian identity was created through such various "national" experiences as the Canadian Pacific Railroad (CPR) and later, the broadcasting system. This rhetoric ideologically constituted those people living in Canada as Canadians (Charland 1986, 202). As historian David Taras (2001) puts it, the challenge of broadcasting in Canada "was to counter American influence by creating a distinctively Canadian mass media culture, one that would generate its own stars, its own memorable and popular programs, and its own allegiances" (120–1).

The role of media in creating a national community is clear in the early work of John Grierson (he would later head the National Film Board of Canada), who recognized the power of representing working people in film in ways that would maintain the status quo (Nelson 1988). On the other hand, we share with our American neighbours an ideology of liberal individualism, which influenced the kind of media industries we created and their attending values (Vipond 1992).

What questions did the old media raise? Does scarcity of some sources of information (or some viewpoints in the marketplace of ideas) lessen the depth of content, or does it in some way diminish the range of common experiences we have as members of our society? Does the commercial origin of much media content influence that content? If it does, then in what ways? How can we detect and study the influences that shape the kinds of content we use to construct social reality? Further, because people often assume the link between media content and social identity, we raise issues about control and ownership of the media. The question arises, how do we structure the media, and how do we place controls on content to achieve desirable social goals? Indeed, in Canada, it is often assumed that the ownership of the means of communication has a greater impact on society than media content in and of itself (Hardin 1985; Raboy 1990).

Approaches to Media Study

In general terms, the study of mass media focuses either on the content or messages of mediated communication or on the media as social institutions. Researchers have evaluated the effects of media messages on audiences or, by investigating media institutions, they have analyzed how the media operate and how the media are structured.

Media Effects

The first approach to the study of media concentrated on the effects of media messages. Early studies assumed that media messages exerted powerful influences on those who experience them (Blumer and Hauser 1939). The basic question from this perspective is, "Do the media have the power to shape, change, or determine the attitudes, values, and, perhaps most importantly, the behaviours of individuals?" At various times in the past 80 years, opinion has swayed from the assumption that the media can influence behaviour so that messages have direct, strong effects, to a more limited view of the influence of media messages that suggests that media content simply reinforces pre-existing opinions, beliefs, and values held by audience members (Lazarsfeld, Berelson, and Gaudet 1944; Berelson 1959; Trend 2007). If media messages are powerful stimuli that can influence our behaviour, government restrictions on certain types of objectionable content might seem reasonable. If, on the other hand, media messages are limited in their ability to influence audiences, then the media should be allowed to provide their audiences with whatever content the people want. Both approaches to **media effects** can be found today.

Fear that the media have a powerful influence on people leads to moral panics arising out of actual or perceived responses to media content. Dr David Walsh, in an interview for the CBC's *the fifth estate* (CBC 2009) supports the view that violence in video games can have a negative effect on young people. When Walsh claims that the computer divides the family, he echoes similar fears that the radio threatened the family during the 1950s because teenagers started to listen alone in their rooms instead of with the family in the living room; similarly, in the early days of cinema, there were fears that youth were vulnerable to bad influences of viewing movies without adult supervision—in the dark, in a room full of strangers.

By contrast, a special issue of *Maclean's* magazine (2008) on the subject of Internet porn argues that parents ultimately have the power and responsibility to monitor their children's Internet use rather than calling for government intervention. Video-game violence and Internet pornography are certainly problematic and socially undesirable forms of media content. Why, then, is such media content readily available? The view expressed in the *Maclean's* article reinforces the assumption that media content has limited effects on our behaviour and that, therefore, it is not the role of government to control or regulate media content.

When people argue that governments should regulate objectionable media messages, they are arguing that media messages are powerful and that at least some media messages are dangerous. Further, when people call for the Canadian government to regulate the media industries in Canada, the issue raised is whether we are shaping the kind of identity we want or whether that identity is unduly influenced by outside sources. (In the Canadian context this raises questions of cultural nationalism, cultural dependency on American culture, and the role of media regulation.) Are we telling enough "Canadian" stories? Once again, if messages can influence our behaviour and if the media do shape identity, a society needs controls over the production of content.

How the Media Operate

The second approach we can take to the study of media institutions is to ask how the media operate. (For examples of this approach, see Tuchman 1980; Schudson 1991; Herman and Chomsky 1988.) For Herman and Chomsky (1988), the main function of the mass media is to foster and spread the values, beliefs, and codes of behaviour that will enable individuals to function within society's institutional structures. We do not have to assume that the media are conscious and deliberate agents of ideology. Rather, the structure of the media as well as the relationships between media organizations, advertisers, audiences, and the larger society all contribute to shape the kind of media content we receive. To help explain these relationships, the authors identify a set of five "filters" that influence the way the dominant media operate as well as how they select and cover the stories presented to the public:

1. The ownership of the media as large, profit-making businesses owned by a small number of owners
2. Advertising as the primary income source for the media

3. The reliance on "official" sources and experts in media coverage, who will tend to present the views and ideas of government, big business, and "experts" funded by business and government
4. "Flak" or negative feedback as a method to influence media coverage
5. A pervasive ideology of anti-communism perpetuated through the media.

While this last filter can be seen as a holdover of a political climate that existed when the filters were first articulated, it can be argued that media coverage in the United States (and to some degree in Canada) still tends to favour capitalism and notions of a free market for goods and ideas as unquestioned components of our society.

This type of research examines the internal and external influences that help determine the information disseminated as well as the tone the media take on particular issues. We can also focus our attention on the news-gathering functions of the media (surveillance of the environment and correlation of relevant information). In this way we can ask how well the news media perform. Are they reliable or biased? Is there a clear distinction between news, opinion, and promotion?

In 2006, after more than three years of research and hearings across the country, the Senate of Canada released a report on Canadian news media. Their report, the third federal study on the news media in Canada in 35 years, urged the government to curb media concentration. One of the targets of the report was Canwest, which was, at the time, the largest integrated media company in Canada, owning the *National Post*, 13 dailies in major cities and 23 papers in smaller cities, Global TV's 11 stations, a handful of radio stations, and an Internet site.

When Canwest bought its newspapers from Southam news in the late 1990s, the new owners alienated journalists by spiking columns that disagreed with the owners' political views, attempting to centralize the production of editorials, rewriting stories, and, ultimately, firing the editor of the *Ottawa Citizen* for publishing a story on the scandal that was to become "Shawinigate" along with an editorial calling for then prime minister Jean Chrétien to resign (McDiarmid 2006).

The Canwest owners' involvement in the editorial and journalistic practices of their newspapers is called "operational" control, where the owners are actively involved in the editorial or news-gathering practices of their papers. Another kind of control that owners can use to shape news coverage is called "allocative control"—concern with how resources (financial, material, and human) are deployed in an organization.

How the Media Are Structured

The choices that editors and media owners make about media content illustrates one of the ways that content is shaped. However, the way the media are organized (as private, commercial businesses; as public institutions; or as global conglomerates) also shapes their relationships with society. Commercial media institutions are corporations that own and operate media outlets for profit. The commercial orientation of the media means that the media must optimize revenues while minimizing production and operating costs. Commercial media create new content or purchase content from media producers in other countries in order to build audiences; that audience attention is then sold to advertisers, who offset the cost of programming and are the primary source of revenues for the media outlets. The commercial pressures that media face can have odd, long-term effects on the cultural life of a society (for examples of research that explores the structure of the media see Bagdikian 2000, Kunz 2006, and Mosco 2009).

A number of large mergers have changed the Canadian media landscape since 2000. In 2001 Quebecor took control of the French-language network TVA; Rogers Media purchased Citytv in 2007; and in 2010 Shaw Communications acquired Canwest Global, and Bell Canada Enterprises (BCE) took ownership of the CTV television network (House of Commons 2011). In Canada's English-language mediascape, the two biggest companies, Bell and Rogers, account for 43 per cent of all revenues. Adding in Shaw and Telus, these four companies account for almost 70 per cent of the media landscape (Fontaine 2013, 1). Figures 11.1 and 11.2 show that, compared to the situation 20 years ago, the major players in Canadian media have shifted from telecommunications (carrier and distribution companies) and print and broadcast (content companies) to vertically integrated communication companies. In 1992 only newpspaper giant Southam was a content producer. Conversely, in 2013 only Telus was primarily a carrier. As telecommunication and media industries have converged into a common communication sector, the market has almost tripled between 1992 and 2013.

In the age of broadcast media (what critical theorist and historian Mark Poster [1995] calls the "second media age"), communication was something that was done *to* us, usually by large, institutional communicators who had specific reasons (sometimes economic, sometimes political) for distributing a standardized message to the largest possible audience. There are practical reasons for this process. For example, in the case of both radio and television in the United States, the media developed as networks rather than as individual stations competing with one another. The networks gave advertisers access to large, national audiences for which the advertisers paid high prices. This revenue allowed the networks to produce programming (sponsored by advertisers) that could be sold to stations (in the United States and Canada) more cheaply than locally produced content (Starr 2004). The networks came to dominate broadcasting for most of the twentieth century. However, the development of media industries based on advertising and commercial programming has created the possibility for media companies to shape their content to satisfy commercial needs or pressures.

Journalist Bill Moyers makes this point, arguing that baseball has changed from a national pastime, a national symbol of sporting identity, to a commodity governed by economic and broadcast requirements. Steroid use is tolerated, even if officially frowned upon, because the game is a spectacle rather than a sport and players feel immense pressure to outperform one another and the stars of earlier generations. Moyers analogizes the situation in baseball to the spiritual or

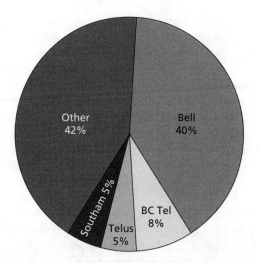

Figure 11.1 Canadian Media Landscape 1992 Showing Market Shares for the Four Largest Private Media and Information Companies.

Note: Total communication market for the year was $25 billion.

Source: CC BY-NC-SA 4.0 Canadian Media Concentration Research Project

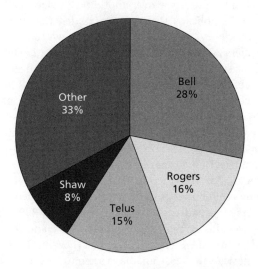

Figure 11.2 Canadian Media Landscape 2013 Showing Market Shares for the Four Largest Private Media and Information Companies

Note: Total market for the year was $73 billion.

Source: CC BY-NC-SA 4.0 Canadian Media Concentration Research Project

moral climate in the United States, where greed and short-term profit are more important than the integrity of sports or politics (Moyers 2007). The same case could be made about pressures to allow violence in junior hockey in Canada because it trains players who want to play professional hockey. In both cases, it is the operation of the media as purveyors of spectacle that subtly change the nature of our cultural activities. Further, as media companies grow larger and become more consolidated, the content produced by writers, directors, musicians, and journalists is undervalued because the companies face greater pressures to make profits and to manage the debt they incur in order to grow larger (Fontaine 2013, 1).

Changes in the Media Landscape

In addition to studying media messages, operation, or structures, students of communication also pay close attention to changes in the media landscape. In particular, we are changing our media consumption habits as we turn to the Internet as a source of information and seem to be losing faith in the traditional media to provide us with reliable information.

In 2009, a survey conducted by the Pew Research Center for the People & the Press reported that nearly two-thirds—63 per cent—of Americans believed that news stories are often inaccurate. In 1985, only 34 per cent of respondents believed stories were frequently inaccurate. In addition, the study found that 74 per cent of respondents thought that the media were biased (that news stories tend to favour one side of an issue over another) (Bauder 2009). The study also showed that more Republicans than Democrats felt that the US media were biased, and that while television was the dominant news source, the Internet had surpassed newspapers as a source of national and international news. Reporting on the results of the survey, Bauder (2009) proposes several reasons for the loss of faith in the reliability of the press, including financial pressures, partisanship, and the effects of competition with the Internet as a source of information.

According to a Pew poll of December 2010, Americans were watching less television and continued to use the Internet for national and international news. And for the first time, a population group—those under 30—were using the Internet more than television for news (Zickuhr 2010).

In Canada, a similar trend is occurring. Canadians between the ages of 30 and 49 are using the Internet as much as television as a news source. Further, significant numbers of Canadians are online. Figures for 2007 show that 95 per cent of 15- to 24-year-olds, 85 per cent of people 45–54, and 70 per cent of those aged 55–64 regularly use the Internet in Canada (Dewing 2012, 1). However, in contrast to the American studies, Canadians seem to trust the media as a source of information more than their neighbours to the south do. Reporting on news coverage of the 2006 federal election, Ray (2008) observes that Canadians tend to recognize the difference between opinion columns and news coverage in daily newspapers. They find opinion columns biased toward particular political viewpoints, but, contrary to the US data, they feel that, in general, news coverage is pretty neutral across the board.

Why do governments investigate the media? Often, the reasons have to do with fears that the media, or certain media companies, are becoming too powerful or that those who control the media may unduly influence the content. Questions that have been asked about the media in Canada over the years have focused on concentration of ownership, concerns over whether the media should be publicly or privately owned or controlled, and the origins and nature of media content (are the programs we watch or listen to Canadian or American, or does media content threaten harm to some segment of the population?). Government commissions on the media have had mixed impact on the nature of the Canadian media system. In some cases (commissions on broadcasting and the arts include Aird in 1929, Massey in 1949, and Fowler in 1957), the answer to the question of whether the government should regulate or influence the operation of the media in the interest of society is yes. In each of the commissions mentioned in the previous sentence, the questions raised by the commissioners had to do with the nature of broadcasting in Canada. On the other hand, for commissions on the press (Davey in 1969, Kent in 1980, and the Senate Commission in 2006), the answer to the same question is no. The reports filed by these commissions did little or nothing to change the patterns of ownership and media concentration that have been characteristic of Canadian (and international) media since the 1960s.

What Happened to the Old Media?

During the 1980s and 1990s, the functions traditionally performed by the mass media became overshadowed by their need to entertain (Postman 1985). Television's traditional network audiences were drawn by the growth of cable content, and the mass audience dwindled except under certain extraordinary contexts, such as the OJ Simpson trial or the funeral of Princess Diana. Businesses became global in desire, if not reach. Similarly, multilateral trade agreements created the economic and regulatory latitude for global business to emerge and thrive. Technologies, such as the computer, became central to the information and communication industries during the 1990s, initiating a period of convergence.

Convergence

During the 1990s technological convergence through the application of computers to the production, distribution, storage, and reception of information made a number of laws and regulations applicable to the media industries seem old fashioned and, at times, ridiculous. For many years, in Canada, cable companies could not enter the phone business even though they provided cables to homes that could carry television signals as well as phone traffic. Similarly, phone companies were not allowed to use the phone lines to bring television into the home. In particular, since the same process of digitization was used to create text, sound, images, and moving images as well as to distribute those messages, it made little sense to structurally separate content-providing industries (such as radio or television stations) from distribution industries (such as the telephone company or cable television companies), which had been the case in Canada. (See Ridout 2003 for a discussion of shifts in telecommunication policy in Canada.)

During this period, the organizations that produced and distributed information and communication content also began to converge. Industries that were formerly separate were also converging into large multinational information and communications entities. Further, by the end of the 1990s it seemed that Canada needed large industrial actors to compete with an increasingly globalized information and media sector. Thus, in Canada, like other countries, mergers and acquisitions among the media and telecommunication sector created giant conglomerates.

Finally, laws and public policies governing the media, career opportunities in media and public sectors, social and personal issues arising from media consumption, and even theories of the media and their role in society changed to reflect the fact of convergence. Under the banner of technological convergence, media companies argued that earlier industrial regulation no longer applied to the emerging information industries. They complained that governments were too slow to adapt to the speed at which the information society was becoming a reality (see Barney 2000).

Fragmentation of Audiences

The pressures facing the traditional media players during the late 1980s and throughout the 1990s became apparent through the decline in audiences. It was not so much a loss as a fragmentation of audiences, who looked to other sources for the media content they wanted.

Since then, the traditional television networks have tried a number of strategies to recover their audience. The focus on reality TV, for example, is an attempt to consolidate the 18- to 34-year-old demographic by integrating the viewing experience with cellphone use, phone use, online discussion groups, etc. Online, viewers are able to see raw material and extras not aired as part of the regular programs. The networks use new media to create interest in their content: Internet advertising promotes programming; online games keep viewers interested in shows like *The Walking Dead*; and gimmicks involve viewers more deeply—for example, the fictional writer Richard Castle posts comments on Facebook and Twitter between seasons of the television series (*Castle*) in which he is a central character.

Another strategy used by television to recapture audiences was the development of reality television geared to global markets. During the early 1990s, reality TV was the only format of television production that was not deficit financed. According to Ted Magder (2009), there were several reasons for this success: prepackaged formats became popular as the basis for program production, product placement and brand integration became a source of revenue for program producers, TV programs became springboards for multimedia exploitation of creative property, and the importance of European program suppliers in the US market grew. Global television formats are one successful response to the changes facing the traditional media over the past 20 years.

Technological Adaptation

The broad effect of the Internet on the traditional media has been to give them a common technological infrastructure. This has forced them to compete against one another as never before. The Internet has lowered the cost of entry into the media market and anyone can now create media content. We see the effects of this shift in the challenge blogging poses to traditional newspaper reporting; in the movies (think of the viral marketing campaign used to create a buzz around *The Blair Witch Project*, and the "Are you serious" viral campaign to promote Christopher Nolan's *The Dark Knight*; a recent example of this sort of viral marketing is Ryan Reynold's use of Twitter and Instagram to build and maintain interest in his *Deadpool* film); and in the way YouTube challenges television by providing a medium for people to watch both traditional TV content and new forms of video created specifically for the Internet.

The convergence of computer, telecommunications, computers, and mass media systems is bringing about some fundamental changes in the way the mass media function. Mass media sources are becoming more numerous and, at the same time, less professionalized or authoritative. Their ability to act as gatekeepers that set the agenda for public discussion is also being diminished. Messages are customized for smaller and more specialized segments of the audience, sometimes more accurately described as "communities," who use personal forms of address, than as audiences. The media narrowcast to these segments rather than broadcast to a homogeneous audience. Audiences are likewise becoming smaller and less anonymous than they were formerly. The media know more about their audience members, who, in turn, have a greater range of effective means of providing feedback to the producers of media content—and even of participating in the creation of that content. For some, this is a sign that the audience is becoming more powerful as we move away from a notion of the passive mass media to interactive media (Straubhaar and LaRose 2000, 28).

However, a number of factors have contributed to a bumpy transition for the media in this century. The Web challenged conventional television as a delivery source (by allowing users to download programs through torrents and to watch old media content on YouTube or Netflix, etc). Indeed, viewing habits changed to the extent that television no longer orders people's evenings and, therefore, no longer provides reliable audiences for advertisers. As an alternative to network broadcasting, the Web has yet to provide a reliable audience to advertisers.

Characteristics of New Media Systems

For many researches, it is not enough to identify "new" media simply as those that follow earlier media. Something about digital, networked communications allows for a qualitatively different media landscape. For Paul Levinson, the significance of what he calls "new" new media is the fact that we now consume media at our own pace once it has been posted online (for example, when we engage in binge viewing—watching a number of episodes of a program—on Netflix), but we also produce content and consume content produced by a worldwide community of consumers and producers (Levinson 2013). Jenkins, Ford, and Green (2013) cite the "spreadable" quality of new media content— the videos we share that become viral phenomena and the diversity of our engagement with both amateur and professional content—as being the most pertinent quality of the media landscape. According to Mark B. Hansen (2009), the "newness" of new media does not refer to a common technological system used by formerly different types of media but to the way we incorporate the logic of computing (searching, storing, and distributing information) as part of our social lives. Finally, we must recognize that new media does not simply replace what came before. We still receive and process images and information through reading, listening, and watching old media while also interacting with and responding to the content we create and share through new media (Jackson, Nielsen, and Hsu 2011).

In her important study of digital culture, *Hamlet on the Holodeck*, author Janet Murray (1998) identifies four qualities specific to our experience of digitally mediated content:

1. *Interactive*: First, computer programs are responsive to our input, so a digital environment can change the way our experience unfolds in response to the commands we enter through the keyboard, mouse, or other device. Murray calls this "interactivity."
2. *Immersive*: Second, digital environments are "immersive": a user has the ability to change the nature of the interactions she or he has in the digital media with ease. The digital environment is "responsive" and compliant.
3. *Navigational*: The third, "navigational" component is evident in applications such as Facebook or Wikipedia. We know where we are in the digital space on the computer screen by engaging in the interactive process of navigation. When we enter commands on the keyboard or move the mouse across a pad, a visual marker—the cursor—moves to specific locations on the screen.
4. *Encyclopedic*: Finally, digital media is often "encyclopedic." When we watch television, we watch a particular episode of a specific program broadcast at a specific time. In the digital environment, however, we can access the entire series as well as production information and biographical details of the actors, and we can interact with other viewers. More importantly, there is so much information in a digital environment—more information than we could use in a single visit—that we can forget its constructed nature. Murray suggests that new forms of interactive media will take advantage of these properties.

Mobility and the Third Screen

Perhaps one of the most profound characteristics of the new media environment relates to how we engage with media content. Today, more and more of us watch, listen, read, and respond to media content while we are on the move.

The evolution of cellphone technology is often described in relation to the tasks the devices are able to perform: the first and second generations (1G and 2G) consisted of devices that could handle voice and text messaging. Next, 3G cellphones and networks added media content, including TV, while 4G networks began the move to seamless connectivity between our phones, our tablets, and the Internet.

Key to understanding the importance of mobile media is that we are constantly connected to the wireless network and, increasingly, to the Internet with multipurpose devices. Smart phones and tablets take the place of computers in that they allow us to make phone calls and send text messages and email; we can browse the Internet and play music and video files; and we can even record audio, video, and photographs, which can be immediately posted online. The devices are always present, and we use them on the move. Further, we are linked to others in ways and to an extent that was impossible in the age of mass media.

Since the early 2000s, mobile devices have been marketed heavily as media devices: "The idea of a third screen as mobile TV took hold as Sprint and other American and Canadian carriers upgraded their networks in order to offer synchronous and asynchronous broadcasting of TV to cell phone viewers" (Nicholson 2011, 77). In a report prepared for the Library of Parliament, Theckedath and Thomas (2012) write that while "people have been talking about convergence since the end of the 20th century, it was in 2007 with the introduction of the iPhone and 2010 with the introduction of the iPad that Internet-enabled smart phones and tablets became realistic platforms for mobile video-streaming, including television broadcasts" (1).

How Are Digital Communications Distinct from Traditional Mass Communications?

So, how are the characteristics of digital communication distinct from those of traditional mass communication described earlier? First, regarding the production of information, in the new media landscape the distinctions between professional, organized communicators and amateur or individual communicators are increasingly blurred. We still consume content provided by media organizations, but we also create information: emails, user profiles, accounts on electronic shopping sites, videos, etc. Some people even engage in activities that resemble the work of traditional media practitioners: blogging, for example. Many argue that such user-generated content undermines the authority and popularity of professional media content (Keen 2007).

Second, traditional distribution networks, which were technologically and often industrially specific to a particular medium, have been challenged by the common infrastructure of Internet and mobile communication devices. Now, different forms of media content reach us through the same devices. However, we can understand the Internet as a site of tension between different philosophies regarding the production and distribution of content. For many years, the Internet could be understood as an environment of "generative" technology: people identified problems with the technology and solved them, thus creating an environment of innovation and the sense that the Internet expanded due to individual efforts. From the generative perspective, computing devices can be modified and software programming can be created to fulfill a variety of needs by any number of creative individuals or companies. On the other hand, with the rise of mobile devices such as iPhones, iPads, and smart phones, a competing view of the Internet has emerged that treats computing devices as "tethered appliances" that require a user to obtain all software and content from the company that provides the hardware. From the perspective of tethered appliances, the new media environment more closely resembles the old media environment in which a relatively small group of people or companies has access to the means of mass distribution (Zittrain 2008).

Mobile communication has made the Internet central to communications in Canada. The old concerns about concentration of ownership in newspapers and broadcasting has been replaced by concerns over who controls access to the Internet and mobile broadband (Theckedath and Thomas 2012). This concern is reflected in a recent Canadian Radio-television and Telecommunications Commission (CRTC) decision. In 2013 Bell offered its mobile phone subscribers access to 10 hours of streamed television for $5 per month while charging the same subscribers up to $40 per month of data charges for streaming YouTube, CBC, or Netflix. The CRTC argued that by giving preferential treatment to their own TV services, Bell was being anti-competitive and could inhibit the growth of other Internet-based TV services (Winseck 2015).

Finally, audiences have been recast as users and participants rather than just recipients. The old media economy focused on the production and control of distribution. Radio and television networks sold the attention of audiences to advertisers, who subsidized or paid for programming. In a real sense, the media turned audiences into commodities. In the new media environment, on the other hand, we engage in media in active, participatory ways. We share the things that interest us, endorse amateur and professional content, and interact with traditional media producers in ways that can be fruitful and, at times, frustrating for the traditional media. For example, fans of the Twilight films were so involved in online discussions and real-time behind-the-scenes video on set that the production crew found it unnerving to have their work documented so extensively and immediately (Jenkins, Ford, and Green 2013).

In the new media environment, we also turn ourselves into commodities through the very acts that seem, on the surface, to give us a power and independence not experienced in traditional mass communication. As we exchange messages and information about ourselves on sites like Facebook or LinkedIn, we are encouraged to participate in social media, where our interactions themselves are the content and the raw material for both the sites and third parties to turn into information commodities. (For examples of how we transform ourselves into "media selves" and "commodity signs," see Couldry 2009 and Hearn 2009.)

Concerns and Criticisms about New Media

Indeed, our social media practices have given rise to extreme behaviour in the form of **cyber bullying** and online harrassment. In the wake of such activities, 18 US states have passed laws that target Internet harrassment and **cyber stalking**. In 2013, Nova Scotia's Cyber-Safety Act was the first attempt in Canada to regulate online harrassment. It was, however, a controversial piece of legislation, and in 2015 the Supreme Court of Nova Scotia declared the Act unconstitutional (Todd 2014). In 2015, the Government of Canada proposed a security bill that would make it illegal to promote terrorism or terrorist organizations online. Such electronic laws can be seen as attempts to control certain forms of mediated content and raise issues about free speech and media effects similar to earlier attempts to regulate media content in the print and broadcast industries.

These new online activities of media consumption, surfing, and social networking have been criticized (as has media content in the past) for the ways they dull our critical faculties. Often, writers highlight negative changes that have arisen from the adoption of new forms or tools of communication. Such critiques are often attacks on contemporary media. For example, Nicholas Carr's article "Is Google Making Us Stupid?" (2008) raises a number of issues about the power and influence of media. He is not the first to criticize media in this way (Postman 1992).

Carr begins with some observations about his own experiences of mediation. Where once he used to read and contemplate, using the Internet as his main medium of information has changed the way he thinks—skimming on the surface of a vast sea of information. He concludes that we may be in the middle of a sea change in terms of how we think. Google is the example he cites as a company that is using the computer to do the work of the mind. Where McLuhan (1994 [1964]) described the "global village" of mass communications as a prosthetic extension of the human nervous system, Carr worries about the success of just such an imagined prosthetic.

For Carr, life moves too fast for us to sit back, contemplate, and digest the torrent of information at our fingertips. In the end, Carr makes a contribution to contemporary discussions about the power of media and its ability to influence us. The deluge of media images gives us what media scholar Todd Gitlin has called "feeling lite"—media is all about conveying feeling, creating a reaction or an emotional response rather than presenting a reasoned argument or facts for deliberation on issues. For others, the acts of self-promotion implicit in Facebook and Twitter posts or in the practice of posting "selfies" create a culture of narcissism (CBC 2013). In the end, for such critics, the contemporary media environment creates a perfect condition for political disengagement (see Gitlin 2002, Hedges 2009).

Is there a counterargument to Carr's perspective on Google and new media? Yes. Johnson (2005) argues that today's popular culture is actually making us "smarter" by teaching us new skills: there are games that force us to probe and telescope; television shows that require us to fill in the blanks over time; software that makes us sit forward, not lean back. For Johnson, these aspects of contemporary culture demonstrate a more than 30-year trend toward increasing complexity.

A recent study reported by the BBC suggests that children who use a variety of communication tools are more likely to read and write than their classmates who use fewer communication tools and settings such as face-to-face interactions or telephone conversations (Kleinman 2009). According to the 2009 UK study conducted by the National Literacy Trust, children who engage in a variety of forms of communication activities have stronger core literacy skills than students who neither blog nor use social-networking sites. Indeed, the BBC reported that there is a strong correlation between technology use and wider patterns of reading and writing.

While the BBC article reported that primary school teachers are reluctant to encourage kids to use computers, the teachers do recognize that there might be benefits in incorporating children's passion for texting into teaching and learning methods (Kleinman 2009). Most significant in this report is the recognition that we have to learn new forms and techniques of communication and new forms of **media literacy**, or "mediacy," to adapt to new social realities. This is a much more compelling insight than the simplistic argument that our old literacy skills are on the decline because of new media.

Conclusion

With more Canadians using the Internet and digital media than ever before, it is possible to argue that we are regular participants in a new media landscape. The old mass media have gone through a process of technological, industrial, and regulatory convergence over the past 25 years, resulting in a single communications sector that includes vertically integrated companies that create and distribute traditional print and broadcast and that control much of the broadband and Internet networks in the country. Audiences have fragmented and have migrated to new sources of information but have also become "users" and content providers in the new media environment, requiring of us new skills and awareness of the importance of mediated communication.

Review/Summary Questions

1. How has the assumption that ownership of the means of communication has a greater impact on society than media content change as a consequence of the adoption of new media?
2. In what ways is a concern about the effects of media content still important?
3. What are the effects of convergence on the new media landscape?
4. In what ways does mobile communication change our experience of media content?
5. Why is media literacy important in an era of digital and mobile communication?

12 Should Policing Be Privatized?

Curtis Clarke

Introduction

> Some authors have warned of potential negative effects of this commodification
> of policing, that is, of its packaging and promotion as a thing that can be traded.
> (Ayling and Shearing 2008, 43)

Recent quantitative and structural changes in the nature of security have
realigned the operational prominence of public policing and blurred the
boundary between private and public providers. As Ian Loader (2000) points
out, this fragmentation of providers has ushered in a "plethora of agencies and
agents, each with particular kinds of responsibility for the delivery of policing
and security services and technologies" (323).

The resulting transformation raises numerous questions with respect to
the role of the state, the assurance of accountable policing, and whether or not
the public interest/good can be effectively protected by the emerging network of
providers. In the context of this transformation, should policing be privatized?
Or is a more appropriate question one that asks whether the state will remain
a focal point in the provision and accountability of policing? A corresponding
question would centre on how the state might formulate its connection to
policing, given the contemporary conditions of diverse providers (Loader and
Walker 2001). Ayling and Shearing (2008) further suggest that "new forms of
policing will challenge conceptions of state centrality in the protection domain
and raise questions about the extent of state regulation that is needed and about
the appropriate loci of accountability and responsibility for service providers"
(44). While these are important points from which to begin our response,
formulating an effective response is not so simple. In order to do so, we must
understand how the current landscape of policing has been transformed. To
begin, let us briefly outline what we mean by policing.

Policing: A Brief Explanation

The activity of policing is closely aligned with **governance** (see Chapter 14). **Policing** is a process of regulating and ordering contemporary societies and individuals. Governance and the activity of policing are thus used as terms to "denote governmental strategies originating from inside and outside the state" (Jones 2003, 605). This notion of governance has been woven into much of the current analysis of policing, and it expresses a broad function within a system of formal regulation and promotion of security (Jones and Newburn 1998; Loader 2000; Jones 2003; Murphy and Clarke 2005). A corresponding layer of analysis focuses on the institution or specific state agency tasked with order maintenance, law enforcement, and public safety. In this analysis, our attention is drawn to the formal structure and organizational practices of these agencies, not to the broad function of social control. In this context, policing refers to

> those forms of order maintenance, peacekeeping, rule or law enforcement, crime investigation and prevention and other forms of investigation and associated information-brokering; which may involve a conscious exercise of coercive power; undertaken by individuals or organizations, where such activities are viewed by them and/or others as a central or key defining part of their purpose. (Jones and Newburn 1998, 18)

Traditionally, many of these tasks and functions were considered the sole purview of the public police. And yet in the current era of transformation, these very tasks and functions have become the foothold of the private sector's perceived encroachment on public policing authority. These regulatory, investigative, and enforcement activities are, in fact, the site of intense debate with respect to the public/private nexus of policing, the crux of which rests on the issue of public accountability. Burbidge (2005) notes the following:

> While the public police are governed by and accountable to democratically elected governmental authority and to the public, private police officers, even when performing the same policing functions as their public counterparts, are not subject to the same form of democratic governance and accountability. (67)

Although the issue of accountability remains a central theme, it is essential to note that private providers do indeed offer similar services to those provided by the public police. The fundamental concern is how public policing shed many of these tasks, thus creating an opportunity for private providers to assume a level of prominence. As the following section argues, the transformation was the result of broad neo-liberal governance policies and a perceived crisis of ineffective order maintenance.[1]

The Shifting Landscape of Policing

In the era of public service rationalization, public police had adopted various strategies of managerial and organizational reform. Operationally, this meant "eliminating, re-engineering, decentralizing, and privatizing" various types of police services. The resulting elimination or downloading of some traditional police services, coupled with an inability or reluctance to meet new policing and security demands, created a new market for services previously provided by public police. In addition, the rapid growth of mass private property and space, technology, and new modes of business created a range of new policing and security needs that could not be satisfied by the public police (Shearing and Stenning 1982).

As a result of this unmet demand, a mix of public and private sources increasingly provide alternative policing and security services. In the public domain, individual citizens, community groups, agencies, and police-sponsored or "partnered" community policing groups adopted various modes of policing and protection. Governments, private companies, and citizens who wanted more personalized and/or sophisticated policing/security increasingly created their own in-house police and security services or contracted with an expanding number of **private security** or hybrid public/private policing services. Philip Stenning (2009, 1) describes this landscape as a plural policing environment that is characterized by fragmentation and a transfer of police services as a result of neo-liberal strategies of fiscal restraint and decentralized governance.

The rationalization of public services, such as health, education, and policing, was made easier by the use of mystifying reform rhetoric that both legitimated and masked shifts and reductions in traditional service, promoting them as progressive improvements. The ambiguous but powerful rhetoric of community policing/integrated policing had been particularly effective, offering both a critique of the modern full-service model of professional public policing as unresponsive and ineffective and a rationale for a more limited model of public policing (Murphy 1998, 9).

The realignment of policing under neo-liberal policies required a rapid adaptation from a service that "bore many of the structural characteristics of its organizational (and operational) origins in the nineteenth century" (Savage and Charman 1996, 39). Reform had been stoked by diminished confidence in the adequacy of public police services to achieve the outcomes desired of a modern police service and a growing demand for police services to adapt to the changing political economy of governance.

From a neo-liberal perspective, the monopoly of public policing represented a strategy of inefficiency, ineffectiveness, and lack of accountability. These alleged failings were cited to stress the need to rework or reconceptualize the police function in ways that would redefine the essential nature and scope of public police service. This critique has forced policing to grapple with the need to re-examine its role, its structure, and how it was to be judged. Unfortunately, the result of this re-examination had been a further blurring of private and public policing functions.

This is not to suggest that this transformation resulted in detrimental operational and organizational outcomes. On the contrary, many public police services are now more effective and efficient with respect to their designated mandate of order maintenance and law enforcement. What this had achieved was an increased public/private blurring, whereby certain functions were relegated to private actors (Stenning 2009). The focus of this transformation has stifled the debate surrounding the issue of policing as a public good—because the objective of the realignment has been the elimination, re-engineering, decentralizing, and privatizing of various types of police services, not the assurance that policing will remain a public good.

A Question of Public Good

Ian Loader (2000) suggests that the provision and supervision of policing is secured through government, beyond government, and below government. Within these sites, one notes alternative models to the previously accepted state-centred responsibility of dispensing and governing security. In this context, the traditional link between the state and police is replaced with a model that connects both state and non-state nodes in the governance process (Johnston and Shearing 2003; Shearing and Wood 2003). However, the question still remains as to whether or not a diversity of security providers can be responsive to the concept of policing as public good.

For centuries, security and the state have been synonymous. Adam Smith, the dean of classical liberalism, is famous for stating that protecting citizens from harm is a duty of the government: it is a service that government must provide. Karl Marx argued that "security is the supreme social concept of civil society" (cited in Jones and Newburn 1998, 33). Unfortunately, the backdrop to the current era of transition in policing is a governance trend toward a fragmented and pluralized network of security in which citizens may not broadly share security interests or achieve equal levels of security. This trend has undermined the importance of state-coordinated security as a fundamental public good. The provision of security has been couched in the economic rhetoric of efficiency, effectiveness, and creation of private goods rather than in terms of the public good.

Furthermore, it affirmed the importance of private interest and the pursuit of specific, self-defined "security requirements without reference to any conception of the common good" (Loader 2000, 386). The state, with varying degrees of enthusiasm, had turned to business and the market as mechanisms to provide public goods, such as education and health care. In the realm of public security and policing, the private sector was given responsibilities that in some settings effectively made it the key provider of perhaps the most basic public good: public safety. Thus the move toward satisfying self-defined security requirements did little in the way of ensuring that the private agencies performing more and more state actions were upholding any measure of democratic accountability (Valverde 1999).

In a post-9/11 world, the question we now grapple with is how the state might (re)formulate principles of accountability and regulation in order to address not only broadly shared security interests but also the governance of a disparate multi-organizational security and policing landscape. And while the emergence of this question may indicate a potential shift in governance, it does not suggest that the dichotomy between private and public interests no longer exists—nor is there a renewed appetite for a heavy-handed regime to ensure public security. What it does suggest is an evolving governance environment in which the provision of goods (i.e., public safety) may be achieved through the co-operative actions of multiple stakeholders.

Although the provision of a secure environment depends on the joint actions of various players, it also relies on the state's ability to coordinate the organizational apparatus of the integrated, multi-functional security and policing providers. Moreover, it is incumbent on the state to "bring reflexive coherence and forms of democratic accountability to the inter-organizational networks and multi-level political configurations within which security and policing are situated" (Loader and Walker 2001, 27). One alternative would be to replace the previously accepted state-centred responsibility of dispensing and governing security with a model that connects both state and non-state nodes in the process of governance (Johnston and Shearing 2003; Shearing and Wood 2003). "Within this conception of governance no set of nodes is given conceptual priority," and the level of contribution of each node is developed through negotiation or collaborative processes (Johnston and Shearing 2003, 147). Johnston and Shearing argue that "by emphasizing that the state is no longer a stable locus of government, the nodal model defines governance as the property of networks rather than as the product of any single centre of action" (2003, 148). Moreover, governance is then considered the practice of shifting alliances as opposed to the "product of state-led steering and rowing strategies" (148). The issue that these models raise is whether we have any assurances that they may serve the desired outcome of enhanced security and policing—or whether they merely represent a theoretical framework that has little operational value.

A Reconfigured Connection between State and Policing

As noted previously, some people would contend that the reformulation of the state's central position has been undermined by the downloading of responsibility to corporations, municipalities, and citizens. In other words, how can the state expect to articulate a position of prominence when in fact it has previously reduced its significance in the realm of policing? This is indeed a critical concern, one that is both echoed and supported by Johnston and Shearing's (2003) assertion. And yet I would argue that the current realignment of policing actually strengthens the state's grip on the tiller. It is a realignment that "flows from an appreciation of the status of policing as a public good" (Loader and Walker 2001, 11).

Jones and Newburn (1998) argue that it is the existence of a diverse network of providers that has forced the state to refocus its efforts to steer policing and security. Loader and Walker (2001) further argue that a "positive (rather than pejorative) connection between policing and the state can be (re)formulated and defended under contemporary conditions" (11).

This differs from Johnston and Shearing's (2003) perception in that the state does play a central role both in coordinating collaborative alliances and in assuring accountability. Here, the joint actions of various players are both connected and coordinated by the state through reconstructed positions of governance. Within this formulation of governance, the state continues to maintain a primacy in the negotiation and collaborative processes involved in providing the public good of policing. This perspective is effectively presented in the following passage:

> Within the normative framework of the liberal democratic society, it is only the state or national government (and not the private sector) that has the capacity to mobilize all of the ingredients that, together, provide policing services that ensure the security and safety of the community. The state, as the embodiment of the values of society, is uniquely capable of ensuring public security, characterized by a monopoly of the legitimate use of force, coordinated governance, collective provision and communities of attachment. (Burbidge 2005, 66)

To illustrate the central prominence of the state and its capacity to mobilize a range of stakeholders, let us examine two points of connection at which the state formulates the principles of accountability, regulation, and civic coordination: the monopoly of legitimate coercion and the collective provision of policing.

Legitimate Coercion

While the services provided both by private and by public policing providers may seem indivisible, there remain distinct differences, differences that are overlooked if we merely compare tasks and functions. As the following statement notes, status alone is no longer a clear determinant of difference:

> Where the public police and private security are performing functions that are to all appearances the same, their differing status becomes even more difficult to appreciate. (Police Futures Group 2005, 3)

This debate over differences is most keenly argued with respect to the authority and legitimacy of the use of force: the monopoly of legitimate coercion. And while the use of legitimate force is indeed a site of contention, it also serves as a mechanism by which the state reinforces its governance prominence. Since it is the state that both grants and regulates the legitimate use of force, it therefore has the capacity to impose a range of regulatory parameters on all providers of policing and security.[2] Max Weber (1948) argued that "the right to use physical force is ascribed to other institutions or individuals only to the extent which the state permits it. The state is considered the sole source of the right to use force" (78). One understanding of Weber's claim would suggest that as representatives of the state, the police are legitimately "empowered to use force if force is necessary." It is the police who are "equipped, entitled, and required to deal with every exigency in which force may have to be used, to meet it" (Bittner 1990, 256). Reiner (1993) argues, "The police are the specialist carriers of the state's bedrock power: the monopoly of the legitimate use of power. How and for what this is used speaks to the very heart of the condition of political order" (cited in Jones and Newburn 1998, 35).

These interpretations suggest that only the state has the right to deliver legitimate violence and thus can limit the capacity of private policing providers to offer the full range of security and enforcement. The distinction to be made is that

> private security has no powers delegated by government, other than those possessed by any citizen, the scope of their activities is necessarily limited to civil matters. . . . [I]t has the powers and protections granted all citizens in the Criminal Code and the delegated rights of clients who are property owners under provincial trespass and landlord tenant acts. (Police Futures Group 2005, 4)

Stenning (2009) aptly summarizes this power differential in the following passage:

> While the public police are sponsored and mandated by society generally (through legislative and executive government provisions) and are accordingly given special powers, duties and immunities in serving the public interest, private police share none of these attributes; they serve no special status, enjoy no powers nor have any duty or responsibility toward the public interest, beyond those of the ordinary citizen and are assumed and expected to serve the private interests of those who employ them. (Stenning, Philip. 2009. 'Governance and accountability in a plural policing environment - the story so far.' *Policing* February 8: pp. 2)

Regardless of the limited statutory powers granted to private security providers, they do "perform many of the functions hitherto regarded as the prerogative of the public police" (Burbidge 2005, 68). Loader and Walker (2001) argue that while the monopoly of legitimate coercion is indeed a central point of authority, it continues to be a "somewhat limited basis for establishing the state-police nexus and it is in numerous ways being further undone by the contemporary fragmentation of policing and state forms" (13).

The concern that this raises has to do with the accountability of the private sector (especially regarding the use of force) since private police are not governed by the same oversight structures as the public police are. The reality is that "while the public police are governed by and accountable to democratically elected governmental authority and to the public, private police officers, even when performing the same policing functions as their public counterparts, are not subject to the same form of democratic governance and accountability" (Burbidge 2005, 67). Stenning (2009) suggests that the regulation of private policing

> tends to reflect a business regulation model rather than a model of public service governance. Government involvement in such regulation is typically limited to settling and enforcing minimum standards of service (and sometimes qualification and training) through licensing and certification and protection of clients from fraud and malpractice. (5)

It is within this context that the state has both the responsibility and the authority to address the current governance deficit. From a public good perspective, the state must exercise a regimen in which private policing is regulated and audited and the objective of public good is ensured. Some (but not all) private security providers want more legal police powers, such as the powers of search and seizure and arrest, the use of force, and greater access to police intelligence information. However, this desire is tempered by a reluctance to become subject to the constraints and limits of public accountability, liability, and the courts. Most private security executives recognize that by having a more limited role, with limited public and legal responsibilities, they actually may have more operational freedom than public police.

While the granting of expanded legal powers to private security is a complex public policy question, one cannot ignore the implications of not moving to impose broad regulatory frameworks.[3] As the landscape of policing and security evolves, "so should the governance and accountability arrangements with respect to the exercise of police powers that impinge on the rights and freedoms of citizens" (Burbidge 2005, 73). Examples of this policy shift can be noted in governance changes flowing from the *Report of the Independent Commission on Policing for Northern Ireland* (Patten 1999); Bill 88: An Act to Amend the Private Investigators and Security Guards Act (Ontario 2004); the *Government MLA Review of the Private Investigators and Security Guards Act* (Alberta Solicitor General and Public Security 2005); and the Private Investigators and Security Guards Act (Private Investigators and Security Guards Act 2010). The challenge confronting each of these initiatives has been to achieve an appropriate balance between those who argue for a **state-interventionist approach** and those who support the **minimalist-government approach**. In other words, can the providers of policing be effectively held accountable through market mechanisms, or can accountability be achieved only through the regulatory mechanisms of the state (Burbidge 2005)? A more important consideration is how these governance frameworks might ensure "the protection and vindication of the human rights of all" (Patten 1999, 18) and "promote an explicit set of democratic values" (Jones 2003, 623). It is precisely because of these considerations that the state cannot relinquish its regulatory capacity or its ability to steer the provision of policing.

Conclusion

We began this chapter by asking whether policing should be privatized but then quickly discarded that question for another set of questions. It is not that the question of whether we should privatize policing is unimportant; rather, it is just that in reality we are already there to a certain extent. There is little disagreement between scholars and police leaders as to whether or not the landscape of policing has shifted significantly toward that of a plural policing environment (Stenning 2009). This is why we side-stepped our initial question and began to tease out another strand of questions that highlight concerns aligned with issues of accountability, assurances of the public good, and the function of the state in steering diverse providers. These are the issues that have monumental implications for how we as a society are governed and protected, and thus we must be constantly mindful of them. Whether or not we embrace a private, public, or hybrid model of policing, the critical question remains: can the public good of policing be maintained? The answer to this question lies in the capacity of the state to steer the process of policing and ensure that the diverse providers are held accountable to the principle of policing as a public good. It is a question that becomes even more problematic to answer when concerns of economics, sustainability, and expanding mandates confront governments, communities, and law-enforcement agencies. Therefore, a more appropriate line of questioning is this: "How will new forms of policing challenge the role of the state in providing equitable policing, and how might state regulation ensure that all providers are held accountable and responsible for public security and safety?"

Review/Summary Questions

1. In your view, can a hybrid version of public and private models of policing effectively protect the public? What are the potential dangers of such a model?
2. If the state is no longer the exclusive policing authority, what is the relationship between policing and democracy?
3. How will economic sustainability, decreasing crime rates, and the desire for more collaborative strategies of law enforcement affect policing?
4. Do you think that the public good is jeopardized when a hybrid model of private and public policing is adopted?

Notes

1. The current political debate centres on the economics of policing. It is a debate that is driving a renewed critique regarding the efficiency of existing police models/operations. The breadth of this discussion is succinctly outlined within the recent Report to the Standing Committee on Public Safety and National Security (Economics of Policing), May 2014, 41st Parliament, Second Session. The report draws attention to the need for multiple agency integration and the redefinition of core responsibilities. The elimination of needless duplication and tiered policing are prominent themes. See report: http://www.parl.gc.ca/HousePublications/Publication.aspx?DocId=6583312

2. Criminal Code of Canada section 25(1), *Protection of persons acting under authority,* states:

   > Every one who is required or authorized by law to do anything in the administration or enforcement of the law a) as a private person, b) as a peace officer or public officer, c) in aid of a peace officer or public officer, or d) by virtue of his office, is, if he acts on reasonable grounds, justified in doing what he is required or authorized to do and in using as much force as is necessary for that purpose.

   Section 27, *Use of force to prevent commission of offence,* is also of interest with respect to the authority to use force and the differentiation between public police and citizens (i.e., police/private security).

3. Across Canada and other jurisdictions, such as the United Kingdom, there is a growing awareness that the legislation governing the private security industry needs to be modernized. . . . In order to enhance public safety and increase the efficiency and effectiveness of the industry, these jurisdictions have focused on amendments to licensing, training and equipment. . . . Events such as Sept. 11, 2001, have reinforced the need to reform the current legislative and regulatory framework of the private security industry. (Ontario 2003, 5)

13 What Do Official Statistics Tell Us about Ourselves?

Nob Doran

Introduction

My recollections of my first term in the honours social science undergraduate program at the University of York, England, are strongly marked by the sociology seminars I attended as supplements to the weekly lectures given to the whole first-year cohort. The first seminar topic was entitled "In what ways do sociological explanations differ from common sense ones—indeed do they?" And it was here that I was first introduced to a world of scholarship completely different from anything I had ever experienced before. Whereas the formal lectures often took for granted the "factual" nature of "**official statistics**," these seminars exposed me to an alternative approach that documented how these "official statistics" and the type of sociology that used them (I later found out that it was called **positivist sociology**, signifying that it was a form of social science modelled on insights from the natural sciences) were integrally based on the mundane "common sense" assumptions that *tacitly* informed their compilation.

More important, this academic insight seemed to fit with what I already knew about the "official statistics" process. Growing up on a Luton "working-class"[1] council estate[2] and frequently hearing of encounters between acquaintances and police officers, as well as having had one or two of them myself (over issues like cycling without a light or cycling the wrong way down a one-way street), I was aware that it was common knowledge that "official statistics" relating to crime and delinquency were compiled from the everyday practices of police officers. They decided to apprehend some people formally while dealing with others informally. And from sociology seminars such as these (which seemed to better explain my experiential world than the emphasis on the factual nature of "official statistics" that I was receiving in the formal lectures), I went on to discover other related critiques of official statistics. Although I did not know it at the time, these critiques had first emerged in the 1960s and early 1970s. By the time I entered university, they were not uncommon. Moreover, the points they were making helped to change the way that sociology understood itself and also changed the way that I understood myself. So let us take a look at some of the studies that intrigued me in those early days of my intellectual and scholarly formation.

Everyday Knowledge versus Official Statistics: Learning from Ethnomethodology

My first seminar reading (Douglas 1970b) had already alerted me to this alternative intellectual route. But I went on to discover other insightful analyses from similarly trained scholars. Douglas himself had written a book (1967) on the problems involved with the official statistics on suicide, but it was from Atkinson's work (1971, 1982) in this area that I probably learned the most.[3]

Drawing on his own empirical research, Atkinson proceeded to demonstrate the mundane, taken-for-granted, common-sense knowledge that competent coroners use on a daily basis in order to make their decisions about how an unexpected death should be recorded. According to Atkinson, suicide is "essentially a socially rather than a naturally defined form of behavior" (1971, 168). Thus, researchers need to examine how social definitions are produced in everyday social life. When Atkinson examined the coroners' practices, he discovered that interpretive decisions resembled certain predicaments that judges face in courts of law when weighing evidence (1971, 174). That is, competent coroners use an array of informal common-sense methods to help them come to a verdict regarding unexpected deaths.

For example, coroners will weigh considerations such as the following: the presence or absence of a suicide note (suicide notes are commonly understood as being good indicators of a suicide); the mode of death (certain ways of dying, such as hanging, are commonly understood as indicative of suicide, while others are routinely treated as probably not indicative, such as road deaths); the location and circumstances of death (an overdose taken in the middle of the woods, for example, is more likely to be understood as suggesting a suicide than an overdose in bed); and the life history and mental condition of the victim (coroners routinely assume that certain biographies are indicative of suicide).[4] But—and this was the crucial point—there is no mathematical formula for precisely determining how these different clues should be put together to unambiguously determine that an unexpected death was in fact a suicide. Both the layperson's reasoning about suicide and the coroner's reasoning employ similar informal methods. Each weighs and sifts through evidence before coming to a decision *for all practical purposes*, based on the information available.

Other early and influential studies that examined the ways in which "official statistics" were produced included Cicourel on fertility (1967, 1973), Garfinkel on suicide (1967), Sudnow on deaths (1967), Cicourel on juvenile delinquency (1968), and Cicourel and Kitsuse on educational decision-making (1963). Other studies examined the mundane methods used to produce other socially relevant but not necessarily "official" statistics. For example, MacKay's (1974) work examined the everyday methods used by teachers to produce supposedly objective scores for children's reading abilities from the standardized tests they administer. Garfinkel's (1967) work included an examination of the mundane common-sense methods that went into the production of quantitative studies of psychiatric admissions (see Sharrock and Anderson 1986, 44–7, for an interesting Canadian example).

Although different in their substantive areas of investigation, most of these studies shared a common theoretical perspective. They pointed out a radically new direction for empirical social research. In contrast to the conventional sociology of that time, this school of **ethnomethodology**, as its founder Garfinkel named it,[5] prioritized quite different concerns. As has already been shown, ethnomethodology posited that official statistics could not simply be accepted as "social facts" to be utilized for positivistic analysis. Rather, these statistics were "practical accomplishments" (Garfinkel 1967) produced by the routine yet often tacit and taken-for-granted methods employed by their compilers.[6] And it was this concern with "sense-making" that became central in the ethnomethodological perspective.

In fact, the ethnomethodologists invited other sociologists to study this process of sense-making and to make it a central feature of their analyses. And in order to prioritize the study of people's sense-making activities, older sociological conventions had to be radically altered. Garfinkel, for example, argued that it was no longer tenable to treat the "social actor" as a "judgmental dope." Rather, he or she must be treated as a "practical, rule-using analyst." In other words, the dominant sociology of that time had tended to see the individual as acting in accordance with a certain "normative" system (internalized through the socialization process and providing him or her with a set of "norms" to *choose* to follow).[7] In contrast, the ethnomethodologists drew attention to the interpretive rather than the normative basis of social life. For them, we all are social actors living in an eminently practical world where rules act more like signposts.[8] As laypeople, we are constantly analyzing and interpreting our surroundings in order to make sense of what is going on around us while simultaneously acting in that social world.

From this engagement with the ethnomethodological approach, I learned some early and very valuable lessons—not just that "official statistics" are compiled from the mundane, common-sense assumptions about how our social world routinely works (which are then tacitly put into practice by, say, coroners) but a number of foundational theoretical lessons as well. Perhaps most important, I learned that the social world can only be known from within (Turner 1974, 204–5) and that the sociological researcher cannot escape using his or her own "cultural competence" in order to make sense of his or her everyday world. Just as native speakers of English (or any other language) make sense of each other because they are constantly using a socially shared language (yet this is simply taken for granted by everyone involved), sociologists could also benefit from seeing social life as being structured like a language. And this view had consequences for future research. Just as linguists might study language systematically to show the underlying linguistic patterns taken for granted by native speakers, and just as anthropologists might study a foreign culture to display the meaningful pattern that culture has for its own members, the ethnomethodologists proposed to carry out somewhat similar analyses in the study of the mundane social world that we all routinely share.

Yet despite the force of these early ethnomethodological arguments, I nevertheless felt that the approach still lacked any explicit discussion of features that seemed quite integral to everyday life. Questions of power and conflict were everyday features of my life and the social world in which I lived; yet ethnomethodologists rarely paid attention to these key aspects of social life. Fortunately, in my early intellectual formation I did find some writers who took these questions of power in the everyday world quite seriously. And I learned the most from a feminist scholar—Dorothy Smith.[9]

Everyday Power Relations within "Official Statistics": Learning from Feminist Scholarship

I was first formally exposed to the work of Dorothy Smith in my second or third year as an undergraduate. I was introduced to an analysis (Smith 1978) in which Smith built on her existing ethnomethodological skills to display the "common sense practices" by which a group of friends routinely came to agree that another friend of theirs, K, was becoming mentally ill.[10] However, Smith's intent in that pioneering paper was not just to document these common-sense practices but also to argue that they worked as mechanisms for excluding someone (1978, 50–2) and as strategies for freezing someone out of a relationship (1978, 25). And, as I was soon to find out, this concern with how people get excluded became a central theme in much of Smith's subsequent work. In fact, much of the rest of her career is devoted to developing a "feminist sociology" called **institutional ethnography** (Smith 1987), which analyzes exactly how women have been and still are excluded from what Smith calls the "ruling relations" (1999, 73–95).

But it was not long after this first encounter with Smith's work that I discovered her own powerful critiques of statistics (1974a, 1975). They were not only insightful but promised an understanding significantly different from the analyses developed by other ethnomethodologists. What Smith especially wanted to draw attention to was the transformative power of certain official discourses on everyday experience such that people's (especially women's) subjective experience, their lived "actuality" (1974b, 257–66) as she soon began calling it, gets excluded, marginalized, or discarded. And official discourses, such as statistical ones, play a significant part in this process.

Smith's early work in this area isolated three related targets for analysis: first, the statistics routinely produced by (certain) sociologists in their empirical research; second, the official statistics routinely used but not necessarily produced by sociologists in their research; and third, the prevailing official statistics concerning the relationship between women and mental illness. She deals with the first two issues in her groundbreaking article "The Ideological Practices of Sociology" (1974a), and the third in an article published a year later. In this early work, it is apparent that she had learned much from ethnomethodology but now wanted to move in a more critical direction. And for this she looks to Karl Marx for help. That is, she combines the ethnomethodological insistence that ordinary people's taken-for-granted, common-sense reality constitutes a paramount reality[11] (all other realities, even social scientific ones, are parasitic on it) with Marx's concept of **ideology**. This allows her to claim that social sciences, such as sociology, are concretely engaged in ideological work. Let us examine her claim more closely.

For Smith, social science and ideology should be opposing terms: we need to be able to differentiate them. And just as Marx in his day was able to examine the science of economics and show its ideological nature, Smith subjected sociology[12] to similar scrutiny. For Marx, this necessitated critically analyzing concepts that nineteenth-century economics took for granted: the "division of labour," "exchange," "competition," and so on. Specifically, Marx examined the historical and institutional structures that produced such concepts. So whereas economics viewed its concepts as "natural"—as being outside any history or institutional structure—Marx insisted on relocating them in their specific social and historical contexts. And, as a consequence, he showed that these concepts were ideological. A century or more later, Smith wanted to follow Marx's method. If we want to get beyond ideological knowledge, we have to pursue analysis through the concepts of the existing social sciences (including economics, sociology, etc.) to their other side—to the "practical activity of actual living individuals" (Smith 1974a, 42). It is only through such a process that we are able to pass from ideology to knowledge.

But whereas this (1974a) article pointed out the ideological nature of the statistics produced by sociologists themselves, another article a year later (1975, reprinted 1990a) focused on the ideological nature of "official statistics" (at least those of mental illness). Here Smith elaborates on the exact nature of her critique of "official statistics" on mental illness but also clarifies an explicit feminist focus on women's shared experiences and culture. Moreover, her feminist approach is distinctly influenced by her ethnomethodological training. As she points out in the article, whereas other feminist scholars had critiqued the official (US) statistics on mental illness primarily in terms of their accuracy, Smith wants to do something quite different.[13] Building on her prior work on ideology, she wants to show how the statistics are worked up in the first place so as to produce a certain "reality" of mental illness, a reality that is taken for granted by professionals but that has been compiled by the transformation of the actual lived experience of women.

Specifically, Smith says that we cannot divorce mental illness from the practices of psychiatry that produce it. And building on her earlier claim that "the actualities of living people become a resource to be made over into the image of the concept" (1974a, 51), she shows how something similar is at work in the social production of "social facts," such as mental illness. For example, a psychiatric diagnosis of depression that focuses on a "withdrawal of interest . . . a slowing of mental and physical activity" may act as a set of instructions for a physician to select out of the actual everyday experiences of someone only those particulars that can match this abstract description. In this process, according to Smith, the psychiatric grid is "specifically inattentive to the actual matrices of the experiences of those who are diagnosed" (1990a, 129). Thus, Smith gives us this account written by a working-class woman experiencing the 1930s Depression years:

> This constant struggle with poverty this last four years has made me feel very nervy and irritable and this affects my children. I fear that I have not the patience that good health generally brings. When I am especially worried about anything I feel as if I have been engaged in some terrific physical struggle and go utterly limp and for some time am unable to move or even think coherently. This effect of mental strain expressed in physical results seems most curious and I am at a loss to properly explain it to a doctor. (Quoted in Smith 1990a, 128)

Smith goes on to say that this account and this woman's life could quite easily be converted into a case of "depression."[14] Yet the woman herself makes no mention of mental illness. Instead, as Smith points out, "she speaks of arduous work, commitment to sustaining children, exhaustion, perhaps of fear and anxiety, of an unbearable load that is daily borne. She shows us strength rather than illness" (1990a, 129). Yet this "lived actuality" is discarded in the psychiatric working up of the case. And this point is of crucial importance because, as Smith discovered when she talked to other women who had been labelled mentally ill, "the threat of invalidation or discounting recurs again and again in experiential accounts" (133). In other words, the problem with statistics on women's mental illness is not so much their accuracy but, rather, their power to invalidate or discount the experiences of the women who have been so labelled.

Class-Based Experiential Knowledge versus "Official Statistics"

In many ways, Smith's work not only advanced the original insights of the ethnomethodologists with regard to our understanding of social statistics (official and otherwise) but her concern with how the everyday is infused with issues of power, control, and authority suggested an important redirection of those original critiques. Nevertheless, I was not totally satisfied with Smith's own theorizing on this subject. Although I had been impressed with her redirection of the ethnomethodological insights, I found her utilization of a relatively straightforward Marxism rather difficult to digest. Specifically, Smith has always preferred to use Marx's own work rather than that of later Marxist scholars in developing her feminist theory, yet for me it was unclear to what extent Marx's own descriptions of working-class exploitation could still be productively used a century or so after his death.

I had been brought up in a (supposedly) working-class home, with my father working in manual jobs all his life, including 23 years in a car factory (I lasted three weeks there). Yet I was also a product of the British welfare state (which among other things introduced the possibility of a university education to students like me), so the classic texts of Marx that I was formally taught at the University of York seemed almost as foreign to my lived experience as the introduction to the positivist sociology that I had also experienced there. Moreover, the lack of reception that my burgeoning ethnomethodological interests met from most of the lecturers at York alerted me to the everyday power relations inherent within academia. So it might not be too surprising to hear that I left York feeling a certain degree of frustration with the academic enterprise. Unfortunately, my struggles at the micro level were also being matched by macro-level developments. That is, I graduated into the aftermath of a socio-economic and political crisis, the severity and global effect of which only became clearer over time. Yet its effects on my life and employment prospects were immediate and dire. With the thoroughgoing implementation of "Thatcherism" underway, I escaped to Canada to improve my employment prospects by taking an MA and waited for things to improve. Thus my life experiences meant that I could not have the easy attraction to classic Marxist texts (such as *The German Ideology*) that Smith had, despite the appeal of much of her micro-work. So I had to search further afield for some other way of figuring out not only my original welfare state/working-class upbringing but also the rapidly changing macro-social world that was now pushing me in completely unexpected directions. And it was a number of post-structuralist scholars (Foucault, Hacking, Baudrillard, and especially Donzelot) who taught me a critical approach that not only addressed this welfare state/working class relationship (Doran 2004) but that also insisted on painstaking genealogical analysis so as to uncover the "ignoble origins" of social phenomena (such as "statistics").

Nevertheless, the fundamental insights regarding "official statistics" that I had learned in my earliest days of university life have stayed with me. In fact, much of my own empirical research has built on these ethnomethodological and feminist insights and has developed them in interesting ways. Ethnomethodologists taught me to always contrast "experiential" knowledge with "official" knowledge, while feminists taught me to examine the process by which official knowledges transform experiential knowledge. But by beginning from a "classed" experience and not just a gendered one, I have come to realize that this latter process is not simply one of "marginalization" but that it also involves **codification** (Doran 1994, 1996, 2008) and cultural "incorporation" (Doran 2001, 2003) as well. And I discovered this process because I had dutifully searched for the "ignoble origins" of those statistics compiled specifically on working-class bodies. In other words, I had carried out a **genealogy from below**. With regard to "codification," this gets accomplished, in part, via the introduction and collection of statistics, which reframe and transform an emerging, embodied truth-telling, cultural voice into an "official" discourse with quite different concerns and priorities.[15] For example, when the embodied, cultural voice of working-class children first emerged in the 1830s, these "factory children" articulated a shared demand that their "health" be protected. They were the first generation to grow up working in factories, and their common-sense, "paramount reality" was that factory life was destroying their "health." But, within a decade, that experiential voice had been "codified." Official statistics started getting compiled on factory life, and these statistics began suggesting that accidents (rather than health) were the major problem within factories (Doran 1996). In other words, the factory children's experiential concerns with their "health" were quickly displaced onto the narrower concern with "accidents." But not only were these factory children's shared concerns displaced by this process, their actual voices were replaced as well. It is now the factory inspectors with their official reports and statistics who get listened to by parliamentarians and law makers; the young workers' own voices no longer even appear at this level of official discourse. Their shared experiential concern with "health" has now been codified into the official, but disembodied, textual concern with "accidents," instead.

Conclusion

To conclude, this chapter has been concerned with displaying the importance of a critical awareness of "official statistics" (see Table 13.1). But I have not been content with simply suggesting that these statistics may be inaccurate in some way or another (as the ethnomethodologists implied). Rather, I have also tried to show what these statistics do. As Smith documented, official statistics have tended to disqualify (women's) voices, and I have learned some important lessons from that research. But because my lived experience was powerfully influenced by growing up in a "working-class" family, and not just a patriarchal one, my own work has gone beyond this feminist concern with "disqualification" to explore issues of "codification" and "incorporation" as they have emerged at particular points in our history. So whereas the current critical scholarship on "official statistics" is increasingly going in a historical and political direction,[16,17] few of these analyses juxtapose the "official knowledge" created by these statistics with the "experiential knowledge" that is transformed in that process.

Table 13.1 Critical Awareness of Official Statistics

Critical Approach	Understanding of Official Statistics
Ethnomethodology	Official statistics are "practical accomplishments" produced by their compilers' use of "mundane common sense reasoning," which they share with other lay members of society.
Institutional ethnography	Official statistics are "ideological transformations" of people's (especially women's) lived "actualities." Via this process, women's subjectivities are marginalized, discarded, and excluded.
Genealogy from below	Traces the ignoble origins of "official statistics" as attempts by the powerful to "know" and "control" a newly emerging, and oppositional, cultural voice (e.g., the working class). This process works to "codify" this voice and to transform these oppositional subjectivities so that they can then be "incorporated" into a somewhat transformed dominant discourse.

Finally, what has also been implied throughout this chapter is that anyone's (including your own) receptivity to scholarly material does not depend only on its persuasive ability or on the claimed accuracy of its analysis; it also depends on the situated embodiedness of you, the reader. Although sociologists have been rather slow in recognizing this fact, it is now being realized that how we as readers "decode" any text depends on the personal experiences that we bring with us to the reading experience. In other words, your understanding of your own age, class, gender, ethnicity, etc., will affect how you decode any text. But what is equally important for you as students to realize (especially as you are now in the very process of becoming "educated" about your "self" and your social world) is that we invent and create our "educated selves" through this process as well. What I have tried to do in this chapter is to make that process more explicit by attempting to show how I decoded the texts that I encountered in my education and what I learned (about myself and my societies) in the process.

Review/Summary Questions

1. What does it mean to think of a suicide statistic as a "verdict" rather than a "social fact"?

2. When Smith looked at the statistics on mental illness in women, her focus was not on their "accuracy or otherwise." What was her focus?

3. Upon examination, the "facts" of suicide produced by coroners were shown to rest on mundane common-sense assumptions about suicide,

shared by everyone. Give some examples of these mundane common-sense assumptions.

4. This chapter is continually concerned with the contrast between "experiential knowledge" and "official knowledge." How did the first statistics on life in factories "codify" young workers' experiential demand for their "health" to be protected?

Notes

1. When I was small, Luton was a large industrial town that had been extensively surveyed by sociologists interested in examining the changing fortunes of the industrial working class (Goldthorpe et al. 1968a, 1968b, 1969). So when I went to university I discovered that sociologists generally labelled families like ours "working class." Today, there is little industry left, yet Luton is still being surveyed. Recently, it was at the top of the list of "crap towns" in the UK (Jordison and Kieran 2004).

2. Although I know of no easy cultural equivalent to the "council estate" in Canada, I have heard terms like HLM (*habitation à loyer modéré*) used in French culture and "the projects" used in US culture to describe superficially similar phenomena.

3. In part, this may have had something to do with the fact that Atkinson's work on the "interpretive foundations" of suicide seemed to suggest a serious problem for positivist sociology, especially in the format pioneered by the academic founder of the discipline, Émile Durkheim.

4. As one of Atkinson's coroners (1971, 181) stated with regard to a suspect's life history, "broken home, escape to the services, nervous breakdown, switching from one job to another, no family ties—what could be clearer?"

5. Garfinkel named it thus in part because he wanted to stress the similarity between this type of research program and studies like *ethnobotany* or *ethnomedicine*. Just as the latter were concerned with examining lay (ethno-) understandings of botany or medicine, ethnomethodology was concerned with examining the lay understandings of the social world that people ordinarily use in their everyday activities. That is, it was concerned with showing the "lay-methods" that people use to make sense of social life (Garfinkel 1974). For a contemporary discussion of the name and its utility, see Francis and Hester 2004, 198–214.

6. This concern with studying different aspects of social life as "practical accomplishments" can be succinctly demonstrated through an example. Garfinkel encouraged his students to go home and act as lodgers or boarders in their own homes for an hour or so. What this experiment vividly demonstrated was the usually tacit work that goes into the "practical accomplishment" of routine family life. When the students slightly adjusted their routine methods (behaving politely, talking formally to their parents), they produced a quite different understanding of family life. Frequently, the routine orderliness of family life was temporarily but seriously threatened as parents desperately tried to "make sense" of what was going on.

7. This normative approach was heavily influenced by the structural-functionalist sociological perspective developed by Talcott Parsons (1902–79). From this perspective, one might see norms as being routinely installed in children so as to give them the energy and directions for acting in socially appropriate ways in the future. More formally stated, these norms act as "potent energizers motivating lines of effort and striving, on the one hand, and as bases for selecting and integrating courses of action, on the other" (Gouldner 1970, 191).

8. Wittgenstein, a philosopher who has had a tremendous influence on many sociologists and ethnomethodologists, drew attention to this understanding of rules. Signposts may suggest a route forward, but they do not compel us to follow this route. For example, you may choose instead to take a more scenic route, or you may choose to follow a different route, perhaps one that is less congested at that time of day. See Wittgenstein (1953, 80) for more details.

9. Of course I also learned a tremendous amount from other feminist scholars throughout my entire intellectual formation, especially writers whose critiques targeted the power relations inherent in the world of social sciences (e.g., Smart 1976, 1989; Harding 1986; Haraway 1988; McRobbie 1980; Hartsock 1987). Yet Smith's ethnomethodological attention to the specific, empirical ways in which power gets constituted has not only remained a constant source of inspiration but provides a specificity sometimes lacking in other critiques.

10. In this powerful analysis, Smith systematically documents how a story written by one of the friends, Angela, to show how K became recognized as mentally ill uses a number of "common-sense" methods to produce itself as a "plausible" account of someone becoming mentally ill, an account that any competent reader would tend to agree with after an initial reading.

11. A good discussion of this progression can be found in Smith 1987, 69–78. Here, she makes clear her debt to the pioneering work of Schutz on these issues. See Schutz (1962) for further discussion.

12. What Smith means by "sociology" here remains rather imprecise, unfortunately. However, from the context she seems to be focusing on one of the contemporary positivist versions that had emerged at that time in response to perceived problems with both the structural-functionalist and Marxist interpretations of social life.

13. That is, although Smith begins by showing the problems involved in "reading" statistics as some type of representation of reality, she really wants to show that "reading" them in this way, even by feminist scholars, may be missing something more fundamental. Thus, she cites several feminist scholars who examined the statistics on women and mental illness and proposed to explain the high rates either in terms of women's oppression (1990a, 109) or in terms of women's roles in modern industrial societies tending to produce higher rates of mental illness than among men (112). Yet in both cases these arguments are based on the examination of statistics that show higher rates of mental illness for women. Now, although Smith does point out that the Canadian numbers do not seem to support the types of conclusions that the American feminists Chesler, Grove, and Tudor make (and she gives some reasonable suggestions as to why the numbers might be counted differently by different analysts and in two different countries), her real aim is to move beyond this conventional paradigm, which simply wants to frame the issue in terms of the accuracy (or otherwise) of the statistics. Instead, she wants to focus on the social organization of these statistics.

14. In another article (1990b), she shows the mundane techniques by which this social process is carried out.

15. Foucault's final lectures (2005, 2010, 2011) deal with this problem of how an embodied self may be able to "convert" itself into a truth-telling subject, despite the agonistic environs that simultaneously work to prevent such an emergence (Doran forthcoming). And although Foucault mainly restricts himself to the "self" in Ancient Greece, he explicitly suggests there may be affinities with the rise of the working class in the nineteenth century.

16. The early "genealogical," "governmentality," and "state formation" writings (Hacking 1982; Rose 1991; Curtis 2001; Corrigan and Sayer 1985) were all instrumental in drawing scholars' attention to the historical construction of "official statistics" at the macro level. And these works were especially useful for displaying the connection between forms of knowledge and forms of governing. Moreover, recent research in this area seems to be furthering this general line of inquiry (Haggerty 2001; Rusnock 2002; Bayatrizi 2008a, 2008b, 2009; Saetnan, Lomell, and Hammer 2011; cf MacDonald 2010). In contrast, because my own research has been more influenced by Donzelot's (1984) historical work on statistical thinking (due to its explicit concern with issues of class) and Smith's prioritization of embodied experience, my research has gone in a decidedly different direction.

17. The recent controversy over the cessation, and subsequent re-introduction, of the Canadian Mandatory Long Form Census has certainly alerted scholars to the overtly political nature of modern "counting." For a discussion of the original decision by the Harper government, see Haan (2012); Cormack, Cosgrave, and Harling Stalker (2012); McDaniel and MacDonald (2012); Ramp and Harrison (2012); and Yeo (2012).

14 Who Governs Whom in Canada?

Dawn Moore

Introduction: What Is Governance?

The answer to the question "Who governs whom?" may seem obvious. In Canada, we are governed by our various levels of government (federal, provincial/territorial, municipal). While it is true that these bodies are responsible for our legal regulation, if we think more broadly about governance, we see that it is carried out by a variety of people in different ways. **Governance**, simply put, includes all the different ways in which people are encouraged to behave in certain ways (and not in others). In order to understand the complexities of governance it is helpful to start by looking at some of the different ways theorists have tried to explain how and why we follow rules and codes of behavior (both formal and informal) as well as who benefits from different kinds of governance.

What Are the Different Ways We Can Think about Governance?

The Collective Conscience and Forms of Solidarity

Émile Durkheim, as noted in the book's introduction and elsewhere, was one of the first Western thinkers to argue that society exists apart from nature and is shaped by uniquely social forces. For Durkheim, the question "Who governs whom?" was not as important as the question "What governs whom?" The "what" for Durkheim was morality. Durkheim argued that societies have what he called a **collective conscience**—the shared morality or the set of values that everyone holds in common. The whole point of governing in a society, according to Durkheim, was to reaffirm and protect the collective conscience. For example, a society has a shared value that murder is wrong. When a murder happens, it offends that value and threatens the collective conscience—as though the murderer is saying "I don't care about the shared values of this society: I am challenging them." At this point, according to Durkheim, governance kicks in. A society responds to the murder because murder is wrong according to the collective conscience. The murder serves a function because it allows the whole society to get together and reaffirm its collective belief that killing other people is not okay. In punishing the murderer, the society can act out this belief.

The case of Robert Latimer serves as a good example of how we can use Durkheim's idea of the collective conscience to understand responses to Criminal Code infractions in Canada. Latimer was accused and eventually convicted of killing his disabled daughter, Tracy, who suffered from acute cerebral palsy. The case wound its way to the Supreme Court of Canada (SCC) as Latimer defended himself by framing his actions as a mercy killing, qualitatively different from the kinds of killings prohibited under the Criminal Code definition of first degree (or premeditated) murder. Latimer argued, and eventually partially convinced the courts, that what he did was an act of compassion that did not deserve the harshest penalty available in Canadian law (a life sentence with no parole eligibility for 25 years).

How does the notion of the collective conscience help us to understand the case of Robert Latimer? In looking at this case, Durkheim would tell us that it has a certain functionality. The question of whether or not someone has the right to take another person's life in order to end suffering is an essentially moral one. Latimer's actions give society a chance to revisit the moral questions that arise out of such a situation. Does mercy killing merit the same punishment as killing based on revenge? Does mercy killing merit any punishment at all? Does one person have the right to decide when another person's life should end? In opening up both the public and legal debate on these questions, Latimer's case allowed Canadian society to re-evaluate its stance, to examine its collective conscience. Ultimately, the courts, in what many would argue was the best reflection of public opinion at the time, offered a softened response to Latimer that suggested that his crime was not as heinous as some but still maintained that what he did was wrong both morally and legally. So the case of *R. v. Latimer* was a chance for Canadian society to reaffirm its collective conscience around the notion of mercy killing.

Of course, this is not what actually happened in the Latimer decision. There never was and never will be a collective voice of Canadians who feel the same way about the Latimer case. The press coverage over the eight years it took for the case to wind its way through the courts shows a country divided on the issue, with citizens arguing all sides of the debate. The fact that there was not a collective and single voice of Canadians responding to the Latimer case illustrates a common criticism of Durkheim's ideas: it is difficult to imagine a society in which a collective conscience might exist. Given the diverse nature of our society, large numbers of people will inevitably disagree with one another on moral issues. Canadian law is full of examples of this: Canadians have differing opinions on abortion, the decriminalization of marijuana, the death penalty, prostitution, the use of fetal stem cells, and so on. While it is true that when these morally loaded cases arise they do give Canadians a chance to revisit the issues and engage in public debate as well as raise the potential for law reform, the results of the debates are not likely to reflect any sort of collective conscience.

Let us turn to another way of thinking about governance in order to determine whose will gets reflected in attempts to make and change law.

Ideological Domination

Another way to examine how governance happens in Canada is to look at how different groups are governed. There are many different ways by which we can define different groups in Canadian societies. Groups might be defined on the basis of age, ethnicity, sexual orientation, and so on. In terms of governance, many social scientists are interested in how the question of social class organizes people into groups that are then governed differently.

The idea that people are governed on the basis of their social class is most famously attributed to Karl Marx (1970 [1859]), who argued that a society's economic structure dictates who gets to be in control in that society and who does not. Marx was writing about society just after the Industrial Revolution. While Marx's ideas continue to have considerable influence on how people think about issues of governance and power, many social thinkers who came after Marx felt that his sole focus on economic structure was overly simple and did not accurately reflect the complicated structures of governance in capitalist societies. One theorist who took Marx's ideas and embellished them in an attempt to reflect these more complicated issues was Antonio Gramsci.

Gramsci's (1992) biggest concern was what he called **ideological domination**: ways of thinking and governing that keep some people on top, to the disadvantage of everyone else. According to Gramsci, capitalist European and North American societies were governed by pervasive ideologies or ways of thinking that came from and benefited the ruling class. This ideological domination served to make sure that one group of people and their way of governing stayed in power.

According to Gramsci, there are two different ways by which ideological domination can happen. First, people can be coerced. As noted above, there are many examples of societies governed through brute force and oppressive laws. The witch crazes of the Middle Ages, the colonization of the Americas, the Nazi regime, Khmer Rouge, the Cold War between the US and the Soviet Union and the "red scare," the Iron Curtain, and, most recently, the rise of the Taliban and ISIL (Islamic State of Iraq and the Levant) are all examples of regimes changing the ways people think and act through the use of fear, intimidation, and violence.

The second way that ideological domination can occur does not involve such coercive and brutal means. There are many subtle ways by which people can be governed with their consent. For example, even though there is no law dictating that we behave this way, we all tend to address certain people (doctors, judges, heads of state, religious leaders, and even university professors) by their formal titles and surnames while expecting that these people will respond to us using our given names. This practice immediately affirms that the people with titles are more powerful than those addressed by only a first name. By continuing to follow the convention of using titles, Gramsci would suggest that we consent to a power structure that subordinates us. We consent to this power even though it offers no benefit to us and we face no formal punishment if we fail to conform.

Discipline and Normalization

As noted in Chapter 1, the practice of governing individuals and populations is not always as overt as those described above. The French intellectual Michel Foucault (1977) noted that governance often comes in extremely subtle forms. For Foucault, **discipline** is governance on a subtle and ubiquitous scale. To be governed by discipline means to be governed thoroughly on an individual level. Foucault suggested that military training was the ideal example of this kind of governance. As in prison, the strict regime of the military training camp means that a person's every action is tightly regulated. Mealtimes, bedtimes, rest times, training times, means of travel (marching in step), conversation (addressing superior officers by correct rank title), and even hygiene and dress are all regulated through military training. The intent is to create a perfectly trained soldier who will behave in the same way as every other soldier without having to be forced to do so. There are three characteristics of this kind of power, which operates through discipline: (1) hierarchical observation, (2) the use of normalization, and (3) consequences that are varied and subtle.

First, discipline involves hierarchical observation, which means that someone (or something) is watching. In the military, we see hierarchical observation in the form of commanding officers who watch over their trainees' every move, ready to correct an error in uniform or a failure to complete a task in the proper sequence. Prisons have hierarchical surveillance in the form of officers watching over prisoners directly as they go about their days (and nights) and also through the prison's architectural design. One of the most popular designs for prisons, particularly when governments first started to build them in the eighteenth century, was borrowed from Jeremy Bentham. He called his model for a prison the **panopticon**. Canada's oldest prison, the Kingston Penitentiary in Kingston, Ontario, is designed exactly on this model.

The panopticon looks like a wagon wheel with a central hub and "spokes" in the form of cell ranges coming out from the middle. The central hub is the guards' tower, designed so that guards can see down each of the cell ranges and control the locking and unlocking of all doors (including cell doors) without ever having to leave the central hub. In addition, the hub is designed so that it is impossible for prisoners to know whether or not a guard is watching them. The term *panopticon* literally means "see everywhere." And while guards can see out, prisoners cannot see into the hub. The panopticon is still used as a basic design for prisons because it allows for constant surveillance of prisoners by very few staff. Because prisoners never know for sure whether or not they are being watched, the expectation is that they will behave themselves simply because the possibility of being watched by someone in authority always exists.

Our urban spaces contain various versions of the panopticon that we encounter every day. Technology has brought us surveillance cameras, which have become standard features in banks, shopping malls, government buildings, and even universities. More and more urban centres in high-crime areas are also equipped with surveillance cameras as a way of curbing criminal activities. The idea behind the use of these cameras is the same as that of the panopticon. That is, people are more likely to behave themselves if they think they are being watched, regardless of whether or not the cameras are actually recording anything or if anyone will actually view the surveillance tapes. This kind of watching is an extremely passive and subtle form of governance. No one is actually doing anything to anyone, but people still monitor their behaviours as though someone were watching them.

The second characteristic of discipline is that it operates through the use of norms. A norm is a generally accepted idea of how a person ought to be. Foucault makes clear the importance of the norm as a tool of governing in his analysis of norms and madness. In his well-known text *Madness and Civilization* (1988), Foucault suggests that many of our ideas about insane behaviour come out of scrutiny of behaviours that can just as easily be understood as deviating from a particular norm. Foucault called this kind of governance **normalization**, referring to the ways in which certain ways of being are viewed as "normal," making alternate ways of being "abnormal" and thus subject to governance. Until 1973, for example, homosexuality was considered a form of mental illness: its symptoms and treatment were detailed in the *Diagnostic and Statistical Manual*— the handbook of psychiatry. People who were revealed as homosexual could be institutionalized as a way of "healing" them (see Chapter 4). At the beginning of the 1970s, the Ontario legislature was deeply involved in attempting to "cure" the homosexuality of prison inmates because it saw same-sex relationships within prison as indicators of an individual's higher chance of reoffending or committing additional "deviant" acts.

Most people now accept that there is nothing sick about or wrong with people who are attracted to members of the same sex. The designation of homosexuality as a psychiatric illness was much more about the fact that people who engaged in homosexual activities went against the norm of heterosexuality deeply ingrained in our society. People eventually started to challenge the idea that homosexuality was an illness by showing that homosexuality is common and that people engaged in same-sex relationships are as "normal" as anyone else in society. Canadian law is now moving more and more toward embracing same-sex relationships as part of the norm of Canadian society. In the cases of *M. v. H.* as well as *Egan and Nesbitt v. Canada*, the Supreme Court of Canada (SCC) recognized that same-sex couples were entitled to benefits similar to those of opposite-sex couples (such as

Canada Pension Plan survivors' benefits) and also liable to the same obligations (such as spousal support and equal division of a shared home on dissolution of a relationship). The most recent SCC decision concerning the normalization of homosexual relationships in Canada was the Same Sex Marriage Reference in which the Court said it was illegal to exclude same-sex couples from the existing definition of marriage.

The third aspect of a disciplinary regime is that the consequences for failing to adhere to expected or prescribed behaviours are also varied and subtle. Those caught through panoptic surveillance transgressing prison rules of conduct by, for example, passing something to another prisoner may have privileges taken away, such as seeing visitors or receiving mail. Students caught skipping school and therefore failing to adhere to a set schedule might be given a detention or have their parents called in to meet with the principal. If you are rude to your friends, engage in offensive behaviour, or gossip behind other people's backs, you might find yourself ostracized, gossiped about in turn, or made fun of. The point is that the consequences of failing to comply with the governance structure in a disciplinary regime are not necessarily punitive in the sense that the criminal law is punitive. Instead, these consequences come in the form of what Hunt and Wickham (1994, 21) describe as "micro-penalties and rewards."

Who Has the Right to Govern?

Governance can take place in all manner of relationships and can be understood from a wide variety of perspectives. But how does governance actually happen in Canada? What does the law tell us about who gets to govern whom and how these relationships are meant to work?

On the broadest scale, governance in Canada is divided among different forms of government. With some overlap among jurisdictions, the federal government, for example, is in charge of a wide range of areas, including international relations, income and excise tax, the Criminal Code, national defence, the environment, treaties with First Nations, fisheries, air travel, immigration, and employment. The provinces are meant to deal primarily with education, highways, health care, social services, liquor law, casinos, utilities, and drivers' licences. Municipal governments are in charge of local by-laws, pet licences, parking laws, city streets, property taxes, fire and ambulance services (and, in some cases, police), and some social services.

Canada also has forms of Indigenous governance. The Constitution Act of 1982 recognizes Aboriginal rights as outlined in the various treaties that were struck during colonization. This acknowledgement also includes the right of Aboriginal communities to govern themselves. Indeed, notions of self-government are becoming more and more central to the ways in which the Canadian government deals with First Nations peoples. In large part, the increased move toward self-government is a bid by the Canadian government to rectify the wrongs done to Aboriginal peoples throughout colonization and in its aftermath. Historically, the involvement of European governments in Aboriginal affairs has been disastrous for Aboriginal peoples, resulting in the loss of life, health, safety, culture, land, autonomy, and children.

Aboriginal communities work toward self-governance because they want to be able to dictate their own affairs and shape their communities independent of the Canadian government. Models of self-governance vary from community to community. Communities that have adopted a self-governance model do not, however, exist outside Canadian law: they are still governed by legislation, including the Criminal Code and the Child Protection Act. The administration of these laws, however, and the establishment of other forms of law and governance often fall to local government. Band councils, for example, can be responsible for a wide range of governing practices, including issuing licences; policing communities; enforcing Aboriginal laws; and running Aboriginal courts, health care, education, family matters (such as adoption, marriage, divorce, and child protection), hunting and fishing regulations, housing, social services, and resource management. In many cases, Aboriginal communities will work in conjunction with non-Aboriginal governing bodies in order to fully administer all the different forms of governance within the framework of limited resourcing. Aboriginal communities that have established their own policing systems, for example, may have one or two officers who do the day-to-day work of policing (dealing with traffic violations, responding to small-scale crimes, performing crime-prevention work, and educating the public). However, when a major crime, such as a murder, occurs, these small police services often simply lack the resources to deal with the crime adequately. In these situations, the local band council will often seek the assistance of a larger police service, such as the Royal Canadian Mounted Police (RCMP), which may come into the community for a specified period of time to assist with the investigation.

In Canada, then, the formal right to govern is assigned through legislation to various levels and forms of government. That is a good deal of power given to a small number of people. How do we make sure that our governments do what they are supposed to do? How do we make sure that they do not abuse their powers?

How Do We Control the Right to Govern?

The democratic structure of Canadian governance is one way by which we put limits on state powers. Our federal government is made up of three different branches, which are meant to keep each other in check. The executive branch consists of the prime minister and cabinet. These are the people who are directly responsible for drafting the laws and policies used to govern the country. Most of the decisions made by the executive branch have to be approved by the legislative branch of government. Parliament is the federal legislative branch, comprising the House of Commons and the Senate. Legislators debate and vote on pieces of legislation and are expected to reflect the will of the public. Finally, we have the judicial branch, and in Canada the highest level is the Supreme Court. The Court's duty is to hear cases pertaining to all areas of Canadian law and render final decisions on those cases. It has the power to uphold, strike down, and interpret or otherwise direct amendments to laws. Typically, but not always, the Supreme Court addresses cases that it deems to be of national importance. Often, that is defined by whether or not the case raises questions about the constitutionality of a certain law or whether a law conforms to the principles set out in the Charter of Rights and Freedoms. As such, the Supreme Court can also decide to not hear cases. Such was the case with Hassan Diab, a Canadian citizen whom France wished extradited to stand trial for charges of terrorism in relation to the bombing of a synagogue in the 1980s. While the lower courts in Ontario agreed that the case the French government had built against Diab was built on flimsy evidence, they also concluded that it was not up to them to decide the merits of that evidence. Given that Canada has an extradition treaty with France, the lower courts ruled that Diab should still be returned to France to face the charges. In refusing to hear Diab's appeal, the Supreme Court tacitly agreed with the lower courts, reinforcing its own limits and establishing a precedent that, notwithstanding requests for extradition that might result in torture or death, there was nothing unconstitutional or indeed unlawful in honouring France's extradition request. Diab was deported the day after the Supreme Court ruling.

The Charter of Rights and Freedoms

The Supreme Court often hears cases in which a citizen claims that a certain law or practice of government is unfair. In order to make such a claim, the citizen (or group of citizens) often appeals to the highest law in the land—the Charter of Rights and Freedoms. The Charter was enacted in 1982 along with the new constitution, and it is the supreme law of the country. This means that all other laws must conform to the principles set out in the Charter, and many scholars see it as the ultimate check on governance in Canada. The Charter applies only to matters between the citizenry and the state, which means that issues of private law (such as a dispute between two businesses over a contract) are not governed by the Charter. It can only govern the laws and actions of a Canadian government.

The Charter sets out seven general areas of freedoms for all Canadian citizens, guaranteeing freedom of thought, conscience, religion, association, the press, expression, and assembly. It also outlines the rights of Canadians, such as the right to vote; to move about the country; to be taught in French or English; and to life, liberty, and security of person as well as rights upon arrest; rights to equality; rights to have the government function in both official languages; and the right to be protected from discrimination. Many of the legal disputes that reach the Supreme Court concern disputes around these rights.

The recent case of *R. v. NS* is a good example. This is a case in which NS (in some cases courts elect to use initials rather than names to protect identities) accused two family members of sexual assault. When the case came to trial, NS wanted to testify while wearing her niqab. The accused argued that by concealing her face with the niqab NS was interfering with their rights (as enshrined in the Charter) to a fair trial by literally denying them the ability to face their accuser. NS countered that if the courts requested her to remove her niqab they were infringing on her right to free religious expression (also enshrined in the Charter).

When the case made it to the Supreme Court the court held (with differing opinions) the decisions of the lower court that NS could be compelled to remove her niqab while testifying. What is important about this case is that even though only one judge dissented in this judgment, two very different reasons were given by the other judges as to why NS could be asked to remove her niqab. Justices McLachlin, Fish, Deschamps, and Cromwell argued that courts must always strike a balance of right—in this case, the right to religious freedom and the right to a fair trial—and that this must happen on a case-by-case basis. In so doing, they sent the case back down to the original court, giving the lower court judge the authority to decide whether or not NS should remove her niqab. Justices LeBel and Rothstein offered a different argument. They asserted that the right to a fair trial was paramount and if NS's wearing of the niqab impeded that right (by allowing her to conceal her face especially during cross-examination) then she ought to be asked to remove the covering. Justice Abella, the only dissenting judge, argued the inverse to LeBel and Rothstein. She reasoned that religious freedoms were fundamental and that the wearing of the niqab did not impede a fair trial because it covered only the witness's face. Other aspects of her demeanour, such as her voice and gestures, and her words themselves were still available to the court and gave the court plenty of information to work with in terms of discerning her reliability.

The case of NS raises a number of important questions about the application of Canadian law and how adjudicators are meant to balance out competing rights. Importantly, the case also shows us that even among the top judges in the land there are often vastly different answers to the questions posed. This in turn reflects the way our legal system is often described as a living tree—growing and changing with different features and different challenges depending on the context in which it finds itself.

What if You Don't Want to Be Governed in a Specific Way?

Despite what Durkheim would have us believe, there are many laws and practices of governance in Canada that people simply do not agree with or do not conform to. Our governing structures and practices, both formal and informal, are constantly changing and being re-evaluated. Indeed, the history of governance in Canada shows many instances of people working to resist governing structures and to change them.

One of the most famous examples is the case of *Muir Edwards et al. v. Canada (A.G.)*, also known as the Persons Case because the decision finally rendered declared that women are "persons" under Canadian law. The case was brought forward in the late 1920s by five women (known as the Famous Five): Henrietta Muir Edwards, Irene Parlby, Nellie McClung, Louise McKinney, and Emily Murphy. The women had gone to court in Canada to find out whether or not women could become members of the Canadian Senate. The law concerning appointment to the Senate stated that senators had to be "persons," and the question these women posed to the court was whether or not women constituted "persons." All levels of the courts in Canada concluded that women were not, in fact, persons. However, the women persisted in appealing these decisions until the case ended up in the British House of Lords. (During this time Canada still had significantly strong ties to the UK, which meant that the highest court in the UK, the House of Lords, had the final say in Canadian legal disputes.) The decision written by Lord Sankey found in favour of the women, arguing that women were indeed persons under Canadian law and as such could become senators. The case was a landmark for women's rights in Canada since it was the first time in Canadian history that women had gained this kind of legal recognition.

The limitation here is that any form of litigation is extremely expensive, and, for the most part, individuals seeking legislative changes are not eligible for any sort of government assistance in paying legal fees. Even the most straightforward legal case can cost $10,000. A case that involves a Charter challenge is likely to run into the hundreds of thousands of dollars in legal fees and ancillary costs. As a result, while technically all citizens have the right to launch legal challenges, the reality is that unless lawyers or law firms are willing to take on a case as a form of "cause lawyering" (meaning the work is pro bono, or for free, because they have a political interest in the case) most forms of litigation are well out of the financial reach of most Canadians.

Conclusion

When we think about different ways of understanding the relations of governance, there are a number of different perspectives we can adopt. We can understand governance through the lens of morality as Durkheim suggested. Alternatively, we could see governance as a product of social inequality and domination as Gramsci did. Foucault, on the other hand, asks us to look at governance through the lens of discipline or "micro" governing strategies.

Canada has a complicated formal system of governing that is largely informed by the Charter of Rights and Freedoms. As the most important law in the country, the Charter is used to challenge other laws and governmental practices—but, as a "living tree," it is a law that is meant to be interpreted and reinterpreted as it grows and changes. Still, people and popular movements can have an impact on governing and are capable of changing the governing structures that regulate a society. The case of women becoming legal "persons" in Canada reminds us that people can and do resist forms of governance and work to change rules they find unfair.

Review/Summary Questions

1. Does governing happen only from the top down? Can you think of examples in which people's actions influence the ways in which we are governed?
2. Can you think of any legal issues on which Canadians agree? If so, how do you know that everyone agrees?
3. What kinds of ideological domination affect your life? Is the university a place of ideological domination?
4. What do Hunt and Wickham mean by "micro-penalties and rewards"? Can you think of any other examples?
5. Is there ever an instance in which it is justifiable to take away someone's rights? What criteria should be used in making that decision?

PART III

Critical Sociological Imaginations

The final part of the book turns to the critical engagement of various topics, often using theoretical concepts and substantive issues raised in the first two parts. Part III considers how subjects and social milieus interact in complex ways in specific areas of Canadian society. These interactions are at times enabling for subjects and at other times disabling. And because the chapters are driven by sociological imaginations, each one asks questions concerned with critically understanding and engaging in an aspect of what it means to govern and be governed in Canada—both right now and in the future. In so doing, the chapters critically theorize the character of Canadian society and sociology.

Chapter 15, "How Do We Help the Environment?" addresses a topic of increasing concern not just to Canadians but also to people around the world. Rather than take for granted that everyone agrees that certain phenomena are environmental issues, Myra Hird critically examines how some things are highlighted in the media, and/or by governments, environmental groups, movie stars, and so on, as urgent environmental issues, while other things—that scientists may argue are equally or more urgent—are not. Hird argues that phenomena such as global warming, biodiversity loss, and ozone layer depletion are not self-evident environmental issues but, rather, depend upon claims-making that involves the valuation of different knowledges. For instance, scientific claims often compete with industry and political claims about the severity and urgency of climate change. Hird goes on to examine how power shapes whose knowledge gets to define not only what an environmental issue is but also how it should be addressed. Finally, Hird's chapter considers how environmental issues are governed—that is, how issues are acted upon—within a broader societal context in which other issues, such as employment, are viewed with equal or greater interest.

Chapter 16—"What Is Sovereignty for Indigenous People?"—addresses a crucial issue in Canadian society. Vanessa Watts frames this chapter as a critique of the concept of **sovereignty** itself, pointing out that sovereignty is a Western colonial concept that was introduced to Indigenous peoples over hundreds of years of colonialism, which many people argue continues today. Indigenous peoples, Watts argues, have different relationships with their communities and environment, one in which sovereignty can only be understood in relation to a specific place and time (i.e., *sovereignty* is not a generalizable term that can be universally applied). Watts goes further to argue that long-established and effective governance structures and practices within diverse Indigenous societies were radically and often violently rejected by colonial interests that sought to replace Indigenous knowledges with colonial rule. Watts concludes by detailing the struggles Indigenous people have faced, and continue to face, in establishing the right to self-determination.

On a related theme, Chapter 17—"What Is Sovereignty in Quebec?"—enlists an analysis of a macro-governance. Rather than rehashing long-standing ideological arguments for or against Quebec sovereignty, Philippe Couton offers a distinctly sociological approach that reflects on the underlying assumptions necessary to sustain these ideological positions. One such assumption is that the natural condition for any given society is independence. Couton forcefully argues that nation-states are not homogeneous entities that can adequately speak for the diverse populations that they claim to embody. Another assumption that Couton criticizes is that societies naturally evolve to claim independent power. He argues that "although there might be an evolutionary component to sovereignty . . . the way the issue is handled at the political level continues to matter a great deal"—as evinced, for instance, by events surrounding the adoption of Canada's Charter of Rights and Freedoms. Couton concludes by considering the viability of post-sovereignty forms of government that do not rely on the precondition of homogeneity inherent in the modern nation-state.

Chapter 18—"Is There Justice for Young People?"—raises questions that are likely to resonate with many young people in Canada. Bryan Hogeveen extends his examination of governance to a group that the Canadian government historically helped to define as "youth." In order to respond to the chapter title's question, Hogeveen focuses attention on different visions of justice, which allows him to make a clearer argument about the areas in which youth justice in Canada is lacking. Hogeveen notes that current public portrayals of today's youth (for instance, those presented by the media) often associate young people with criminality and irresponsibility. These (mis)perceptions are reflected in changing approaches to youth justice. Paradoxically, such public perceptions continue to influence policy even though youth crime rates are steadily declining. Hogeveen provides several examples of the ways in which Canadian youth are governed through discourses of criminality and risk, thereby indicating a new regime for regulating young people that, Hogeveen argues, is far from just.

Chapter 19 is entitled "Women and Prison: Who and Why?" In it, author Kelly Hannah-Moffat asks important questions about the relationship between gender, crime, and incarceration. Hannah-Moffat provides an overview of the prevalence and characteristics of women in Canadian prisons, the reasons women end up in prison, the struggles they face when they are released, and initiatives to implement women-centred or gender-responsive punishment. Hannah-Moffat points out that although only a small minority of women commit crimes—most of which involve theft, fraud, or sex work rather than violence—women who have been convicted of a violent crime are overrepresented in prisons. Further, women are less likely than men to repeat offences, and repeat female offenders are less likely than men to escalate the severity of their crimes. She goes on to provide evidence that structural factors—racialization, social class, poverty, mental illness, early victimization, being in a violent intimate relationship, and so on—are key to explaining how women end up in prison. Given that approximately 70 per cent of women in prison have children, the implications of women's incarceration extends far beyond the individual woman to her family, and to society as a whole; for instance, families and provincial agencies (such as the Children's Aid Society in Ontario) must ensure that the children of imprisoned women are adequately cared for. The chapter closes with a consideration of the multiple difficulties women face when they are released from prison, including unemployment, fractured families, and societal marginalization. She also critically examines recent attempts by the government and prison systems to adopt a gender-centred approach to women's incarceration, emphasizing the need to better understand the structural forces that lead women into crime and women's unique experiences within the prison setting.

Chapter 20—"How Is Aging a Critical Sociological Problem?"—explores the relevant topic of aging within Canadian society. Stephen Katz considers the key categories of social organization and stratification that are used to make sense of the implications of the steady rise in the elderly population: population, life course, generation, and gendered age. Katz argues that each of these four ways of classifying people within particular age categories emphasizes particular features (consumption, gender, and so on) that often do not accurately reflect the experiences that elderly people have in their daily lives or the impact that elderly people have on Canadian society. For instance, Katz argues that "apocalyptic demography" presents a distorted picture of a future Canadian society in which elderly people increasingly drain the economy through intensified demands on the health-care system. Katz argues that this portrait obscures important factors, such as intergenerational interdependence and the wide range of volunteer services that elderly people contribute to Canadian society. In this chapter, Katz considers critical economic, social, and political consequences that an aging population means for a future Canadian society.

In Chapter 21—"What Is Global Inequality?"—Amy Kaler broadens the discussion beyond Canadian society to consider how sociology contributes to our better understanding of how people around the globe have or do not have access to fundamental resources, such as clean water, health care, education, and income. Kaler's chapter considers the important distinctions between three terms: difference, inequality, and inequity. The differential use of these terms, Kaler argues, profoundly influences the way that we both understand how people fare in the world, and also what (if anything) can and should be done to assist people's life chances. When people's circumstances are understood as merely differences—differences in education, health, wealth, and so on—we are encouraged to see these circumstances as the outcome of individual choices or the "fact" that everyone is simply different from each other. Some people work hard, earn an education, and enjoy the fruits of their labour while other people choose to not work hard and therefore have fewer opportunities in life. Worse still, understanding inequity as merely differences between people encourages forms of racism, sexism, and disablism that consider some people as incapable of or unwilling to apply the necessary effort to achieve, thus justifying either people's inaction in helping them, or justifying the use of social programs (such as the disastrous residential school system in Canada) that further disenfranchise people. Understanding inequities as difference, in other words, denies the profound influence of power and injustice in structuring people's lives. Inequality, Kaler goes on to argue, also obscures how we understand social, economic, and political relations between people because inequality is focused on the premise that the solution to inequity is simply the equal distribution of resources. Only by examining inequities in society will we understand differences in life chances as an issue of social justice, rights, and global responsibility.

In Chapter 22, R.A. Sydie addresses the perception that social theory is "abstract, difficult, and of dubious relevance to everyday life." In responding to the question "What Use Is Social Theory?" Sydie begins by noting that early social theorists (e.g., Martineau, Durkheim) formulated theories about people's "personal troubles" as well as the societies of the time. They did so with the aim of developing harmonious and peaceful social formations. Their theories served this aim, not as irrelevant abstractions but, rather, as direct explanations of everyday practices designed to point the way toward better relations with others. We all theorize whenever we try to make sense of our practices. What distinguishes sociological from everyday theorizing, however, is its commitment to critique. Sociological theory is useful because it raises basic questions about the very foundations of everyday social relations, and it does so with the aim of undoing specified negative (unjust, unequal, tyrannical, etc.) conditions. Theorizing demands a self-questioning social theorist who understands the precariousness of being simultaneously creator and creature of the social relations criticized. With this in mind, Sydie explores how various modern social theorists developed universal explanations of "order and progress" when offering theories of modern society. She examines how current (postmodern) conditions have undermined modern social theory, including its emphasis on homogeneous, universalizing images of progress, knowledge, and society. This undermining has demanded new approaches to the concept of society—to address the challenges that racial, ethnic, cultural, social class, age, ability, sexuality, and gender diversity bring to the assumption of a national identity, for example—and opened the way for new forms of social theorizing. However, Sydie is clear that "the important point that should guide the social theorist if she is to play a useful and important role as a public intellectual is that she should not simply diagnose the critical issues of our time but also offer a critique and thus reveal the way in which personal troubles are public issues."

In Chapter 23—"What Questions Has Sociology Deserted?"—Lorne Tepperman asks us to consider some of the questions sociology asked some 50 years ago but has yet to answer. His plea is for sociology to return to some "deserted questions" that could be addressed with "scientific skepticism, empirical rigour, and statistical testing." For example, Tepperman calls for sociology to reopen discussions on Marx's concept of alienation, especially as it refers to the dehumanization of people as cogs in a capitalist machine, which in turn leads to a raft of social problems. And what about the enormously important contributions of labelling theory, which highlighted the social effects of labelling people? Although it may not be possible to avoid social labelling, Tepperman notes that sociology would benefit from a return to the study of "conditions under which labelling has harmful effects." Equally, he questions the wisdom of sociology apparently deserting questions regarding such key concepts as social distance, social mobility, anomie, altruism, and the idea that there may be universal features to group dynamics. Tepperman rightly urges sociology students to engage with influential figures in the history of the discipline, and to grapple with the key questions that they raised—even if some of these appear to have been abandoned. This may, he suggests, serve as "a reminder that important sociological problems do not disappear simply because we choose to ignore them."

Chapter 24—"What Does the Future Hold for Canadian Sociology?"—is a fitting end to this book. In this chapter, George Pavlich considers how sociology has aided Canadian society in better understanding itself and our place in the world, and how this work might continue in the future. And, as Pavlich points out, sociologists are not just imagining what a future Canadian society might look like, but how the discipline of sociology will continue to reformulate itself to meet the challenges of the twenty-first century and beyond. As such, imagining the future is as much about sociologists critically examining the tenets of our own discipline—what assumptions and premises we may continue to make, and which ones will face challenges—as it is about predicting a future Canadian society. This critical lens, turned inward toward our own discipline as much as outward to Canadian and the world, will, of necessity, focus on how to maintain sociology's relevance in helping to resolve both long-standing issues, such as poverty, and emerging issues, such as global warming. Rather than restrict itself to a particular, and therefore narrow, line of analysis, Pavlich demonstrates how sociology's open-ended imagination will continue to encourage the formulation of new concepts, which will in turn help us to understand Canadian society in new, challenging, and productive ways.

15   How Do We Help the Environment?

Myra J. Hird

Introduction

In a 1991 lecture, Howard Newby announced that "environmental change . . . is as much a social as a natural science issue" but that sociologists have been slow to analyze environmental issues (in Irwin 2001). Why did Newby need to make the claim that environmental issues are as much social issues as they are material issues? And how do we explain sociology's late arrival to environmental discussions, especially given the number and range of pressing environmental issues facing Canadian society?

Twenty years after Newby's statement, environmental concerns are emerging as a key field within Canadian sociology. Important texts, such as Andil Gosine and Cheryl Teelucksingh's *Environmental Justice and Racism in Canada* (2008) and Julian Agyeman, Peter Cole, Richard Haluza-DeLay, and Pat O'Riley's edited collection *Speaking for Ourselves: Environmental Justice in Canada* (2010), as well as the recently formed Environment Cluster of the Canadian Sociological Association, examine the relationships between our society and the environment. There is historical precedent for this approach: early social scientists, such as Auguste Comte and Herbert Spencer, devised theories based on evolutionary principles such as adaptation. For his part, Karl Marx argued that different environments (climate, soil, temperature, and so on) lead to different divisions of labour in society. But, overall, the tendency within academia has been to assume that the environment refers to material things and that society refers to the cultural aspects of the world. As a consequence, the physical sciences (chemistry, biology, engineering, physics) are associated with studying the environment, while the social sciences and humanities are associated with studying the human or cultural aspects of society.

Undergirding this disciplinary separation is a long-standing view that the natural environment is separate from human-made environments. Another way of saying this is that the natural environment has long been considered asocial and somehow removed from human concerns. To be sure, Marx, Émile Durkeim, Max Weber, and other founders of sociology took for granted that the environment provided resources for human consumption and utility (coal, lumber, water, and so on). But this background was viewed as external to the business of being human, and to human concerns. Durkheim (1952 [1897]), for instance, argued that social observations (suicide, for example) must be explained by social facts rather than by material or natural facts.

As such, the environment was mostly defined as something beyond the reach of human beings—indeed, as separate from social life. And we may go further here to say that Western thought has strongly supported the principle that to be human is to overcome or to transcend nature. Consider, for instance, Friedrich Engels' statement that "the earth's surface, climate, vegetation, fauna, and the human beings themselves have infinitely changed, and all this owing to human activity, while the changes of nature . . . which have occurred in this period of time without human interference are incalculably small" (2001 [1883]). Or consider Marx's even more explicit claim that nature passively gives itself up as resources to human capital: "Natural elements entering as agents into production, and which cost nothing, no matter what role they place in production, do not enter as components of capital, but as a free gift of Nature to capital" (Marx 1993 [1894], p. 745). And no one attempted to secure humanity's separation from nature more than Immanuel Kant, who introduced the proposition that the faculty of reason indelibly separates humans from all of nature (Uleman 2010).

For some time now, this stark division between humans and the environment has been called into question. Defining any space as purely natural is becoming more difficult, and acting as though humans are not part of the environment, or indeed as though they do not depend fundamentally on the environment, is becoming equally problematic. Growing concerns with global warming, biodiversity loss, fossil fuel depletion, and many other issues make it clear that we can no longer afford (if we ever could) to see ourselves as distinct from, or to transcend and control, the environment. We are creating much more nuanced and complex understandings of how the environment and how we as a species are co-constituted. In other words, we are learning that environmental issues are the result of complex material, institutional, racial, political, class, gender, economic, and other factors. Sociology can be at the forefront of this endeavour.

Of course, concern for the environment, and the specific impact of human attitudes and behaviours toward other organisms and the Earth, features in every culture throughout human existence. In the late 1940s and into the 1950s, for example, deep concern with the invention of the atom bomb and its effect on the future of humans, other animals, and the planet occupied the conscience of at least one generation. Albert Einstein, who in 1939 warned US President Franklin D. Roosevelt that the Germans were attempting to construct an atomic bomb and who urged the US to begin its own bomb development, later devoted himself to cautioning people about the devastating effects of this particular turn in the arms race. Today, we have shifted our attention to other pressing environmental concerns, such as climate change and species extinction. The particular shape that environmental concern takes in any given generation is intimately dependent upon social factors, such as culture, politics, and economics. The most recent discussions among geologists about whether or not we as a species have precipitated a new geologic period—called the Anthropocene—further indicate our concern with the magnitude of our human impact on planet Earth.

What Is an Environmental Issue?

At first glance, environmental issues may seem obvious to identify and without need of further explanation. For instance, as we are bombarded with news of species extinction, biodiversity loss seems to be an uncontroversial issue that needs to be urgently addressed. But environmental issues are not fixed or necessarily self-evident. What gets identified as an environmental issue is always the result of *claims-making*. **Claims-making** involves stakeholders—people who have a stake in a particular thing—who turn an object or event into an issue. **Climate change**, for instance, is a set of events (change in average temperature among other things), that becomes an environmental issue because stakeholders—scientists, industry representatives, politicians, journalists, environmental activists, community group representatives, students, and others—have turned this set of events into an issue: climate change. Stakeholders make assertions about a particular object or condition, trying to convince others of the veracity of their claims. These claims, in turn, may help propel a particular object or event into the public's attention, or they may help to dismiss a particular set of events as not really an issue worth focusing on. As such, claims-making is always interactive in the sense that those engaged in claims-making engage with other stakeholders (whether to agree or disagree, form alliances, and so on).

So how and why do some things get turned into environmental issues while others do not? And further, why do some issues (such as climate change) seem to be sustained as issues (i.e., kept in the public eye), while others (such as ozone layer depletion) seem to fade from public concern? To answer these questions, we need to consider that it is actually rather difficult to make environmental issues public at all. When we consider the vastness of the globe and all of the myriad changes taking place in the oceans, the land, and the atmosphere, few of these changes garner public attention. There are several reasons for this. First of all, environmental issues are complex, often involving numerous and diverse stakeholders, who are making competing claims about the seriousness, veracity, and scope of a given issue, as well as how that issue should be resolved. For instance, while the Intergovernmental Panel on Climate Change's annual reports identify climate change as a real and urgent issue, the fossil fuels industry and conservative politicians deny that climate change exists or insist that if it does exist, it is the outcome of human impact on the planet.

Second, environmental issues involve material things: a diverse array of living and geologic forces that impact how an environmental issue is understood. For instance, the *E. coli* 0157:H7 outbreak in Walkerton, Ontario in May 2000 brought together bacteria, viruses, animals, water treatment, monitoring operators, international trade laws, doctors, the media, and other stakeholders (see Harris Ali 2004). A third reason why it is difficult to bring environmental issues to the public is that many environmental issues are routinized within our society. Water comes out of our taps, garbage is taken from our streets before we wake up, toilet-flushing takes our sewage from our homes, and exotic fruits appear on our grocery shelves in the middle of winter. As Bruno Latour observes, it is "all those institutions [that] appear on the surface to be apolitical, and yet in their silent, ordinary, fully routinized ways they are perversely the most important aspects of what we mean by living together" (2007, 817). Other reasons include the fact that most people are not suffering from any given environmental issue. Thousands of people may be affected by a coastal oil spill, but this is a tiny fraction of the world's population. Moreover, and as we will shortly see, the majority of people may well benefit from environmental issues—for example, billions of people benefit from the depletion of fossil fuels and carbon emissions by using cars. And, finally, an environmental issue may simply not have the media "traction" to sustain the public's interest for long. As news and entertainment increasingly merge, complex and not easily resolvable environmental issues may lose out to celebrities' latest controversies.

In an influential article called "Up and Down with Ecology—The Issue-Attention Cycle" (1972), Anthony Downs argues that public interest in environmental issues is not typically sustained: things tend to go through a cycle consisting of five stages:

1. *Pre-problem stage*: During this initial phase, an actual material thing may be at its worst, but the public has not yet become aware that there is an issue.
2. *Alarmed discovery and euphoric enthusiasm*: During this stage, the public is aware of the issue, and strong claims are made that something can and should be done to solve the issue. The assumption here is that environmental problems are external to society; that is, environmental issues can be resolved without altering consumer lifestyles and other aspects of society.
3. *Realization of the cost of significant progress*: At this point, it becomes clear that solving an environmental problem will require substantial sacrifices by an enfranchised portion of the world's population. This is referred to as the **democratization of privilege**, which refers to the fact that what the privileged portion of society deems to be environmental deterioration, the rest of society sees as improved living standards. Take, for instance, carbon dioxide (CO_2) emissions from the use of cars. People in affluent countries may lament the increase in car use in countries such as China and India. But people living in these countries may well argue that they are simply now enjoying the mobility that relatively affluent people in Canada and elsewhere have enjoyed for years.

4. *Gradual decline of intense public interest*: Once people realize that environmental issues are tied to social issues—that oil spills and nuclear power plant accidents are linked to society's insatiable desire for cheap energy, for instance—public interest tends to wane. Some people may feel threatened by the realization that their lifestyles would need to change in order to make significant progress on an environmental issue; others may become bored or feel helpless. And by this time, another environmental issue is being brought to the public's attention.

5. *Post-problem stage*: During this final stage, a new issue replaces the (now) old issue, and committees, programs, or policies are brought in to deal with the old issue. These may resolve the problem, or they may serve as a way for people to move their attention toward a new issue.

In describing these phases of public attention, we begin to see the many challenges to sustaining the public's interest in any given environmental issue.

Whose Knowledge Gets to Define Environmental Issues?

At first glance, it may seem obvious that science is the most powerful source of knowledge about environmental issues. Steve Shapin notes the following:

> Few observers disagree when it is said that science has changed much about the way we live now and are likely to live in the future: how we communicate, how long we are likely to live and how well, whether the crucial global problems we now confront—from global warming to our ability to feed ourselves—are likely to be solved, indeed, what it will mean to be human. (2010, 381)

Modern science explicitly values objectivity, **reliability**, **validity**, accuracy, and testability. At the same time, we know that science not only reflects but influences societal values and that it is increasingly contested through what is known as *scientific controversies*.

Scientific controversies refer to disagreements about the validity and reliability of a scientific claim. Sometimes these controversies stem from questions about the validity of a particular scientific discovery or invention. We have all become familiar with the oscillation of scientific findings on diet- and exercise-related matters. Coffee consumption, for instance, goes through regular cycles of scientific proclamations about it being either healthy or unhealthy. At other times, controversies concern scientific misconduct. For instance, a 2013 article describing the Southern Beaufort polar bear population survey only reported data from 2007 to 2010 and did not include available data beyond 2010, which shows that the polar bear population has continued to increase (Bromaghin et al. 2013). The statistics before 2010 provided the results that the Polar Bear Specialist Group needed to ensure that the bears' "threatened" status remained intact. Other scientific controversies, such as **Climategate**, regularly pepper the news and have raised the public's skepticism toward science. Another way of looking at this is to say that contemporary science is more democratized, with non-scientists (e.g., industry, community activist groups, politicians, and members of the public) increasingly commenting on, and influencing, science. (We will come back, in the final section of this chapter, to the particularly powerful role that industry plays in creating, defining, and governing environmental issues.)

Western science and technology has always borrowed, taken, imitated, and otherwise incorporated knowledge about nature from Indigenous and non-Western cultures. Long before French and British explorers tracked through Canada, Aboriginal and Inuit peoples had developed ways of finding out about and understanding nature and had also developed sophisticated and practical technologies to enhance their survival in a variety of climates and environmental conditions. The pressing issues of global warming, species extinction, sustainable agricultural practices, and environmental degradation in general may now be making this incorporation explicit.

Canadian government officials, researchers, and members of the public have begun to call for a more open exploration of **traditional ecological knowledge** (TEK) about the environment. In *Native Science: Natural Laws of Interdependence* (2000), Gregory Cajete contrasts Western and Indigenous ways of understanding the environment. Arguing that Western science is mechanistic—that is, it seeks to determine causal laws underwriting the cosmos—Cajete argues that Indigenous knowledge allows a holistic approach to understanding the relationship between humans and our environment. Indigenous knowledge, writes Cajete, "attempt[s] to gain comprehensive understanding rather than piecemeal analysis; a pursuit of wisdom rather than the accumulation of data . . ." (2000, 61).

TEK understands humans to be part of the environment rather than somehow standing outside or apart from the world. Put another way, all living organisms, and the Earth itself, are co-dependent upon all other living and nonliving organisms. A number of researchers point to the ways in which Indigenous peoples have learned, through generations of trial and error, to survive and thrive in specific environmental contexts (Flannery 1994; Pyne 2001; Raffles 2002; Trafzer, Gilbert, and Madrigal 2008; Vale 2002). For instance, Aboriginal people are known to have worked with, rather than fought against, the dry climate in Australia, strategically setting and lighting fires in order to steer fires in particular ways, to improve the land's condition, and to maintain passages through the land for humans to traverse (Clark 2008; Langton 1999; Yibarbuk 1998). These fires were also strategically lit to better capture and kill animals for food, clothing, and implements (Franklin 2006).

This is knowledge accumulated by people who have lived within particular geographical regions over many generations. This intimate knowledge has at times been very different from the knowledge of how to live in other climates and geographies (for instance, Europe) that colonialists brought to Canada and other

New World countries. "Experience," writes Clark, "counts . . . and as a rule the longer a people or a species or a mixed community has inhabited a region, the greater the range of variation they will be conversant with, the more attuned they will be to its characteristic shifts, peaks and troughs" (2008, 5). Mike Davis (2001) details the dire consequences that faced Indian people when Indigenous and colonial ways of coping with the agricultural environment in India clashed during the Victorian era (1837–1901). "When one group," notes Clark "has the power to impose inappropriate responses to environmental stress and extremity on another, these repercussions can be catastrophic" (2008, 2).

Focusing on different human experiences with the environment, and the ways in which all species survive through adapting to the viscidities of the environment, is a way of escaping representations of Indigenous peoples as harmoniously living with nature (Massey 2005). It also provides a way of keeping in mind that trial-and-error can be very costly when it goes wrong (as must have been the case at times) and that the "debt—immeasurable and unredeemable—that is owed to those unnamed others whose trials and labors ultimately . . ." enabled current species (including humans) inhabitation (Clark 2008, 6). Focusing on different human experiences with the environment also encourages us to acknowledge that there are environmental events that no peoples—Indigenous and settlers included—can predict or adapt to, such as the devastating impact of meteorite hits, which no amount of improvisation and adaptation can prepare us for (Bryson 2005).

The relationship between science and TEK is not straightforward, and a number of environmental sociologists are exploring how TEK and science variously work together, speak past each other (Henri 2012), and/or serve political and industry interests (Agyeman, Cole, Haluza-DeLay, and O'Riley 2010).

How Are Environmental Issues Governed?

As we see, a number of complex factors determine whether or not a particular object or event will come to the public's attention, and be sustained, as an environmental issue. Now we need to consider how an issue is governed. Governing refers to how an environmental issue is controlled or managed. Two of the main ways in which environmental issues are governed in contemporary Canadian society are through the concepts of "risk" and "individual responsibility." Let's consider risk first.

The German sociologist Ulrich Beck is most closely associated with the concept of risk. His first book on risk, *The Risk Society*, was published around the same time as the Chernobyl nuclear accident, and this coincident timing helped to focus public attention on risk as a key way of understanding environmental issues. Beck argues that risk is a way of ordering reality, of making reality calculable. It is a way of turning uncertainty (*When exactly will all of the polar ice caps have melted?*) into a quantifiable number (the risk of all of the polar ice caps melting within the next decade). Beck argues that modern Western society practises a circular logic: science and technology create the catastrophes and we then call upon science to define and control the consequent risks. For example, the nuclear scientists and engineers who created nuclear reactors are also called upon to define the risks of high- and low-level radiation. In other words, the usual solutions to environmental disasters—more science, further technological development, stricter regulations—create more problems. As Beck forcefully writes, "the origin of risk consciousness . . . is truly not a page of honor in the history of (natural) sciences. It came into being against a continuing barrage of scientific denial, and is still suppressed by it. . . . Science has become the protector of a global contamination of people and nature" (Beck 1992, 70).

Modernity, for Beck, does not promise to eliminate hazards; rather, it offers a way of calculating these hazards, and commerce then offers a way of financially compensating when hazards transform into tragedies. Another way of thinking about this is to say that environmental issues are increasingly beyond individual control, involving numerous stakeholders, institutions, and power exercised in direct and indirect ways. Risks are now global in scale: radiation from the 2011 Fukushima nuclear disaster in Japan has now reached the shores of British Columbia (CBC 2014c). Insurance is based upon these risk calculations: insurance does not undo the damage done to human health or the environment; it monetarily compensates people for the damage. It is clear that the benefits and costs of established and new technologies are not evenly distributed across society. And this means that issues of fairness and justice are central to risk assessment.

One of the main features of risk is that it is not objective. As François Ewald observes, "Nothing is a risk in itself; there is no risk in reality. But on the other hand, anything *can* be a risk; it all depends on how one analyses the danger, considers the event" (1991, 199). This means that different people can have different perceptions of risk: people actively interpret environmental issues, and the risk to themselves, their family, and other people, based on a number of factors. Donna Haraway (1988) calls this **situated knowledges** and speaks to the fact that there isn't a single public that simply needs to be educated about science (known as the deficit model), but that there are several publics with different understandings that may each be valid within their own context.

Environmental concerns, in other words, do not stand apart from other aspects of people's everyday lives. People talk about local pollution, trust in local and national politicians, employment, poverty, race, and housing as a single concern. Local residents also have a contextual knowledge that scientists visiting a region to test for contamination and issue a report do not have. And so there can be a profound divide between the situated or contextual understanding of risk that gives weight to local experience and brings together different kinds of evidence, and arms-length scientific evidence that calculates risk based on averages. So, the risk assessments issued by industry representatives and scientists may be met with considerable skepticism from local residents and, indeed, wider society (Wynne 2006).

The second way that environmental issues are governed is through individual responsibility. Michel Foucault argued that a particular form of governmentality operates in modern societies by targeting populations and their "security." Such governmentality works through various "political technologies" characterized more by guidance and empowerment than by coercion and violence. This governmentality is, above all, a way to get individuals and populations to govern themselves by acting "responsibly" rather than being governed haphazardly by the state. An excellent example of individual responsibilization within environmental studies concerns the recycling of waste. Many people in Canada recycle (and more Americans recycle than vote), and the general consensus is that recycling is a good thing: it demonstrates our care and concern for the environment. But research on recycling shows that it is more complicated than this (see for example MacBride 2011). Recycling hasn't decreased rates of resource extraction, and indeed, recycling has actually *increased* the production of garbage: when people know there is recycling in place, they actually increase the amount of waste they produce. For example, Figure 15.1 shows that when diversion (which primarily means recycling) goes up in Ontario, so too does Ontarians' waste generation.

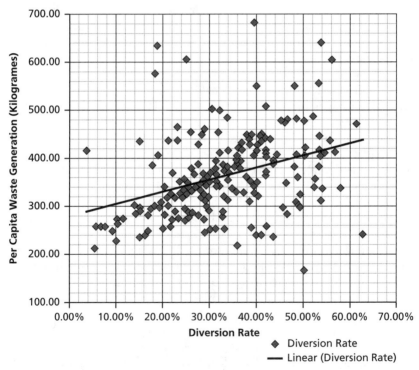

Figure 15.1 Ontario Municipalities Waste Diversion X Per Capita Waste Generation in KG

Source: Graph created by Scott Lougheed, Waste Diversion Ontario. 2012. *Municipal Data Call: 2012 Diversion Rate by Municipality.* The source of the materials is http://www.wdo.ca/. The use of these materials by Oxford University Press is done without any affiliation with or endorsement by the WDO.

Recycling also releases hazardous wastes through by-product emissions; increases pollution from transportation; has zero impact on resource conservation; doesn't reduce health risks; and may use toxic chemicals to re-process materials. And the "dirty little secret" of recycling is that a good proportion of recycled material ends up in landfills (see Hird et al. 2014). From a governmentality perspective, recycling is popular because it focuses on individual behaviour—the good, responsible, environmental citizen—rather than addressing reducing waste production or increasing producer responsibility, both of which would require a societal reorientation away from consumption. Much of the waste studies literature, unsurprisingly, focuses on individuals' behaviour regarding municipal solid waste, even though this represents a very small fraction of the waste produced in Canada, most of which is produced through mining, agriculture, industrial development, and the military.

These two brief illustrations of the governance of environmental issues demonstrate that the management of environmental issues is complex and involves multiple interested parties (often termed stakeholders), institutions, and practices. Since sociology studies these how institutions and practices interact, it is well placed to study how environmental issues are governed in different political, economic, geographical, and social contexts.

Is Sustainability Good for the Environment?

All of the factors involved in how environmental issues are defined and governed lead us to a consideration of **sustainability**. Sustainability is an extremely popular term used to describe our relationship with the environment. The well-known Bruntland Report, *Our Common Future*, produced by the World Commission on Environment and Development in 1987, defines *sustainability* as "development that meets the needs of the present without compromising the ability of future generations to meet their own needs" (World Commission on Environment and Development 1987, 1). Looking closely at this definition, we see that it emphasizes development, which is a highly contentious theme to put to the forefront when considering environmental issues from a global perspective. As Indian environmental activist Vandana Shiva notes, "'development' [means] destruction for women, nature, and subjugated cultures, which is why, throughout the Third World, peasants and tribals are struggling for liberation from 'development' just as they struggled for liberation from colonialism" (1988, 1–2).

Shiva points to the fact that the Global North and Global South often have very different (and indeed opposing) environmental goals. In the North, we prioritize habitat protection whereas in the South, the priorities are to alleviate poverty and inequality. The relationship between the environment, poverty, and inequality is clear: according to a recent Oxfam report, the richest 1 per cent of the world's population will own over 50 per cent of the world's wealth. More than a billion people live on less than $1.25 per day (Oxfam International 2015, 1), and most people in the world who do work are non-unionized and have temporary jobs with low wages. For many people in the Globalized South, *development* means consolidating control over their economies through World Bank and International Monetary Fund loans and structural adjustment (i.e., paying back these loans) through currency devaluation, interest rate increases, trade barrier removals, privatization, deregulation, and control over agricultural practices— all of which increase local poverty and inequality.

There are numerous examples of extremely wealthy American and European corporations controlling what crops are planted in regions of the Global South. Often, these crops suit the needs of people in the North rather than the subsistence farmers in the South. (This is also known as *land grabbing*.) **Environmental justice** is concerned with **environmental imperialism**, which refers to the appropriation of land (forests and agriculture), rivers, lakes and oceans, and homes by foreign corporations and governments for their own profit. We need to carefully consider, then, exactly who benefits from the focus on sustainability.

Conclusion

In sum, sociologists offer critical insights into how we as a global society may best help the environment by focusing on the ways in which environmental issues "transcend personal, local, national and global scales" (Stoddart and Ramos 2015, 72). To do this, sociologists focus on issues such as risk, uncertainty, governance, and expertise in order to determine the intended and unintended consequences of environmental initiatives.

Review/Summary Questions

1. Is sustainability good for the environment? Is it good for people?
2. How can members of the public evaluate scientific claims without specialized technical knowledge?
3. How can traditional ecological knowledge (TEK) and scientific knowledge meaningfully inform each other about environmental issues, given the hegemony of scientific knowledge in Canadian society?
4. Should we focus less on individual actions and more on corporate and government actions concerning the environment? And, if so, how might we do this?

16 What Is Sovereignty for Indigenous People?

Vanessa Watts

Introduction

There are many understandings of what sovereignty actually is and where it derived from for Indigenous peoples. From a statist perspective, **Indigenous sovereignty** is something that is *granted* by the authority of the state itself (Alfred and Corntassel 2005). Therefore, Indigenous sovereignty is a sovereignty that is circulated within and by state power. From an Indigenous perspective, sovereignty for Indigenous peoples pre-existed statist notions of recognition. And yet, upon encountering Indigenous sovereignties, imperial nations *did* recognize the legitimacy of these nations—hence, the emergence of the treaty-making process in Canada. In this chapter, I will examine how Indigenous sovereignty is traced through three different mechanisms. First, I will explore where Indigenous sovereignty came from and how was it represented at the point of contact between Indigenous people and colonialists. Second, I will examine social theory's engagement with Indigenous sovereignty. Finally, I will discuss sovereignty from an international perspective. At the end of this chapter, you will gain insight into how sovereignty is oriented in often contradistinctive frames (Indigenous and Canadian) and how these frames attempt to manifest sovereignty amid colonial confrontations.

In order to gain insight into this perspective, we must explore how Indigenous sovereignty was designed prior to contact with imperialist notions of sovereignty. Fred Kelly, Hereditary Chief of Onigaming, states the following:

> The four concentric circles in the sky—*Pagonekiishig*—show the four directions, the four stages of life, the four seasons, the four sacred lodges (sweat, shaking tent, roundhouse, and the Midewe'in lodge), the four sacred drums (the rattle, hand, water, and big ceremonial drum), and the four orders of Sacred Law. Indeed, the four concentric circles of stars

is the origin of the sacred four in *Pimaatiziwin* that is the heart of the supreme law of the Anishinaabe. And simply put, that is the meaning of a constitution. (Watts 2006, 77)

For **Anishnaabe** peoples, like most Indigenous nations, sovereignty is place-based and spiritual, and incorporates all elements of creation (animals, rivers, plants, rocks, etc.). The land is considered female, and so women too are regarded as sacred (Green 2007). The ideas put forth above speak to a constitution that is demonstrated and exercised out of place. Anishnaabe people understand their sovereignty as emerging from a cosmology that is particularly locatable. That is, as Chief Kelly explains, to look above and observe constellations at a designated time of day, month, and year and to derive meaning from what is observed means that those who look up belong to a particular place below (land) in order to have a designated perspective. While ownership of land is a complex issue for Anishnaabe and other Indigenous peoples, it is understood that people are *of* the land and are responsible for it. This stands in contradiction to the common colonial practice of assuming that Indigenous peoples were constantly transient and that, therefore, land in the "New World" was virtually unstructured and uninhabited (Doyle 2014). Our responsibility to place is fundamental to notions of Anishnaabe sovereignty. This responsibility is imbedded in the land that we come from—we are citizens of place. This idea becomes problematized when attempts to reconcile land title with the state continue to be unresolved, as I will discuss further in the chapter.

Because the nature of Indigenous sovereignty is place-based, sovereignty cannot be exported to another's land. This would negate the tenets of polycentrism under which all Indigenous nations on Turtle Island[1] exemplified. It would also be materially impossible to do so as our constitutions are founded in place. This understanding of sovereignty is lost, however, when evaluated against an imperialistic frame, in which Indigenous sovereignties are observed as archaic or anti-intellectual (Howard and Widdowson 2008). It is better understood as a completely distinct frame of reference in which colonizing another nation was an alien idea for the Anishnaabe.

Indigenous sovereignties are not focused on the rights of their citizens but, rather, on the roles and responsibilities individuals have within the collective (Watts 2007). In Western terms, this is understood as a form of participatory democracy, wherein individuals are free to stay within the collective (or nation) or are free to leave. This is best exemplified in the **Haudenosaunee Confederacy's** *Kainere'ko:wa,* or **the Great Law.**

Social Implications and the *Kainere'ko:wa*

The Great Law is the constitution of the Haudenosaunee (Iroquois) peoples and serves as a basis for Haudenosaunee sovereignty. It originated in the year 1142 (Fields and Mann, cited in Johansen 1995), making it one of the longest-running democracies in world history. The *Kainere'ko:wa* brought together six nations into a confederacy: the Mohawk, the Seneca, the Onondaga, the Cayuga, the Oneida, and eventually the Tuscarora. These nations belonging to the confederacy have considered themselves collectively sovereign for almost a millennium and have operated with the goal of maintaining peace among nations.[2] The premise of the *Kainere'ko:wa* was to embrace other nations wishing to live in peace and participate in this democratic union.

The Grand Council of Chiefs is one of the many democratic processes outlined in the *Kainere'ko:wa* (Wallace 1990). The five nations have a designated number of hereditary chief titles (or *Hoyaneh*, meaning "good men") for each of the clans of the nations. These chiefs compose the 50 members of the Grand Council. The Onondagas are the Firekeepers. They are responsible for bringing forth issues to be tabled at the Council for discussion. The Mohawks and the Senecas are the Elder Brothers and are expected to be the first to discuss the issue or conflict at hand. Once they have come to a decision, they defer to the Cayuga and the Oneida (the Younger Brothers) for a similar discussion. If both sides come to a mutual agreement, the Onondagas confirm the decision. If the two sides are irreconcilable, the Council must meet again for two more days in order to achieve a resolution.

This design is both democratic and sophisticated. The Grand Council is premised on the idea of peace and common resolution. Though the hereditary chiefs are male, it is the women who possess the authority to install and remove chiefs. These women are known as **Clan Mothers** within the confederacy. They are considered the heads of clans, and it is in their estimation to name a chief. If the selected chief conducts himself personally or politically contrary to the *Kainere'ko:wa*, the Clan Mother can "dehorn" him, or remove his title. Haudenosaunee women, like many Indigenous women, are central to governance. Given their authority over leadership, they are also integral to the economy, social life, child-rearing, and property.

During the Victorian era and even, arguably, in contemporary times, perspectives on gender roles classified women as the weaker sex (Butler 1988). The stronger male counterpart was required not only to protect the woman, but to act on her behalf. The division of the public and the private domains demonstrated this deference to male authority. While there is a division of gender roles in traditional Indigenous systems, they are oriented differently in terms of power:

> In our community, the woman was defined as nourisher, and the man, protector, and as protector, he had the role of helper. He only reacted: she acted. She was responsible for the establishment of all of the norms— whether they were political, economic, social or spiritual. . . . (Kane and Maracle 1989, 12)

This same "protector" idea, when placed in a different frame, constitutes an alternative understanding of gender. Though men are considered to be protectors, this is not due to a stronger intellect or physique. Rather, the "protector" is understood as being responsible for ensuring that women's authority is maintained. Haudenosaunee women were active contributors to the economy, working in agriculture and developing sophisticated systems of farming that have been incorporated in Europe and all over North America today. They held judicial powers over selected leadership, and could veto any decision made by the Grand Council that might result in war (Wallace 1990). In terms of property, when a man and woman were married, the man was expected to live with the woman's family and live on their property. In the event of separation, the man was expected to leave and was not entitled to any of the woman's property.

Given this example of an equitable and democratic sovereign union, why is it that the *Kainere'ko:wa* and other Indigenous constitutions have not been inherently regarded as legitimate by the Canadian state? There are multiple intersecting reasons for this. First, Indigenous sovereignties were, and are, viewed as a barrier to the colonial enterprise, which, according to Marx, is the accumulation of capital and the establishment of private property. Indigenous communities or, legally, "reserves" in Canada are categorized as Crown land and are not considered **fee simple property**. Canada created reserves for Indigenous peoples in order to establish an apartheid system wherein incoming settlers would be able to flourish.

The reserve system was a result of the historic treaty process that began in Canada in the seventeenth century. From an Indigenous perspective, the objective of the treaty-making process was understood as two sovereign nations negotiating how to live in a shared territory. The *Kaswentha,* more commonly known as the **Two Row Wampum**, was first negotiated between the Haudenosaunee Confederacy (representing the *Kainere'ko:wa*) and the Dutch in 1613. This treaty was reaffirmed with the British in 1677 in the Silver Covenant Chain Treaty. It was again reaffirmed, as were all other treaties in Canada, in section 35 of the Constitution Act, 1982.

The Two Row Wampum signified how two distinct sovereign nations could exist alongside each other into the future. In it, there are two purple rows of wampum and three white rows of wampum (or shell). The purple represent two vessels travelling down the river of life. The vessels are separate and are not to interfere with one another's course. The white wampum represents the three principles of the treaty: peace, friendship, and respect. The intention of this international treaty was as follows:

> We will not be like Father and Son, but like Brothers. [Our treaties] symbolize two paths or two vessels, travelling down the same river together. One, a birchbark canoe, will be for the Indian People, their laws, their customs, and their ways. The other, a ship, will be for the white people and their laws, their customs, and their ways. We shall each travel the river together, side by side, but in our own boat. Neither

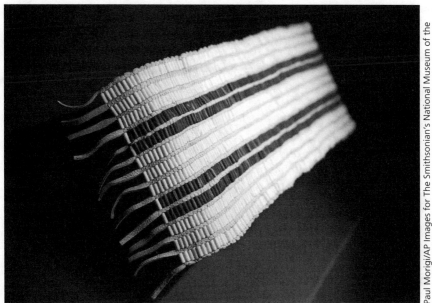

The Two Row Wampum signified how two distinct sovereign nations could exist alongside each other into the future. The dark rows (purple) signify vessels travelling down the river of life—separate and not interfering with one another. The white wampum represents the treaty principles of peace, friendship, and respect.

of us will make compulsory laws nor interfere in the internal affairs of the other. Neither of us will try to steer the other's vessel. (Wilson 2000, 115)

Sovereignty for the Haudenosaunee Confederacy preceded any contact with Europeans, but again was recognized and ratified by newly forming colonial governments. Further, these colonial governments were deriving *their* sovereignty from nation-to-nation agreements with the Haudenosaunee and other Indigenous nations in Canada.[3] This means that non-Indigenous citizens of Canada are inheritors of this treaty relationship just as Indigenous people are—*we are all treaty people.*

Social Theory and Indigenous Sovereignties

In the eighteenth century, when European ideologies began to form a stronghold in Upper and Lower Canada, a generally held belief was that European modes of politics and religion held a racial and intellectual superiority. Indigenous spiritualities, on the other hand, were classified as "pagan" and regarded as deficient and godless (Bönisch-Brednich and Trundle 2010). While spirituality was assumed to be irrelevant to the colonial pursuit, the Canadian state recognized that it was central to Indigenous sovereignty and that Indigenous sovereignty was a barrier to the appropriation of lands. As such, Indigenous ceremonies were banned from 1885 to 1951 by the newly implemented Indian Act of 1876. Such ceremonies were not simply the pagan rituals that the colonial government had dismissed them as, but understood as a much more powerful and meaningful point of access between Indigenous peoples and their sovereignties.

Similarly, the primacy of Indigenous women's authority was integral to the dignity of Indigenous sovereignties. Yet this fundamental difference of gender delegation against the colonial frame was seen as a barrier to the colonial imperative. This played out in Canadian policy until 1985 when Indigenous women were forced to legally relinquish their Indigenous identity in order to become Canadian citizens (Anderson 2000). It was further entrenched into policy during the residential school era when Indigenous women were legally forbidden to mother their children: during this period, Indigenous children were forcibly removed from their homes. Consequently, daughters were trained by government and church-run schools to abandon their traditional gender roles in favour of a more Victorian identity wherein they were no longer useful to public/political life (Milloy 1999).

Despite the end of the residential school era in 1996, Indigenous women continue to face violence. In Canada, missing and murdered Indigenous women represent the most devastated population. Despite comprising only 4 per cent of the total female population nationally, they make up 23 per cent of the female victims of homicide as of 2013 (RCMP 2014). Andrea Smith (2005) intersects these high rates of violence against Indigenous women with the continued efforts to suppress Indigenous sovereignties. She argues that because Indigenous women are so intimately tied with the power and authority of Indigenous nationhood, they simultaneously exist as the barrier to continued colonial pursuits of Indigenous territory by the state. Therefore, they occupy one of the most vulnerable positions in Canadian society because of the power of Indigenous sovereignty that they represent culturally.

Indigenous issues such as these are the areas that sociologists have traditionally been concerned with: that is, analyzing social inequalities as phenomena rather than within the context of "sovereignty." Imperialism has dictated that culture is merely a category rather than a basis for sovereignty, as sovereignty was a special term reserved for colonial states. Sociology has been primarily concerned with the cultural artifacts of pre-contact Indigenous societies as well as sociological phenomena resulting from contact (i.e., issues of poverty, health determinants, access to education, etc.). That is, how do Indigenous populations fare within a statist frame? This would include orienting Indigenous cultural signifiers and phenomena amid heteronormative standards of what constitutes "good health," "proper parenting," "justice," etc. This also assumes that Indigenous populations and cultures are framed within and by state regulations—the underlying assumption here being that Indigenous cultures are not synonymous with a notion of sovereignty but, rather, that they should operate within the multiculturalist mosaic of Canada.

State-sponsored sovereignty or **self-government** for some Indigenous peoples is tantamount to rejecting the original teachings and laws of our nation and thereby colonial law and rule. This, in turn, amounts to recognizing the state's power in terms of *how much* sovereignty we are "allowed" within a Canadian frame. Taiaiake Alfred (2005), a Mohawk scholar, rejects the notion that Indigenous peoples should accept a diminutive sovereignty allocated by the state. He argues instead that self-determination is the true pathway toward reconstituting Indigenous place-based sovereignty:

> It is still true that the first part of self-determination is the self. In our minds and in our souls, we need to reject the colonists' control and authority, their definition of who we are and what our rights are, their definition of what is worthwhile and how one should live, their hypocritical and pacifying moralities. We need to rebel against what they want us to become, start remembering the qualities of our ancestors and act on those remembrances. This is the kind of spiritual revolution that will ensure our survival. (Alfred 2005, 32)

Continued efforts to achieve statist recognition will never accomplish a revitalization of our original constitutional designs, according to Alfred. Rather, choosing to define and practise Indigenous sovereignty within a statist regime would ultimately act to recognize the power that the state claims to wield over us. Thus, Indigenous nations may risk losing the intent and breadth of original systems of sovereignty by choosing "rights" over sovereignty.

The rights-based discourse emerged out of the modern and post-modern age of Western liberalism. The transition to a more individualist-based society constituted a relationship with the state that was based on the interplay of **nationalism** and entitlement (Smith 1999). Will Kymlicka (1995) argues that, despite this, there is still a space for multi-nationalistic ideals within the state:

> Self-government rights devolve powers to smaller political units, so that a national minority cannot be outvoted or outbid by the majority on decisions that are of particular importance to their culture, such as issues of education, immigration, resource development, language, and family law.

Self-government for Indigenous peoples and their communities is a commonly pursued avenue of sovereignty arising out of the land claims process. It arose out of the Inherent Right to Self-Government policy in 1995 as a potential solution to land title disputes. This is a constitutionally protected right in Section 35 of the Constitution Act, 1982. While the self-government path does increase the powers that an Indigenous community can possess, it is out of a process of devolution of state powers, not a restitution of the multiplicities of Indigenous sovereignties. In negotiated self-government agreements, the limited autonomy that is accorded to Indigenous communities cannot equal or supersede the sovereign powers of the state (Aboriginal Affairs and Northern Development 1995).

In sum, the orientation of Indigenous sovereignty in Canada (and certainly in other nation-states) must adhere to the liberal undertones of a unified nationalism. This exists in opposition to the original intents of treaty-making, which, from an Indigenous perspective, framed a relationship of one sovereignty *with* another—not one sovereignty *within* another.

Sovereignty: From Turtle Island to Geneva

On 25 October 1924, the Haudenosaunee Confederacy representing the *Kainere'ko:wa* were having a council meeting at Six Nations of the Grand River in southern Ontario. Their meeting was interrupted by the arrival of the RCMP, who, upon entering the Council House, seized several of the wampum agreements that had been made with the Crown. From the vantage of the Canadian government, this was an act of symbolic and physical removal of sovereignty for the Haudenosaunee Confederacy. The Confederacy existed as one of the last traditional governance systems in Canada that had not forcibly adopted an Indian Act–elected council regime. The traditional chiefs were removed from the House, and the doors were padlocked. Five days later, a new council was created, complete with a newly elected chief. Despite the low number of Haudenosaunee people supporting the new Indian Act regime, they received federal support (both policing and fiscal) to install this new system.

The tipping point for Canada's intervention in Haudenosaunee sovereignty might be seen in the year before the raid, when Chief Deskaheh, who spoke for the Haudenosaunee Confederacy, travelled to Geneva to address the League of Nations (now known as the United Nations) as a representative of the *Kainere'ko:wa*. Though he had the support of four member nations to speak, Canada contravened this support and successfully removed Deskaheh from the agenda. There is no doubt about the embarrassment that Canada would have felt at this moment during the international forum. That one of its "citizens" would act to oppose its sovereign claims over Indigenous peoples was perceived as an act of defiance. Deskaheh was heard informally after the forum had closed but would not be officially recognized by the League. On the issue of sovereignty, Deskaheh stated the following one year after the raid in 1925:

> To punish us for trying to preserve our rights, the Canadian Government has now pretended to abolish our government by Royal Proclamation, and has pretended to set up a Canadian made government over us, composed of the few traitors among us who are willing to accept pay from Ottawa and do its bidding. My home is on the Grand River . . . You

would call it Canada. We do not. We call the little ten-miles square we have left the "Grand River Country." We have the right to do that. It is ours. We have the written pledge of George III that we should have it forever as against him or his successors and he promised to protect us in it. (Deskaheh. (1925) 2005. "The Last Speech of Deskaheh." in *Akwesasne Notes* 2005: 48)

The wampums were eventually returned to the Six Nations community but not without the newly elected system being the only recognized form of government for the people of Six Nations. Despite this, the Haudenosaunee Confederacy is still in formation today and continues its council meetings and other governance proceedings.

On 13 September 2007, over 80 years after Deskaheh's visit to Geneva, the United Nations announced its new international instrument after 25 years of deliberation: the **United Nations Declaration on the Rights of Indigenous Peoples** (UNDRIP). Four member nations voted "no" to this declaration (which was not legally binding): the United States, New Zealand, Australia, and Canada. UNDRIP included 46 articles, which addressed issues ranging from authority over economy and political practices to the rights to have access to traditional territories. These articles were anchored within the framework of self-determination and the rights of Indigenous peoples to determine for themselves how they would live. Self-determination, as Alfred (2005) points out, could be the best strategy for Indigenous peoples going forward in reclaiming their sovereignty. So how does UNDRIP's orientation toward self-determination advance this idea of sovereignty?

UNDRIP was received with both adulation and criticism by Indigenous peoples internationally. Some argued that UNDRIP was a landmark recognition for Indigenous peoples and could serve as a basis for more equitable policy-making in nation-states (Assembly of First Nations 2013). However, we know that UNDRIP was not legally binding and, therefore, could not compel nation-states who adopted it to enforce its recommendations. In terms of sovereignty, UNDRIP ultimately states this in the second-to-last article of the declaration (Article 46):

Nothing in this Declaration may be interpreted as implying for any State, people, group or person any right to engage in any activity or to perform any act contrary to the Charter of the United Nations or construed as authorizing or encouraging any action which would dismember or impair, totally or in part, the territorial integrity or political unity of sovereign and independent States. (United Nations 2008, 14)

UNDRIP, while recognizing the need for nation-states to adopt more equitable policies and support a self-determining process for Indigenous peoples, essentially barred any language around sovereignty, unless it applied to state sovereignty. And, in doing so, it protected the sovereignty of the state.

Interestingly enough, Canada's rationale for initially refusing to vote in favour of UNDRIP was that UNDRIP might act to undermine the special and many treaty relationships it has with Indigenous nations. In other words, an acknowledgment of a nation-to-nation relationship with Indigenous nations was cited as a reason to refuse UNDRIP, as it might intervene on previously negotiated sovereignty agreements—indeed this formal acknowledgement was a surprise to many Indigenous peoples.

Eventually, Canada did choose to adopt UNDRIP in 2010 because of international pressure following New Zealand's, Australia's, and the United States' reversal and subsequent endorsement. However, consciousness-building in Canada toward reconciliation was no doubt interrupted by this initial refusal to adopt UNDRIP, and it certainly damaged efforts at reconciliation, to say the very least. One could argue that while the spirit of recognition has improved at the United Nations since Deskaheh's travels, the practice of recognition remains largely the same. The Declaration was a proud moment for Indigenous peoples, both because we had the ear of the world in the celebration of unity and because of the fact that indeed we had not vanished but were powerful. It remains to be seen, however, almost a decade later, whether Canada will incorporate the articles outlined in UNDRIP and move toward more of a nation-to-nation relationship—one wherein each nation recognizes each other across the river.

Conclusion

A constructed narrative in Canada historically held Indigenous sovereignties as generally archaic and far less robust than European notions of what constitutes a nation-state. Yet the Canadian state's systemic attempts at disempowering these sovereign nations only reaffirm that Indigenous sovereignties were feared because of how powerfully they were expressed in Indigenous societies.

For Indigenous nations, sovereignty never left. For Canada, however, there remains only one supreme sovereignty. The reconciliation of these two contra-assertions continues to be fraught with complexities. We know that one sovereignty is much younger than the other, and necessitated the dispossession of Indigenous peoples and lands to achieve it. Yet we also know that Canada entered into a treaty-making process with Indigenous nations and that, whatever the intention, the process itself represented a constitutive reality for Canadian sovereignty.

So what is Indigenous sovereignty? It is something that is spiritual, place-based, sophisticated, historic, fought for, alive, and practised. It is also met with objection or distillation when proposed and organized within the Canadian body politic. Yet we know that just as Indigenous nations derive their sovereignty from place and from the spirit world, Canada derives its sovereignty from the existence of Indigenous nations. This demonstrates two crucial realities: (1) in order for Canadian sovereignty to be legitimate, the sovereignty of Indigenous nations must be empowered; and (2) Indigenous nations were not, and cannot be, conquered.

Review/Summary Questions

1. How have the principles of the *Kaswentha*, or Two Row Wampum, been demonstrated in the contemporary relationship between Indigenous peoples and the Canadian government? How have they not?
2. How can social theory contribute to Indigenous notions of sovereignty?
3. How is the *Kainere'ko:wa*, or Great Law, distinct from Canadian political values? How are the two similar?
4. How would describe your relationship to treaties?
5. Should the United Nations Declaration on the Rights of Indigenous Peoples have a place in the relationship between Canada and Indigenous nations? Why or why not?

Notes

1. "Turtle Island" refers to North America generally, and is used by many Indigenous peoples to refer to their homeland.
2. There are Haudenosaunee communities in both Canada and New York State, but most are concentrated in southern Ontario and upstate New York. There is one community where all six member nations live together: Six Nations of the Grand River in southern Ontario.
3. Refer to the Numbered Treaties in Canada for more information.

17 What Is Sovereignty in Quebec?

Philippe Couton

Introduction

There are three simple and divergent answers to the question asked in the title of this chapter. The first is provided by proponents of sovereignty who argue that Quebec has long suffered oppression at the hands of the British Empire and its successor state, Canada, and would be better off as an independent country. The conquest of 1760 and the subsequent repression of various uprisings; the ensuing political, economic, and cultural domination by anglophone elites (even within Quebec); and the ongoing lack of recognition of Quebec society's uniqueness all point toward the necessity of independence (Bourque 2001). The quest for sovereignty is furthermore described not just as a reaction to perceived humiliations but as the collective affirmation of Quebec's distinctive culture and identity (Beauchemin 2008). Second, opponents of sovereignty conversely describe what they often call "separatism" or "secession" as a product of narrow nationalism that seeks to protect and defend a particular ethnic group at the expense of both the larger Canadian society and minorities within Quebec. They further argue that sovereignty is democratically illegitimate, violates international law, and goes against the global trend toward greater diversity and pluralism (see Pratte 2008).

A third, less ideologically charged, answer that is often provided by social scientists points out that as a historically and culturally distinct community within the larger Canadian political entity, Quebec lacks what many other such communities in the world enjoy: full political control over its own destiny. The sovereignty movement seeks to obtain independence in order to achieve this control, to protect the distinctiveness of Quebec culture, and to pursue social and political objectives with tools that are currently in the hands of the federal government. This quest for independence simply follows a global process that has seen the world divided into more or less clearly defined cultural units (nations) endowed with their own sovereign political institutions (states). Where this process has not come to completion for historical reasons (conquest, colonialism, etc.) in many other parts of the world (Scotland and Kurdistan, for example), groups similarly seek to achieve sovereignty by either peaceful or violent means. Like these other communities, Quebec has developed into a thriving, unique society that now wishes to achieve the last stage of a fully mature social and political entity: independence (see Venne 2001; Cardinal and Papillon 2011).

All three answers contain elements of truth. Preference for one depends on a variety of personal, cultural, and intellectual factors. There is certainly no right or wrong answer since each reflects particular political inclinations not amenable to simple right/wrong determinations. In any case, the point of this chapter is not to lend support to any particular viewpoint but to help disentangle the assumptions that underlie all three answers and that often remain under-analyzed. Only once these considerations are better understood can a person make a fully informed, critically minded choice about Quebec sovereignty. To this effect, the rest of this chapter provides a discussion of the following key assumptions: the "naturalness" of political independence; the concept of nation; independence as the endpoint of an evolutionary process; nationalism as an ideology; and the idea of sovereignty itself.

(Un)Natural Independence

The first of these assumptions is the idea that the natural condition for any significant social group is political independence (synonymous with sovereignty). This is not always the case, although political independence remains a strong and durable aspect of modern social and political life throughout the world. A first argument against the presumed naturalness of independence is the clear lack of "fit" between state and nation, which is a near universal dimension of most of the countries existing in the world today. Few states can legitimately claim to be the home of a single, culturally homogeneous nation (Keating 2004). That is, few political entities (states) govern a single, culturally homogeneous population (a nation); conversely, a very large number of culturally distinct groups do not enjoy a state entirely of their own. Canada is certainly one of the best examples of this as a true **multinational state** and one of the most diverse places in the world (Laczko 2000).[1] Quebec itself is of course just as diverse, with large Aboriginal groups, linguistic minorities, and rising immigration levels. Even some of the oldest nation-states in the world are home to sizable, culturally distinct minority groups, including France, China, and many others.[2] And many of the oldest cultural groups in the world do not live in states of their own (nearly all Aboriginal peoples in the Americas, for instance). If language is one measure of the expression of a distinct culture, there are several thousand languages in the world today but only about 200 independent states.

The "naturalness" of the sovereign nation-state is therefore more myth than reality; moreover, it is a potentially dangerous myth at that. One of the legacies of Western political history is the notion that states should encourage cultural uniformity within their populations, and that they should mould the nations over which they rule in order to obtain a fit between state and nation. As Rae (2002) puts it, states are typically nation-forming states, and this process has very often been based—even before the advent of nationalism on a world scale—on **pathological homogenization**: the imposition of a single culture on the entire population. Quebec and other parts of Canada have periodically suffered from efforts at eradicating French as well as other non-English cultural traditions. The idea that most Western democracies have been and continue to be ethnically neutral (i.e., that they tend to not favour a particular ethnic group) is therefore simply untrue (Kymlicka 2000). All have promoted and continue to promote one culture (sometimes more) that is believed to be that of the nation the state governs. What nevertheless remains true is that a number of nation-states are home to several large cultural groups that coexist in relative harmony (Canada, Switzerland, and India are examples). Yet the norm remains that most nation-states tend to be the home of one dominant group, from which comes the notion that political independence is the natural condition of culturally distinct communities (Italy is for Italians, Brazil for Brazilians, etc.).

In the case of Quebec, the argument is easily extended to say that Quebec should become a "normal" country with the attributes of these other nation-states, although even strong proponents of Quebec sovereignty agree that Quebec has become less a single, homogeneous community and more a "community of national communities," as Bourque (2001) puts it. No proper attempt to understand Quebec sovereignty can therefore rely on the putative naturalness of political independence. Quebec is not exceptional in having to share sovereignty with a larger entity. Some fit between state and nation is common in most countries, which does lend some support to the assumption, but even that is changing as some of the discussion below shows. On the other hand, most other existing states have been relatively free to promote a specific culture (through educational, cultural, and other policies), and Quebec understandably also wants to have this de facto aspect of nation-states at its disposal.

What Is a Nation?

The concept of nation itself is the second assumption that needs to be analyzed in order to better understand Quebec sovereignty. If Quebec is to achieve independence in the name of the dominant nation that resides on its territory (Québécois, French-speaking Quebecers), what is this nation? Nations have attracted considerable attention from social scientists, historians, philosophers, and others, generating a large literature, including a number of classic works (e.g., Gellner 1997; Anderson 1991). There is little agreement on exactly how to define a nation, but major parameters of the discussion have emerged. First is the question of whether nations have always existed or are a fairly recent product of modern social life (often termed the constructionism/primordialism debate). A loose consensus has emerged that sees nations as we understand them—large communities, territorially bound, sharing a common language and culture—as historically fairly recent. France, for instance, although one of the oldest countries in the world, has only truly shared a common language for the past century or so, and parts of its territory were disputed even during the twentieth century.

Likewise, the current territory of Quebec was finalized only in the early twentieth century, and Aboriginals, who have national claims of their own, populate very large parts of it. People within Quebec have only been identifying themselves as members of the Quebec nation (Québécois) since the middle of the twentieth century. Prior to this point, the dominant identity was French-Canadian or simply Canadian. But this is not very different from what has happened elsewhere in the world. Before the development of mass public education, mass media, and other aspects of modernity, most countries were marked by a high level of linguistic and cultural diversity, and most still are. The transition to greater national homogeneity is facilitated by various administrative instruments, including censuses, representative politics, mass education, and so on (Anderson 1998, 43; Laczko 2000). The process of nation-making is not unproblematic, however. Some have described the process as the serialization or homogenization of individuals into largely constructed communities. Most national categories are, after all, the product of institutions and administrations. Quebec fits this general pattern and has only recently become a relatively unified society. Basing one's opposition to sovereignty on the recentness of Quebec nationhood is, therefore, not very helpful. Indeed, few nations have any solid claims to ancient histories as homogeneous cultural entities.

One thing is clear, however: despite their relative newness, nations are tremendously resilient. Several ideological currents of the past predicted that nations would disappear. Liberals were hoping that a global, peaceful culture would emerge, while Marxists thought that classes would replace nations as the predominant form of social and political identity. Currently, a number of commentators claim that globalization is eradicating national borders and that we are about to enter a post-national world (Cohen 1996). The reality is, however, that a number of "new" nations are emerging and a number of old ones are making new claims to autonomy. For instance, Aboriginal peoples in Canada—including in Quebec—and in other parts of the world are positioning themselves as nations and demanding some measure of self-determination. Another striking example of the resilience of ethno-national identity is its resurgence after the collapse of the Soviet Union in 1989 (Laitin 1998). Despite the best efforts of the regime to repress or remove national minority groups for over 70 years, they resurfaced and sought their independence in the wake of the disappearance of the Soviet Union. Quebec, in other words, is certainly not alone in wanting sovereignty as a nation, and there is little reason to believe that claim is irrelevant in today's world.

Evolution toward Independence?

A third and related dimension to be considered is whether or not societies, and Quebec in particular, follow a slow, evolutionary development that necessarily ends in political independence. As some of the above indicates, there is some truth to this view. The world seems to have evolved from fairly simple human groupings into large empires (Roman, Greek, then British, French, etc.), almost all of which eventually split into sovereign states, some very recently. This phenomenon would also address the issue raised above: if so many cultural and linguistic groups have not reached sovereignty, it is simply because they have not yet experienced the full evolutionary process that leads to sovereignty. In some cases, the process is still unfolding, and this could be the case in Quebec as well as in Scotland, Kurdistan, and many other nations.

The history of Quebec is well known and thus needs only to be briefly summarized here to further illustrate the point. (See Dickinson and Young 2000 for details.) Quebec emerged as Canada's second-largest and sole majority-francophone province over the past two-and-a-half centuries. Once a French colonial possession, what is now Quebec was conquered by the British in 1760. At that time, only about 60,000 French colonists lived in New France. Over the following decades, inflows of English-speaking immigrants from the newly independent United States and from the British Isles came to outnumber francophones in British North America. New provinces emerged east and west of Quebec, most of them almost entirely anglophone. But despite these forces (conquest, English-speaking immigration), Quebec managed to survive and indeed thrive under British institutions. By the early twentieth century, thanks to a high birth rate, Quebec was more than holding its own demographically. And thanks to strong institutions both religious (the Catholic Church) and secular (growing political institutions), Quebec managed to preserve its culture and identity. By the 1960s, Montreal was emerging as one of the world's great cities (with the consecration of Expo 67 and later the 1976 Olympic Games), and Quebec was undergoing massive social and political change: the role of the church was declining, while the provincial government was taking a more active role in a number of areas, including education, culture, health care, and so on. During this period, political parties promoting Quebec independence emerged and were successful at the polls. The logical outcome of this long history might seem to be some form of independence for Quebec, just as other countries have formed and developed elsewhere in the world, building their institutions, creating a unique culture, and achieving full independence. Quebec is in many ways in a similar position: long included in the British Empire, then in Canada, it has been attempting to evolve into a fully independent nation-state.

But leaving the argument at this level would miss several important points. First, the idea that Quebec should become an independent country is not new. Jules-Paul Tardivel, for instance, was an early proponent of Quebec independence. His 1895 novel *Pour la Patrie* summarized his political position, which failed to generate much support during his lifetime. Nationalists of various stripes have argued and struggled for independence over the past two centuries. For example, Lord Durham's infamous 1839 report aptly summarized the situation as "[t]wo nations warring in the bosom of a single state." However, the debate about the difference between sovereignty and federalism was not always as stark as it is today. Indeed, a number of early French-Canadian nationalists were also staunch federalists. Earlier versions of Quebec nationalism included the work produced during the interwar period by Lionel Groulx, whose organic, traditional view of the nation was decidedly anti-liberal (Boily 2004). The notion of sovereignty did not become a central aspect of Quebec and by extension Canadian politics until the 1960s, culminating in the first referendum on sovereignty in 1980. It was only during that period that the Quebec provincial government slowly constructed a large bureaucracy able to challenge some of the power of the federal government, particularly during the 1960s and 1970s, a period known as the **Quiet Revolution**. In this sense, however, the Quebec nation is actually the product of Canadian **federalism**, forcing a large number of Canada's francophones to identify with the Quebec territory and later with its institutions (Bourque 2001). Yet this might still seem to support the evolutionary view of Quebec sovereignty: only once its institutions were fully developed did the population of Quebec express strong support for independence.

There are, however, other explanations for the timing of the rise of the sovereignty movement. One is the influence of global anti-colonial struggles; French-Canadian nationalism was reinterpreted through this prism during the 1950s and 1960s. French-speaking Canadians had long struggled for some measure of self-determination and against Anglo domination (from the uprising of the late 1830s to resistance to conscription during the two world wars), but only in the second half of the twentieth century did this struggle become a full-fledged independent movement centred on Quebec. This new dimension of the fight drew direct inspiration from similar struggles in Algeria, Vietnam, and Cuba, among others. A second explanation is simply the emergence of a new class of politicians and public servants who had a significant stake in the developing Quebec institutions. This class formed the backbone of the sovereigntist movement.

Another, more clearly supported explanation points to the tremendous influence of political events on the sovereignty movement, especially during the period that followed the first referendum. Quebec's position within Canada has been ambiguous and hybrid for at least 50 years: neither sovereign nor completely integrated (Laforest 2001, 299). But the recent nationalist movement has been particularly affected by the patriation of the Constitution in 1982 and by the events that followed it. In brief, for historical reasons the process of amending the 1867 Constitution of Canada had been left in the hands of the British government. Prime Minister Pierre Trudeau decided to "patriate" the Constitution, meaning to bring full control over the constitution from the UK to Canada. At the same time, Trudeau decided to add a Charter of Rights and Freedoms to it and to provide for court-based enforcement of its provisions. This proved to be a divisive process, and Quebec felt cheated both by the way it unfolded and by the substance of the Charter, which failed to clearly recognize that Canada consisted of two founding societies. Two agreements were subsequently attempted, the Meech Lake (1990) and Charlottetown (1992) accords, both of which failed, only adding fuel to the fire. To this day, a number of politicians and commentators feel that the entire process was illegitimate, possibly in breach of legal principles, and that the basic principle on which Canada had been founded was broken (Laforest 2001). The Charter was perceived to be a centralizing document that recognized a range of individual and collective rights but distinctly failed to recognize Quebec as such. It was seen as undermining provincial autonomy and weakening the ability of Quebec to be a nation (Kymlicka 1998). One of the consequences of this protracted process was dramatically increased support for sovereignty in Quebec, leading to the election of a Parti Québécois government in Quebec in 1994, a strong showing by the Bloc Québécois in federal elections, and near victory for the "yes" side in the 1995 referendum.

The role of this divisive political process confirms that support for sovereignty does not follow a steady evolutionary path but is strongly influenced by political events. A large proportion of Quebecers, sovereigntists and federalists alike, were angered by the constitutional process and further inflamed by the bungled agreements. Support for sovereignty receded significantly in later years to the point that, in the 2003 election, the Parti Québécois (PQ) lost the province to the Liberals, who remained in power in the next two elections in 2007 and 2008. The PQ briefly returned to power in 2012 but lost the 2014 election after a failed and highly divisive attempt to pass a **Charter of Values**, broadly viewed as targeting Muslim immigrants. The Bloc Québécois, the federal-level pro-sovereignty political party, continued to enjoy strong electoral support after its first sweeping victory in 1993, until its surprising near-total collapse in the 2011 election. This would tend to confirm that although there might be an evolutionary component to sovereignty (the development of institutions, etc.), the way the issue is handled at the political level continues to matter a great deal. Quebecers regularly support some form of independence when federal politics seem to short-change them, but are quick to turn away from versions of nationalism perceived as exclusionary (like the ill-fated Charter of Values).

Is Nationalism an Ideology?

The fourth key assumption of the sovereignty question is the circumstances under which nations emerge and the claims that are most commonly made in their name. In other words, what is the nature of nationalism, and how does this apply to Quebec? Historians have long pointed out that nations are a product of the rise of democratic ideals. Nations are in that sense very similar to the "people" that putatively govern in a democracy. The beginning of democracy, in revolutions and reform movements in Europe and North America, occurred in the name of the people or the nation in opposition to the ruling class (see Hobsbawm 1992). It is only fairly recently that nationalism has become associated with destructive and politically extreme political ideologies and movements (e.g., Nazism, as well as the wars that ravaged parts of the former communist Europe in the 1990s). No single ideology is clearly and uniquely associated with nationalism, which has been a force of both emancipation and oppression—even genocide—in recent history. Simply equating the quest for national independence with narrow tribalism or claiming it is purely a liberation movement is therefore inaccurate. Just as elsewhere in the world, the movement for Quebec sovereignty has had its share of extremists (but far fewer than in, for example, Ireland; see Cormier and Couton 2004), although the Quebec movement has been thoroughly democratic and peaceful in recent decades.

A related and important aspect of the question is usually presented as a tension between liberal individualism and communitarianism—or, to put it differently, between the idea that the ultimate source of freedom and autonomy resides in the individual and the opposite notion that it is found in the community. This issue emerges in a number of debates, not only about Quebec sovereignty but about the rights and objectives of a range of minority communities the world over (e.g., similar national minorities in Belgium, Spain, Indonesia, and parts of Africa; immigrant groups in many Western countries; Aboriginal communities in former European colonies). Debates on the issue tend to present most nationalist movements as primarily communitarian and thus as posing a threat to the core value of Western democracies: that is, individual liberty. However, this is usually not the case and clearly not as far as Quebec is concerned (see Kymlicka 1998, 2000). There is no evidence to indicate that Quebec's aspiration to sovereignty is based on a stronger commitment to collective values than to individual autonomy. In fact, substantial evidence indicates that Quebecers tend to be more liberal and individualistic in their attitudes and behaviour than English-speaking Canadians—for example, in terms of respect for traditional institutions, such as marriage and religion. Sovereigntist parties and individuals have embraced many of these liberal attitudes. On the other hand, there is also some evidence that Quebecers are more attached to their collective culture (with higher rates of domestic cultural consumption, for instance). It would therefore be inaccurate to characterize the Quebec sovereignty movement as ideologically homogeneous and either liberal or authoritarian. Like most other political movements, it contains several often contradictory trends and tensions.

Photos.com/Thinkstock.com

Quebec citizens celebrate Saint Jean Baptiste Day in Montreal. Is the Quebec aspiration to sovereignty based on collective values or on individual autonomy? Can it be characterized as one or the other?

Sovereignty to Post-Sovereignty

The final issue that needs to be fully unpacked in order to better understand the question of Quebec's independence is the concept of sovereignty itself. We have just read that nations, nation-states, and nationalism are neither easily defined nor understood. This is also the case with sovereignty. On the one hand, it is a key feature of the world today. We take it so much for granted that we rarely stop to think about it: the world is divided into a finite number of sovereign, independent countries over which no greater power exists. But this too is undergoing profound changes. The trend toward **post-sovereignty**—that is, toward forms of governance that do not rely exclusively on the traditional statehood—is only in its infancy, but it is slowly unfolding (Keating 2004). Indeed, a range of processes is challenging the traditional understanding of sovereignty, including international organizations. The European Union, for instance, is weakening the traditional power of the individual state to the point where a number of movements in Europe are mobilizing around a more regionalist perspective than around simple nationhood (Keating 2004). In other words, what is happening in Europe is a slow but profound reshaping of the nature and location of political authority. This is also happening on a more modest scale in North America, where part of the sovereign authority of states has been delegated to the institutions of the North American Free Trade Agreement (NAFTA). Quebec, in fact, has confirmed several times that it intends to remain in NAFTA in the event that it achieves sovereignty. Some have even argued that NAFTA may actually facilitate the transition to sovereignty by providing a level of political and economic stability above and beyond Canada.

Other processes are challenging the traditional sovereignty of states as well, including multinational corporations, transnational actors (immigrant groups, for instance), and global technological changes. (States can do little to stop the flow of information.) In a number of countries, including Canada, competing groups and institutions dispute sovereignty. Quebec is the most significant contender in Canada, but First Nations come a close second, with a number of less important groups making occasional claims (proponents of Western Canadian separatism, for instance).

The most provocative conclusion of this line of reasoning is that state sovereignty no longer really matters. Whether or not Quebec achieves sovereignty will not change many of the processes mentioned above. Quebec will still be part of global networks of trade, migration, and information flows, just as Canada minus Quebec will remain connected to them. Yet this too would be an exaggeration. Both the federal and provincial governments in Canada have tremendous powers and responsibilities as yet unequalled by non-state actors. In fact, many see the state as the last barrier against the homogenizing forces of globalization, and some argue that Quebec would be better able to be a successful member of a globalizing world as a sovereign nation-state (see Venne 2001). Others point out that remaining in a larger multinational entity is the best way for Quebec, and for francophones throughout Canada, to stave off the threat of globalization (Pratte 2008).

Conclusion

How does the foregoing discussion help to answer the question contained in the title of this chapter? Quebec's quest for sovereignty remains high on the list of critical, unresolved issues facing Canada. After two referendums—1980 and 1995—and several decades of active political mobilization, including electoral victories by nationalist parties both provincially and federally, the question of Quebec sovereignty remains unresolved. The choice is largely, but not solely, in the hands of Quebecers. What matters most is that we understand all the issues at stake and how best to address them.

First, it is clear that portraying Quebec sovereignty and its associated movement and ideas as simplistic oppositions (nationalism against pluralism, etc.) is at best unhelpful and at worst politically dangerous. The movement is obviously part of a much greater global story in which nation-states have emerged as the basic unit of political reference. But there is nothing inevitable about that story in the world in general, as the trend toward post-nationalism and post-sovereignty illustrates, or in Quebec, as the ebb and flow of the sovereignty movement confirms. A range of historical administrative and political factors has influenced the sovereignty movement. It cannot merely be characterized as a simple yearning for national homogeneity or in opposition to federalism or diversity. Nor is it simply a liberation movement: by most measures, Quebecers enjoy very similar social and political conditions as in the rest of Canada and do not suffer from any significant level of oppression.

And Quebec itself is changing rapidly. The province is becoming increasingly diverse, although it has always maintained a conflicted relationship with immigration and cultural diversity. Immigrants have historically gravitated toward English North American culture, leaving many in Quebec unsure about the consequences of immigration (as the recent debate on reasonable accommodations illustrated; see Bouchard and Taylor 2008)—to the point that some have accused governmental institutions of fostering the subordination of immigrant communities in the name of maintaining a fictitious national unity (Fontaine 1993). This accusation does not entirely reflect Quebec's recent success in the field of immigration. The province has secured nearly full control over immigration from the federal government and has been attracting more and more francophone newcomers. In 2009, for example, over 60 per cent of immigrants to Quebec spoke some French, more than double the 1980 proportion (Institut de la Statistique du Québec 2010). Partly as a result, Quebec culture is becoming increasingly diverse—to the point that an important intellectual current within Quebec literature and social sciences identifies Quebec as a "new world" society, more influenced by North American than by European cultural practices (Theriault 2002). Similarly, others have pointed out that Quebec culture is moving away from a sharp distinction between nationalism and cosmopolitanism, finding instead a more complex mode of belonging somewhere in between (Maclure 2003). The strong attachment of most Quebecers to their culture is beyond doubt. But it is also clear that today, as well as in the past, sovereignty is viewed as only one of the many options available to ensure the development of this culture.

The debate over Quebec sovereignty may take several routes in years and decades to come. Some have argued that a gradual evolution is unfolding, particularly in Europe, away from locating political authority simply at the level of the national state, and that a kind of "third way" of handling the desire for national sovereignty is emerging (Keating 2004). Quebec may very well embrace this new trend and become one of the many places in the world that sit somewhere between traditional sovereignty and its current, already hybrid status. Canada may also follow a similar route, further sharing its sovereignty with multinational institutions and sub-state communities (Aboriginals, provinces other than Quebec, etc.). In that sense, both Quebec and Canada may follow what some have identified as two contradictory global trends: one toward increasing pluralism and multiplicity and one toward "unmixing" and consolidation (Cornell and Hartmann 1998). On the one hand, migration and ethno-cultural diversity is on the rise in much of the world, but on the other hand, nationalist movements seeking independence from larger political units have also dramatically strengthened (e.g., in Quebec, but also in Eastern Europe, parts of Asia, etc.). How these forces will play out to decide the future of Quebec and Canada is for history one day to decide.

Review/Summary Questions

1. Why does a significant part of Quebec's population want political independence?
2. Is Quebec already sovereign?
3. Should all nations have the right to become sovereign?
4. Is a nation necessarily a sovereign nation?
5. Is Canada a sovereign nation?

Notes

1. Canada received about 250,000 immigrants in 2013, the majority from Asia. See Canada, Citizenship and Immigration (2014) for details.
2. A few exceptions exist, notably Japan.

18 Is There Justice for Young People?

Bryan Hogeveen

Introduction

Is there justice for youth? This chapter confronts the regrettable conditions many youth face in Canada—especially those from the most disadvantaged backgrounds—and reaches the conclusion that there is little in the way of justice for them. First, I explore differing conceptions of justice in a section that underscores the (dis)connection between rights and justice. Next, I highlight three particularly lamentable instances of injustice experienced by young persons—child poverty, racism confronting Aboriginal youth, and the dislocation of girls under law. The final section examines the silencing of young people in Western society and urges us to listen to youthful voices.

What Is Justice?

Ours is an era in which war, prison overcrowding, genocide, ethnic cleansing, and vigilantism are all too often rationalized in the name of justice. But what, exactly, is **justice**? A significant problem in answering this question centres on the fundamental ambiguity of the word *justice* itself. It can refer to the bureaucratic structure for administering the legal process. Canada boasts a federal Department of Justice, which embodies and reflects this convention. It can be used in law and legislation to imply the impartiality of the system (e.g., the **Youth Criminal Justice Act** [YCJA]). Moreover, *justice* suggests a connection with law-and-order campaigns in which victims declare that they are owed **retribution** for pain suffered. In this context, "justice being done" means an ethic of punishment that delivers obvious signs of unpleasantness to offenders. This kind of justice can also reflect the public's desire to amend law, often in relation to existing but flawed legislation that seemingly promotes injustice. Until 2003, when the YCJA became law, Canadian youth were governed under the **Young Offenders Act**

(YOA). Throughout the period leading up to legislative change, the YOA was consistently hailed as inequitable for not sufficiently taking into account the victims of juvenile deviance. Newspaper headlines suggested that federal young offender legislation was to blame for victimization and that tougher legislation would prevent the harm done to the injured (Hogeveen 2005).

For many, justice is intimately connected with inalienable and omnipresent rights enshrined under legislation. For example, the **Charter of Rights and Freedoms** (Canada 1982) guarantees Canadian citizens and permanent residents the following rights and freedoms: freedom of conscience and religion; freedom of thought, belief, and expression; freedom of association; the right to vote; and the right to life, liberty, and security of person. Nevertheless, until very recently youth did not enjoy access to these guarantees in the same way that adults did. The movement toward assigning rights to children went through three fundamental stages. It passed from (1) a laissez-faire philosophy in which children were considered parental property, to (2) a humanitarian and sentimental rationale of children as a separate class of partially formed individuals, to (3) the current discourse of children as people entitled to individual rights (Covell and Howe 2001).

A turning point in rights allocation for youth occurred on 20 November 1989, when the United Nations Convention on the Rights of the Child was unanimously adopted. A convention is an expression not only of a moral stand but "also of a legal agreement and international obligation" (Covell and Howe 2001, 20). In 1991, Canada ratified the convention, which comprises 41 articles divided into two broad categories:

1. Civil and political rights, which include the right to self-determination and protection from arbitrary arrest
2. Economic, social, and cultural rights, which include the right to health care and education and freedom of religion

According to Hammarberg (1990), human rights and protections set out by the Convention can usefully be divided into three broad groups, often referred to as the "three Ps":

1. *Provision*: Rights of provision imply that youth must be afforded basic welfare, which includes the right to survival and development, education, and to be cared for by parents.
2. *Protection*: Articles under the protection rubric ensure that children are sheltered from abuse, economic exploitation, discrimination, and neglect.
3. *Participation*: Youth are also accorded the right to participation, which involves freedom of speech, freedom of religion, and the right of expression (Denov 2004).

Despite Canada's agreement to abide by the convention's conditions, substantial gaps remain between the state's promise and reality. One of the greatest concerns for youth advocates is the general lack of awareness among young people about the Convention and the rights they are guaranteed. A study of high school students by Peterson-Badali and Abramovich (1992) found that very few youth could identify the most basic legal principles, such as the youth court's age jurisdiction (12–17). Moreover, when asked with whom their lawyer could share privileged information, many young people were certain that their legal representative was obliged to inform their parents and the judge what they revealed in confidence (Feld 2000; Doob and Cesaroni 2004). To what extent are rights meaningful if young people are unaware of their implications and how they are exercised?

Equating rights with justice is spurious at best. Rights conventions are of little utility when their intricacies are not widely known, understood, or distributed. They tend to float above relationships among individuals and provide little guidance on the ethical responsibility of one person to another. Rights discourses provide very little direction to those addressing inequality and subjugation in an unjust society. Rights and social goods are not equally distributed throughout the Canadian population. Socio-economic status and **class** play a significant role: people on the margins are grossly overrepresented in poverty and incarceration rates. Is this a just state of affairs? If working-class and minority youth have become the foremost clients of coercive state services and, at the same time, experience higher rates of poverty, it is not as a result of some innate propensity toward crime and unemployment. Rather, it is because they are trapped at the intersection of three transformations distinct to the **neo-liberal** organization of society that have targeted the visibly different and the socially marginal: (1) economic globalization, (2) the dismantling of the **social welfare** net, and (3) the intensification of penal strategies. These have all contributed to greater inequality and unequal distribution of scarce societal resources in favour of the affluent (Wacquant 2001). During the late 1990s, to paraphrase the title of Jeffrey Reiman's (1979) seminal work, the rich were getting richer while the poor were receiving prison. If the goal of justice is to ensure equal distribution of resources and goods to societal members, it would appear that Canada is moving in a most peculiar direction, especially as the situation pertains to young people.

Justice and the Poor?

Child **poverty** continues to rise as the gulf between the rich and the poor widens (Canadian Council on Social Development 2010). Apart from Germany, Canada leads the way among Organisation for Economic Co-operation and Development (OECD) countries in measures of income inequality (Organisation for Economic Co-operation and Development 2008). While the rich continue to benefit and grow their personal wealth, the marginalized and impoverished see social assistance subsidies slashed and real incomes erode. Between 1986 and 1996, as measured in constant dollars, Alberta welfare benefits for a single individual deemed employable were slashed by 42.5 per cent, while single parents with a child saw their benefits eroded by 23.6 per cent (Canadian Council on Social Development 2004).

As poverty rates have continued to climb, the net traditionally put in place to soften the impact has been stripped away. Even the benefits available to ameliorate the conditions of the most vulnerable—Canada's children—are currently being clawed back by the state. For example, the National Child Benefit provides families with annual incomes of less than $22,615 with $126 per month for the first child and decreasing amounts for subsequent children. However, under a scheme initiated by the federal government, only working families are now allowed to keep the money while those most in need—individuals on social assistance and disability pensions—are denied support payments altogether (Della-Mattia 2004). Compare this with the almost $43 million per year that the Alberta government doled out to subsidize the local horse-racing industry (Markusoff 2007). A growing group of destitute individuals, who require the greatest assistance, are having to scrounge for the crumbs that remain after services that the government deems more important get their cut.

Youth are hit the hardest by these changes. In 2010 the Canadian Council on Social Development (2010) reported that almost 10 per cent of children under the age of six lived in low-income families, and, despite early signs of economic recovery, food bank usage has continued to climb (children and youth under 18 comprised 43 per cent of food bank clients [Food Banks Canada 2010]). The council's 2003 report, *Campaign 2000: Report Card on Child Poverty in Canada* (Canadian Council on Social Development 2003a), provided convincing evidence that over a million children in this country live in poverty. These figures establish that more children are poor than in 1989, when Parliament unanimously pledged to eradicate child poverty by the year 2000. Poverty, however, is not an equal opportunity oppressor. In 2010, the Council presented evidence that marginalized populations (i.e., children of recent immigrants and **Aboriginal** peoples) and children in lone female–parented households are at the greatest risk of experiencing poverty (Canadian Council on Social Development 2010). The Council's 2010 report also confirmed that young people are overrepresented among Canadian food bank users and that Canada ranks poorly on infant mortality rates among OECD nations (Canadian Council on Social Development 2010). Despite persistent need, governments have been reticent to loosen budgetary purse strings to ameliorate adversity and hardship brought about by systemic poverty and the onset of the most recent fiscal crisis.

To manage the excesses of, and fallout from, the current economic climate, state officials have resorted to pruning child welfare budgets and cutting jobs—a far cry from extending social welfare assistance to needy parents. The Children's Aid Society (CAS) of Halifax, for example, was forced in 2002 to cut a million dollars from its budget over a mere six months (Mills 2002). Funding cuts of this magnitude have serious and often severe implications because child welfare workers become overextended and managers feel pressure to reduce spending. In this desperate environment, youth in need have routinely been denied essential helping services, such as treatment sessions and educational programs. For example, after the provincial government cut $1.1 million in funding, the British

Columbia Ministry of Children and Family Development axed school meal programs, early academic intervention, and school-based support workers for inner-city schools (Douglas 2002).

In such an overburdened system, children are being placed in foster homes that meet only minimal standards. Bob Rechner, child advocate for Alberta, stated that "when funding for foster homes and resources are tight, it's not surprising standards may not be strictly adhered to. There are many great foster homes in this province. Unfortunately, there are some retained as foster homes that probably shouldn't be, but there aren't alternatives" (Johnsrude 1999). The solution to this problem offered by Manitoba's Child and Family Services is particularly deplorable. Confronted by a lack of adequate foster homes and insufficient funding, child welfare officials rented a floor in a hotel to house youth awaiting placement. A single, barely qualified staff member who entertained his or her charges with television, supervised them. For some youth, this was their home for more than a year. The most vulnerable children in Canadian society, therefore, appear to be short-changed and denied essential services as a result of shrunken social welfare spending (Blackstock 2003). It should come as no surprise that many of these youth become inmates in Canadian penitentiaries.

While Canadians favoured tax breaks for corporations and the richest segments of society, they campaigned at the same time for increased rates of incarceration for young people—the most costly (both economically and socially) mode of penalty (Hogeveen 2005). This situation is particularly troubling when we consider that a great number of young people are incarcerated for relatively minor forms of deviance. Throughout the 1990s, a great number of inmates were sentenced to prison for such "heinous" breaches of public order as failure to comply with court orders and property-related crimes (Hogeveen 2005).

More troubling still is that individuals warehoused in Canada's centres of detention are almost exclusively from the most marginal classes. Instead of distributing welfare benefits to the poor and destitute, Canadians have placed this class under the authority of the criminal justice system. While social welfare schemes were shrinking, programs that coercively targeted the poor were expanding. Consider the amount of relief that could be administered for the resources devoted to incarcerating excessive numbers of young people. Reflect on how much tuition could be paid with the $50,000 to $100,000 required to detain one young person for a year. Indeed, set against the backdrop of the type of crimes for which these youth are being detained, this expenditure seems extreme. Throughout the 1990s, when the tendency to lock up juvenile offenders was at its peak, so too was the erosion of welfare. One could interpret this as an indication that a new control regime was emerging for marginal and destitute youth, characterized by eroding social programs and a greater emphasis on punitive justice practices.

In effect, centres of detention had become the social service to which the poor and oppressed had the readiest access. With the rising cost of post-secondary education and toughening criteria for welfare eligibility, the criminal justice system might be the state service most available to the subjugated and marginalized.

Canada seemed to have embarked on a path toward managing youth poverty and inequality through an integrated control complex. The system was no longer asked only to deter and punish crime; it would now regulate the lower segments of the social order and defend against the discardable, derelict, and superfluous (Bauman 2011; Wacquant 1999).

Justice and Indigenous Youth?

Throughout history, Aboriginal peoples have been subjected to intrusive and invasive modes of state-level control aimed at reform, assimilation, and sub-jugation (Anderson 1999; Hogeveen 1999; see also Chapter 16). Wherever the Euro-Canadian state encountered Indigenous people, the Native land was quick-ly vacated to make way for white settlement and capitalist expansion. Among the tools of Anglo **colonialism** employed to regulate and shore up the Anglo vision of the country's founders were the North-West Mounted Police (forerun-ner of the Royal Canadian Mounted Police [RCMP]), laws, reserves, children's forced adoption by white families, and residential schooling. With the closure of residential schools and with many Indigenous peoples now living off reserves, institutions of detention are now on the front lines when it comes to controlling the Indigenous "other."

Government reports and investigations consistently point to a gross over-representation of Aboriginal adolescents at the most punitive end of the system (Royal Commission on Aboriginal Peoples 1993; 1996). (See Figure 18.1.) Peter Carrington and Jennifer Schulenberg (2004) suggest that Indigenous adolescents are 20 per cent more likely to be charged when apprehended than non-Aboriginal youth. Moreover, Aboriginal youth are more likely to be denied bail, to spend more time in pre-trial detention, and to be charged with multiple offences (often for administrative violations) (Roberts and Melchers 2003; Statistics Can-ada 2000). While Aboriginal youth accounted for 5 per cent of the total youth population in 1999, they occupied 24 per cent of the beds in Canadian detention centres. More tragic is the situation confronting Indigenous youth in Canada's Prairie provinces. In Saskatchewan and Manitoba, three-quarters (75 per cent for Manitoba and 74 per cent for Saskatchewan) of youth sentenced to custody were identified as Aboriginal, while less than 10 per cent of Manitoba's youth popu-lation is Aboriginal (Statistics Canada 2000). No group has been more touched by Canada's appetite for youth incarceration than the First Nations. A Canadian Bar Association report suitably titled "Locking Up Natives in Canada" provided evidence that a 16-year-old Aboriginal male had a 70 per cent chance of serving at least one prison stint before turning 25. The report further states that "Pris-on has become, for young Native men, the promise of a just society which high school and college represents for the rest of us" (Jackson 1989, 216). Situated in the context of the racist practices and policies of the Canadian state, centres of detention are the "contemporary equivalent of what the Indian residential school represented for their parents" (Jackson 1989, 216).

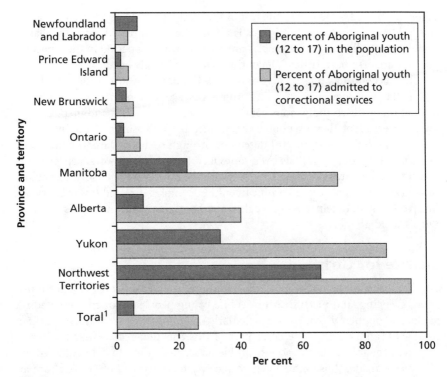

Figure 18.1 Aboriginal Youth Admissions to Correctional Services, by Province and Territory, 2010/2011

Source: Statistics Canada, Canadian Centre for Justice Statistics, Youth Custody and Community Services Survey.

Buttressing this systematic subjugation of those considered alien to the national body is the coincident dismantling of welfare programs during a period of intensified poverty among Indigenous peoples—especially children. Not only are Aboriginal people highly overrepresented among the street population, they are more likely than the general Canadian population to be living in urban poverty and inhabiting living quarters deemed overcrowded (Canadian Council on Social Development 2003b). According to Aboriginal activist Cindy Blackstock (2003), Canada's Indigenous peoples would rank seventy-eighth on the United Nations' Human Development Index (HDI)—which measures poverty, literacy, education, and life expectancy. Canada itself consistently ranks first. The HDI, developed by Pakistani economist Mahbub ul Haq, has become the standard means of measuring overall well-being, and especially child welfare, through three basic categories:

1. Long and healthy life, as indicated by life expectancy at birth
2. Knowledge, as measured by adult literacy rate
3. Standard of living, as derived from gross domestic product per capita

When compared to people in the rest of the world, Canadians are well situated. But hidden among facts and figures is a long silent, oppressed, and subjugated population. Colonialism, it seems, is not an embarrassing period in the long-forgotten Canadian past. Instead, it continues to rear its ugly head.

This section has offered a glimpse into the brand of justice that the Canadian state considers First Nations groups deserve. Colonialism has produced a situation in which Indigenous youth are subjected to **racism** and inequality at almost every turn. They are poor, hungry, excluded, and criminalized. Instead of responding to these disgraceful outcomes through social welfare, the incarceration/punitive continuum has been mobilized to regulate its worst aspects. The upsizing of the state's penal sector along with the downsizing of its social welfare institutions have constituted an incarceration complex directed toward surveilling, training, and neutralizing recalcitrant Aboriginal youth who exist outside Euro-Canadian mores.

Justice for Girls?

Youth, especially the poorest and most marginalized, face pervasive discrimination, silencing, and **victimization**. While young people are often presented in media and popular discourse as particularly troubling, they are at the same time troubled (Tanner 1996). The latter part of this equation receives far less scrutiny than the former but is no less problematic. According to data gathered by Statistics Canada, those most likely to receive the sharp end of "justice" are at the same time the most vulnerable to crime as well as to social and economic subordination and are thus most in need of protection. Youth are highly overrepresented as victims of crime. In 2009, youth between 15 and 24 were "15 times more likely than those aged 65 and older to report being a victim of a violent victimization" (Perrault and Brennan 2010). The same study revealed that girls were overrepresented as victims of violent crime, especially sexual deviance (Perrault and Brennan 2010).

Throughout history, the youth justice system has tended to neglect girls both as victims and as offenders. This is not surprising given that young girls have been highly underrepresented in crime statistics. Early criminologists and youth justice officials used this underrepresentation to bolster the view that wayward girls must somehow be defective. Discourses around female deviance embedded in traditional criminology illustrate this tendency. The founders of criminology, such as Cesare Beccaria in 1778, Charles Hooton in 1939, and Otto Pollak in 1950, portrayed female offenders as a defective lot, the product of inferior breeding as well as biological and anatomical inferiority (Snider 2004). By the turn of the nineteenth century, offenders were considered mentally weak, but following the logic set out above, female "deviants" were "more terrible than any man" in that they were "less intelligent, more passive, more deficient in moral sense, but stronger in sexual instincts" (Snider 2004, 232). Flowing out of this discourse were "capricious and arbitrary status" offences—a category of offences that applies solely to youth, which if committed by an adult would not result in arrest (i.e., drinking, incorrigibility, truancy, and curfew violations)—that aimed to control female sexuality by incarcerating those who flouted norms of **emphasized femininity**, which stressed the importance of piety, domesticity, and above all monogamous heterosexual marriage (Snider 2003).

Juvenile court officials cast a wide net over what they deemed "sexuality." Girls did not have to be caught in the act to be admonished by state actors. Franca Iacovetta (1999) charged that parents often brought their girls to the attention of police on the basis of neighbourhood gossip. Indeed, the mere suggestion of sexual activity could initiate state proceedings against young girls. Throughout the late nineteenth and early twentieth centuries, girls were routinely incarcerated for such aberrant conduct as holding hands with boys or being out after dark in the wrong part of town in the company of a male companion.

Not only was girls' sexuality policed through juvenile court and industrial school intervention, race relations were also governed through state-sponsored intrusion. A familiar refrain from white Anglo-Celtic elites who dominated social, economic, and political life during the early twentieth century was that "the nation" was in danger of decline (Valverde 1991). In the eyes of many, "nation" was a generic term that referred to those of Anglo descent while racialized "others" were viewed with increasing suspicion. By the 1910s, a widely accepted racial hierarchy was firmly established in Canada. This ordering was not solely structured by skin colour but also by degrees of whiteness. The mostly British upper-middle-class professionals who spearheaded **eugenics** constituted themselves and "the nation" in opposition to immigrants from other cultures. Anglo-Celtic elites, bolstered by eugenics discourse, created a purportedly common-sense racial logic that associated whiteness with the "clean and the good, the pure and the pleasing" (Jackson 2000; Roediger 1991; Morrison 1992). It followed, then, that "white" girls found associating with boys considered "other" required training and reformation for the good of "the nation."

Such was the case in 1939 when Velma Demerson's father, with police in tow, stormed into the apartment she shared with her Chinese lover. The officers arrested her under the 1897 Female Refugees Act, which allowed for the indefinite detention of girls and women between 15 and 35 suspected of drunkenness, promiscuity, and pregnancy outside of monogamous union. Velma was 18, pregnant, and in love. Pregnancy before marriage was one thing: that her boyfriend was not white was quite another and a source of embarrassment to her father. Velma was sent to Belmont House—a female house of refuge—for being promiscuous, for being illegitimately pregnant, and for consorting with a Chinese man. There she spent six weeks working in the laundry before being transferred to the Mercer Reformatory. For her "crimes" she was detained in a seven-by-four-foot cell with bars on the door to prevent her escape. Demerson gave birth to her son inside the institution, with neither her parents nor her partner at her side. Soon after his birth, her son was taken away. Women like Velma suffered tremendously within institutional walls without having committed any crime. In recent years, Demerson has sued and demanded an apology for her suffering from the Canadian government. She has received the latter but still awaits financial compensation (Demerson 2004).

Injustices experienced by girls and young women continue under contemporary youth justice regimes, in part because they remain "too few to count" within the youth justice system (Adelberg and Currie 1987). Despite some modest increase in numbers, female young offenders constitute one-fifth of all cases appearing in youth court. Their infrequent appearances before magistrates and in centres of detention helps to explain why relatively few youth justice resources are set aside for female offenders—it does not, however, excuse it. This condition is felt throughout the youth justice process as more and more female youth are subjected to institutional arrangements, risk assessment, and programming designed by men on the basis of boys' experiences. Given that theoretical foundations have been developed out of male experiences, females are excluded as subjects of knowledge and authorized knowers. The implications are profound. Existing theories of crime and deviance predict the greatest deviance by the most marginalized, alienated, and devalued by society. However, this condition applies to women much more than it does to men. Yet despite being devalued and alienated, girls do not commit crime at anywhere near the rate of boys (Reitsma-Street 1999). Thus, it would be useful if theoretical interpretations of juvenile criminality and the programming that flows from it reflected girls' experiences. However, that has not been the case.

Voices of Youth?

Canadian institutions function to censor youth and fix them in a subordinate position. No one has to state overtly that youthful voices are deemed less intelligent, barely cogent, and inferior to adults; it is simply understood. Indeed, pervasive discourses such as "children should be seen and not heard" function to entrench the view that youth are somehow less than and "other" to adults. However, this discourse is anchored in much more tacit ways. The fact that youth are not given the right to vote until they reach their eighteenth birthday speaks volumes about their silence (Mathews 2001). Moreover, when we consider the terms *teacher*, *politician*, and *judge*, we automatically assume that we are referring to adults. But do youth have nothing of value to contribute to these important domains? It would seem not. They find themselves on the outside, invited to participate only when something is being imposed on them—without, of course, any choice on their part. This order of things does not need to be taught in schools: it just is.

According to social theorist Pierre Bourdieu, every established social order necessarily makes its own arbitrariness seem a natural condition (Bourdieu 1977, 164). In Canadian society, where traditional hierarchies based on age remain relatively stable, our order of things appears self-evident, innate, and ordinary. Or, to put it succinctly, in Canadian society the majority of people are fully aware of their social positions and conduct themselves accordingly. In this order, there remains little room for many youth to manoeuvre into a more equitable position. It appears that the normative social order is fated to be replicated generation after generation. Those who benefit from the established order prefer not to unsettle the status quo. It is only the subordinated who have an interest in pushing back societal limits in order to expose the capriciousness of the presupposed order. Therefore, youth are left the task of unsettling the traditional norms that silence them.

In Edmonton, Alberta, a group of enterprising youth despondent over their silence has challenged contemporary orthodoxy by establishing and administering the world's only "youth for youth" restorative justice program. A well-established definition of restorative justice suggests that it is an alternative criminal justice process whereby "parties with a stake in a particular offence come together to resolve collectively how to deal with the aftermath of the offence and its implications for the future" (Marshall 1996, 37). In opposition to traditional youth justice processes in which adults predominate, the Youth Restorative Action Project (YRAP) was created, designed, and implemented and is currently administered by youth. It is made up entirely of young people—between 14 and 21, ranging from honours students to ex-offenders and recovering drug addicts—who consult with offenders to decide on appropriate sanctions within the frame of restorative justice. Adults are accorded no decision-making power and are almost entirely excluded from proceedings except in rare instances when they are called upon to provide clarification on technical points of law. YRAP paves the way for new discursive potentials and novel understandings that recognize the injustices and exclusions contained within established youth justice practice.

Unfortunately, YRAP is the exception rather than the rule. Youth continue to be silenced and nullified in matters that affect them directly. Only when the norms that reinforce adult privilege are exposed and the resulting social order is no longer considered inevitable can amendments be suggested.

Conclusion

Given the silencing of young people, their experiences of poverty, the racism that confronts certain segments, and the dislocation of girls in juvenile justice, we may conclude that there is no justice for marginalized youth. But what would justice look like? Given that those for whom justice remains elusive are subjugated, marginalized, and racialized populations, justice—broadly conceived—would imply an ethic of how to be just with/to the "other." The problem, however, is that universal pronouncements such as the Canadian Charter of Rights and Freedoms and the UN Convention on the Rights of the Child provide little guidance toward this end. We should, therefore, not be fully satisfied with such endeavours. Satisfaction with the application of conventions and charters reduces the language of justice to questions of rights and conceals the tyranny over the poor, the Indigenous, the female, and the silent.

Canadians cannot be satisfied with contemporary action toward the "other"—who are downtrodden, excluded, and intruded upon. There must be something more—something better. There is but one answer, which is to "listen to the unspoken demand . . . [since] the beginning of all evil is to plug one's ears" (Bauman 2001a). Let there be no mistake: listening to the "other" is just a beginning. Hearing and acting ethically toward the disempowered is something altogether different. Thus, giving voice to the voiceless demand is a necessary initial foray into being just—but not its infallible guarantee.

Marginalized, impoverished, female, and racialized young people routinely confront countless barriers. This chapter has demonstrated that despite claims of Canada being one of the most tolerant and livable countries, there remains little in the way of "justice" for young people. We have seen that the social welfare net is continually under attack and that social supports are dwindling. Yet nefarious services that deliver pain and deprivation continue to be well supported by the Canadian state. Homeless young people, Aboriginal youth, and girls are among the most affected by this intrusive regime. At the same time, marginalized young people are ceaselessly silenced and denied a voice in matters directly pertaining to their well-being. If there is ever to be "justice" for youth, novel ways of being and thinking about being with young people that might involve law, but that will certainly move beyond it in very important ways, are needed more now than ever.

Review/Summary Questions

1. What understanding(s) of "justice" does the author suggest pervade the contemporary Canadian scene? What examples does he use to illustrate this?
2. To what does the author attribute burgeoning rates of poverty experienced in an era of opulence? Why are youth affected most?
3. How does the author suggest that the state has responded to the impact of funding cuts on the poor and marginalized?
4. To what extent do young people understand and know the rights granted to them by the United Nations Convention on the Rights of the Child? Why does the author argue that familiarity with their rights is fundamental to "justice" for youth?
5. Compared to their male counterparts, for what reasons were and are girls brought into the criminal justice system?

19 Women and Prison: Who and Why?

Kelly Hannah-Moffat

Introduction

Women constitute a small proportion of incarcerated individuals worldwide, but are also the fastest-growing prison population. Although this increase echoes the rise in the overall prison population of many countries, studies in some countries have shown that the number of female prisoners is increasing at a faster rate than that of male prisoners (UN, 2014). In the United States, for example "the number of women in prison . . . is increasing at nearly double the rate for men" (Carson and Golinelli 2014). A similar pattern is evident in England and Wales, Australia, Mexico, Europe, South America (UN 2014), and Canada (Public Safety Canada 2013; TBC 2012; Dauvergne 2012), despite decreasing crime rates overall (Perrault 2013). Although Canadian women prisoners are still a minority when compared with men, it is important to clarify why their incarceration rates are increasing and how the face of Canadian women's imprisonment is changing.

Scholars explain the **criminalization** of women and their **pathways to prison** in different ways. Many argue that sanctions of imprisonment are over-used and unnecessary. Some maintain that the increased numbers of women in prison (as well as changes in the "type" of women in prison) are a by-product of changes in the nature and severity of women's crime and their increased opportunities to commit a broader range of drug-related, economic, and property offences; others argue that the increases are the result of social and structural factors, such as changes in policing and sentencing patterns (Mauer 2013, Chesney-Lind and Pasko 2013, Sharp 2015, Stubbs 2015). Another common argument is that the preferential or chivalrous treatment women once enjoyed has dissipated: the media and popular culture often portray women, particularly young girls, as more aggressive and violent and often focus on sensational accounts of heinous crimes involving women (Chesney-Lind and Pasko 2013). However, empirical evidence consistently shows that women tend not to commit serious crimes and that women who offend tend to have experienced social exclusion caused by poverty, racism, mental illness, and/or the trauma of physical and sexual violence (Balfour and Comack 2006, Sharp 2014). In many countries, women are imprisoned due to poverty and an inability to pay fines; a large proportion need help for developmental disabilities, mental-health issues, or substance dependence; and many are actually victims of crime but are imprisoned due to discriminatory legislation and practices (UN 2014). This chapter will provide (1) information about the number and characteristics of women in Canadian prisons; (2) an overview of the explanations of women's pathways into prison and the struggles they face upon release; and (3) a description of the concept of women-centred or gender-responsive punishment.

Number and Characteristics of Women in Canadian Prisons

Before discussing the number of women in Canada's prisons, it is important to point out that relatively few women compared to men commit crimes (22 per cent). And those who are involved in crime tend to have committed property crimes, such as theft under $5000 or shoplifting, fraud, administration of justice (e.g., failure to appear in court, breach of probation condition, etc.), or drug-related offences; only a small percentage of all female convictions are for violent crimes (21.5%) (Mahony 2015). Women are also overrepresented in prostitution-related crimes. Women in provincial or territorial prisons, in fact, are typically there for non-violent offences (PSC 2013). Yet women who resort to violence are often sent to prison; consequently, prison population statistics and detailed examinations of imprisoned women's histories (particularly for Aboriginal women) typically indicate that they are incarcerated for crimes involving interpersonal violence (assaults, robbery, manslaughter, and murder). This is especially true for women serving federal sentences (more than two years in custody). Data on female violent crime shows that

> similar to their victimization, females are most likely to commit acts of violence against their spouses or other intimate partners. In 2009, among those females accused of a violent offence, the most common victim was a spouse or other intimate partner (33.4%), followed by an acquaintance (26.3%), other family members (34.9%) and lastly a stranger (5.5%). (Mahony 2015)

In 2012, 49.4 per cent of federally-sentenced women were serving time for a violent crime and 72.4 per cent of the Aboriginal women incarcerated in federal prisons were serving time for a violent crime (PSC 2013).[1]

Whether instrumental or defensive, women's violence *must* be understood within a wider socio-economic context. When placed in context, there is little evidence to support the claim that women overall are becoming more violent or aggressive. A Canadian study revealed that 9 per cent of federally sentenced women who had committed homicide as an act of self-defence were sex workers protecting themselves against assault or unwanted sexual relations by customers (CSC 1998; also see Balfour and Comack 2006).

Generally, women are less likely than men to become repeat offenders, and when they do reoffend, their crimes tend not to escalate in severity (Kong and AuCoin 2008). Consequently, women are less likely than men to receive a prison sentence and are more likely to receive a community sentence of probation, regardless of the severity of the crime (Kong and AuCoin 2008). Exceptions are women convicted of interpersonal violence, prostitution, and drug possession crimes; these women are *more* likely than men to be sent to prison.

Women have consistently represented a small proportion of all offenders and of those sentenced to imprisonment. Women accounted for 15 per cent of overall admissions to adult correction services in 2013–14. Women were sentenced to community supervision (20 per cent) more often than custody (13 per cent) (Mahony 2015). In 2012–13, women comprised only 12 per cent of offenders in Canada's provincial/territorial prisons, 13.9 per cent of those in federal prisons, and 13 per cent of those in detention centres on remand (Calverley 2010). In early 2012, there were 603 women incarcerated in Canada under federal jurisdiction. Women in federal penitentiaries tend to be concentrated in Ontario and the Prairie provinces, which consistently have larger proportions of women prisoners overall compared with other regions (CSC 2007). Yet, women are less likely than men to receive a prison sentence (26% versus 37%) and when sentenced to custody their median sentence lengths are generally shorter compared with men (Mahoney 2015). Roughly two-thirds (67.8 per cent) of women and just over half of men (52.9 per cent) who are sentenced to custody receive a sentence of one month or less, and 91.9 per cent of women and 85.1 per cent of men receive a sentence of six months or less (Public Safety 2013).

Similar to many other countries, Canadian prison populations are disproportionately comprised of racialized individuals. The nature of **racial overrepresentation** varies by each country's demographics. In Canada, Aboriginal persons are overrepresented in all areas of the criminal justice system. For example, in 2013–14 Aboriginal persons represented about 3 per cent of the Canadian population; yet they comprised approximately 24 per cent of the incarcerated adult population (CSP 2014). During the same period, Aboriginal women accounted for 36 per cent of women serving a custodial sentence in the provincial/territorial system, while Aboriginal men accounted for 25 per cent of men serving a custodial sentence in this system (CSP 2014). The number of incarcerated Aboriginal women in prison increased steadily from 108 in 2003–04 to 191 in 2012–13, an increase of 76.9 per cent. The increase for incarcerated Aboriginal men was 45.8 per cent for the same period (from 2193 to 3197) (CPS 2013). Aboriginal women have acute and multifaceted needs and often have experienced pervasive substance abuse and physical and/or sexual abuse. Moreover,

Aboriginal women are more frequently housed in the maximum-security units of prisons (CSP 2010), and they are often younger than their non-Aboriginal counterparts when they come to prison. The disproportionate representation of minority women in prison is a global phenomenon. Sokoloff points out that while African Americans represent only 13 per cent of the total American population, about 50 per cent of the female inmate population is African American. Indeed, black women are seven times more likely to be incarcerated than white women (Sokoloff 2005, 129; also see Mauer 2013). In Canada, we have a significant population of black women: in 2011 there were 55 black women inmates serving time in federal penitentiaries (mostly Ontario), representing 9.12 per cent of the incarcerated women population (OCI 2013).

Clarifying the changes in the number of women in prison is a complicated and nuanced process. In Canada, women may face different forms of imprisonment, as determined by the length of sentence. If a woman's sentence is more than two years, she serves it in a federal prison; if her sentence is less than two, on the other hand, she serves it in a provincial prison. Women can also be imprisoned while waiting for their trial (remand). Although federal admissions constitute only about 3 per cent of women sentenced to prison, women's imprisonment at the federal level has increased since the 1980s (Gartner, Webster, and Doob 2009). Admissions of women to provincial prisons increased until the early 1980s, remained relatively stable until the early 1990s, and subsequently declined. Remand prisoners, however, are the most rapidly increasing population of Canadian women in prison (Gartner et al. 2009); these women have been denied bail and are being held in prison awaiting trial. Kong and AuCoin report that "since 1995/1996, the number of women in remand has more than doubled and has pushed the total number of women in provincial/territorial custody up 30%" (2008, 12; also see Porter and Calverley 2011).

Aboriginal persons are overrepresented in remand, and Aboriginal women are remanded more often than men (Perreault 2011). This change in remand numbers is important because these women are often not yet convicted of a crime, and this form of incarceration has significant costs for the accused: research has shown that these individuals can feel pressured to plead guilty; live in harsh conditions with few programs; and can lose their jobs, homes, and/or custody of their children (Kellough and Wortley 2002, Canadian Civil Liberties 2014).

The increase of women in federal prison populations and the decrease in provincial populations can partially be explained by the fact that five new federal prisons for women opened across the country in the 1990s. In the past, judges may have been reluctant to sentence women to federal custody because there was only one federal prison for women (located in Kingston, Ontario). This prison was fiercely criticized for its inability to appropriately and safely meet the needs of women prisoners and for the often vast distances between women and their families and communities of origin (Hannah-Moffat and Shaw 2001). Another possibility for the increased number of women in federal prisons is that women offenders and their lawyers consider federal prisons to be better resourced in terms of programs and therapeutic services than provincial prisons.

Some have suggested that the "type" of women sentenced to imprisonment has changed over the past 30 years, but this broad claim is difficult to verify empirically due to limited data and a variety of complicating methodological factors. The female prison population is aging, and many older women are experiencing significant health problems, including mental-health challenges, with fewer external supports (Michel et al. 2012). However, demographic data about women currently housed in Canadian prisons suggest that their circumstances and experiences are largely related to economic instability, political conservatism, punitive crime control, exclusionary social policies, and the persistent decline of the social safety net—resulting in cuts to benefits, health and social services, welfare, and housing (see, e.g., Hermer and Mosher 2002). Each of these factors contributes to increased criminalization, and they affect women differently than men.

Approximately 75 per cent of women prisoners report having children, and many are simultaneously involved with family courts and children's aid societies. Many of these women are at risk of losing their parental rights because they do not have access to legal aid or advocacy. Children usually live with their mother (often a single mother) before prison, and most wish to live with their mother once she is released from prison. During their mother's prison term, they usually live with another family member or in a foster home. Mothers have limited contact with their children; given the remote location of many prisons, contact is possible only through telephone calls and letters. Many mothers lose legal custody as a result of their criminal history (Arditti and Few 2006; Celinska and Siegel 2010; UN 2014).

Many female offenders report that substance abuse played a major role in their offences or their offending history (Derkzen et al. 2012). Indeed, recent data on federally sentenced women indicate that 59 per cent of these women self-reported current or previous drug addictions and 37 per cent reported current/previous alcohol addictions (CSC 2010). Derkzen et al. (2012) reported that 80 per cent of the women they studied had experienced a long-term dependence on at least one substance. Aboriginal women offenders, in particular, report high levels of substance misuse. Studies have also consistently demonstrated that women prisoners are less educated: prior to incarceration, many have not graduated from high school (Brown 2006). They are also frequently unemployed or underemployed at the time of incarceration and lack basic job skills and/or employment experience. Single-parent status for part or all of their children's lives often complicates their access to meaningful employment. Incarcerated women also reportedly have a much higher incidence of mental illness, childhood sexual abuse, and severe physical abuse than women in the general population (Bingham and Sutton 2012; OCI 2014). For many women prisoners, prison offers the first access to help for their problems (Comack 1996).

Pathways into Crime and Prison

Empirical studies have demonstrated differences in the motivational factors that lead to women's use of violence, involvement in drug and property crimes, and patterns of substance abuse, as well as how factors such as drug use are connected in gender-specific ways to initial and continued prostitution and other crimes (e.g., Blanchette and Brown 2006; Bloom, Owen, and Covington 2006; Daly 1992; Hannah-Moffat and Shaw 2001; Heimer and Kruttschnitt 2006; Moretti, Odgers, and Jackson 2004). Even when women and men's offences are similar (e.g., assault, fraud, or murder), the context of offending and the offender's relationship with the victim tend to be different.

Research about the pathways to prison among female offenders has revealed various ways in which women end up in prison. Much of this research is based on an incarcerated sample and explores how a number of different life-course trajectories can explain how women become part of the prison population. Gender-specific adversities appear to work to produce and sustain women's **criminality**: histories of abuse, mental illness tied to early life experiences, addictions, economic and social marginality, homelessness, and violent relationships (Bloom and Covington 2006). Many scholars have argued that profound differences between the lives of men and women shape their patterns of criminal offending (Steffensmeier and Allan 1998). The next sections will discuss some of the factors that contribute to women's incarceration.

Economic Marginalization and Street Life

As noted, women entering prison are often poorly educated. While 80 per cent of the general female population has progressed beyond grade nine, only about 50 per cent of women in prison have achieved this level of education (CHRC 2004). Traditionally, women (especially Aboriginal women) experience higher rates of poverty and earn lower wages than men and non-Aboriginals. Prior to incarceration, many women live in poverty with their children and rely on welfare or social assistance. In 2005, social assistance rates for single-parent families in Canada ranged from 27 per cent below the poverty line (in Newfoundland) to 52 per cent below the poverty line (in Alberta) (National Council of Welfare 2006). Women who were employed upon entering prison generally report low-skill employment in sales and services industries, child care, and housekeeping (CSC 2010). Aboriginal women are twice as likely to be unemployed than non-Aboriginal women, especially between the ages of 15 and 34. On average, Aboriginal women in large urban centres cannot earn enough money to meet their own basic needs or support a family (Statistics Canada 2006b). Such economic marginalization increases women's exposure to and involvement in crime.

When women are poor and/or unemployed, they are more likely to enter into street life and become involved in illegal markets. For example, they may be forced to trade sexual services for a meal or to avoid sleeping in a cold public park when city shelters are full ("survival sex"). Some may return to abusive relationships or high-risk environments, increasing the risk of further legal problems. Stable housing is positively associated with employment, the ability to access government benefits, mental and physical health, and familial support. When women are homeless or marginally housed they are more likely to become victims of physical and/or sexual violence and find it more difficult to provide for their children and secure sufficient employment.

Daly found that street life was a common pathway to female offending:

> Whether they were pushed out or ran away from abusive homes, or became part of a deviant milieu, young women begin to engage in petty hustles or prostitution. Life on the street leads to drug use and addiction, which in turn leads to more frequent law-breaking to support a drug habit. . . . Their paid employment is negligible because they lack interest to work in low-paid or unskilled jobs. Having a child may facilitate . . . [state aid]. A woman may continue lawbreaking as a result of relationships with men who may also be involved in crime. Women are on a revolving criminal justice door, moving between incarceration and time on the streets. (Daly, Kathleen. 1992. 'Women's pathways to felony court: Feminist theories of law breaking and problems of representation.' *Southern California Review of Law and Women's Studies* 2(1): pp. 3-14)

Simpson et al. (2008) also found that women who engage in street life tend to have extensive criminal records, to have served a number of jail or prison sentences, and to have numerous criminal acquaintances that encourage further law-breaking. Johnson (2006) reported that most incarcerated women (50–75 per cent) have histories of illegal drug use, and substance abuse is pervasive among women in prison. Women's addictions are different from men's in terms of the types of drugs they use and their reasons for using, highlighting the need for women-specific resources (Hannah-Moffat and Shaw 2001). For example, women in prison often report using drugs and alcohol to numb the pain of past traumas or to cope with their immediate circumstances (e.g., working in the sex trade for economic survival). Some women make direct links between their substance use and their conflicts with the law (Comack 1996). The depletion of publicly funded addiction counselling and treatment programs in the community has resulted in prisons becoming a default option for women with substance addictions (Pollack 2009).

Violence and Formative Years

Most criminalized women have suffered multiple **traumas**. Several studies have reported that violence (trauma from childhood sexual assault) is an important precursor to adult drug abuse and offending, and that women who experience disruptive family life gravitate toward abusive adult relationships (Brown 2006; Salisbury, Van Voorhis, and Spiropoulos 2009). Simpson et al. (2008) also found that many incarcerated women had experienced violence (physical and/

or sexual) as children and adults, and that many of these women went on to be violent themselves. Similarly, DeHart (2008) found that victimization appeared to be directly related to **delinquency** and criminal activity: through child corruption or perceived force, provocation, or pressure to commit crime (also see Balfour and Comack 2006). For example, during their formative years many incarcerated women had caretakers who provided them with drugs and alcohol, forced them to steal, and/or prostituted them. In adulthood, these women often use similar criminal strategies. Many also use defensive violence during adulthood to stop abuse from partners or to prevent the assault or threat of assault on their children or families. These cumulative experiences of victimization can affect women's mental and physical health and their psychosocial functioning, influencing family and work life. They often contribute to women's externalizing of their anger and using violence, which can lead to their initial contact with the criminal justice system (DeHart 2008). Aboriginal women in the general population are twice as likely as other women to be victims of emotional and physical abuse, and significantly more likely than non-Aboriginals (54 per cent versus 37 per cent) to report the most severe and potentially life-threatening forms of violence: being beaten or choked, having had a gun or knife used against them, or being sexually assaulted (Statistics Canada 2006b). Unsurprisingly, these experiences are also more prevalent among Aboriginal women in prison.

Early victimization (childhood sexual abuse) increases a woman's risk for future victimization (Carbone-Lopez and Kruttschnitt 2010). DeHart (2008) reported that victimization can generate or intensify mental illnesses, drug and alcohol abuse, feelings of worthlessness and withdrawal, low self-esteem and shame, as well as suicidal ideation and attempts. Furthermore, abuse in the home (particularly at early ages) can push women and girls to the streets, where lack of housing, social support, and shelter spaces places them at further risk of violence, criminal involvement, and even premature death.

Mental Health

Mental-health needs constitute an area of growing concern among imprisoned women. Studies about criminalized women have highlighted the range and density of their needs. Correctional scholars report that women in prison outnumber men in all major psychiatric diagnoses with the exception of antisocial personality disorder. Gender differences also appear in the behavioural manifestations of mental illness. For example, women in prison reportedly suffer from depression at twice the rate as men (and federally incarcerated women are three times more likely than federally incarcerated men to be moderately to severely depressed). Incarcerated women are less physically and sexually threatening and assaultive than men; instead, women prisoners tend to be more self-abusive and to engage in more self-mutilating behaviours, such as slashing (Laishes 2002). A study conducted in New Zealand found that compared with women living in the general population, criminalized women had a higher prevalence of mental disorders, including schizophrenia, major depression, and post-traumatic stress (Brinded et al. 2001). A recent CSC study reported that 94 per cent of a sample of women in prison had experienced symptoms consistent with a diagnosis of a psychiatric disorder and that 85 per cent had experienced diagnostic symptoms of more than one disorder[2] (Derkzen et al. 2012). According to the Office of the Correctional Investigator (2014), 62.6 per cent of incarcerated women are pre- scribed some form of **psychotropic medication** to manage their mental-health symptoms. Many women in prison are struggling with past histories of abuse and trauma as well as adjusting to life in prison, which is often re-traumatizing.

Once in prison, women require specialized services to address their health difficulties. International scholars estimate that approximately 10 to 13 per cent of female prisoners have self-injured during their current sentences (Meltzer et al. 2002). And self-injury is a significant problem among women in the Canadian prison population. One study of 26 female inmates admitted to a psychiatric cen- tre found that 73 per cent had engaged in self-injurious behaviour prior to their admittance (Presse and Hart 1999, cited in Fillmore, Dell, and The Elizabeth Fry Society of Manitoba 2000). Furthermore, in a Canadian study of self-harm- ing women offenders and corrections staff, interviews with offenders revealed that they used self-harming to help them cope with a variety of issues: to deal with isolation and loneliness; as a cry for attention and nurturing; as a form of self-punishment and self-blame; as an opportunity to feel something; as a way of distracting and deflecting emotional pain; as a release and cleansing of emo- tional pain; as an expression of painful life experiences; and to obtain a sense of power and control (Fillmore and Dell and The Elizabeth Fry Society of Manitoba 2000). Over the past five years, moreover, incidences of self-injury have tripled; Aboriginal women are disproportionately represented in these rates. Although a small number of women (37 of a sample of 264) accounted for 36 per cent of the incidences in one study, prisons are not equipped to manage this disturbing pattern (OCI 2013). The Office of the Correctional Investigator (OCI) and an On- tario Coroner's inquest into the death of Ashley Smith have raised a number of concerns about how correctional officials manage self-harm as a security problem rather than as a health problem (OCI 2013).

Recent research suggests that the "pains of imprisonment" are a major con- tributing factor to self-harm among incarcerated women (see CCSA 2006; Fill- more and Dell and The Elizabeth Fry Society of Manitoba 2000). These "pains" may include negative relationships with staff and other prisoners, confinement in segregation, stressful living conditions, and rigid and arbitrary rule enforce- ment. The high prevalence of mental-health difficulties among incarcerated women has been linked with their experiences of trauma, violence, and drug use (Booker, Loper, and Levitt 2011) and is further complicated by the limited number and quality of community-based psychiatric services. Mental-health difficulties complicate the experiences and management of women once they arrive in prison and require prison and health-care systems to work together in prisons and in communities to treat women and to prevent future incarcerations.

Gender-Specific Approaches

Women face complex challenges: they must often simultaneously deal with multiple challenges that are not easily prioritized and disentangled. For more than 30 years, international research has demonstrated that crime is gendered and that gender matters in shaping criminal justice responses to women and in the differential effects of policies (Hannah-Moffat and Shaw 2001; Carlen 2002). There is no "one-size-fits-all" policy, and criminal justice organizations and policymakers are starting to understand this fact. Indeed, many now recognize that corrections policies need to respond to both gender and culture. Research conducted in Canada as well as by the United Nations has revealed the importance of gender sensitivity and the need to rethink women's prisons without using the male prison as a reference point (see UN 2008). Acceptance of the premise that women are *different but equally entitled* to the protection of the law and fair treatment under the law signifies tremendous progress. Proponents of this approach stress that an effective system for female offenders must be structured differently from a system for male offenders. Many argue that policies, programs, and procedures that reflect gender-based differences can make the management of women offenders more effective, increase resources, improve staff turnover, prevent sexual misconduct, improve program delivery, decrease the likelihood of litigation against the criminal justice system, and improve the gender responsiveness of services and programs (Bloom, Owen, and Covington 2003; Hannah-Moffat 2010; Wright et al. 2012).

Material republished with the express permission of: Edmonton Sun, a division of Postmedia Network Inc.

Julie Bilotta gave birth to her son (both pictured above) while being held at the Ottawa-Carleton Detention Centre in 2012. The guards allegedly disbelieved her pleas that she was in labour, and did not call paramedics for nine hours; her son was born breech in her holding cell. The incident led to a review of the province's policies on pregnant prisoners.

In the early 1990s, Canadian women's prisons underwent significant restructuring in response to a renowned report by the Task Force on Federally Sentenced Women: *Creating Choices* (CSC 1990). This reform was intended to redress a long history of sexism and neglect in women's corrections by developing an alternative women-centred correctional model that focused on the unique needs and experiences of women (Hannah-Moffat and Shaw 2001; Hayman 2006).[3] It provided a conceptual template for the reform of women's imprisonment and led to the eventual closure of the notorious and degraded Prison for Women (P4W) in Kingston, Ontario. The federal government's acceptance of the Task Force's recommendations enabled feminist-inspired knowledge of women prisons and "treatment" to filter from feminist critiques into Canadian penal policy and eventually into the managerial regimes of women's prisons.

During the reform, the five principles set out in *Creating Choices* (empowerment, meaningful and responsible choices, respect and dignity, a supportive environment, and shared responsibility) were integrated into corporate documents about women prisoners in Canada. Correctional officials and feminist researchers began to produce a body of knowledge about women prisoners and gender-sensitive treatment and confinement, which started to alter correctional practices. For example, more knowledge about women's trauma and experiences with male violence informed the development of cross-gender staffing practices. Knowledge about women's relationships with their children informed the development of various forms of parenting accommodation. Knowledge about women's mental-health problems and self-injury led to the development of peer support programs and mental-health strategies. Critiques of prison classification systems, moreover, inspired a new generation of gender-informed risk-need assessment research: a persuasive and comprehensive body of research about women's correctional programming has evolved from Canadian and American studies about gender-responsive correctional strategies (Bloom et al. 2004).

The CSC characterizes its women-centred prisons as a human-rights milestone, and its acceptance of the Task Force's progressive recommendations made it an international leader in women's corrections. However, its commitment to **gender-responsive policy** has met multiple operational difficulties over the years, and Canada's progressive attitude has been overshadowed by ongoing public condemnation of the CSC for failing to protect the human rights of women prisoners and for ongoing gender discrimination. The initial adoption and creation of Canadian women-centred prisons was hasty, poorly conceptualized, and based on scant theoretical and empirical research about how gender should inform penal programs. The well-intentioned labels of "gender sensitive" and "women-centredness" have been attached to a wide range of improvised and poorly adapted programs and managerial processes without substantial consideration of how gender should be operationalized. As demonstrated in the next section, even the provision of a gender-responsive template has not resulted in significant improvements in how gender has been addressed in penality.

A number of well-documented operational and systemic problems remain in Canadian women's prisons (Parkes and Pate 2006; OCI 2008; Hannah-Moffat 2010; Dell, Fillmore, and Kilty 2009).

The Revolving Door: Reintegration and Continued Social Marginality

Community sanctions and measures would likely serve the social reintegration requirements of a vast majority much more effectively and inexpensively than imprisonment (UN 2014). From 2003 to 2012, the number of women in the community under supervision increased by 20 per cent (McConnell, Rubenfeld, Thompson, and Gobeil 2014). Studies have found that women do not have sufficient access to resources in the community upon release and that they face contextually different issues upon **reintegration** than men, even though their problems may be labelled the same (e.g., addiction, homelessness, unemployment, and housing). The lack of services and supports for women leaving prison contributes to their continued involvement in the criminal justice system and often to their return to prison. Marginalized and criminalized women have considerable needs and extremely few available resources. For example, many women offenders report concerns about the lack of opportunities for vocational training in prison, which limits their job opportunities upon release (Pollack 2009; Carlton and Segrave 2013). Nonetheless, women prisoners tend to be more successful on parole than men and are less likely to breach their conditions of release (OCI 2014). When women are returned to prison for parole violations, it is typically because of a failure to report to their parole officer, rather than for the commission of new offences (McConnell, Rubenfeld, Thompson, and Gobeil 2014).

Upon reintegration, women face many unique challenges. International research has demonstrated that, when they leave prison, women face the same overwhelming problems they faced prior to entering the system (Richie 2001; Carlton and Segrave 2013). Some of these persistent challenges include meeting basic needs, accessing safe and affordable housing, securing child care, reuniting family, finding employment, obtaining identification, opening bank accounts to deposit or write cheques (e.g., for rent), and acquiring social assistance.

Safe housing is a major challenge for many women leaving prison (Martin et al. 2012). Empirical research (Home Office, n.d.) suggests that addressing severe accommodation problems can reduce the risk of reoffending by as much as 20 per cent. Failure to find housing is a major cause of parole revocations, reoffending, and returning to prison (Martin et al. 2012). Additionally, when women are unable to find and maintain housing, they risk losing their children.

To address some parenting issues, CSC has piloted an initiative called Child Link, which allows women prisoners to maintain remote contact with their children via video conferencing (OCI 2014). If a woman maintains her relationships with her children throughout her incarceration, she is more likely to successfully reintegrate after prison, although she will still face a number of challenges in the correctional environment and may not regain custody of her children.

Homeless women, like incarcerated women, are far more likely than their male counterparts to have young children in their care and to be dependent on public assistance. Upon being released from prison, many women are unable to secure housing; as a result, they live in environments that are conducive to reoffending, while they are subjected to increased police surveillance. Being homeless or precariously housed is clearly not conducive to pro-social living.

Obtaining sustainable employment, and employable skills, is crucially linked to women's ability to meet their basic needs in the long term, to parole success, and, eventually, to desistence from crime. Women's ability to meet their basic needs upon release requires sustained economic independence: they need access to employment or some form of income to support them and their children. As noted earlier, many women report having insufficient job skills, education, or experience prior to incarceration or upon release. Interviews with imprisoned women have revealed how they are pulled toward high-risk situations and illegal activities as financial and housing options are exhausted (Koons et al. 1997; Richie 2001). When women are underemployed or unemployed and consequently cannot access safe, affordable housing, they rely on families, past social networks, welfare, and/or community agencies. Living with family can be a positive experience for some women, but for many it is not. Ongoing dependencies on friends, families, and social agencies for basic needs, such as food and housing, can erode self-esteem, dignity, and sense of self-worth (Barker 2009). Economic need can also push women back into negative relationships with men and may act as a catalyst for re-entry into criminalized activities, such as prostitution or drug-dealing.

Conclusion

Both American and Canadian studies have reported that homelessness and mental illness together are strong predictors of involvement with the correctional system (Gaetz and O'Grady 2006). Mentally ill persons who are homeless are particularly vulnerable to frequent involvement with the criminal justice system. Several surveys (including Canadian studies; see MHCC 2009) have shown that of the homeless population, those who report psychiatric illness or hospitalization are most likely to have a history of arrest or incarceration. As discussed, criminalized women are affected by a range of emotional and mental-health problems that are not well managed in the community and that pose significant challenges to their reintegration.

Many women enter prison expecting to receive treatment for drug and alcohol addictions and mental-health conditions (Pollack 2009). The prospect of getting treatment has actually led many women facing shorter sentences to request federal sentences in order to access treatment options. However, once they enter the federal system, they quickly discover that prisons are punitively focused and that institutional programs are not always available or helpful. Indeed, many women report that institutional and post-release programs did not adequately prepare them to manage their addiction in the community (Richie and Johnsen 1996). Because few resources are available to assist them after prison, they continue to struggle with abuse and trauma issues (trust, relationships, and safety). Their access to programs and services is also limited by the stigma of parole or ex-prisoner status. Although scarce, resources are crucial to break the unique cycle of crime that faces women in prison.

Review/Summary Questions

1. Describe the pathways that lead women to prison.
2. What are the main characteristics of the prison populations and women in prison?
3. What barriers do women face upon release from prison?
4. How could we reduce the number of women being sent to prison?

Notes

1. Approximately 514 women are incarcerated in federal institutions/treatment centres across Canada, and 567 women are held under federal supervision in communities across Canada (CSC 2010).
2. The most notable elevations were seen with post-traumatic stress disorder (PTSD) (52 per cent), major depressive episode (69 per cent), and antisocial personality disorder (83 per cent).
3. Conditions at P4W, combined with a series of deaths of Aboriginal women in custody and mounting political pressure due to a potential section 15 Charter of Rights case, led to the establishment of the historic Task Force on Federally Sentenced Women in 1989 and its now 20-year-old report, *Creating Choices*, which the CSC routinely refers to as a foundational document.

20 How Is Aging a Critical Sociological Problem?

Stephen Katz

Introduction

Sociologically, age is one of the most fundamental principles of social organization and stratification. Gerontology, the professional field that studies aging and old age, was founded in the early twentieth century by scientists influenced by psychology, biology, and medicine. Like pediatrics and its identification of childhood as a distinct part of the life course, gerontology focused on the special physical, emotional, psychological, and social changes that are part of the aging process (Achenbaum 1995; Katz 1996). For example, the gerontological psychologist G. Stanley Hall pioneered these ideas in his two influential books, *Adolescence* (1904) and *Senescence* (1922), and theorized adolescence and old age as particularly modern stages of life. In the latter twentieth century, gerontology became more interdisciplinary and spread its research across the arts, sciences, and social sciences, crossing paths with sociologists of aging who work on demography, policy, and social inequality. Both gerontologists and sociologists also attack popular ageist notions of decline and promote more positive accounts of aging creativity, wisdom, productivity, and resilience. Their goal is to understand aging as a successful part of life, the knowledge of which provides all age groups with the insights to develop equitable approaches to health, work, and intergenerational relations. With this brief background in mind, the following chapter looks at how social gerontologists and sociologists understand the aging process through four key categories of social organization and stratification: (1) population, (2) life course, (3) generation, and (4) gendered age. Our discussion explores these categories from a critical perspective, identifying certain problems and limitations. Conclusions offer some thoughts and questions about future trends in aging societies.

The Aging Population and the Problem of Apocalyptic Demography

Demography is the field of research that studies populations. Demographers typically identify age populations as statistical aggregations based on features such as median ages, fertility and mortality rates, dependency ratios, migration patterns, and life expectancy probabilities. Demographic data can be used in diverse ways, but generally demographers and gerontologists highlight three current age-related trends in industrialized societies: (1) an unprecedented growth of aging populations, (2) a decline in fertility rates, and (3) a widening gendered longevity gap as women outlive men. Traditionally, the age of 65 was used to mark the onset of old age because of pension and retirement policies. While we know that 65 is hardly old anymore, it is still an important chronological designation of the older or "senior" population, which in Canada has increased every decade since 1921. Statistical data on Canada (e.g., Statistics Canada 2011b; 2012a) reveals that in 2006 13 per cent of the Canadian population was over 65 and by 2041 that figure will almost double to 24.5 per cent. In addition, the 80+ population is and will be the fastest growing age group due to declining mortality and lengthening life expectancy. These demographic trends are also illustrated by median age calculations that divide the population into its younger and older halves. A median age over 30 indicates a population that is "older" rather than "younger," and in Canada in 2011 the median age was 39.9.

Given these demographic data and population predictions, most government analysts, policy-makers, health-care leaders, and economists agree that these trends and median ages will have critical economic, social, and political consequences. People may be living longer, but longer lives also mean more injury, disability, illness, and dependency, which in turn require more social services, community support, and health-care resources. Some of these concerns are encapsulated in mathematical dependency ratios. A dependency ratio reflects the extent to which dependent populations, such as children and older people, rely on a wage-earning working population who pay taxes and provide the support for dependent populations. In Canada in 2006, the aged dependency ratio was 210 elders per 1000 15- to 64-year-olds and 250 dependent youth per 1000 15- to 64-year-olds. So the combined dependency ratio, old and young, was 460/1000 or 46/100. That rate is expected to rise to 60/100 in the next couple of decades, and by 2056 the total ratio is predicted to be 84/100 (Wister and McPherson 2014). In addition, our fertility rates are dropping and indeed there are far fewer children and younger people than in earlier post-war decades, with the current average being 1.5 children per family. While immigration in Canada is responsible for some population growth, it hardly offsets the drop in fertility rates or the fact that more people will be moving out of the workforce than moving into it.

While demographic data provide essential diagrams of our aging populations, these data have also been distorted through the usage of popular metaphors such as "the grey tsunami" and "greedy geezers" that depict the growing aging population as an uncontrollable threat to national prosperity and welfare viability. For this reason, critics have labelled such a distorted picture **apocalyptic demography** (Gee and Gutman 2000), an age-blaming discourse of intergenerational injustice supported by media portrayals of older people at play, going on cruises, and receiving undeserved financial investment and pension rewards. As a corrective, the critics remind us that in reality there is much more intergenerational interdependence and co-operation than antagonism (see Kemp 2005). Further, when we revisit the demographic data, we see that dependency ratios can be very limited if used to assume that older people are economically dependent just because of their age. Increasingly, greater numbers of older people past retirement age perform essential work as volunteers, grandparents, and domestic caregivers, even if such work is unpaid and undervalued. If we look carefully at the 1996–2041 period, the total combined dependency ratios have been and will continue to be relatively modest compared to the 1950s–60s period, when the boom in fertility rates created large populations of children who required family supplement support, new schools, and health programs. Unfortunately, the apocalyptic demographic stereotype maintains that supporting children is a worthwhile investment while supporting older people, who have worked throughout their lives to build Canada's welfare policies and education systems, is a diversion of resources.

Thus, demography is not just a statistical knowledge but a political one as well, where population data are used to support ageist stereotypes of risky older populations or justify neo-liberal agendas to transfer reduced welfare services and health-care budgets to individual responsibility. As such, we can consider the knowledge generated by demographic gerontology as an example of Michel Foucault's idea of a "bio-politics of the population" (1980b), whereby the historical division of peoples is part of the evolution of governmental power.

The Life Course and the Problem of the Aging Body

The "life course" is a second analytical category that connects the aging process to social organization and stratification. By understanding how changes in life occur along social contours and structured identities, life-course researchers challenge earlier lifespan and human development models that biologized and naturalized age categories. For example, Glen Elder, Jr., in his book *Children of the Great Depression* (1974), is one of the first gerontologists to situate people's life courses within historical circumstances intersected by individuals, families, cohorts, and generations. While **generation** is discussed in the next section of this chapter, the concept of age **cohort** is important here because it joins individual biographies to cultural experiences within historical events, such as wars, technological revolutions, or economic fluctuations. For Glen Elder, Jr., the children of the Great Depression in the 1930s form a cohort because their transitions through life were and always will be always shaped by their experience of the Great Depression. Since his work, life-course research has grown rapidly in social studies of aging. By the 1990s, it was rare to find sociological work on aging untouched by the life-course perspective, and in 1997 the American Sociological Association's section on aging was renamed "Sociology of Aging and the Life Course." On a practical level, life-course data have become vital to advocacy groups lobbying for better health, labour, retirement, education, and pension programs (see Marshall 2009).

Critical writers have also extended the life-course literature to include issues of policy, diversity, gender, and transnational movements (Calasanti and Slevin 2006; Grenier 2012). Anthropologists, moreover, deconstruct the notion of a universal life course in their work on diverse societies (Sokolovsky 2009). Global researchers look at life courses in term of "linked lives" that span continents, cultures, and economies (Dannefer 2003b; Phillipson 2009, 2013). The idea that our life courses are linked is not just a theoretical notion but also one experienced in our everyday lives. For example, when child garment workers in Southeast Asia make cheap and fashionable clothing to help us look young, they are prematurely aging due to their harsh working conditions and lack of educational opportunities. Wearing their clothes links our lives and their life courses together. In all these ways, the life course is a useful category that adds temporal, global, and subjective complexity to static demographic population diagrams.

However, despite the progressive nature of life-course research, a central problem is the absence of the aging body. Since life-course models tend to combine time-based and age-based phenomena within pre-structured trajectories, transitions, pathways, and strategies (see Dannefer and Kelley-Moore 2009), the body's role in later life appears as a rather passive and homogeneous result of health, risk, and longevity factors. Instead, we need to see aging bodies within life courses as material, experiential, and cultural forces of their own. For example, Wainright and Turner's work (2003; 2006) with the Royal Ballet of London explores the idealization of youthful bodies, where dancers learn to perform the style, stamina, and competence of an elite physical capital that rewards them with prestigious roles, despite the shortening of their careers due to increased injuries and longer recovery times. Similarly, Emmanuelle Tulle (2008) writes about older Masters-level long-distance runners, whose bodies provide the means for expressing and understanding aging. In addition to dance and sport, research on the materiality of embodied aging in relation to dress (Twigg 2013) and dementia (Kontos 2011; Kontos and Martin 2013) demonstrates the phenomenological interplay between biological age, biography, and culture. Such critical and ethnographic investigations bring the body back into the life course and thus enrich our understanding of how cohorts move through time in embodied ways.

Generation and the Problem of the Commercialization of "Boomers"

Generation is a third category of social organization and stratification based on age. It was introduced into social thought by Karl Mannheim in his essay "The Problem of Generations," which broadened the idea of generation to include factors of identity, consciousness, history, and location 1998 [1952]. In his essay, Mannheim wrote that only in a "utopian, imaginary society" could social life be envisioned as one generation living on forever because in reality we live in a society where "the transition from generation to generation is a continuous process"

(170). Each subsequent generation has "fresh contact" with the legacies left by previous generations, such that "generations are in a state of constant interaction" (180). Further, "whether a new *generation style* emerges every year, every thirty, every hundred years, or whether it emerges rhythmically at all, depends entirely on the trigger action of the social and cultural process [original emphasis]" (191). Especially innovative in Mannheim's work was a focus on the relationship between generation and class and their combined role in the intergenerational transmission of culture (Edmunds and Turner 2002). Today culturally formed generations such as **Generation X** or the **Woodstock generation** would fit well within Mannheim's perspective. But Mannheim also asked why some generations realize their potentialities and develop "a distinctive unity of style" (192) while others remain latent. Mannheim would have viewed today's **boomer generation**, with its economic power, political clout, and sense of historical self-importance, as exemplary of a distinctive unity of cultural style and potentialities. Born between 1946 and 1964, the boomers are defined by the bulging size of their cohort relative to adjacent generations and by the particular post-war conditions in which they matured: national prosperity, the relative political peace of the Cold War, new media and communication networks, affluent consumerism, and rapid social change. In turn, the populous boomer generation created new lifestyles and forms of expression that dismantled the traditions separating young and old, producing an extendable youth culture identified with rebellion (Gilleard and Higgs 2005).

The problem is that boomer discourse, itself a product of popular demography and marketing, stereotypes the very people it represents (along with a boomer kinship network of "empty nesters," "snowbirds," "seniors," "zoomers," etc.). Yet few journalists, marketers, or popular demographers are prepared to delve into the detailed gerontological research on cohorts, life-course trajectories, and intergenerational relations or consult the critical perspectives stemming from feminism, disability studies, political economy, and the humanities that deepen such research. As a result, a popular boomer vocabulary has become a pseudo-authority on aging, health care, housing, and retirement, even while it ignores important sociological data on inequality and population diversity. This homogenizing vocabulary also sidelines the realities that not all boomers are prosperous, healthy, educated, and politically empowered, and the lauded ideals of individual choice and liberating lifestyles are themselves part of a larger political economy of post-war and late capitalism. In other words, the boomer generation has become imagined as a commercialized lifestyle rather than understood as a deeper sociological phenomenon (Katz 2013; 2014).

Gendered Aging and the Problem of the Gendered Life Course

A fourth and final analytical category is gendered aging; that is, the gendered nature of aging populations, life courses, cohorts, and generations. We are always studying older women and men when we study aging; thus, the intersection between age, sexuality, and gender is at the core of the sociology of aging. In Canada, women, generally, outlive men so that women make up 57 per cent of the 65+ population and 70 per cent of the 85+ population. This situation leads to the problem of what Neena Chappell, Lynn McDonald, and Michael Stones (2008) refer to as the **gendered life course**. If women often outlive their spouses, are more often alone and single, and have become one of the poorest groups in the country, then the gendered life course appears to be a series of detriments and accumulated disadvantages for women (see Dannefer 2003a). While premarital heterosexual cohabitation has since the 1970s become an increasingly accepted norm, surveys illustrate that when such cohabited relationships break up, the female partner—who in many cases has been living with an older partner—is often left with fewer resources, less education, and lower status. This pattern applies to marriage, divorce, and child-rearing as well, where women have been found to have histories of more part-time, "casual" work and more interrupted careers. They are also more likely to be caught in a "sandwich generation"; that is, sandwiched between the time between caring for children and caring for older parents and other family members. Single women, despite their greater longevity, generally have lower pensionable incomes than men and are also less privileged by Canadian tax and pension systems. Thus, for Canadian women between the ages of 75 and 79, half are widows (compared to 16 per cent of men), and 40.1 per cent of 75+ women live alone compared to 27.4 per cent of men (Chappell et al. 2008, 124–5). When these facts are added together with the wage gap and gender discrimination in the workplace, the impoverishment of older women is built into the gendered life course from an early age.

vm/iStock Photo

Older women are often depicted through a "misery perspective" and are viewed as weaker, more risk-prone, and generally more vulnerable than older men. Is this depiction reflective of reality or a product of sexist, ageist determinants?

These data on the gendered life course are not sufficiently reflected in aging research. While most researchers have identified a "structural lag" between the realities of aging and inadequate social policies, few combine this critique with a "gender lag" between aging research and gender inequality. For example, Clary Krekula (2007) argues that the image of women in sociological and family studies is usually that of a young mother of small children, while older women in families are portrayed through a "misery perspective." Further, much of the sociological literature on aging women assumes a masculinist standpoint that women universally perceive and accept that declining sexual attractiveness is part of the aging process, while critical research has shown this is not necessarily true (Öberg and Tornstam 2003; Dumas et al. 2005).

A good example of why gendered aging needs to be part of aging research is the issue of falls and falling. Although older women fall more often and suffer more injuries than older men do, gender rarely figures into the professional research. The patronizing double image that naturalizes women as both physically weaker and more risk-prone (especially after menopause) yet reviles feminine strength and risk-taking as unfeminine, encourages older women to see their own bodies as vulnerable (Grenier and Hanley 2007; Horton 2006). In addition, gender differences in the risks and experiences of falls have culturally sexist determinants. Women are often given a higher number of medications compared to men, which can cause dizziness and loss of stability. A British study also found that in cases of injury recovery at home, female carers encouraged autonomy, self-esteem, and reasonable risk-taking, while male carers practised more protective and sometimes coercive caring styles, especially where the care recipient was female (Horton and Arber 2004).

These and many other examples of gendered aging have been advanced in feminist gerontological models that link women and aging, sexism and ageism, and social and gendered inequalities (Clarke 2011; Sandberg 2011).

Conclusions and Future Trends

The previous sections have critically argued that aging populations, life courses, generations, and gendered age groups fit together as categories of social organization and stratification. In this concluding section, we want to ask how such categories are merging into trends for the future or into what Settersten and Trauten have called a "new terrain of old age" (2009). We know that the issue of rapidly growing aging populations in light of social resources and national stability is part of this new terrain. However, Settersten and Trauten have other trends in mind, both reassuring and troubling, that are worth thinking about. For example, they predict that there will be more flexible lifestyle choices for older people but also more risks and vulnerabilities, especially financial ones. The constant diminishing of social safety nets and the pressure for older people to take care of themselves today and into the future mean that aging becomes more of a coercive individualized process. This could mean a greater impact of class, race, and gender divisions on access to supports for health and independence in later life. Another trend will be that, as populations age, families will increasingly be called upon to take care of older kin members even as more families are affected by growing rates of divorce, unemployment, immigration, and uncertainty. To support their families, older workers may also be pressured to delay retirement. As Chris Phillipson predicted (2006), such changes will be reflected in global relations as aging, retirement, and the restructuring of national welfare budgets come to be seen as part of a worldwide crisis of aging. Paradoxically, as life expectancy may be expanding, the security of aging may be eroding, as the globalization of life courses involves the dislocation of traditional places of residence, the disruption of long-term jobs and lives, the transnational control of financial pension capital, and the degradation of sustainable environments.

The relationships between young and old, outside of apocalyptic scenarios, are also changing in future-oriented ways. Young people are experiencing prolonged transitions to adulthood, longer periods spent in education, less certainty about starting careers, later marriages and family-making, more part-time work and job-changing, and more mobility between homes. In the future, the idea of a "linear" life course will no longer apply (Settersten and Ray 2010). There are also innovative developments in intergenerational opportunities that foretell how education might change in the future. For example, The Intergenerational School (TIS), founded in Cleveland in 2000 by Peter and Catherine Whitehouse, with classes for 224 inner-city students of all ages, is organized according to individualized learning needs. In addition to regular teaching and administrative staff, there are dozens of volunteers who teach, support, study, and mentor. At the TIS, children learn about respecting older adults by interacting with the older adults among them, including persons with dementia, from whom the children learn first-hand about their society's living history. The Whitehouses claim that the success of their school is due to a principle of **intergenerativity**. Compared to *generativity*, which is "the creation of new internal ideas and behaviors," *intergenerativity* is about "sharing change across boundaries" and connecting "otherwise divergent fields of human endeavor" (George, Whitehouse, and Whitehouse 2011, 392).

Finally, the prospects and promises of new biomedical, pharmacological, cosmetic, prosthetic, and genetic technologies for extending life will raise a host of ethical questions about enhancement and longevity (Hogle 2007; Turner 2009). We are already able to modify the body to such an extent that the boundary between culture and nature is becoming blurred (Katz and Gish 2015). When gerontologists Bernice Neugarten (1974) in the United States and Peter Laslett (1987) in the UK stressed the distinction between multiple later life categories, they emphasized the uniqueness of the "third age" (55–80) as a period mainly characterized by independence and healthy lifestyles (see Carr and Komp 2011). They also darkened the "fourth age" (80+)—or old, old age—as a period of decline, disease, and finality, which Gilleard and Higgs (2010) argue is like a black hole exerting a gravitational pull on those otherwise capable of maintaining a distance from the signs of dependency. However, the fourth age—or old, old age—has become a time increasingly available to longevity procedures, creating what medical anthropologist Sharon Kaufman calls a new era of **reflexive longevity** (2010a; 2010b). For Kaufman, the medical interventions offered to increasingly older patients, despite their age, are creating new tensions around life prolongation and the meaning of a natural lifespan. One of these tensions is figuring out how, when one is nearing the end of life, to measure the worth of more future living against the risks that come with it. Thus "longevity-making" is not just about privileged access to medical treatments but also a reflexive practice that involves choice, ambivalence, obligation, experimentation, and responsibility. Kaufman asks an important question: "What kind of subject emerges when longevity becomes a reflexive practice" (2010a, 228)? Perhaps this is the ultimate question when it comes to measuring human life; that is, how do we ourselves measure age and think about our futures as biotechnology promises to advance our lives beyond traditional expectations? These kinds of ethical questions about aging touch all of us and break apart the anti-aging cultural narratives about life that have us believe we should always want to be younger than we appear to be. As Molly Andrews argues (2012), when we try to imagine our futures we also must permit ourselves to expect old age. Otherwise how can younger people see themselves in and learn from older people if they are taught to deny and despise aging? Hopefully, this chapter has provided some answers to these questions from the perspective of a critical sociology of aging.

Review/Summary Questions

1. What do the critics mean by "apocalyptic demography," and how does their critique help us to understand the age stereotyping of the aging population?
2. What are some of the advantages and limitations of the life-course perspective in social gerontological research?
3. How are today's "boomers" a "special generation," according to Karl Mannheim's sociological definition of the term?
4. Why is it essential to include the "gendered life course" in any analysis of aging in Canada?
5. Why will the relationship between personal ethics, biomedical technologies, and longevity become increasingly important in the future?

21 What Is Global Inequality?

Amy Kaler

Introduction: "Everybody's Different"

"Everybody's different." This may seem like the most obvious statement in the world. Of course we are all different. The purpose of this chapter is to move away from clichés about difference and to consider how one might think sociologically about the reality that no one is exactly the same as anyone else in the world. To do so, we will employ concepts of difference, inequality, and inequity, and we will broaden our investigation to think globally about the "distant others" who populate the world as well as about the people we know, or know about.

As an example, your life as a university student in Canada is undoubtedly different from the life of, say, a paddy farmer in Bangladesh, or a refugee in a camp in Lebanon, or a social worker in Morocco. Your life is probably quite different from the life of someone with fame and fortune, such as Bill Gates or Rihanna (or your sociology professor!). What else can we say about these differences? Are they simply variations, much like the difference between dark blue and light blue, or between salty and sweet? Some differences are simply the result of individual preferences. You like chocolate, your friend likes strawberry. You like rap, your parents like classical. Maybe the preferences are more profound and long-lasting: you may have preferred to pursue post-secondary education full-time while some of your high school classmates preferred to go directly into the workforce; or you may decide to marry young while your cousin chooses to remain single for most of her adult life.

However, some differences can't be attributed to just individual preferences and decisions. These are differences that confer distinct advantages to some people and disadvantages to others, which take the form of resources or opportunities that are unevenly distributed so that some people have more than others. These are the differences we call *inequalities*, which we discuss next.

Inequality

You're probably familiar with many forms of **inequality** from your sociology courses: economic inequalities, for instance, which result in some people being poor and unable to afford the necessities of life while others have all the luxuries they could ever want; other people are ranged in between these extremes. Money isn't the only thing that is unequally distributed, of course—many other resources are concentrated among some people at the expense of others. Political power is one example, as is access to health care and education or to clean air and water. The result is that some people have more comfortable or more fulfilling lives than others, not because of anything they have chosen to do or not do but because of social inequalities.

One perspective would be that inequality is the way of the world and not much more needs to be said about it. It's unfortunate, but it's inevitable. Some people would agree with iconic punk rocker Joe Strummer of the Clash, in "Bankrobber," when he sings, "Some is rich/And some is poor/That's the way the world is/But I don't believe in lying back/Sayin' how bad your luck is." The bank robber in Strummer's song believes that inequality is inevitable, but he finds his own individualized way of redressing that inequality: he robs banks. (Or, as Strummer wrote, "He just loved to live that way/And he loved to steal your money.") Obviously, this is not a solution to economic inequality that could be implemented on a large scale!

Other perspectives on the inevitability of inequality are a bit less lighthearted than the fictitious bank robber. Some people who work in global development and relief programs have encountered an acceptance of inequality that shades into callousness. For instance, I worked on a project that was intended to help reduce infectious disease mortality in a very poor, conflict-burdened part of the world. I learned second-hand that some friends of friends had doubts about whether this was a good use of Canadian taxpayers' money. These friends of friends pointed out that life in this part of the world had been nasty, brutish, and short for as long as anyone could remember. People there endured chronic hunger and famine, and environmental devastation was accelerating. In these conditions far away, it was sad that men and women were dying from treatable diseases, but perhaps this was just nature's way? And what kind of quality of life would they have if they did recover from disease? The inequalities in life expectancy and health status between this region and most of Canada were understood as simple facts of nature, like the laws of gravity, and efforts to redress these disparities—to redistribute opportunities to be healthy—were seen as well-intentioned but naive. Needless to say, I did not agree with this view of global inequalities, and neither do most other Canadians, from what I have seen. (However, it is often much easier to frame the suffering of people far away as a matter of inevitability or fate than the suffering of people close to home, or of people whom we know.)

Inequity

If we choose to not see inequalities as inevitable—if we see them as evidence that all is not right in the world—then we understand such differences as **inequities**. Inequities are different from inequalities in two important ways. First, when we say that something is inequitable, we are saying that *it could be otherwise*. For example, consider research that reveals racialized practices in hiring and research, such that employers tend to favour resumés from candidates with typically "white" surnames (Bertrand and Mullainathan 2003). When we call this an inequity we mean that there is no reason why candidates with "non-white" surnames must inevitably be disadvantaged. We can imagine a world in which perceived racial category is not a hindrance to hiring. The fact that these candidates are disadvantaged is due to actions stemming from human biases and prejudices, and these biases and actions could be corrected if people chose to do so. Second, when we say something is inequitable, we mean not only that it *could* be otherwise but that it *should* be otherwise. This brings inequity into the realm of morals and ethics. The differential job-seeking experiences of people of colour and white people are not simply different, they are wrongly different because discrimination on the basis of race is wrong. Similarly, differences in life expectancy in different parts of the world are inequities because it is wrong that some people should run the risk of death from disease at a young age while other people can look forward to many healthy years.

Why are these situations wrong? The answer to that question depends on the moral orientations of the person who is answering. Some people would answer from a **compassion orientation**, according to which we as human beings are obligated to do what we can to reduce suffering. Such a compassion orientation is reflected in the teachings of many religions, which emphasize kindness and helping the less fortunate. For example, *zakat*, or giving to the poor, is one of the five pillars of the Muslim faith. Similarly, the Jewish faith espouses the concept of *mitzvot*, or "kind acts to others," as part of the process of *tikkun olam*, or "healing the world." Indeed, many faiths and cultural traditions embrace variations of the injunction to show both empathy and compassion by treating others as one would like to be treated oneself. This obligation to show kindness to other humans is so universal it is often referred to as the Golden Rule. Implicit in all the formulations of the Golden Rule is the notion that showing kindness is a moral obligation, not a means of getting what one wants. In other words, we should show compassion to other people because it is right to do so, not because we expect that we will be rewarded.

Other people might answer from a **justice orientation**, according to which inequities represent breaches of universal norms of fairness or ethical behaviour, which must be redressed. Inequity is a form of injustice, which calls out for action to change it and to make the world a more ethical, fairer place. Examples of this justice orientation to inequities can be found in reparation movements, which call for the return of property or goods that were illegally seized from people in the past, or for harms that people suffered. In the United States, for example, the reparations-for-slavery movement calls for the transfer of resources to African-American communities in reparation for the damage done by slavery in past centuries. This movement is not based on sentiments of kindness or compassion for the difficulties facing many African-American communities but, rather, on the idea that African-Americans were unfairly deprived of their lives and their possessions for the financial benefit of whites, and the belief that this historical inequity requires some form of redress.

In Canada, in 2007, the federal government attempted something similar with the Indian Residential Schools Settlement Agreement, which provided transfers of money to Aboriginal Canadians who had been put in these schools as children; they had been unjustly deprived of their culture and their connections to their families, and many had suffered abuse by teachers and staff. Clearly, no amount of money will remove the effects of childhood trauma or make everything okay, but it is necessary nonetheless. The payment of this money reflects a belief that the negative life experiences of many Aboriginal Canadians as compared to their non-Aboriginal counterparts are not merely inequalities in areas such as health and education, but are inequities because they are the result of injustice in the form of long-term racism. This racism was not natural or inevitable—it *could have been otherwise*—and, indeed, it *should have been otherwise* because racism is wrong.

Why Does Inequity Exist?

Why do inequities persist? If human beings are basically moral creatures, with a sense of right and wrong, why do some people have so much while others have so little? Certainly, some inequities are the result of greed and callousness—I want what I want, and I don't care who gets hurt in the process of my getting what I want.

A lack of empathic imagination—the inability to understand (or the choice not to think about) the sufferings of other people—may also be a culprit. For example, environmental activists often point to these characteristics in efforts to make sense of why we continue to destroy the planet, despite evidence that our high-consumption practices, as individuals and as states and corporations, are causing disproportionate amounts of suffering to people far away (and will cause suffering to our own descendants, as the planet continues to heat up). Given the knowledge that extreme weather is devastating people in coastal regions of Asia, why do people in Canada persist in buying enormous suburban houses whose construction and location results in heavy consumption of oil, gas, and other fossil fuels? Perhaps we do not see a connection between our habits and the extreme weather conditions of communities far away? Perhaps we do not believe that we are responsible for the people in those communities, even if we do see a connection? Perhaps it is difficult to see the people in those communities as similar to Canadians, so it is easier to ignore their plight?

The late sociologist Derrick Bell, in the unlikely form of a science fiction story, provided an insightful analysis of how inequities become understood as simply inequalities or differences. His subject was racial disparities in the United States, but his ideas can be transferred to many other forms of inequity. In "The Space Traders," written in 1992 and included in his book *Faces at the Bottom of the Well*, Bell imagines the arrival of extraterrestrials in the United States at the dawn of the new millennium. They are benign, even friendly, and they offer the US government the proverbial offer you can't refuse: they will provide endless clean energy and an infinite supply of gold free of charge. The only thing they ask is that all black Americans be handed over to the aliens for transport off the planet. The aliens will not say, however, what they plan to do with the black Americans.

At first glance, this sounds like an appalling form of inequity—why should a specific group of citizens be taken away from everything they know and sent off to face an unknown future for the benefit of other citizens? However, Bell goes through all the machinations through which this inequity gets reframed simply as inequality. Yes, black people are being asked to endure unequal sacrifice, but isn't that always the way it is when the nation must be protected? During wars, soldiers, whether conscripted or volunteer, suffer much more than people on the home front, and yet we all agree that these soldiers' sacrifices are necessary, even noble. Do we really know that the aliens' intentions are to harm these people? Perhaps they are being transported to a better future than the one they face in the US. Perhaps they won't mind being taken away from their lives in the US as much as white people would. Indeed, perhaps the United States would be better off without African-Americans, as they do not contribute as much to economic growth because they are poorer.

Gradually, in the story, the national mood shifts to support for the aliens' offer, and the story ends with the African-American population being forced onto the alien ship in chains. (It's important to note that in Bell's story, not all whites want to accept the aliens' offer, and some try to help their black neighbours escape once it becomes clear that "the trade" is going ahead. Similarly, some black leaders contemplate a strategic show of support for "the trade." Reactions to this extreme racial inequity are not simply the result of racial identity but engage more complex processes of justification and changing world views.)

Bell's point is to show how inequities become understood as simply inequalities or differences between groups. Using his sociological imagination, he demonstrates how we rationalize inequity and make it seem acceptable or even inevitable. If we did do so, what might we see when we look at the world?

Global Inequalities and Inequities

Sociologists and other social scientists have developed different ways to conceptualize and measure global inequality. We can look at inequalities between countries, comparing them across indicators that measure national outcomes in areas such as health, education, and income. For illustrative purposes, we will concentrate on health, with reference to other indicators.

Opportunities to be healthy are not evenly distributed across the world. Global health researchers Solomon R. Benatar and Ross Upshur suggest that up to one-third of global disease is the result of poverty (Benatar and Upshur 2010). In particular, these researchers note that "Ninety-five percent of tuberculosis cases and 98% of tuberculosis deaths are in developing countries" (Benatar and Upshur 2010, 1217). Tuberculosis, which is easily treated in high-income countries with strong health-care systems, can be life-threatening if it is contracted in a country with fewer resources. Paul Farmer, a renowned anthropologist and physician, recalls his first encounter with tuberculosis in Haiti:

> I went to rural Haiti, and as chance would have it I ended up in the town of Mirabelais. While I was there I saw an episode that has stuck with me: a young woman coughed up bright red blood. I had never seen anything like it in my life. She was referred to a clinic elsewhere and I later heard that she'd died. (PIH 2014)

Farmer's medical training in the United States had taught him that tuberculosis had been cured, and that there was an array of drugs available to treat it. However, in Haiti these drugs were not available. Rather than regarding this as a tragedy or a purely clinical matter, Farmer's experiences in Haiti led him to found an organization, Partners in Health, which both provides treatment and also foregrounds the global inequities that put people at risk for the disease and prevent them from being treated for it. For example, a huge hydroelectric dam in Haiti, which was financed by the American government and provided power to the homes and businesses of the wealthy elites, also created the conditions for cholera and other infectious diseases to spread rapidly among the peasants who were displaced (Kidder 2003).

Activists in Indonesia campaign in front of the Pasar Gede, Surakarta to prevent the spread of tuberculosis. Why do sociologists consider tuberculosis an issue of social inequity?

Partners in Health's two-track approach to medicine—treating ill-health as a form of social inequity as well as a biological issue—has been successfully scaled up to fight malaria and other infectious diseases. Farmer says his work is "less about assisting the distant needy and more about repairing a broken world" (Arnst 2006, 20), an approach that sets him apart from other medical practitioners who might not see sickness as a form of inequity. Farmer and PIH have both a compassion orientation and a justice orientation to the global inequities that are revealed in health.

What is true for health is also true for other measurable indicators of well-being, such as education and income. In terms of education, we can see inequality among countries through differences in access to primary education in developing countries. The United Nations Education, Scientific and Cultural Organization (UNESCO) found that globally 74 countries are facing a chronic teacher shortage—more than a third of all the countries in the world. The situation is especially acute in sub-Saharan Africa, where post-secondary teacher training is prohibitively expensive and where many of the teachers who do get trained end up leaving the public education sector because they have better prospects and higher wages in private employ. Moreover, UNESCO argues that countries in sub-Saharan Africa face the worst of this situation. UNESCO suggests that these countries account for over half of the global teacher shortage and that this shortage will severely limit the quality of, and access to, primary education in various areas of the world (UNESCO 2015).

The evidence for income inequality is even more extreme. For instance, one study reports that the average income of the top five per cent of wage earners in India barely equates to the relative wealth of the lowest five per cent of American wage earners (Milanovic 2013, 206). It's difficult to get truly accurate figures on global wealth distribution because wealth isn't always measured in money. (Think, for instance, of societies in which wealth is based on land tenure or hereditary entitlements.) However, researchers from Oxfam estimate that the wealthiest 1 per cent of the world own more than half of the total assets of the world (Hardoon 2015). Indeed, Hardoon's research team estimates that the wealthiest 85 billionaires in the world own as much wealth as the poorest half of the world's population.

However, using national figures doesn't always give the true picture. A country with a high average income may have a vast range of internal inequality, with a few very rich people and a lot of very poor ones. Similarly, a country with a long life expectancy may contain groups of people whose life expectancies are shorter than the national average.

One example of an internal disparity in health is seen in access to emergency health facilities. This is noticeable in Canada, where 22.5 per cent of the population live further than an hour from an emergency health-care facility. Nearly all of these people live in rural or remote areas of the country (Hameed et al. 2010). Perhaps not surprisingly, rural Canadians suffer from poorer health and are more likely to die as a result of a traumatic injury. In addition, some researchers have noted a further lack of rural health data, which is likely the by-product of an urban bias in health research (Fleet et al. 2013).

When we look at education in Canada, York University researcher Mai Nguyen argues that "the historical consequences of colonialism that resulted in diminished sense of self-worth, self-determination, and culture" have placed Aboriginal Canadians at a disadvantage within the education system (Nguyen 2011, 229). Nguyen suggests that currently only 43 per cent of Aboriginal youth (ages 14–24) are enrolled in school compared to 50 per cent of non-Aboriginal Canadian youth (Nguyen 2011, 234). The legacy of the residential school system, and the cumulative effects of dispossession and racism, compounding over generations, are only now becoming recognized as powerful influences on the life experiences of First Nations youth today. For many years in Canada, these forms of racism and the inequalities they produced were treated by most white Canadians much as Derrick Bell might have predicted—they were rationalized as necessary and even beneficial for Aboriginal Canadians.

Income inequality also remains an issue in Canada. For instance, recent female graduates of post-secondary institutions make 6 to 14 per cent less than their male cohorts in their first five years after graduation. This difference largely remains intact even if one accounts for personal circumstances and employment differences (Boudarbat and Connolly 2013)—in other words, the gender gap between men and women is not just because women choose different career and family paths than men do. And the bad news is that income inequality is increasing. Indeed, the Centre for Policy Alternatives found that salaries of the super-rich in Canada—the top 100 CEOs—were 195 times the salary of the average Canadian worker, up from 1998, when the average pay for the top 100 was "only" 105 times that of the average earner (CBC 2015).

Comparing Inequities

Not only can we look at inequities within societies, we can also compare societies in terms of how inequitable they are. Some countries have managed a fairly even distribution of income, education opportunities, and health access, while others have concentrated these resources among a fortunate minority. The most commonly used tool for measuring inequality in countries is the **Gini coefficient**, or **Gini ratio**. The Gini coefficient works like this: take a variable of interest. (Income is most commonly used, but Ginis have also been calculated for other variables which are not monetary, such as life expectancy or educational attainments.) The Gini coefficient measures how equitably that resource is shared among the entire population. For example, a Gini coefficient of 0 indicates complete equality—everyone has exactly the same income (or whatever the variable of interest may be) as everyone else. A coefficient of 1, on the other hand, represents complete inequality—one person has all of the variable of interest and everyone else has nothing. (Sometimes Ginis are expressed as percentages, rather than decimal points.) Needless to say, coefficients of exactly 0 or exactly 1 do not appear in real life. However, we can compare countries based on their national coefficients.

Countries can be sorted into higher inequality and lower inequality categories. Canada, for instance, is considered a moderately equal country when it comes to income, with a Gini of 0.33. By contrast, the United States, with a Gini of 0.44, is a much less equal country. Ginis are not related a nation's absolute wealth or poverty—Sweden, Serbia, Germany, Kazakhstan, and Pakistan all have lower Ginis (indicating a more equitable distribution of income) than Canada.

Does the degree of inequity matter for the quality of life? Surely, life is pretty comfortable among the elite, whether they are living in a very equal or a very unequal country. However, sociologists and economists argue that the existence of inequity is a social problem that affects everyone, wealthy and poor alike. In *The Spirit Level* (2009), Richard Wilkinson and Kate Pickett argue that high-Gini societies—those with great discrepancies between the wealthy and the rest—have lower levels of social trust and connection and higher levels of a range of social problems, including mental illness, anxiety, and substance abuse. These, they argue, are the effects of living in an inequitable society—they are not solely the result of being rich or poor as an individual.

Changing Global Inequalities

Global inequalities are not static and unchanging, however. Some gaps are growing wider, while others are decreasing, so the world as a whole is simultaneously becoming more and less equal, depending on what measure you are looking at.

For example, the disparity between men's and women's educational achievement has decreased in virtually every region around the globe. Researchers have reported gender parity in educational enrollment in 59 countries in 2006, up from 39 in 1999. In fact, in high-income countries, women have actually come to exceed male enrolment in many situations (Charles 2011, 358).

Similarly, life expectancies in many parts of the world are converging, as public health measures—including childhood vaccination and treatment of infectious disease—extend lives in low-income countries. This wasn't always the case, however—between 1800 and 1950, the gap in life expectancies between the wealthiest and the poorest countries actually grew. However, since the 1950s, enormous gains have been made in some countries that had experienced many deaths at young ages. There are still exceptions to the general trend of convergence—the impact of human immunodeficiency virus (HIV) in southern Africa, for instance, or rising male mortality in eastern Europe—but overall, the opportunity to live a long life is much more evenly distributed than it was 100 years ago.

At the same time, other disparities are growing. Oxfam reported that since 2009 global wealth has become increasingly concentrated among the richest 1 per cent of adults. In 2009, the globe's wealthiest 1 per cent controlled approximately 44 per cent of the globe's wealth, but by 2014 this number had increased to 48 per cent (Hardoon 2015, 2–3). And as we have already noted, income inequality in

Canada itself appears to be getting worse, if we look at the discrepancy between the highest and the lowest paid workers.

Conclusion: Pressing Inequities

In this chapter, we have distinguished among difference, inequality, and inequity. The first two might be considered inevitable, natural, or unproblematic, but when we describe something as *inequitable*, we understand it as something that can be, and ought to be, changed. Some people approach inequities from a compassion orientation, which leads them to feel pity or sympathy for others who are suffering from the sharp end of inequities, while other people approach these considerations from a justice orientation, in which inequities are viewed as intrinsically unfair and immoral.

Given that compassion and justice are principles that most people would adhere to, why do we allow inequities to persist? Derrick Bell offers a graphic and vivid account of how even the most shocking and overt inequities can be framed as simple facts of life, or even as necessary for the benefit of the majority. In your everyday life, in your conversations with friends, or in the media, you may have encountered variations on these ideas.

Whether they are rationalized, excused, or ignored, inequities manifest themselves between countries and within countries. Using examples from health, from income, and from education, we've seen how vast the differences are between countries, and even within Canada. We have also introduced techniques for measuring inequities, such as the Gini coefficients, so that we can identify societies with greater or lesser degrees of inequity, and see where Canada ranks.

Inequities are not fixed and permanent features of our world, however. We have seen how dynamic inequities can be as some gaps are growing wider while others are closing. Technological advances and historic changes contribute to the closing of some of the worst gaps, but the committed work of activists like Paul Farmer also drives the quest for equity forward. Global inequities are neither inevitable nor natural—they are produced by human actions and choices, and can be undone by the same means.

Review/Summary Questions

1. What is the difference between inequality and inequity?
2. What are Gini coefficients used for?
3. How does a justice orientation differ from a compassion orientation?
4. How might tuberculosis be considered a disease of inequity?
5. What global inequities affect your everyday life or your life history to date?

22 What Use Is Social Theory?

R.A. Sydie

Introduction

Theory is the "act of viewing, contemplating, considering," and it usually involves some imaginative interpretation of what is referred to as "data"—which for social theorists is the raw material of everyday life. **Social theory** is "first and foremost *a way of thinking* about the human world" (Bauman 1990, 8; emphasis in the original).

The term *theory* often generates negative reactions because it is assumed to be abstract, difficult, and of dubious relevance to everyday life. This is ironic because the founding mothers and fathers of social theory regarded their theoretical work as critically relevant and significant to finding solutions to the problems of everyday life. Harriet Martineau (1983 [1869], 2, 335) defined social theory as the science for the discovery of social laws and therefore the "eternal basis of wisdom" for the development of "human morality and peace." Émile Durkheim maintained that abstract theory would not be "worth the labour of a single hour if its interest were merely speculative" (1989 [1893], xxvi). As a result, these early social theorists saw the theoretical X as an essential explanatory part of any practical Y.

The key element in the development of social theory was the conceptualization of society as an autonomous entity, separate from its individual members. For nineteenth-century theorists, it seemed clear that the social was different from, and in contrast to, nature and that modern society was markedly different from traditional or primitive societies in other parts of the world. For classical social theorists, the new concept, "society," was the object of scientific investigation, which would provide solutions to the various social problems that modernity had produced. Most classical social theorists were from Western, largely European or North American societies, and they assumed, on the basis of "evidence" from ethnographic and anthropological reports, that the West was modern and the "rest" were primitive or backward. In this light, social theory was seen as a vital contribution to social progress for Western societies and as the means to bring primitive societies into the modern world under the benevolent guidance of Western "experts." As Saint-Simon wrote in 1814, the "Golden Age of the human race is not behind us but before us; it lies in the perfection of the social order" (136).

It was the clear, scientific eye of the social theorist that would provide the directions for the perfection of the social order. Without necessarily agreeing with the specifics of Marx's predictions for a new social order and how it might be achieved, classical social theorists generally endorsed the notion that the "philosophers have only *interpreted* the world, in various ways; the point is to *change* it" (Marx 1947 [1846], 199). Social theory was to break out of previous philosophical or abstract modes of thinking about the world and produce tangible *scientific facts* that would provide the basis for social change and the establishment of worldwide "human morality and peace" that Harriet Martineau predicted.

While the optimism of the early theorists has been considerably modified in current theoretical work, nonetheless social theory remains committed to addressing the pressing social issues of our time in the hope of alleviating the various troubles that affect individuals in their everyday lives (Smith 1978). It is *how* these troubles can be understood theoretically that generates different solutions for social change. Many of our current public problems may seem to be similar to those addressed by the classical social theorists, but the social, political, economic, and physical contexts are often profoundly different and require somewhat different theoretical perspectives. For example, the former modern/traditional (primitive) distinctions break down in the wired global world we inhabit, where even subsistence farmers carry cellphones. But the same imaginative interpretation of the raw material of everyday life, which was the foundational method for classical social theory, remains the same because theory is, as indicated, "a *way of thinking* about the human world" (Bauman 1990, 8).

What Is Social Theory?

For classical social theory, the solutions to modernity's problems varied, but they were framed by a confidence that theorists could produce objective and hence irrefutable knowledge about the social world as opposed to past philosophical, religious, or ideological constructions of social reality. As Comte (1975, 37) remarked, by discovering the invariant laws governing the social, the theorist could determine "what *is*, what *will be*, and what *should be*" so that past theological or metaphysical abstractions and fantasies by which theorists had explained the social world could now be rejected. The "real" nature of society would be revealed and humanity freed to pursue "Order and Progress" through **positivist sociology**.

Theoretical thinking is therefore not merely contemplative; it also involves some imaginative interpretation of what can be called *data*—which for social theorists is the raw material of everyday life. We all make sense of our world in a theoretical manner and make decisions about our conduct and responses to our world based on those theoretical suppositions, most especially if we are encountering problems. For example, in the 1960s Western women began to question the assumption that their supposedly natural destiny as adults was to be wives and mothers. Betty Freidan's book *The Feminine Mystique* (1963) discussed the sense of malaise that women (especially North American, educated, middle-class women) felt about the social pressures to realize their "femininity" solely through their roles as mothers and housewives. She called the malaise the "problem that has no name" because women did not articulate these personal troubles. Women blamed themselves for their discontent, feeling that there was something wrong with them, especially because the suburban American woman was the "envy, it was said, of women all over the world" (Freidan 1963, 13). This seeming personal problem that produced a sense of personal failure eventually became, through informal discussions and grassroots organizing among women, a collective issue that coalesced into a mass movement for women's liberation. As women realized that they experienced a common problem, they began to theorize the reasons for their situation and their discontent. Their collective theoretical analysis of the problem was summed up in the slogan "the personal is political." That is, the individual and personal "no-name" problem was revealed as a political, ideological formulation of gender power relations that oppressed women for the benefit of men. The outcome of feminist theorizing on women's position and relationships in society generated a radical re-thinking of how power operates, how it structures gender relations, and what constitutes the political.

Theory is useful in making sense of the world. But if theorizing is something that all of us do, then what special claims can social theorists, or any other specialist, advance in respect to their theoretical efforts? What sets social theory apart from our everyday sense-making? The answer lies in the distinction between criticism and critique. In the example above, women may have *criticized* the causes of their discontent, but the theorist does not rest with finding fault or venting frustration; he or she tries, instead, to produce a **critique**. Critique goes beyond mundane criticism to ask "What is the evidence?" and, most important, "How might it be different?" The theorist examines the social and cultural context in which this discontent arises as well as how, and how much, it affects the lives of others in order to understand how to make a positive, constructive difference. That is, as stated in the introduction, the theorist's "sociological imagination" translates "personal troubles into public issues" (Mills 1959, 187).

What Do Theorists Do?

Social theorists explain and interpret "personal" troubles to make sense of the social world and provide signposts as to how to effect change. Dahrendorf (1973, 58) suggests that "[t]wo intentions were the godparents of sociology. First, the new discipline was supposed to make the fact of society accessible to a rational understanding by means of testable assumptions and theories," and, second, sociology was supposed "to help the individual toward freedom and self-fulfillment." It was the clear, scientific eye of the social theorist that would provide theoretical directives for the perfection of the social order and advance individual happiness. The problem is that these two intentions often produce antithetical results. The perfection of order can just as easily constrain rather than promote the freedom and happiness of individuals. It is this dilemma that confronted classical social theorists in their examination of modern society.

For the classical social theorists, the critical public issues of modernity were capitalism, industrialization, urbanization, secularism, bureaucratization, excessive individualism, and alienation. In particular, the alienating nature of modern life seemed to be inevitable given the demands of a capitalist, industrial social structure. Rationalization and objectivity are essential to the success of capitalist modernity, but they are Janus-faced, offering an illusion of individual freedom but *only* as long as individuals control themselves and fall in line with the regimented demands of modern capitalism. Max Weber observed that capitalism involves the objective, impersonal pursuit of wealth "stripped of its religious and ethical meaning," but this in turn produces "specialists without spirit, sensualists without heart" (1904–5, 182). This rational, regimented treatment of people and things eliminates "respect, kindness and delicacies of feeling." But if the capitalists who are interested only in the pursuit of wealth are "reproached with callousness and brutality," they reject the accusation, claiming they are acting only with "logical consistency and pure impartiality" and not with any "bad intentions" (Simmel 1990 [1900], 434), a point that many bankers and economists would have endorsed prior to 2008 and perhaps still do.

Unfortunately, it was often the work of the social theorist that contributed to the fulfillment of Dahrendorf's first intention. Some social theorists provided facts that enabled state bureaucracies to produce more sophisticated, alienating, and constraining social structures and conditions that invariably ran counter to the second intention of providing for human freedom and self-fulfillment. The bureaucratic structures of modern states are designed to be efficient and effective means for the objective application of rational legal rules for the pursuit of good social order and progress. But those same bureaucratic structures ensure that any idiosyncratic needs and desires of individuals in the pursuit of their personal freedom and happiness are controlled, regimented, and/or denied. Indeed, modern states are about "red tape"—about setting rules, about administration, management, surveillance, and supervision of all individual citizens. And it is the social theorist, as the expert, who provides reliable information on how to prevent deviance from social norms, any breaching of the rules, anything "haphazard, erratic, unanticipated and accidental" from occurring (Bauman 2000, 76). This is not to say that social theorists deliberately set out to preserve or augment the powers of the modern state. However, the work of those who insist on the *scientific* status of theory, and see it as providing *objective knowledge* of society, is useful for policy-makers and politicians seeking to control populations.

The social theorist as scientist reveals the "what," "why," and "how" of social problems but, as a scientist, cannot take over the role of politicians or administrators to determine what, therefore, "should" be done.

Complicity with modern institutions of power and authority was not overtly duplicitous on the part of social theorists, however. On the contrary, such complicity was often done with the best of intentions. For example, the abstract population surveys and classifications sorted by age, sex, class, race, etc., produced by social theorists concerned with poverty and inequality provided the impersonal "objective" basis for the bureaucratic management of a welfare state ostensibly to solve those problems. But many individuals involved with welfare-state bureaucracies often find that the statistical category to which they are assigned does not fit the realities of their lives and their specific needs. Social theorists are alert to the dangers of co-option, especially by undemocratic, authoritarian regimes, but the social engineering of state bureaucracies is necessarily dependent on social theory. As a result, the second, emancipatory intention of using the theorist's expertise to advance the freedom and self-fulfillment of individuals may well be contradicted by the implementation of their research findings.

Classical social theorists produced useful analyses of the nature of modernity, but as a *science* of society the reviews and results have been mixed. The social problems identified as characteristic of modernity—capitalism, industrialization, bureaucratization, excessive individualism, alienation, and secularization—remain problematic, generating personal troubles and producing public problems, but how they are manifested and theorized has changed. For example, the extremes of wealth and poverty have increased as capitalist enterprises consolidate their global reach, seemingly indifferent to any coherent control or regulation by governments. Industrialization is a global phenomenon and one that has often sidelined the former industrial powerhouses of the West only to introduce horrendous working conditions for many industrial workers in the southern hemisphere. The presumed disinterested objectivity of "pure" science is challenged by various problems with the aftermath of the discoveries. For example, drugs developed from medical breakthroughs may generate unexpected, often dangerous, side effects. Engineering innovations, moreover, may result in unforeseen problems of environmental degradation. And confidence in science is challenged when it is revealed that top scientists have "cooked" their results. The social problems caused by excessive individualism and alienation, of central concern to classical theorists of modernity, remain and are exaggerated by the simulated, wired, abstract world we inhabit—where, for example, "friends" are only encountered on screens and an enemy can be depersonalized as a blip on the computer and easily erased. Racial and gender inequities persist and have generated genocidal conflicts. Secularization, regarded as the inevitable result of modernity, has not materialized in quite the manner foreseen by classical theorists. On the contrary, in the most powerful, capitalist, liberal democracy—the United States—religion remains a critical determinant in all dimensions of social and political life. In addition, the fundamentalism that affects all religious denominations has become a decisive, divisive, and murderous factor in global politics.

There is, therefore, considerable skepticism about the social theorists' hope that a reformed, scientifically based modernity can usher in a golden age of order, progress, happiness, and self-fulfillment. One theorist even contends that current "[t]heory discussions have little bearing on major social conflicts and political struggles or on important public debates over current social affairs" (Seidman 1991, 132). Nonetheless, social theory's ability to explain society remains important precisely because of the abstractions of social power and the sense that social problems—especially current global ethnic, religious, and racial conflicts—seem to be inevitable, intractable, and beyond individual capacities for change. The theorists' task is to tackle such problems, guarding against the ethical dangers of a "pure" science that may dispense with the "real" and make it easier to condone or ignore inhuman actions. As Mills points out, it is the ethical danger of abstraction that "hides" the humanity of individuals affected by "efficient, rational, technically clean cut" actions. Such actions are "inhuman acts because they are impersonal" (1963, 238).

Currently, for some theorists, modernity is no longer an issue; we are now **postmodern** and therefore we confront a different social universe that requires different ways of explaining the social. But what is postmodernity? Can it present a more positive future for all individuals? And what is the use of social theory if we are postmodern?

Postmodern Social Theory?

The confident assertion that scientific knowledge can act as a progressive force for the freedom and emancipation of humanity by revealing the "truth" about social and political reality is, according to postmodern theorists, a delusion. In fact, truth claims need to be treated skeptically because they are invariably claims to power (Foucault 1977). For example, one of the truth claims advanced by many social theorists (as well as by scientists, theologians, and medical practitioners) well into the twentieth century was that women were unfit for intellectual pursuits. Among the several reasons advanced for this "truth" was the claim made by many physicians that "the physical organization and function of woman naturally disqualify her for severe study, and an education essentially popular and largely ornamental is alone suited to her sphere" (Rothman 1978, 27–8).[1] Unalterable physical and mental difference was the "truth" of gender. As a result, patriarchal power was biologically ordained, immutable, and inevitable. But it has become clear that sex is not a biological binary that separates women from men at birth and that gender is a variable social/cultural designation.

The postmodern perspective views all knowledge as contingent. Plurality, diversity, difference, complexity, and hybridity replace confident **universalizing** classical theories, the "grand narratives" that claimed to produce the "truth" about the nature of social life. But if social theory has to abandon its generalizing, universalizing ambitions (Featherstone 1988), then what remains? How can the theorist claim any authority to speak about the social when such reflections are regarded as simply variants on language games or culturally specific notions, none of which can claim any privileged status? More troubling is the question of the sincerity of the postmodern position. The idea assumed by Western intellectuals in the past that their modernity gave them the authority to speak "of"" or, more arrogantly, "for" primitive, traditional Others may have been rejected, but can we be sure that current postmodern theory is not another variant on this old theme? For example, can the subsistence farmer in Africa or the exploited garment worker in South Asia understand his or her world as a postmodern space in which individuality is prized, lifestyle choices and playful consumption are the order of the day, and contingency is embraced as making life worthwhile? Or is this another Eurocentric/North American, universalizing theoretical stance?

Whatever the answers to these questions, it is clear that it cannot be business as usual for social theorists (Bauman 1992, 54). The critical point is that social theorists can no longer claim that the classical concept of "society" is the basic, fundamental theoretical concept. The classical concept was always tacitly tied to the idea of the nation-state. Although it may have been recognized "theoretically" that nation-states were not closed entities, most theorists continued to confound the idea of society with the idea of the nation-state as the framework for analysis. In addition, the primary models of society that theorists used were Western democratic states. The use of "society" in this way is what enabled social theorists "to speak of social laws of regularities, of the normative regulation of social reality, of trends and developmental sequences" (Bauman 1992, 60). As indicated, it was this conflation that made social theory useful to nation-states, especially Western nation-states, in their control over the "less developed" or "less advanced" sectors of their own or other "primitive," "uncivilized" societies.

The nation-state/society is a porous concept, and global social order today is governed more by the needs and dictates of transnational corporations, non-governmental organizations (NGOs), and international consortiums and agencies. In addition, nation-states no longer need to employ the old coercive, disciplinary practices of modernity to ensure order and legitimacy. Social order and citizen compliance can be secured more easily by "seduction" (Baudrillard 1983). Coercion and control can be exercised through persuasion, impression management, and image manipulation. Seduced by consumer culture, bombarded with infomercials and slick advertising, and tempted by the constant creation of new "needs," the satisfaction of which is "guaranteed" to transform the self in new and desirable ways, citizens have great difficulty in finding ways to articulate their personal troubles as public issues.

Seduction, however, is limited, if only because there are multiple sectors of power that compete for citizens' affections. Furthermore, people are not robotic dupes. For example, the "crisis" of voter apathy, or, more realistically, voter cynicism, is partly explained by voters' realization that elections do little to alter the fundamental mundane, practical problems of everyday life (Habermas 1975).[2]

The "crisis" is largely one for political elites whose legitimacy is rendered questionable when it rests on poor voter response, although consistent poor responses may have the paradoxical effect of forcing political attention onto pressing social problems in the hope of regaining voter confidence.

While a self-enclosed notion of "society" is difficult to sustain, and global forces tend to generate a fatalistic approach to solving local, national, or international problems, social change is not always a top-down process. Most of us still identify ourselves as citizens of a nation-state, and the continued proliferation of grassroots pressure groups indicates that not everyone is a solitary, postmodern individual, lost in the crowd, feeling "unimportant, lonely and disposable" (Bauman 1990, 68).[3] Problems that may seem overwhelming, constraining, and even inevitable can yield to citizen pressure. As a result, social theory is still needed to convert personal troubles into public issues by helping to make sense of the abstractions of social power and how the various "forces" that appear so constraining are developed and maintained, and how they might be resisted and changed. It is the social theorists' "special business" to help us to make sense of what seems to lie outside "the scope of everyday practices" (Smith 1987, 161).

And So, What Is the Use of Social Theory?

The classical narratives of social theory may no longer hold up, but the "post" of postmodernity does not necessarily mean a radical rupture with the social and political issues addressed by those narratives. If postmodernity is understood as "after" rather than "anti," this "clears the ground for new political and social strategies which embrace difference, pluralism and the incommensurability of culture and values" (Turner 1990, 12). The important point that should guide the social theorist if she is to play a useful and important role as a public intellectual is that she should not simply identify the significant issues of our time but also offer a *critique* and thus reveal the way in which personal troubles are public issues that can result in the formation of solutions to these issues. Social theory must be *in* the world and claim the "right to expose the conceit and arrogance, the unwarranted claims to exclusivity of others' interpretations, but without substituting itself in their place" on the understanding that the choices made about "how to go on" in this world are not waiting to be revealed but must be worked for (Bauman 1992, 214). Social theorists still need to "engage (and enrage) the public," recognizing that they will never win a popularity contest among those who claim power and privilege (Agger 1991, 185). In the complex, risky global world we inhabit, the "vocation of the social theorist is . . . to be positively—as opposed to negatively and nostalgically—analytical and *critical*" (Robertson 1990, 57).

Conclusion

There is as much need for social theory today as there was in the past. The confidence in the first intention—making the fact of society accessible to rational understanding—may have been reformulated by a healthy skepticism about scientific claims, but this needs to be balanced by the recognition that scientific theory and practice is still a necessity, all the more so because it is currently under siege from religious zealotry that hinders the pursuit of the second intention—helping individuals realize freedom and self-fulfillment. It is the second intention that is the critical, ethical basis for the social theorist to adopt as a goal when reflecting on current problematic public issues and suggesting solutions.

Review/Summary Questions

1. What does "the personal is political" mean for social theory?
2. What are the two "godparents" of sociology?
3. How do modern bureaucratic structures counter human freedom and self-fulfillment?
4. What, according to the theorist Mills, are the ethical dangers of abstract theorizing?
5. What is wrong with confounding the idea of the nation-state with the idea of society?

Notes

1. University or college education was especially dangerous to women because of the "periodical *infirmity* of their sex," which, on a monthly basis, "unfits them for any responsible effort of mind, and in many cases of body also" (quoted in Rothman 1978, 25).
2. It should be noted that the issue of voter apathy also seems to be a problem for Western nations. Newly enfranchised citizens in many parts of the world have often had high and enthusiastic voter participation. And in those parts of the world where a version of democracy involves ensuring that the votes confirm the continued power of the current dictatorship, Western-style apathy must seem inconceivable if not frivolous.
3. For example, the collective euphoria expressed by Canadians over the 2010 Winter Olympics was an occasion for the expression of national, patriotic pride for many citizens and certainly for the Canadian athletes.

23 What Questions Has Sociology Deserted?

Lorne Tepperman with the assistance of Zoe Sebastien

Introduction

In recent years, I have read a lot of material outside my field of immediate research interest—problem gambling—to prepare a new textbook that introduces students to sociology. In doing this, I have learned a great deal about many different fields of sociology but from new sources using somewhat less familiar perspectives: postmodernism, critical race theory, cultural studies, intersectionality theory, and so on. Though it is exciting to confront new ways of thinking about the world, it is also puzzling that much of the new work doesn't try to answer the original sociological topics that attracted me, and other sociologists, to the field 50 years ago. This brief chapter is about this problem.

Some Background

Before looking specifically at a few of the topics sociology has neglected—that is, stopped actively researching—I will briefly describe how sociology looked half a century ago.

Fifty years ago, the dominant sociological belief in North America was **positivism**—a conviction that you could make sociological laws through empirical analysis. One of the books that impressed young students then with its sheer boldness was by Bernard Berelson and Gary Steiner. Titled *Human Behavior: An Inventory of Scientific Findings* (1964), the book tried to codify everything sociologists knew about various topics close to Berelson's heart. These included public opinion, political behaviour, the effects of reading on people's attitudes, mass communication, and so on. The book may have been misguided even then: likely, it was never possible to codify all of social science knowledge, and it never will be. That is because too many social principles are conditional or contextual: how they work depends mainly on the particular setting, situation, or demographic mix.

Yet early sociology, before (say) 1970, mostly believed that discovering and documenting the scientific laws of society was possible. Another example is a book by my former teacher and mentor, George Homans. That book was titled, simply, *The Human Group* (1950). Based on an interesting variety of group studies, the book aimed to discover universal principles that would apply to all groups at all times and places. In this way, it assumed that we could understand the practices of a present-day juvenile gang by studying nineteenth-century Irish peasants or understand the operation of a winning basketball team by studying a small, preliterate Australian tribe.

Homans was right, to a degree: there are universal principles of group dynamics, and sociology has come a long way toward understanding them. (For example, the principles concern leadership, group ritual, cohesive norms, goal-setting, and the like.) However, today psychologists, social workers, and management experts are doing new work on this topic while sociologists have mostly moved on to other topics without ever having discovered how we can build a winning team, a happy family, a contented classroom, a productive workplace, and so on.

Whatever the current state of sociology, given the positivistic mindset of sociologists when I first entered the field, it is understandable that the very first research project I worked on—and a typical one—was empirical and positivistic in nature. In the summer after my third undergraduate year, I was hired at the former Addiction Research Foundation of Ontario (which is now the Centre for Addiction and Mental Health [CAMH]) as a research assistant to sociologist P.J. Giffen, a specialist in deviance and addictions. My job was to write a report on a group of 50 first-time offenders, who, several years earlier, had been arrested for drunkenness for the first time ever. I was to find out which of them had gone on to become repeated or chronic drunkenness offenders, who, in turn, stood a good chance of ending up as alcoholics on "skid row." My little study was to fit into a larger study of skid row alcoholics that Professor Giffen and his collaborators had been working on for years.

I analyzed the interview data that had already been collected, gathered new information about the later arrest records of these first offenders, and carried out an elementary statistical analysis of the results. The data showed that first offenders with the least education, least occupational status, and (most important) fewest social and family contacts were most likely to become chronic offenders. These were people—all men—without much **social capital**, cultural capital, human capital, and money. In time, they would be arrested repeatedly, beginning a long downward spiral that would see them pass repeatedly through jails, hostels, and, occasionally, hospitals. Some would finally die on the streets, in hostels or shabby rooming houses. Their problem, however, was not an above-average level of alcohol addiction; it was a below-average level of social attachment.

This finding about first offenders—so simple yet so powerful—hooked me on sociology. It showed me that sociology could play a role in studying social problems, making social policy, and understanding the plight of poor and isolated people—society's victims. Later, in social theory classes, I learned that this had always been the purpose of sociology. Indeed, sociologists had always tried to study the facts of social life and to develop hypotheses, principles, and even "laws" and apply these to improve people's lives and build a better society.

Auguste Comte, who first conceived the idea of "sociology," imagined a science of human societies that would help humanity make social as well as technological progress. Karl Marx, in turn, imagined that a systematic, sociological study of history would help end inhuman exploitation. The left-leaning sociologists of turn-of-the-century England, Canada, and the US, moreover, believed that sociological research could help improve the lives of the poor, the weak, and the oppressed.

Moreover, when I came into sociology in the early 1960s, a youthful wave of idealism once again supported the idea that sociology could fix society by studying it, criticizing it, and coming up with new and better ways of doing things. Sociology classrooms at that time were filled with idealistic young people who opposed the Vietnam war, racial oppression, nuclear adventurism, and the historic mistreatment of women; and the discipline responded accordingly.

Of course, that was a long time ago. With the rise of **postmodernism**, we have become more skeptical today about the possibility of progress or even social improvement. It has become obvious that a century-and-a-half of positivistic sociology has not been enough to erase capitalism, racism, sexism, or many of the other social ills that concerned earlier generations. However, despite the critical self-consciousness of our postmodern condition, we must still admit the empirical truth—that there has been social progress and that it is likely that some of it resulted from the efforts of sociologists and their students.

Some Deserted Topics

The question now is, are none of the goals of early sociology relevant anymore? Should sociology have "deserted"—or, at the very least, neglected—the topics and research questions that were so dear to many nineteenth- and twentieth-century sociologists, or should we reopen a discussion of these topics? My answers, respectively, are that, no, we should not have deserted those goals, and, yes, the discussion must be reopened and continued. To understand my answers, however, we must begin by discussing the questions themselves and some possible reasons—reasons that are unfounded and unjustifiable—for their abandonment in the first place.

Alienation

First, consider the question of the causes and effects of **alienation**. The concept of alienation was popularized, though not invented, by Karl Marx in his "early manuscripts" of 1848. In these manuscripts, Marx used the term *alienation* to suggest a dehumanization that resulted when people were treated as objects or mere cogs in the wheels of capitalism. Subject to exploitation and humiliation, people became estranged from their work, from the things they produced at work, from other workers, and even from themselves. In effect, Marx asserted, they became machines.

In the late 1950s, Melvin Seeman (1959) rebooted the concept by combining it with several other sociological and psychological ideas, such as **anomie**, estrangement, isolation, and meaninglessness and by then developing empirical measures of these concepts. His work launched a surge of new research on alienation throughout the late 1950s and 1960s.

However, there has been almost no research on alienation in North American sociology since the 1970s, which seems odd given that ordinary people do not seem to feel less alienated today than they did 50 years ago. Indeed, if anything, we are even more alienated today. For many individuals, the desperate search for meaning and social connection in their lives is unsuccessful; as a result, they feel unhappy, demoralized, alienated, and empty. It is perhaps this combination of feelings that leads so many people today to modern "addictions." New addicts consume food to obesity and mass media to idiocy, use drugs and sex to find meaning, and surf the Net endlessly in hopes of contacting anyone about anything—perhaps, merely to confirm they are alive. Today, television and social media seem to have become the "opiate of the masses," as Karl Marx called religion.

My question is this: if people today are still estranged from one another, why have we ceased studying the problem of alienation and ceased seeking solutions to it? We have clearly not found an answer yet. The goal of sociology, however, is to critically analyze society, find its flaws, and then come up with ways of improving it—even if that improvement is only slight, slow, and gradual. Thus, abandoning the question of alienation merely because no progress has been made is unacceptable; I suggest we reopen the discussion. Perhaps, if we do, we will be able to find ways to measure and improve the quality of work life (or school life) and maybe find a way to deal with some of the rampant addictions and mental illnesses our society is currently facing.

Labelling Theory

Consider another equally important yet deserted sociological issue: the effects of **labelling theory**. Labelling theory is taught in every introductory textbook and introductory course; however, the topic does not enjoy the popularity it once did. Labelling theory says that people judge people and put values (or labels) on them: good or bad, beautiful or ugly, smart or slow, and so on. In turn, we tend to live up to or live down to the labels others impose on us. This fits well with Charles Cooley's earlier theory (1902) of the **looking-glass self**, created in 1902, which says that people evaluate themselves according to what they read in other people's eyes. Individuals respond to how others view them, and come to view themselves similarly.

Thus, a person viewed and treated as unattractive will feel unattractive, and even exclude him- or herself from social life, thereby creating a self-fulfilling prophecy and becoming an "unattractive person" with no friends. Similarly, a person viewed as being not very bright will lower his or her academic ambitions, try less hard, and do poorly on tests, again creating a self-fulfilling prophecy and becoming a "slow" person who gets bad grades.

The legitimacy of labelling theory, or the theory of the looking-glass self, was tested and corroborated by psychologists Robert Rosenthal and Lenore Jacobson. In 1968, they published *Pygmalion in the Classroom*, a book discussing the relationship between a teacher's expectations and a student's performance. The set of experiments they conducted, which are described in the book, reveal that when teachers believe a student isn't very bright, they will give that student less help, and his or her grades will, indeed, drop; that student will then test as unintelligent and, in this sense, become so. Contrarily, if the same teachers think a student is smart, that student will get more attention and receive higher grades. Thus, Rosenthal and Jacobson's experiments seem to corroborate labelling theory and show that the way a person labels you can affect the way you see yourself and, in consequence, also affect your performance.

Labelling theory can affect a person's performance in two different ways: externally and internally. Labelling can work internally by attacking people's ambition and self-esteem. In this case, labelling works because people come to expect less of themselves if they believe other people expect little of them. Labelling can also work externally by stigmatizing and excluding people. In this case, labelling works because of the biases and limited opportunities that follow from it. There are many modern examples where it is possible that labelling theory plays an influential role, either internally or externally, on a person's performance.

My question is this: if labelling still occurs and the theory that this labelling influences a person's performance seems to be both plausible and possible today, why has its popularity waned? A likely answer is that labelling theory is not always true. Sometimes labelling has limiting effects, and sometimes it does not. This fact might have been what caused some modern sociologists to view the theory as trivial and not worth pursuing, since it cannot be proven systematically.

This answer, however, is unacceptable. A sociologist's job is to be critical and to use empirical investigation to discover the factors affecting a person's experience in society, no matter whether those factors always have effects or only sometimes play a role. Thus, sociologists must do more to investigate the effects of labelling so as to discover the conditions under which labelling does have a harmful effect, versus the conditions under which it does not. Questions such as "To whom do people tend to give more credence when they receive labels or evaluations?" and "Which labellers have the power to use labels to cause the stigmatization or exclusion of other societal members?" have yet to be answered.

Social Distance

Consider a third deserted topic: **social distance**, the degree to which one ethnic or racial group is willing to be intimate with another, different, group. The psychologist Emory Bogardus (1925) developed this idea in the 1920s, and although social researchers employed it for decades after, it has been relatively unused in the past 30 to 40 years. Bogardus intended to use this concept as a way of measuring the distance or closeness between different ethnic or racial groups. In part, his goal was purely scientific: to discover which groups feel drawn to, or repelled by, which other groups. However, Bogardus also saw social distance as a way of assessing social improvement based on whether or not mixing and assimilation among societal groups was increasing, despite traditional ethnic or racial dislikes. The original Bogardus measure (1925) was a scale that ranks people's willingness to accept members of a certain racial, ethnic, or other group into closer or more distant social relationships. These relationships are listed here from the closest relationship to the most distant:

1. Close relative by marriage
2. Close personal friend
3. Neighbour living on the same street
4. Co-worker in same occupation
5. Citizen in one's own country
6. Temporary visitor in one's own country
7. Someone excluded altogether from one's own country

Today, the question of social distance is still applicable and useful as a possible theory of social progress. Indeed, progress in this sense is clearly visible in that groups have been mixing more and more. Over the past 50 years, social distance among ethnic and racial groups has been generally declining in North America. Ever-fewer signs of overt racism and ever-increasing rates of racial, ethnic, and religious mixing at school, at work, and in marriage confirm this observation. (For rates of intermarriage, see Figure 23.1.) However, although this issue has shown much progress, there are still more aspects to it that are in need of explanation. For example, some societal groups—such as racialized minorities—are still more excluded than other groups, and some groups are still more exclusionary than others. Thus, arguing that the question of social distance was deserted because sociology has already completely answered it is untenable, since this is clearly not the case. Indeed, the exclusivity and exclusion of certain societal groups indicates an area where further investigation into the question of social distance is necessary.

Anomie or Strain Theory

Another equally interesting theory that has received less research attention of late is Robert K. Merton's (1938) "anomie theory," often called "strain theory." The theory argues that seemingly bizarre and unrelated types of deviant behaviour

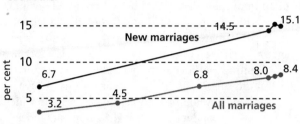

% of marriages involving spouses of a different race or ethnicity from each other

Note: New marriages numbers are from 1980 Census and 2008–2010 American Community Survey (ACS). All marriages are from U.S, Decennial Census data and 2008–2010 ACS, IPUMS.

Figure 23.1 Rates of Intermarriage, 1980 to 2010

Source: "The Rise of Intermarriage," Pew Research Center, Washington, DC (February, 2012), www.pewsocialtrends.org/2012/02/16/chapter-1-overview/.

are actually sensible and related to one another. According to Merton, this kind of behaviour should be seen as a meaningful, "functional" adaptation to anomie, or as the solution to the fundamental problem caused by a gap between people's culturally determined, consumerist-driven desires and their access to socially acceptable ways of satisfying these desires.

Indeed, these so-called adaptations—crime, mental illness, addiction, and other seemingly alienated approaches to living—are what make it possible for capitalism to survive. In this way, they are functional not only to the alienated individual, who is successfully able to devise a new way of living, but to the social and economic system, which is committed to capitalism.

With the rampant and prevalent examples of addictions—possible adaptations to modern-day social and economic issues—Merton's anomie theory seems to be worth exploring now more than ever. And yet, this approach, too, has been largely deserted. Why? Perhaps the reason for the neglect of this theory is similar to the explanation provided for the desertion of labelling theory: namely, that it cannot predict what kinds of people are going to devise what kinds of adaptation, how long they will adhere to those adaptations, or why certain adaptations are more common in certain neighbourhoods, communities, or societies than in others. That does not mean that the approach is without value, however. Sociologists should take up the study of anomie again and try to specify the conditions under which it will give rise to crime rates or addiction rates or rates of mental illness. What sociologists should not do is abandon the question of anomie altogether simply because its conditional influence has not yet been defined.

Baumrind's Theory of Parenting Style

Another example of an important theory that has fallen out of favour concerns the issue of good parenting: Diana Baumrind's (1966) theory about superior types versus inferior types of parenting. This theory asserts that authoritative parenting (which combines firm rules with loving support) is superior to three alternative forms of parenting: authoritarian (rules/no love), permissive (love/no rules), and neglectful (no rules/no love). This theory seems to have incredible potential to explain childhood development and to suggest ways in which society can create conditions that are conducive to that development. Indeed, studies over the past two decades have shown that authoritative parenting is more likely than the other three styles to produce happy, healthy children. These children tend to do well in school, stay out of trouble with the law, get along well with other people, and respect themselves.

Ironically, despite the support for this theory and its potential to be applicable universally, it is often dismissed and even rejected by modern sociologists because "universal" theories such as Baumrind's are subject to a postmodern skepticism about the possibility of finding universally applicable theories at all.

With the decline of logical positivism, the dominant sociological view 50 years ago, came the rise of postmodernism, a late twentieth-century concept in the arts, architecture, and criticism, emphasizing a self-conscious critique of one's own knowledge of truth and general distrust of earlier, previously accepted theories. Postmodern sociologists are, therefore, inclined to oppose the search for universal principles of social life, some even going so far as to deny the existence of any such principles altogether. The adherence of many modern sociologists to postmodernism may explain why even theories like Baumrind's theory of parenting, which profess to be universally applicable, are either rejected outright or regarded with suspicion and distrust.

Postmodern sociologists are skeptical of Baumrind's theory because, as they correctly point out, in various parts of the world, people expect different kinds of parenting and, therefore, may adapt to authoritarian parenting differently than we might do. Thus, any attempt to make a universal statement about the effects of parenting styles on child development would seem to be destined for failure. However, even in light of this criticism, totally rejecting Baumrind's theory seems an unjustified response. What is needed now is a series of cross-national studies to discover the universality, or particularity, of Baumrind's findings, not neglect the question altogether.

The job of the sociologist in this case is to clarify and identify the conditions under which the Baumrind theory holds or does not hold. For example, we may want to find out if the theory is valid in urban regions of the world but not in rural regions; in secular parts of the world but not theocratic parts; and in societies that promote gender equality but not in societies where men routinely subordinate women (and children).

Modernization

Another topic not often studied in present-day sociology, which could also possibly be due to the rise of postmodernism, is "modernization," a topic that not only dominated sociology 50 years ago but also could be seen, in certain senses, as the founding problem of sociology. The founding thinkers of sociology— Marx, Weber, and Durkheim—were all concerned with the likely effects of urbanization, industrialization, political revolution, new technology, new forms of social organization (e.g., bureaucracy, rule of law), and, above all, capitalism. Nineteenth-century sociologists tended to be optimistic about the possibility of "progress," although they may have disagreed about the shape this progress would, or should, take. They all agreed, however, that a modern, literate, urban industrial society carried more potential for freedom and human fulfillment than traditional rural societies. In particular, they heralded the escape from the traditional constraints of religion, caste, class, and provincialism.

At first glance, this case of neglect may seem justified. After all, it is fairly obvious that "modernity" did not give us everything that humanity had expected. We can probably all agree that the twentieth century—however technically and educationally advanced—was a nightmare of war, cruelty, and disappointed hopes. It is hard for us to believe in progress or modernity today, any more than we can believe in capitalism, communism, nationalism, or organized religion as sources of human empowerment. And yet, I will insist that the abandonment of the topic of modernity and its impact on society is still an improper course for sociologists to take. Just because modernization failed to satisfy all of our grand expectations does not mean that we as sociologists should give up on the notion.

Instead, we should find out under what conditions modernity worked reasonably well and under what conditions it failed dismally and try to explain the successes and failures of the past so that we can work to create more successes and fewer failures in the future. Indeed, this question is just as relevant today as it was a century or even two centuries ago, as is evident in the clash between (for example) traditional Islam and modern Western secularism. Learning from historical case studies is one of the best ways to learn how to address the issue of modernization in the form in which it appears and affects society today. The work of postmodernists would, in general, benefit from being more informed by modernization—particularly by the progressive, problem-solving goals that motivated much of the social science work published between 1870 and 1970.

Altruism

Despite the revival of interest in social inequality and social mobility in general (see below), a possible theory for approaching those topics, that of **altruism**, has been abandoned. Altruism is one of the "social sentiments" that was investigated by some of sociology's key figures—including Émile Durkheim and Pitirim Sorokin. It was the great classical economist Adam Smith (2010 [1759]), however, who started the conversation a century earlier when he discussed the "moral sentiments" of society. Altruism as a solution to inequality is based on the idea that human societies are held together by something more than self-interest and that people are more than just profit-maximizers.

Throughout history, people have risked their lives and belongings for grand ideas and for other people. They have often acted in the interest of things larger than themselves; and it is this that often holds societies together. We see this altruism every day in friendships, families, communities, schools, and workplaces. In fact, the only place we do not see altruism is in the marketplace. The question that most intrigued Sorokin toward the end of his life was how we might capitalize on altruism to increase social cohesion and improve general well-being (see, for example, Sorokin 1950).

Despite the potential ability of altruism to provide some tangible solutions to the continued increase in inequality in Canada, this approach has been largely abandoned. Although an altruistic society is conceivably more attainable than the classless society to which Marx had pledged himself, modern sociologists, for the most part, no longer research it. Indeed, while it is possible that creating an altruistic society is the goal of sociologist Amitai Etzioni (1996) and others who promote present-day "communitarianism," we know little more about the conditions that promote altruism than Durkheim or Sorokin did a century ago, and yet altruism is no longer a subject of sociological investigation.

The Resurgence of Some Deserted Topics

Whether we choose to investigate altruism as a possible solution to income inequality or social mobility, the fact remains that sociologists have come to see these topics as increasingly important—and for good reason. Consider, for example, the problem of present-day homelessness. Today, many Canadians, sociologists and non-sociologists alike, are concerned about homeless people, and the recent economic turbulence has only caused homelessness and other, similar instances of social inequality to increase. Although homeless people are hard to count and often nearly invisible, we know they lead lives of quiet desperation, ill health, and, often, great danger. Sociologists today who study social inequality and mobility are taking initiatives to improve their condition, starting with their housing and health care.

What is interesting is that the more we study and understand the plight of the homeless and other socially disadvantaged members of society, the more we are reminded that they are in their current situation not because they are sicker, weaker, or more blameworthy than the rest of us but because they have fewer advantages and resources, such as social capital, cultural capital, human capital, or, simply, money. And so, 50 years later, it seems that we are returning to the basic concern with which we started, the one that attracted me to sociology in the first place, and the one that all of the aforementioned deserted questions were initially initiated in order to treat: that people's lives are often beyond their control.

That is why we study society, why we come up with important questions, why we investigate them as they pertain to our current situation, and why we then use our knowledge to create social safety nets and devise policies of harm reduction.

Income Inequality

Early sociologists had hoped to tackle the issue of income inequality and erase it entirely or, at the very least, avoid and remove its worst harms. Today, we can be certain that sociology did not wipe out income inequality. For a while, the topic of income inequality also seemed destined for the sociological "garbage heap" and a candidate for intellectual desertion.

However, with the recent economic turbulence since 1990 and especially since the financial crash of 2008, sociological research on income inequality has, in fact, increased. It seems that when it comes to income inequality, even if we now know that it is not universally solvable, we have come to recognize that it is still a question worthy of investigation and an important issue for which some kind of solution, however temporary, must be sought. Large numbers of sociologists are investigating this issue again; they are asking how successes have been achieved in this domain and how we can make better social policies, in specific circumstances, to achieve added successes. Although we have long given up the idea of a fully egalitarian society, it seems that we still believe we may be able to make better headway solving at least some of the problems commonly associated with social inequality.

Social Mobility

A closely related topic, social mobility, has also undergone a similar rebirth. Social mobility research—especially, research on intergenerational social mobility—was initially intended to find out whether society was open or closed to talented, educated people from poor families and whether it was becoming more open over time. Such mobility research led one of Canada's greatest sociologists, John Porter, to argue for the expansion of post-secondary education in Canada (and against multiculturalism, which he saw as condoning ethnic enclaves, self-exclusion, and even discrimination). People who studied social mobility were convinced that, even if perfect equality of condition was unattainable, we might at least aspire to achieve equal opportunity; and we could only assess our progress by measuring intergenerational mobility.

Although it was a central topic of sociology in the 1950s, 1960s, and 1970s, by the 1980s the question of social mobility had dropped out of favour and remained virtually unstudied for years. However, with recent economic developments and the resulting increase in income inequality, there has been a correlated resurgence of interest in the question of social mobility, as well. Indeed, sociologists today likely see the question of social mobility as not only related to the question of income inequality but as possibly able to provide some kind of explanation for or solution to it. Thus, with the growing relevance and urgency of the issue of income inequality, related questions, like that of social mobility, have also risen in importance.

Conclusion

In conclusion, many of the topics of study 50 years ago have been given less attention than they deserve, either because they were not universally applicable, in which case we unfairly trivialized them, or because they claimed to be universally applicable, in which case we have become so skeptical that we immediately, and unfairly, rejected them. In both cases, we have not done enough to investigate whether there is, indeed, some truth to the theory or some value in pursuing the question further. Indeed, we seem to have "thrown out the baby with the bathwater," so to speak, and have therefore failed to see not only how these questions are still relevant to society today but, how, even if they are not obviously immediately relevant, they may become relevant in the future.

That past issues can be reincarnated in the form of current issues or future ones is evident in many sociological examples. The "skid-row alcoholic," about whom I wrote my first report, now takes the shape of the homeless man, woman, or child of today. The issues of income inequality and mobility that plagued sociologists of the nineteenth century have become extremely important in today's society, although they are now expressed differently and can be traced to different causes.

These examples, along with many others, should serve as a warning and a caution that important sociological problems do not disappear simply because we choose to ignore them. These "deserted" topics and theories are not dead, as many would like to believe. Instead, they lie dormant or comatose, waiting for the moment in which society changes such that they are brought to the forefront, once again, and sociologists come to deem them worthy of investigation.

This notion of addressing and investigating only those issues that are deemed currently relevant is not a good one. It leaves us unnecessarily vulnerable to future social issues for which we will likely find ourselves ill-prepared. Indeed, even sociological issues that we have managed to solve may, as they often have in the past, resurface in the future in different forms and require different solutions. Society is dynamic and ever-changing; and it is likely, therefore, that our current answers to social questions may, one day, no longer work.

Thus, not investigating issues either because they are difficult to solve, have been temporary solved, or no longer seem worth solving is not a responsible thing for a sociologist to do. It leaves us unnecessarily vulnerable. No, we cannot completely escape our vulnerability to the impacts of future social changes. And, no, we cannot anticipate every possible future question. However, what we can do is prepare ourselves as best as is humanly possible by learning from history, which tends to repeat itself, and by learning how to wield the tools of social investigation that we have inherited from the great sociologists who came before us.

Indeed, by reading the works of these great thinkers, we enter a dialogue with some of the smartest people who ever thought about societies and social problems. It is the continuation of this dialogue and the ability to learn from the past to improve the future that will allow for true progress. When these sociological giants are offering you their shoulders, do not hesitate to show your gratitude and proudly stand upon them. And so I urge you to take up the torch, receive the inheritance these great thinkers have left to you, build on and add to their knowledge, and then use everything you have learned and discovered to improve society and build a better future.

Review/Summary Questions

1. Try to think of some other sociological topics or theories that may be less popular or less regularly studied.
2. Take any social issue today and give an example of a related historical case study that can be used to offer a possible solution to it.
3. What, if anything, do the topics discussed in this chapter have in common?
4. Describe and explain the possible influence that a world view can have on deciding which questions are pursued or abandoned in the field of sociology. (Look at the importance of logical positivism in the mid-twentieth century and postmodernism in the late twentieth century.)
5. What can we do to ensure that important topics, such as these, continue to receive attention?

24 What Does the Future Hold for Canadian Sociology?

George Pavlich

Introduction

Predicting the future of sociology in Canada is an undertaking fraught with uncertainty. As indicated in the introduction, and reflected by the subsequent chapters of this book, its discourses lack an overarching core or canon. Instead, diverse issues, methods, themes, and questions are explored through variously conceived approaches, all claiming the mantle of sociology. As such, any predications should be seen as highly speculative and as emanating from a perspective. Such hefty caveats notwithstanding, sociologists are often passionately drawn to debate on what they take to be possible outlooks for their particular areas of the field. Contributing to that long-standing custom, this chapter offers a speculative response to the title question via three related moves.

Looking back to the modern roots of sociology I start by briefly noting the discipline's fascination with the future, both concerning particular societies and sociology's own development. Sociology is often imagined as a science that can "improve" future societies by offering policy solutions to applied social problems—what some call an **administrative sociology**. Secondly, I refer to a sociological framing of apartheid in South Africa to highlight significant dangers associated with this approach to sociology before turning to Gouldner's (1970) iconic reflections on the future of the discipline in the 1970s. For him, sociology was poised to develop as a critical discourse; his prediction played itself out variously in Canada, especially through calls for transformed sociological imaginations from feminists, political economists, Indigenous peoples, and other critics. Finally, and working out of that critical heritage, I suggest that the future of sociology might be considered in at least two ways: (1) its institutional prospects as a producer of knowledge within current university settings (here I piggyback partly on a reframed **public sociology** working out of current university arrangements); and, (2) its future as a prolific intellectual endeavour that develops new concepts of what it is to be with others to narrate changing historical visions of the social.

I: Sociology's Fascination with the Future

Sociology's fascination with the future is easily discernible from its founding pursuit of progressive, or more advanced, societies to come. For example, as previously indicated in Chapter 22, Comte's positivist sociological imagination promised to explain the moral forces shaping social relations and, thus, enable sociologists to influence paths toward brighter social futures (see Thompson 1976). Equally, Marx's socio-economic analyses sought to transform oppressed capitalist societies and to embrace equal, just, and free communist (or socialist) futures (see Chapter 9 and Chapter 14), a version of which took form in C. Wright Mills's use of sociological imaginations to redress the power of elite social classes. Durkheim and Spencer framed their sociologies on assumptions about the evolutionary development of societies. In general, such thinking echoed early social theorists who were

> . . . intoxicated with the future: they looked into what was about to be and they found it good. The past was a mere prologue and the present a spiritual and moral, even a physical, burden which at times was well nigh unendurable. They would destroy the present as fast as possible in order to usher in the longed-for future, to hasten the end. (Manuel 1962, 6)

In the 1950s and 1960s, a branch of sociology surfaced with a unique object of study: how given societies imagined where they were heading. Framed as a new kind of "sociology of the future," this discourse examined how particular societies conceived of their futures and viewed sociology as a discipline to help bring them into being (Bell 1992). These sociologists did not view themselves as impartial scientists but as "future makers" who were open champions of new societies (Barbara Adam 2004, 16). On a side note, an oft-overlooked variant of this approach had appeared earlier, at the turn of the twentieth century, in Britain. It called upon sociology to generate utopian views of what society ought to be: "There is no such thing in sociology as dispassionately considering what is, without considering what is intended to be" (cited in Levitas 2010, 537). The author of these words continued that "the creation of utopias—and their exhaustive criticism—is the proper and distinctive method of sociology" (537). Who was this author? None other than the famous utopian thinker H.G. Wells, who wrote such classics as *The Time Machine* and *The War of the Worlds*!

In any case, the latter approaches not only drew attention to social futures; they also showed how historical social contexts provided vocabularies for sociologists to imagine their discipline's future. From this vantage, when we speculate on sociology's future in Canada, we must engage with and yet think beyond the conceptual palettes provided by our current social contexts. In his attempt to forecast sociology's development in the late 1980s, Giddens put the matter in these terms: "The concepts, theories and findings generated by sociology 'spiral in and out' of social life" (Giddens 1987, 32). So while our attempts to visualize its future may be bound to specific social times and places, they simultaneous-ly "spiral" out of these in new and not always anticipated directions. One way that sociologists have understood how such spirals happen is through versions of crises facing the discourse. As such, it is useful to return to an iconic framing of a crisis that Gouldner (1970) predicted for "administrative" sociology at the start of the 1970s. To understand his position, though, we need to grasp what he means by "administrative sociology." Although his discussion references Par-sons's **structural functionalism** (see Segre 2012), I shall use the more accessible example of administrative sociology in relation to apartheid in South Africa.

II: Imagining a Coming Crisis: Administrative Sociology and Critical Encounters

It may surprise many to hear that three of the leading architects of apartheid's atrocious racial segregation in South Africa (Cronjé, Verwoed, de Wet Keyter) were administrative sociologists (Pavlich 2014). They tied sociology to existing social forms or to their evolution through social engineering. This version of sociology claimed to use scientific methods to frame and solve social problems through practically orientated policies. Typically, dominant social actors (e.g., state administrators) defined such problems; in South Africa successive colonial governments pronounced a so-called "race problem" to be addressed through policy directives (see Louw 2004). For them, colonization had produced a clash between cultures and societies at different stages of development, requiring dif-ferential resolutions.

Administrative sociologists like Geoffrey Cronjé (1945; 1937) did not ques-tion the state's imperialist, self-serving formulation of the problem, which placed "Europeans" at the pinnacle of social development. On the contrary, he dressed up this "race" problem in scientific language and claimed to have found an unassailable solution: the state should forcibly divide society into separate racial communities to prevent "blood mixing" (miscegenation), which he proclaimed as the source of social problems (Cronjé 1945)! Following the absurdity of that unfounded assertion (Coetzee 1991), he called for the state to keep imagined races socially isolated—in public spaces, in education, in living arrangements, in private associations, in prisons, etc. (Pavlich 2014). The engineered racial groups were then to be provided with unequal resources so that they could develop at their supposedly different paces and stages of development. Clearly, despite con-trary claims, there was little neutrality in this sociology: it was very much on the side of protecting privileges for minority elites of **colonial** societies, who de-scribed themselves as the most socially advanced group. Cronjé thereby provided sociological justifications for maintaining that group's political, economic, so-cial, and cultural advantage.

But what kind of "science" would license this racist thinking? How could sociology defend unequal colonial orders and entrench its claims to different stages of "civilization" as scientifically justified? Certainly, Cronjé peddled a **Eurocentric** sociology informed by the disastrous social engineering of Nazi Germany (Moodie 1975; Coetzee 1991) and by 1930s sociology in the United States. Regardless, it is hard to underestimate the brutal consequences of a sociology that championed apartheid futures. Literally millions of people suffered the attempts to realize apartheid's racial abstractions through sheer force: police intimidation, brutal torture, detention without trial, discretionary bureaucratic measures, etc. The violence of administrative sociology's science became palpable through such events as the Sharpeville massacre, where police fired shots into the backs of fleeing protesters who were voicing legitimate dissent (Lodge 2011).

Of course, not all of administrative sociology's policy solutions would lead to such calamitous moments, but the point to note is that its imaginations harbour dangerous potential because it too readily accepted the state's definition of social problems. This realization prompted critical sociologies to challenge apartheid ideas about society, and it set South African sociology on a different course (Webster 2004). Corresponding sorts of worries lay behind Gouldner's sense that administrative sociology in the US was in crisis and hence his iconic statement about the discipline's critical future.

A Critical Future for Sociology?

Gouldner's book *The Coming Crisis of Western Sociology* opened with a pithy statement about the state of 1970s sociology as it confronted collapsing social orders to which it was once closely attached:

> Social theorists today work within a crumbling social matrix of paralyzed urban centers and battered campuses. Some may put cotton in their ears, but their bodies still feel the shockwaves. It is no exaggeration to say that we theorize today within the sound of guns. The old order has the picks of a hundred rebellions thrust into its hide. (Gouldner 1970 vii)

For Gouldner, this old social order was characterized by free-market capitalism and its associated social welfare state. He showed how functionalism had led many sociologists to the view that existing social, cultural, and political structures are likely to endure if they perform a useful function for a given society. This administratively orientated sociology was bound to the social order, calling only for evolutionary reforms to protracted social injustices. Gouldner detected here a troubling social conservatism that ignored centuries of critical social thought and shackled sociologists to a crumbling welfare state in crisis. More than this, it tied research programs to problems that state agents considered relevant and practical and that they were prepared to fund. Administrative sociology thus allowed such agents to define the parameters of sociological contemplation.

But Gouldner questioned whether such a sociology could survive contemporary financial and legitimacy crises faced by welfare states (Offe 1984). For one thing, many of the "problems" seemed impervious to administrative kinds of solutions. That is, sociology's limited policy reforms could not address the scale of growing social inequalities, or injustice for the downtrodden. As well, for him administrative sociologists had a professional interest in sustaining problems they were supposed to solve, but many were appalled by social exclusions anyway. He described this seeming contradiction in a rather blunt way: "Even if it is the special business of such sociologists to help clean up the vomit of modern society, they are also sometimes revolted by what they see" (Gouldner 1970, 439). That revulsion turned many away from the constraints of administrative sociology and toward more critical or reflexive forms of the discipline.

Thus, Gouldner envisaged the future of sociology in the 1970s as standing at a crossroads. On the one hand, it could expand administrative approaches that were "hardware using, high-science oriented, methodologically empiricist" (Gouldner 1970, 476), and in constant search "for less costly and effective ways of meeting the basic requirements of the *status quo*" (475). Privileging researchers who claimed to solve social problems, administrative sociology would spawn "the new market researchers of the Welfare State and the agents of the new managerial sociology" (500–1). However, for Gouldner, with the rise of such inventions as new media (see Chapter 10 and Chapter 11), this kind of sociology would eventually become indistinguishable from compliant forms of state research or media (e.g., journalism). It might try to distinguish itself by claiming to be a science objectively discovering social facts; but such claims merely disguised its subtle, underlying support for the status quo. Such a sociology also reflected the "timidity" and "fear" of sociologists not wanting to challenge capitalist societies with their growing social oppression. But Gouldner was confident that the counter-cultural movements of the 1970s would inspire sociologists to recognize the social and psychological sources of their *own* biases; that is, in his terms, they would come to understand their "background" or "domain assumptions."

On the other hand, Gouldner saw future possibilities for sociology to cultivate radical, self-aware, and practical engagements with the changing social times. For him, such critical versions of sociology would acknowledge their place in shifting social contexts (i.e., cultivate a **reflexive** imagination) without pretending to produce "neutral" or "impartial" scientific knowledge. Rather, for Gouldner, critical sociological imaginations saw their approaches as always guided by moral values. They would explicitly declare the ideals behind their research endeavours and acknowledge underlying commitments to values such as equality, fairness, justice, etc. This value-orientated sociology would be concerned with "the positive formulation of new societies," with a "criticism of the present" (1970, 503), and with ushering in significant social change.

Accordingly, Gouldner described critical sociologists as "humane" scholars invested in the reflexive and self-aware formulation and, indeed, realization of future societies. Such reflexive, critical sociological imaginations would openly declare, rather than deny, their value commitments. They would locate themselves within, rather than outside, social life, conceiving how to live lives with others in good, true, and beautiful ways. The emerging sociological task was, for

Gouldner, to produce knowledge to free humankind from capitalist oppression. To be sure, the social context that Gouldner questioned has changed, and his language at times reflects a 1960s retro, counter-cultural tone. However, his work provides an important attempt to name dislocations between an older sociology and its changing social context in order to address the critical, rather than administrative, future of the discipline.

Recasting Sociology's Future: Power-Knowledge and Critiques of Society

Gouldner's call for morally reflexive voices reverberated throughout sociology, and encouraged critical forms of sociology alongside civil rights and social movement struggles (Kurlansky 2005). Under the influence of New Left reinterpretations of Marx's ideas (Marcuse 2007), different approaches to feminism (Jagger and Young 2000; Butler 2006), and several civil rights struggles, it became clear to many that what passed as truth in given contexts was directly involved with the exercise of **power relations** (Foucault 1980a; Butler 1997). Critical sociology now increasingly turned to questions of how existing forms of power and knowledge produced subjects, societies, and oppressive subjections. It also examined how new social subjects could emerge to challenge oppressive power relations. As indicated in several of the chapters in this book, the rise of feminist, black consciousness, critical race, Indigenous rights, gay rights, ecological, peace, labour, prisoner rights, and other social movements showed how societies were to be challenged for promoting unequal, unfair, unjust, and outright discriminatory structures (see Carroll and Ratner 1996). In Canada, dissent took various forms (Campbell, Clement, and Kealey 2012), and indeed several First Nations challenged oppressive social legacies of colonial pasts (see Chapter 16). They coupled that challenge with the realization that new kinds of social theorization were needed (Simpson and Smith 2014). Here, the dangers of administrative sociology became clear: administrative sociology was unable to engage changing social forms at scale. Consequently, sociology's wider future—as indicated by a turn to political economy—was to be recalibrated if it was to confront the diversity, class inequities, and elusive exercise of power in Canadian society (Porter 1965).

That sociology had to change if it were to promote effective social transformation became clear from feminist challenges to widespread **patriarchy** that permeated all aspects of society (Sydie 1987). As Chapter 13 indicates, Dorothy Smith's (1991; 2005) standpoint approach to sociology had a profound impact on exposing the complex ways that power and knowledge reproduced gender inequities in society generally but also within sociology itself. Her work showed that validating women's voices and experiences was crucial to challenging patriarchy within the discipline. At the same time, she pointed out how social science and its methods silenced women's experiences. Sociology thus needed to be overhauled to engage subjugated people's voices and experiences, which should shape the future of both society and sociology. Chapter 2, in part, develops the theme through an analysis attentive to the way gender-related legacies limit resistance and voices of subjects who pursue prevailing identities (e.g., "girls"—a theme also developed in Chapter 18). In allied ways, Chapter 19 on the disproportion of incarcerated women shows the deleterious effects of prevalent discourses of crime and punishment just as Hogeveen's discussion of youth justice in Canada points to the value of Canadian critical criminology for examining crime outside of its administrative limits (see Doyle and Moore 2011; Ratner 2006; Hogeveen and Woolford 2006). Equally, as Chapter 3 indicates, the rise of queer theory required significant changes to sociological thought, as did ongoing questions about Quebec (see Chapter 17) and Indigenous (see Chapter 16) sovereignty.

Even though selective, these examples highlight how challenges to various socio-political subjections were matched by claims that sociology had to be mobilized in fresh ways to redress past inequalities. Its imagination required fundamental change to resist rather than sustain oppressive power formations. By the early 1990s, sociological self-reflection continued to worry about the baggage carried from past orders that had rendered sociology ill-suited to engage transforming social orders. Even if some sociologists insisted on the discipline's rosy future (e.g., the "future for sociology and sociologists is bright" [Eitzen 1991]), most detected challenges that implied the need to re-think sociology's future (Crook 2005).

III: Imagining Sociology's Future Today

More recently, debates about the future of sociology in Canada have taken what White (2005) calls an excessively "apocalyptic" tone. Like Sydie (2005), she questions the self-appointed keepers of the discipline who contend *inter alia* that sociology is facing extinction because of an internal erosion (too many "outsiders" are sheltering in sociology departments); because too little applied, relevant (as defined by the self-selected few) empirical work is happening; because theory is disconnected from "empirical" foundations; and because not enough "real" leadership is to be found. And so the list goes on (see, for instance, McLaughlin 2006). However, this imperialist call for sociologists to uniformly pursue some or other pure sociological line may run counter to the intellectual ethos and prolific diversity of sociology's imaginations.

As noted, even a quick glance over the variety of the previous chapters—a small subset of work being carried out in the name of sociology in Canada—confirms the lack of a disciplinary core. Despite or perhaps because of this, the chapters provide rigorous, lively, and heterogeneous narratives that help us to comprehend our unfolding social lives. Sociology seems, then, to be more a shifting patchwork of related discourses than a clearly bordered, consensus-driven discipline. Its imaginations thread the changing warp and weft of a varied discursive fabric, without compelling integration. But even with basic disagreements regarding its role and tasks, many nevertheless identify with and carry out their work in the name of sociology. To be sure, ongoing debate about its borders may perturb those seeking simple, clear-cut disciplinary boundaries, but demanding that its discourses be woven of one cloth would likely stifle the intellectual vibrancy of a diverse concept-creating arena (O'Malley and Hunt 2003).

With this in mind, the future of sociology could be imagined in many ways, but what follows proceeds from this starting point:

> There are two aspects to the future of sociology: social structural and intellectual. On one hand, we ask whether sociology will survive as a discipline at all; on the other, we ask whether there are new ideas to inhabit that structure if it survives. (Abbott 2000, 295)

If nothing else, this somewhat arbitrary point of departure allows us to restrict our speculations to two broad arenas: sociology's future as a discipline in changing regimes of knowledge production within institutional (i.e., university) settings; and, the intellectual ethos that enables an ongoing development of new ideas and debates. Let us briefly consider each of these in turn.

Changing University Structures and Sociology

Addressing the structural dimensions of sociology's possible futures, one might note the growth of neo-liberal (see Chapter 6), corporatized mindsets within universities (Derrida 2004; e.g., Readings 1997). Here, academic disciplines are to account for themselves through empty concepts such as excellence, innovation, accountability, etc. Their practices should be made accessible to new corporate management measures, even if these run counter to a democratic or public education (Brown 2015). Unsurprisingly, such managerial demands do not favour those disciplines unwilling to play the corporate game. Discourses that lack consensus about how they produce knowledge or that have a limited capacity to attract revenue may find themselves in a weakened operational position. The situation is even worse for critical discourses that challenge the very foundations of **neo-liberalism**.

Despite the lip service paid to innovation and interdisciplinary work, sociology is at a disadvantage in these settings because it ". . . has little or no core" (Cole 2001, 14). Indeed, two decades ago an influential sociologist presciently described sociology as a kind of **disintegrated discipline** making its way through changing university structures. He described sociology then as having "many different and incompatible standards for what is good work" and judged its standing "to be precarious in academic settings" (Stinchcombe 1994, 279). Even so, Stinchcombe thought it best to adopt a "wait it out" approach:

> [So] nothing is to be done except to suffer from the fact that deans are not going to like us, and from the fact that inside our departments we will fight each other about how to determine the merit of research and what our curriculum ought to be about. (Stinchcombe 1994, 291)

Whatever one may make of this resigned if conflicted fatalism, perhaps Stinchcombe's prediction was apposite: despite new management tides, sociological discourses have managed to survive, even to flourish in some contexts (Spalter-Roth

2015). They have spiralled in and out of shifting institutional tides, taking advantage of various openings. But in university climates, where neo-liberal and corporate requirements abound (Brown 2015), how might sociology unfold institutionally?

One of the more influential recent responses to this question calls for a "public sociology." This idea was succinctly articulated by Burawoy's (2005) presidential address to the American Sociological Association that reflected on sociology's future in current university settings. Burawoy noted sociology's well-established traditions of studying society empirically (professional sociology), and using such knowledge to advocate for socially progressive policy changes (policy sociology). However, he echoed Gouldner's concerns that such administrative (i.e., "professional" and "policy") sociology may be too invested in preserving societies without assessing their values or potential dangers. By the same token, he worried that critical forms of sociology had tied themselves to dogmas of the new left or had wandered into conceptual (for him, "postmodern") wildernesses detached from timely matters facing today's societies. Burawoy saw possibilities for developing a future sociology by taking advantage of strengths in both administrative and critical or publicly engaged approaches. For him, reflexive "critical sociology" could serve as the "conscience of professional sociology" while "public sociology" could become the conscience of "policy sociology." That is, value-driven critical and public sociology would check "instrumental" approaches geared to solving applied problems. It might also take seriously Chapter 23's call to reframe past questions that current sociological imaginations have—with some intellectual cost—deserted.

Whatever reservations one might have about Burawoy's public sociology (Morrow 2009; Nichols 2011; Inglis 2005), it has certainly struck a chord. His work provides a way of reimagining how sociological discourses can work out of today's knowledge-producing structures, and tie research agendas to publicly framed and critically forged values. However, one may question whether deferring to contextually conceived "publics" would unduly relieve policy sociology of a basic internal responsibility to critically frame the values behind *all* its narratives. I would suggest, too, that sociology's disintegrated discourses are well positioned to promote critiques of existing associational patterns by engaging with and enabling the voices of those subjugated, marginalized, or excluded by such arrangements. In short, working within knowledge-producing contexts of today's universities, sociological imaginations in future could become sturdier vehicles for conceptualizing new patterns of association driven by values that actively engage those who are excluded from specific social arrangements.

Sociology's Intellectual Ethos: The Social and Narrating Its Changing Forms

Within such knowledge-producing contexts one may also refer to the second point noted above: the intellectual prospects for a future sociology. Despite their acknowledged differences, the discourses of this book variously show how our historical ways of associating with others plays out and affects specific issues (e.g., freedom, gender oppressions, how we view the environment or the family, etc.). In important ways, this work offers various conceptions of the social. The precise future of sociology's debates and trends may be anyone's guess, but I think that Canadian sociological imaginations—whether subjectively orientated, structural, or critical—suggest two looming shifts: namely, (1) a recalibration of the social as an object of analysis, and (2) a revaluing of critical social theorizing as a narrative form legitimately able to conceptualize complex associational patterns.

Concepts, "Being with," and Becoming Social

As noted in the text, Durkheim's (1964) approach proffered the "social" as a discrete and distinguishable object of sociological analysis, positing social facts as the latter's unique building blocks. Over the years, different versions of the social have anchored sociological thinking, as evinced by the images of the social welfare state (see Chapter 6). However, under neo-liberal thinking, the social and its welfare provisions underwent a change: the call was to reduce spending on social services by privatizing state amenities, instituting user fees, and encouraging voluntary community programs. Within such contexts, one saw the rise of a new claim: the social had ceased to exist. Images of society were deemed less helpful for understanding human relations than other concepts, such as family or community, even though Chapter 5 shows how misleading such a claim might be. Regardless, in the early 1980s, the conservative British prime minister Margaret Thatcher confidently asserted that the "social" was dead and had been replaced by family (or community) relations. By implication, sociology had lost its prime object of study and faced a bleak future of fading relevance. That thinking perhaps undergirds former Canadian prime minister Stephen Harper's contemptuous statement about not "committing sociology" when understanding terrorist attacks ("Harper on Terror Arrests: Not a Time for 'Sociology'" 2013).

Yet the social was also seen as a fading idea by some academics. The cultural analyst Baudrillard (1997, 77ff) conceived of the "social" as a historical idea produced by a particular cultural infrastructure. Since the latter had collapsed with the fragmentation of new media and the rise of computer simulation (see Chapter 10 and Chapter 11), Baudrillard argued that the social could no longer materialize as a "reality." He then proclaimed the "death of the social," a position ambivalently engaged by the sociologist Nikolas Rose (1996). On the one hand, Rose thought Baudrillard was too hasty in his allegations of a final death; on the other, he argued that the social's role in "advanced liberal" practices of governance had changed so markedly that it no longer afforded a pivotal idea for governing people in a "post-social age" (as it was under liberal social welfare states) (1996, 354).

But without a fixed sense of the social, has sociology lost its prime object? Does it even then have a future? As Chapter 15 makes so clear, changing images of the social continue to be crucial to such matters of consequence as how we envisage and engage the environment. Along with O'Malley (1999), we might also say that allegations regarding the end of the social have grossly underestimated the phoenix-like nature of the concept. Sure, the welfare state has changed (see Chapter 6), as have the ways in which we are governed in Canada (see Chapter 14) or how we calibrate political sovereignty (Chapter 16 and Chapter 17). Previous chapters also reference changes in how we collectively understand policing (Chapter 12), label/conceive of sexuality (Chapter 3), understand health (Chapter 7), conceive of the family (Chapter 5), consider migrants (Chapter 8), approach aging (Chapter 20) rethink global inequality (Chapter 21), formulate mental illness (Chapter 4), or imagine past approaches to the environment (Chapter 15). However, these chapters do not imply the end of the social per se; rather, they variously show that while we may be witnessing significant changes to how the social was once framed, new forms thereof are simultaneously emerging.

Indeed, common to these analyses is this: to escape inequities and injustices within current contexts requires not that we abandon but, rather, re-imagine the *social*. That is, sociology's intellectual framing need not collapse because the currency of erstwhile versions of the social have declined. On the contrary, such a decline merely opens spaces, as reflected by the chapters in this book, for reimagining new forms of the social, and to imagine future possibilities both for a given society and for sociology itself. Such an approach takes seriously something already mentioned in the introduction: sociology's future is unceasingly bound to analyzing and developing ways to be with others, as conceptualized through changing images, forms, and practices of the social. Just as, say, economics may target concepts of the market, recognizing changing forms thereof, so too may sociology understand itself as considering and helping to bring about changing ideas of the social.

In other words, the future of sociology in Canada may well be tied to a new way of understanding the social: namely, as a wide-ranging and dynamic, rather than a particular or static, concept. Here, sociology could be considered as always involved with contingent ways of becoming social but not with pursuing one absolute version of social being. Nancy's (2000) important discussion of what he calls "the with" provides a philosophical grounding for imagining the social as an open placeholder that is historically replenished. The task of imagining how to be with others at given times/places is endless. Nancy refers to our primordial "being with others" into which we are born, to which we continually respond and that contingently shapes our identities—singularly and in concert—as social subjects. The idea of an open concept of "the with" as always in process defies fixed, essential, and closed concepts of the social and its subjects (Butler 2005). This thinking requires us to acknowledge the dangers of closing off particular ways of being social as if they were necessary, inevitably superior, and so on (e.g., Nazism, Stalinist communism, apartheid, etc.). At the same time, we cannot abandon our unrelenting responsibility to debate, problematize, shape, and critically reflect on how we might be, or ought to be, with others. It is just that no conceptions of the social are absolutely certain, determinate, or necessary—our imaginings might take account of the **indeterminacy** that belies our emerging associations with others.

Shifting Narrative Forms?

Sociology's open-ended imagination will, if my speculations materialize, focus on a central task: creating concepts. Specifically, it will attend to generating concepts with which to narrate, engage, and pursue changing imaginings of the social. Sociological thinking will helix in and out of specific contexts, working with presently accessible vocabularies to apprehend possible social futures. A future sociology that attends to this task will need to develop a capacity, on the one hand, to recognize that the social is always open ended, and, on the other, to offer specific conceptions of the social for given contexts. This seemingly paradoxical mandate may be framed as a question: what tools can sociological imaginations develop for narratives that recognize the social as a permanently shifting and open placeholder while also positively enunciating historically credible versions thereof? I cannot here, of course, respond adequately to such a large matter, but let me at least suggest that such a sociology will work from within, even as it seeks to displace different historical practices of becoming social. That sociology is also likely to be transformed through such work is not to be bemoaned but expected of future-orientated attempts to conceptualize new social forms.

But how exactly might sociology's future narratives engage the "with" through changing concepts of the social? One could, of course, offer many guesses as to how Canadian sociology will revamp its narrative tools and approaches. The introduction has already alluded, for instance, to changing grammars of critique as moving away from modernist judgments against supposedly absolute criteria. For instance, new critical grammars may shape the creation of concepts directed to social possibilities via interpretative practices that separate out, and perpetually open, what appears as closed, fixed, or—worse—necessary understandings of the social (Pavlich 2000). However, I want to suggest the prospect of two changes to sociology's future ways of narrating the social in open ways that turn away from prevalent administrative tendencies: (1) the rekindling of critical social theorizing to frame consequential sociological narratives; and, (2) critically rethinking administrative sociology's ideas about the role of empirical methods.

Administrative sociological narratives have tended to contrast sensory observation with social theory, and to privilege the former over the latter as the ground of scientific knowledge. Here, theory is deemed valid only to the extent that its statements derive from, or are verified (confirmed, refuted) by, the sociologist's systematic observations. But as several chapters in this text (e.g., Chapter 13 and Chapter 22) have argued, social theory's primary role in understanding the social reflects a narrative and interpretative life of its own; it need not require narratives that claim to yield unquestionable empirical facts. In short, one may say that there are many ways to conceptualize the social, including (quantitative and qualitative) empirical narratives, but equally various genres of theory, or combinations thereof (Schneck 1987).

Along these lines, White views social theory as a distinct—rather than empirically derived—practice of concept making:

> [S]ocial theory is necessarily a vocation, one that is textual, and one that demands a rigorous analysis in order to determine the nature of a concept's insights. Such an understanding of social theory mitigates against a "mix-and-stir" approach which involves the careless lifting of concepts from the intellectual context that supports them in order to "apply" them willy-nilly to all manner of so-called "empirically" based sociological projects. This kind of "application" is counter to the ethos of a textually-grounded social theory that seeks to be creative of new concepts and insights. (White 2005, 543)

White's emphasis on conceptualization suggests how social theory's genres always interpretatively involve narrating moving and often contradictory incarnations of the social. For example, sociology may be more actively involved with decolonizing Canadian society, and re-engaging Indigenous imaginings of the social (Simpson and Smith 2014). More generally, I would think that social theory's future will include far greater attention to its role in concept creation and the way that particular concepts enable the narration and possible appearance of new versions of the social. Even if many genres and practices of theorizing the social are possible, I think that Canadian sociological imaginations are poised to develop new horizons of interpretation. In the latter, closer attention will be paid to how concepts are created and how they affect emerging ways to be with others. Specifically, sociological imaginations are likely to change as they critically apprehend the force of emerging concepts and recognize their ability to shape emerging forms of the social.

Over the years, however, a certain tyranny of especially quantitative empiricism has led some to extort this blackmail over the field: either conduct empirical survey research to define the social, and ground theories on such observation, or do not count your work as sociology. However, sociological imaginations include multiple genres by which to narrate how to be with others: qualitative, critical, theoretical, ethnographic, quantitative, etc. Despite the privilege that administrative sociology still permits narrative genres with a quantitative or metric-orientated bent, all may not be well with the underlying data collection, survey, and (as Chapter 13 suggests) the statistical foundations of that privilege.

Akin to Gouldner some decades before, two scholars recently predicted another "coming crisis," this time not for sociology per se, but for its reliance on dated empirical methods in changing contexts:

> Our concern is that in the years between about 1950 and 1990 sociologists could claim a series of distinctive methodological tools that allowed them to claim clear points of access to social relations, but in the early 21st century social data is now so routinely gathered and disseminated,

and in such myriad ways, that the role of sociologists in generating data is now unclear. (Savage and Burrows 2007, 886)

Indeed, as indicated by Chapter 10 and Chapter 11, data are now routinely collected from the Internet and communicated on an unprecedented scale via big data analysis and social media. There, data are used in ways that rarely call on sociological analyses. What might this mean for future conceptualizations and communication of the social?

To be sure, sociology is not now at the centre of debates on how to collect, or analyze, big data in ways that further critical concepts of the social. For this reason, Savage and Burrows argue that "the repertoires of empirical sociology need to be rethought in an age of knowing capitalism" (2007, 895). They envisage a future sociology that links "narrative, numbers, and images in ways that engage with, and critique, the kinds of routine transactional analyses that now proliferate" (Savage and Burrows 2007, 896). In this future, sociologists could be attentive to how the concept of the social, of "being with," is recalibrated through the consumption of new media and, indeed, through the narratives generated out of uses (of corporate or state) to which data accumulations are now put. Perhaps sociology can in future expect to renew and develop a critical, theoretical edge to empirical data collection, carving out a distinctive interpretative engagement with new forms of the social by challenging how information is gathered, interpreted, and "deployed" (Savage and Burrows 2007, 896).

If nothing else, perhaps these two predictions—restoring critical social theory as an intrinsically valuable technique for envisaging how to be with others and a critical reappraisal of "empirical" data—promise an emphasis on being critically reflexive when articulating diverse narratives and concepts of the social. Such changes are likely to require a democratization of methods within the field; but they will also require a critical focus on how concepts are formed—in all their discursive manifestations. For instance, such criticism will likely emphasize sociology's responsibility to those who are excluded by given formulations of the social. A future sociology would then be openly responsible not only to those included by its narratives (whatever the genre) of the social, but equally to those who are excluded and who make these possible.

Conclusion

This chapter has offered a limited speculation on the future of sociology in Canada—as affected by developments elsewhere—by referring to the dangers of a previously dominant administrative sociology whose legacy, though modified in several ways, is still evident in the discipline. I have referred to a pivotal moment of crisis in the 1970s where "domain assumptions" were challenged as sociology opened out to new critical possibilities. This enabled diverse approaches of a disintegrated imagination to face the tribulations of corporatized university contexts and yet seize new opportunities offered there. In short, and to answer the title question, the future of sociology as I see it will continue its questioning path by recovering, from its institutional setting, the means to renew social theory and critically evaluate the privilege granted to claims regarding empirical fact. Sociology will thereby emphasize the role of creating concepts and narrating new forms of the social, tying its discourses as much to receptive versions of the humanities as to social sciences. From these, sociology will likely continue to inspire narratives of social change and possible social futures. In all, sociology's prospects lie with creating robust, democratic, critical, and questioning narratives to re-conceptualize, endlessly, how to be with others via historically deliberated concepts of the "social."

Review/Summary Questions

1. Can one avoid the potential dangers of administrative sociology?
2. Is sociological research inevitably conducted in the interests of particular members of society?
3. Should future sociological research be guided by moral values about how to live with others? What does this mean for its status as a social science?
4. Is the social indeterminate, and what does this mean for future sociological imaginations?

Glossary

Aboriginal Persons who are indigenous to the territory of Canada, including First Nations, Métis, and Inuit groups. Because of the fundamental and internal ambiguities intrinsic to this term, however, it is contested by many Indigenous groups.

adolescent femininity Socially accepted ways to be a teenage "girl."

administrative sociology An approach that considers sociology to be a problem-solving science of society, using impartial methods to develop policies for social improvements.

agency An actor's ability to take self-directed action. While experienced as a "personal" quality, all of our actions, no matter how seemingly autonomous, are constrained by the socio-cultural context of our action.

alienation The estrangement of people from one another, from their work, or from the products of their work; more generally, a sense of distance from social relations.

altruism Behaviour that takes account of the interests of others, in opposition to egoism, selfishness, and self-interested individualism.

Anishnaabe One of the largest Indigenous nations in North America, whose homelands include territories in the provinces westward from Ontario to Saskatchewan, as well as in the American states of Michigan, Wisconsin, and Minnesota. The Anishnaabe include the Ojibway, Algonquin, Odawa, Chippewa, and Saulteaux peoples.

anomie In Merton's use, a gap between cultural goals and social opportunities, created by a strain in the social system of modern capitalism.

Anthropocene Refers to our present time period, in which human activity is of such magnitude and extent that it has affected geological conditions and processes.

anti-psychiatry movement The predecessor of the mad movement, the anti-psychiatry movement flourished in the 1960s when a group of psychiatrists began critiquing their discipline for failing to recognize the moral judgments embedded within psychiatric diagnoses. The movement continues today.

apocalyptic demography A critical term used by age scholars to identify the ageism of popular accounts of aging population growth as economically threatening and socially catastrophic, and to distort the future of intergenerational relations between young and old as competitive, hostile, and inequitable.

assimilation A term associated with the structuralist perspective. It describes the process by which an immigrant becomes part of his or her new society. For some, assimilation is relatively straightforward. The immigrant arrives, may experience some difficulties adapting to the economy, social practices, norms, and culture in the short-term, but as time in Canada increases, he or she begins to adapt and change to act and think more like a Canadian. For others, assimilation is more difficult and time consuming, and many never fully become "Canadian."

bias of communication A term proposed by Harold Innis that all media hold a bias of communication. Different media of communication, for example oral speech or the radio, hold a bias toward either time or space.

Big Pharma The combined economic and political power of the world's largest pharmaceutical companies.

boomer generation A unique grouping born after World War II, whose large demographic profile and growth during the prosperity and consumerism of the post-war period have created dramatic historical shifts in education, work, retirement, consumer marketing, housing, and family structure.

call centre A specialized workplace that provides service and/or information over the telephone. Increasingly, call centres also provide web support, including email handling, fax support, and online chat. Call centres now serve many different organizations in a range of industries.

capitalism An economic system in which production of goods and services are privately owned, and the environment and workers are exploited in the interests of making profit.

Charter of Rights and Freedoms A bill of rights for Canadians that was signed into law in 1982. The Charter makes up the first part of the Canadian Constitution Act and secures liberties and privileges for all citizens, including the right of Canadians to the freedom of thought, belief, expression, mobility, and from arbitrary detention.

Charter of Values A document proposed by the government of Quebec that outlined cultural and normative rights and obligations for Quebec's population. One of its most controversial clauses sought to limit the wearing of "conspicuous" religious signs by public employees, widely believed to target the Muslim headscarf.

claims-making Refers to the act of making statements about something that bear on someone else's interests. For instance, "climate deniers" make statements denying that global increases in temperature are not the result of human activity (see **Anthropocene**). These statements (claims-making) affect the interests of people living in vulnerable geographical areas, as well as people who benefit from no changes in lifestyle (for instance, in the decreased use of fossil fuels).

Clan Mother A hereditary title held by women and passed down to a female member sharing the same clan. There are 49 Clan Mothers in the Haudenosaunee Confederacy among the five nations. Clan Mothers oversee the leadership of the Chiefs and the welfare of the clan. They are accorded great political power within the Haudenosaunee Confederacy, including the ability to install and remove Chiefs.

class According to Marx, the product of, and defined through, relations to the mode of production. That is, either one owns machines or,

conversely, works on these machines. Capitalists control the production of commodities and benefit from their sale. By contrast, workers have access only to their labour power and sell it to owners in exchange for a wage. Contemporary class theorists have expanded this understanding to encompass, among other divisions, the middle classes.

climate change Refers to changes in climate patterns that extend over long periods of time (decades to millions of years). With reference to the **Anthropocene**, climate change refers to changes in weather and climate patterns caused by human impact on the Earth, linked in particular to the increasing use of fossil fuels.

Climategate Refers to a 2009 controversy involving hacked email exchanges between scientists at the Climate Research Unit at the University of East Anglia, UK. The emails seemed to indicate that climate change was a scientific conspiracy and, in the lead-up to the Copenhagen climate summit, were used by climate deniers to make the claim that climate change does not exist. Numerous investigations revealed no scientific misconduct and that the climate-deniers had misinterpreted the scientific data.

codification A process by which the experiential, shared cultural voice of an emerging group is transformed into an official, dominant discourse, such that the original demands are reframed and now make sense differently.

cohort A gerontological term to denote the organization of individuals into birth categories and used to explain the collective subjective experiences of such individuals. The analysis of various cohort characteristics allows researchers to predict changes in labour, education, welfare, fertility, and mortality.

collective conscience A society's shared morality.

colonialism The subjugation of one people to another. In Canada, colonialism refers to the historical and enduring processes (i.e., industrial schools, the reserve system, and outlawing of traditions) of subordinating Indigenous cultural norms to Euro-Canadian ways of being.

community sanctions (also known as *intermediate sanctions, alternative sanctions,* or *community punishments*) Refers to a wide range of court-imposed sentences, which can be financial (i.e., fines) or supervision (i.e., probation, electronic monitoring, community work hours, etc.). Community sanctions are frequently referred to as alternatives to sentences of imprisonment.

compassion orientation (also called **care orientation**) A tendency to evaluate problems of inequality with an emphasis on doing what is kind or merciful or relieves suffering.

constitutional autonomy In sections 91 and 92 of the Canadian Constitution, responsibilities are assigned to the federal and provincial governments, respectively. Responsibility for the social well-being of citizens falls to the provinces. However, because delivering social policy is expensive and can be popular among voters, the federal government has used its constitutional authority to raise and spend money to make its way into this provincial area of constitutional autonomy. Quebec and Alberta have often resisted such incursions.

criminality In criminology, refers to characteristics of being criminal or to forms of criminal activity as defined in criminal law.

criminalization The process of making an act or behaviour illegal; also refers to institutional practices that produce the status of offender or treat an individual as a criminal.

critical communication studies The study of communication and power in society, which situates the question of communication in a wider social context. Approaches to critical communication studies can draw on political economy, cultural studies, Marxist sociology, feminist theory, post-structuralism, critical race theory, and other critiques of knowledge and power in society.

critique Refers to a reasoned reflection on the nature of society and involves a questioning of "taken-for-granted" ideas or values.

cultural studies The changing study of culture in creative, social, and political contexts. Today it has come to mean a multi-disciplinary and usually critical approach to social formations. Often its study engages with popular cultural forms.

cyber bullying The act of harassing, harming, or intimidating a person by repeatedly and deliberately posting negative comments to or about them on the Internet. Cyber bulling can involve the spread of rumours about a person or posting personal or embarrassing information about them on social media.

cyber stalking Similar to cyber bullying in that a person uses the Internet to post information about another person or organization that causes them harm. The cyber stalker also uses the Internet to monitor information about the victim, posting anonymously on discussion boards, using false identities on social media platforms, and emailing or messaging his or her victims directly.

decentralization The shift of responsibility and/or authority from a central body to smaller units. For example, a provincial government might require municipal governments to fund and deliver shelter services to homeless people. Since municipal governments are closer to the people they serve, they might have a more accurate picture of the number of people in need and how best to help them. In such a situation, decentralization can be positive. However, when decentralization does not involve a transfer of funds or only shifts responsibility without a shift of authority to make decisions, it may be less desirable.

deinstitutionalization The movement of people out of psychiatric hospitals and into the community to receive treatment and services.

delinquency Illegal, antisocial, deviant, or inappropriate behaviour.

democratization of privilege Thomas Parkinson's term that refers to the spread of privilege to the general population. For example, the global increased consumption and use of cars democratizes the privilege of car use beyond wealthy members of any society.

deregulation Removing rules in order to enable less inhibited forms of activity and increased freedom. Deregulation can have both positive and negative consequences. For example, deregulating drug approval processes might ensure that the population has greater access to more drugs, but it may also expose people to greater risks due to inadequate safety testing.

detraditionalization A claim made by some social analysts that the demise of conventional institutions—in particular, the nuclear heterosexual family—has liberated us as agents from the constraints of "tradition."

discipline A subtle but pervasive form of governance that shapes individuals' behaviour using techniques and forms of (disciplinary) knowledge that operate outside the law and sovereign models of power.

discourse Refers to symbolic communication through the written, visual, or spoken language-in-use, or shared representation (such as dress to symbolize "gender"). Because this communication is shaped by a set of rules and procedures that demarcate and produce certain dominant and legitimized ways of thinking and acting, discourse is a venue for the operation of power that shapes social "practice." Discourse makes certain ways of thinking and acting possible, but it also makes other ways "unthinkable" (making nonconforming gender practices difficult for many people to understand).

disintegrated discipline A discipline for which there is no consensus of its core approach, methods, and ways to create knowledge—it lacks integration.

division of labour In his earlier work, Durkheim emphasized this concept to suggest that groups are significantly influenced by the way that they organized their labour and divided the tasks required to accomplish functions required for the survival of a given social formation. He noted that changes from "primitive" to "modern" forms of the division of labour were to have important implications for the ways that those societies developed, and for the kinds of subjects (e.g., individuals) they shaped.

economic class immigrant A legal category of immigration in Canada. It refers to a person (including the spouse and any dependent children) who enters Canada for the purposes of obtaining a job, creating his or her own company, or investing a significant amount of money into an existing business. It is the most popular class of entry for immigrants to Canada.

emphasized femininity A term emerging out of the pioneering work of R.W. Connell; the term is corollary and dependent upon hegemonic masculine scripts. Society and the general media constrain the limits of women's behaviour by presenting images of how to "be" appropriately female. For example, mainstream music (i.e., hip hop) imparts lessons in toughness for men and sexual subservience in women. Repeated exposure to such portrayals endorses and establishes the dominant gender hierarchy.

empowerment To transfer powers, often by transferring decision-making authority to persons or groups who are directly affected by specific decisions.

environmental imperialism Also referred to as "eco-imperialism"; refers to the imposition of Western views about environmental sustainability onto non-Western societies and, more specifically, onto developing countries.

environmental justice A legal process that seeks to redress situations in which environmental problems are felt most by those who benefit from them least.

epigenetics The study of how organisms' genes interact with the environment. Epigenetics shows that the environment (including factors such as stress and nutrition) turns genes off and on, and that these gene expressions are passed to the next generation.

ethnic enclave perspective A Marxist theory that explains the development and maintenance of two separate economies one for the mainstream (which is larger, more lucrative) and one for marginalized groups (which is smaller and less lucrative and pays employees less).

ethnomethodology An alternative sociological theory/methodology that examines the tacit, taken-for-granted practices that constitute everyday social life. It focuses attention on the social methods that people use to make sense of their social contexts.

eugenics A term meaning "well-born" or "good genes." Early eugenicists drew inspiration from the biological sciences and assumed that, like livestock, some humans possess "better" genes than others. This mentality was the impetus for campaigns promoting forms of social control aimed at improving the racial qualities of future generations.

Eurocentric (Eurocentrism) A term that refers to certain forms of knowledge or claims to truth that emanate from and/or privilege European ways of life, thinking, and so on.

existentialism A school of philosophical thought that considered human beings, by their unique nature, as partly undetermined. As such, individuals are required to make free choices among possible courses of action. Such freedom was seen as closely tied to moral responsibility, but with the recognition that there are no moral certainties. In this context, human beings must freely choose actions (without any necessary moral guidelines), but then they are also held responsible for the outcome of the choices they make—the source of considerable "anxiety." Under the famous idea of "existence precedes essence," existential thinking emphasized that by freely choosing particular kinds of existence, human beings could, in essence, become authentic and responsible beings.

familialization A shift in responsibility for a service from the realm of the state to the realm of the family. With budget cuts to health care provision, patients are often discharged from hospitals when they are still very ill. In such situations, the state is implicitly relying on family members to maintain the care of the recovering patient, even though those family members may not have the skills or the time to take on this responsibility.

family class immigrant A legal category of immigration in Canada. It refers to people who are closely related (includes spouses, children under age 19, and grandparents only) to someone who is already living in Canada. The

sponsor agrees to financially and socially support these newcomers for a period of between 3 and 10 years after landing.

federalism A system of government that divides power between a central (national) government and various territorial units (provinces, states, etc.). Canada, the United States, and Brazil are examples.

fee simple property A form of real property that involves freehold (rather than leased) ownership.

fictive kin relationships People chosen to be family members that are not legally or biologically related.

Frankfurt School The name given to the Institute for Social Research, which was organized at the University of Frankfurt by a group of Marxist intellectuals in the early 1920s. The School gave rise to well-developed critical theory, and many of its scholars engaged critically with the rise of popular and mass culture, in particular film, radio and television, and other media of communication.

free will The idea that human beings are able to choose ways to act from various courses that might be available to them. Free will and being morally responsible for chosen courses of action are often intertwined.

functionalism (sometimes **structural functionalism**) A school of sociological thought often associated with Talcott Parsons. It has a wide focus that views society as a combination of the functions of the basic elements and structures that comprise it. So, various functioning systems (e.g., education) work because of the functional elements within, but in turn these systems function in relation to other systems (e.g., politics). Such systems should work together but can evolve to advance the society as a whole.

fundamentalism A religious doctrine (typically Protestant, Islamic, or Jewish) that advances conservative interpretations of religious texts to assert a traditionalist vision of society and morality in opposition to trends. Fundamentalism in the twentieth and twenty-first centuries often upholds patriarchal values in gender and family, intolerance of sexual diversity, and opposition to secular and scientific perspectives.

gendered life course Feminist gerontologists contend that aging and the life course are gendered experiences because women not only live longer than men but, compared to men, have more interrupted education and work careers, face greater caregiving responsibilities, and bear the accumulated disadvantages of lifelong financial inequities in their old age.

gender policing Practices that pressure, discipline, or penalize people to make them conform to specific standards of masculinity or femininity.

gender-responsive policy Policy that recognizes quantitative and qualitative differences between men's and women's lives and is responsive to their unique needs and experiences. Such policies are intended to eliminate systemic barriers, cultural bias, and gender bias. (Also referred to as *gender-specific* or *women-centred policy*.)

genealogy from below A form of socio-historical analysis that seeks to carry out genealogical analysis (searching for the "ignoble origins" of dominant discourses) from the standpoint of those whose experiential voices were codified and incorporated in the construction of these discourses.

generation A category of aging that combines chronological age with social location, such that generational distinctions and boundaries are marked by the historical period in which generational members lived as well as the life-course opportunities—such as higher education, life expectancy, and public health—afforded by that particular period.

Generation X Popularized by Canadian author Douglas Coupland in his book *Generation X Tales of an Accelerated Culture* (1991), Generation X, or Gen X, refers to the specific group born between mid-1960s to mid-1980s. Members are characterized by their experience of political change, technological innovation, career uncertainty, social diversity, and "grunge" fashion style. Rock group Nirvana's Kurt Cobain is revered as a celebrated Gen X icon.

Gini coefficient or Gini ratio A statistical measure of economic inequality that describes the extent to which wealth is distributed equally among the members of a given society or country. The higher the Gini coefficient, the more unequal the distribution of wealth in that society.

globalization A process of transnational integration facilitated by information technology. There are cultural, political, and educational aspects (such as cultural exchange, global citizen networks, and the diffusion of health knowledge and technologies); however, the dominant form of globalization is economic. Economic globalization has been driven by free-trade imperatives that facilitate the international flow of capital and investments, often at the expense of governments' ability to legislate and govern in the interests of public health.

governance The guiding of behaviour through law, norms, morality, power structures, surveillance, etc. The process and practices that apply to policing vary significantly given the environment in which policing is applied. Governance in the realm of public policing must take into account legal and constitutional accountability and responsibilities.

Haudenosaunee Confederacy A sovereign, democratic union of the Onondaga, Mohawk, Seneca, Cayuga, and Oneida nations in the mid-twelfth century (the Tuscarora nation later joined in the mid-eighteenth century). This confederation was formed under the principles of peace, power, and righteousness as expressed in messages of peace by the Peacemaker (Huron) and Hiawatha (Haudenosaunee).

health inequities Differences in the health and longevity of different groups that can be attributed to political and social factors (such as poverty) and that, as such, could be avoided. The term *health inequities* is used when health differences between or among groups are known to be unjust. It is distinguished from *health inequalities*, which are differences between or among groups that at not avoidable, usually for biological reasons.

hegemony The social, political, cultural, ideological, or economic dominance of one group or individual over others.

heterosexual matrix A "hegemonic discursive/ epistemic model of gender intelligibility that assumes that for bodies to cohere and make sense there must be a stable sex expressed through stable gender . . . that is oppositionally and hierarchically defined through the compulsory practice of heterosexuality" (Butler 1990 151 note 6). More simply, a biological sex—designated as either "female" or "male"—is necessary to render our gender as "feminine" or "masculine," knowable and "correct" based on common sense.

homophobia Attitudes and practices that disadvantage, discriminate against, or persecute homosexual people and practices. Homophobia can reside in individuals, but it can also be institutionalized and enforced through law, family, religion, media, employment, and so on. (Alternatively conceptualized as *heterosexism* or *heteronormativity*.)

human capital Refers to the investments, such as education, training, and health care, that have been made to make people more able to participate in the economy (Becker 1993). Provincial governments invest in the region's people throughout their lifetime by funding schools, colleges, and universities as well as health clinics, medical offices, and hospitals.

identity Our sense of who we are and who others perceive us to be; identities are formed through social interaction.

ideological domination Ways of thinking and governing that preserve a society's power structure to the disadvantage of those who are ruled.

ideology Originally associated with the work of Marx and his analysis of how dominant political economies maintain their positions, the term has evolved into a more complex and contested explanation of social power in the face of cultural developments such as mass media and entertainment, and new communication and information technologies.

immigrant A person who is living outside the country in which he or she was born. About 3 per cent of the world's population are currently living outside the country in which they were born.

indeterminacy A philosophical idea that refers to the notion that our ways of being together are never fixed, necessary, or essential and so are not "determinate." This means that there are always openings from which new and incalculable ways of being might arise. In other words, this idea suggests that our social history is never closed, which has significant implications for how sociology might approach the social.

Indigenous sovereignty The political condition in which Indigenous peoples in Canada (including Inuit, First Nations, and Indian people) would autonomously govern themselves as a sovereign political community under international law. Sovereignty may include any aspect of economic, political, social, and/or cultural affairs, as well as land use. The degree of this autonomy continues to be widely debated in terms of its probability and practicality amid the national borders and political sovereignty of Canada.

individualism An ideology that gives the individual person rather than the social collective primacy.

inequalities Differences between individuals or groups that create advantages or disadvantages or that confer benefits or penalties in society.

inequities Differences between individuals or groups that create social advantages or disadvantages and that are also unfair or unjust.

institutional ethnography A feminist perspective that combines **ethnomethodological** and Marxist insights to examine how the "ruling relations" tacitly work to exclude and marginalize women (and others) in Western societies.

institutional racism A pattern of inequality by social institutions to treat groups of people differently based on their race.

integration A process of settlement that encourages newcomers to keep some aspects of their former culture while at the same time accepting certain aspects of their new society. It is a two-way process in that the culture and norms of the host society change to accommodate and welcome the newcomers. Integration is the preferred form of settlement for immigrants, according to the legislation set up by the government of Canada.

intergenerativity A model promoted by Peter J. Whitehouse to indicate the benefits of learning partnerships between younger and older generations, particularly in educational settings, and how such benefits can be achieved through combining, rather than isolating, generational experiences and contributions.

justice Takes on many meanings; can signify a system of law, morality, impartiality, and even a village in Manitoba. For Jacques Derrida, its meaning is forever deferred and, thus, cannot be effectively defined or constrained and contained by legality.

justice orientation A tendency to evaluate problems of inequality with an emphasis on doing what is fair and equal.

Keynesian welfare state A system developed after World War II by both federal and provincial governments to provide tax-funded public programs to ensure citizens' basic needs. These programs rested on a premise of shared citizen entitlement and mutual obligation and were designed as economic instruments to shore up the market in times of economic downturn. In Canada, the programs of the Canadian welfare state were particularly important in articulating a shared sense of national identity.

labelling theory An approach to understanding behaviour, especially deviant behaviour, that emphasizes the potentially reinforcing effects of societal labels on a person's behaviour; these effects may be either internal, affecting how the person sees himself or herself, or external, affecting how society sees and, consequently, treats him or her.

LAT ("living apart together") couples A newly emergent family form wherein a committed couple live in separate homes either by choice or by circumstance.

longevity Lifespan, or how long we live.

looking-glass self theory Charles Cooley's theory that a person's sense of self is derived from the perceptions of others, depending in this way on the imagination of our appearance to the other person; the imagination of their judgment of that appearance; and resulting feelings about ourselves, such as pride or shame.

mad movement Groups of psychiatric survivors/consumers who fight against the oppressive techniques used by the mental health system. The groups are best known for Mad Pride events that take place around the world.

mass communication The process of creating shared meaning between mass media and their audiences. The term refers to the process by which a complex organization, using a variety of technologies (machines), produces a steady stream of public messages aimed at a large, scattered, and diverse audience.

media effects The various ways individuals or groups can be influenced by media content. Research on media effects often addresses dramatic issues, such as violence, pornography, or social stereotyping. Debates on media effects often frame discussion on two opposing perspectives either media messages are powerful stimuli that can persuade or influence peoples' behaviour, or media messages have little influencing power. Communication research since the 1960s tends to support the view that repeated media exposure reinforces values and attitudes that a person already has.

media literacy The development and use of a set of skills that enable individuals to interpret and evaluate critically the meanings of messages they encounter in the media. "Media literacy" also refers to an individual's ability to use the tools of communication to produce as well as understand mediated communication.

medium theory A theory that asks what media basically are and what media do. It focuses on the particular type or kind of medium or media of communication separately from the content or meaning conveyed.

minimalist-government approach Here, the state takes an arms-length approach and fosters an environment wherein the private sector provision of police/security service is commercialized and provided like many other commodities.

morbidity The incidence of disease in a defined population.

mortality The rate of death in a defined population.

mother-blaming The tendency to hold mothers responsible (and *not* fathers) for how their children turn out, especially when the child exhibits what society considers a problem, such as obesity, autism, or schizophrenia. Mother-blaming invokes the idea of the "bad" mother to explain such problems.

multinational state A country where people claiming to form distinct nations coexist. Few states have homogenous populations, but few states are truly multinational. Canada, Spain, Great Britain, and India are examples.

nationalism Refers to both an ideology seeking to create or defend a specific culture within a given political unit, and to a process the formation of distinct national states, mostly during a period covering the late nineteenth and twentieth centuries. Some researchers argue that we have now entered a post-national period, but nation states, usually enjoying a fairly high degree of sovereignty, and more rarely cultural homogeneity, remain the most common political structures.

nation-state Two separate but often linked concepts.

neo-conservatism A political philosophy that advocates aspects of a free economy, such as free trade and privatization and the cutting down of social welfare programs, and that actively promotes radical change.

neo-liberal welfare state A systemic reform in the 1980s, reacting against the perceived weaknesses of the Keynesian welfare state. Some social programs were eliminated, while others saw a drastic reduction in funding and a reorientation in delivery. Neo-liberal social programs emphasize individual, family, and community responsibility; choice in the market place; and freedom from the state.

neo-liberalism A social, political, and economic regulatory system that is characterized by (among other things) the freedom of the market, privatizing government services, and shifting responsibility from government to individuals.

NIMBY **(not in my backyard)** Refers to community opposition to a development (often one seeking to support vulnerable populations) because of its proximity to their home.

normalization A governing practice that makes some ways of being "normal" and others "abnormal" and thus in need of interventions.

normative The socially prescribed ideal, correct, or standard way of doing something.

official statistics Numerical information, typically compiled by government agencies, regarding social and other phenomena (such as crime, unemployment, health, suicide, population, etc.).

out-migration The departure of people from a region on a temporary or permanent basis.

panopticon Originally an architectural design for the prison that allowed guards to watch prisoners without prisoners knowing whether or not they were being watched; now associated with broader practices of surveillance through which people are under the impression they are being watched and conduct their behaviour accordingly.

pathological homogenization A process by which a government pursues the creation of a culturally homogenous population, usually by means of violence, expulsion, and fear.

pathways to prison Individual or structural factors that may contribute to an individual's involvement in crime and eventual incarceration. Some factors may include homelessness, mental health difficulties, prostitution, victimization, trauma, poor education, unemployment, substance use, economic marginalization, or lack of social support.

patriarchy The structures and practices whereby males explicitly and implicitly exert power over females, and enjoy economic, political, cultural, and material privileges compared to females; a form of social stratification in which men have disproportionate influence and power, and masculine traits and characteristics are valued more than highly than feminine ones.

policing A process of regulating and ordering contemporary societies and individuals carried out by police—the civil force of a national, provincial, or local government, responsible for the prevention and detection of crime and the maintenance of public safety and order.

political disenfranchisement Not having the opportunity to participate in democratic processes, or to self-govern, particularly with respect to voting.

population health The health of a society's population, usually measured as life expectancy, or the average lifespan.

positivism A philosophical way of thinking founded by French philosopher and social scientist Auguste Comte, which only accepts knowledge based on systematic observation and experimentation.

positivist sociology A form of sociological research that seeks to apply the methods used in the natural sciences to the study of human behaviour; the claim that social knowledge must be scientifically verified by observable facts that will reveal the invariant laws governing social behavior. Auguste Comte is regarded as the "father" of positivist social theory.

postmodern A skepticism about the dogma of universal, objective, scientific knowledge, social progress, or "truth." It recognizes the plurality, complexity, and diversity of social life. (For art and culture the term *postmodern* is often used to refer to more playful, decorative, vernacular styles in contrast to the rigidity of high modernist styles.)

postmodernism A way of thinking that began in the 1960s by emphasizing the importance of plurality, diversity, and relativity in art and then came to apply to world views themselves in the late 1970s; postmodern thinkers maintain that there are many different, equally legitimate ways of thinking and that one should be skeptical of all meta-narratives and universals.

post-sovereignty The idea that many states and communities are less concerned with political sovereignty than in the past. Many European states have ceded part of their sovereignty to the European Union, for instance, and many non-sovereign communities are pursuing forms of autonomy rather than complete sovereignty.

poverty The inability of persons to meet their essential human needs (i.e., food, shelter, well-being, and services). Unlike many other nations, Canada does not institute an official poverty line. Instead, government agencies use other measures to determine poverty. Statistics Canada, for example, uses the Low Income Cut-Off or LICO to this end, which "are income thresholds below which a family will likely devote a larger share of its income on the necessities of food, shelter and clothing than the average family." (http://www.statcan.gc.ca/pub/75f0002m/2012002/lico-sfr-eng.htm)

power relations Foucault used this phrase to emphasize his "relational theory of power." In short, against a dominant view of power as a top-down phenomenon in which subjects are constrained by a visible and central authority (e.g., a sovereign, a king or queen, etc.), Foucault understood power as a "bottom up" affair. Here, the outcome of local clashes of will effectively shapes subjects, their actions, and ultimately the social and political contexts that envelop them. In effect, this means that in his approach to power, Foucault focused on the "political technologies" developed by local relations, and the ways that people's actions helped to structure the actions of others. In this context, freedom and power are not opposed, since power relations shape the freedoms of a given historical moment.

private security The broad term used to describe a wide range of private (non-governmental) security-related activities associated with the protection of private property.

psychotropic medication Prescription drugs commonly used to treat various formulations of mental illness.

public health The arm of government that is responsible for protecting the health and safety of the public and for improving population health. Through legislation (such as anti-smoking legislation and mandatory seat-belt legislation), policies, and programs, public health seeks to prevent disease and premature death.

public sociology A recent approach to sociology framed by Michael Burawoy that calls for a critical re-evaluation of traditions of policy, professional and critical sociology. Among its many contributions is the call for sociology to engage a wider public when developing its research agendas.

quantitative studies Research methods that draw on empirical studies—data collected from a population or group—and that can be precisely analyzed using established statistical procedures. In communication studies, quantitative methods typically involve a controlled research project designed to investigate and measure an aspect of communication.

queer theory A theoretical approach based on analyzing societies and cultures from the viewpoints of lesbian, gay, bisexual, and transgendered people. Queer theory focuses, in particular, on showing how concepts of heterosexuality and masculinity depend on the simultaneous covert desire for, and overt denial of, homosexual attraction.

Quiet Revolution A period in Quebec's history, spanning much of the 1960s, when it experienced peaceful but rapid cultural, political, and social change.

racial overrepresentation A phenomenon that occurs when a racial group has more of its members in some condition (i.e., unemployed, living in poverty, imprisoned) in greater numbers than the group's population would suggest. For example, as Aboriginals make up 4 per cent of the population, you might predict, other things being equal, that they would represent 4 per cent of the prison population. However, in actuality Aboriginals make up approximately 18 per cent of the incarcerated adult population. Thus, as a racial group they are overrepresented in the prison population.

racialized minorities People who, because of their physical or linguistic attributes, are marginalized. They may be immigrants but they may also be born in Canada. It is a term that replaces old phrases, such as visible minority and minority group, and recognizes that language may also demarcate a marginalized group.

reflexive longevity A concept developed by Sharon R. Kaufman in her research on older medical patients to illuminate the ethical dilemmas of negotiating life-prolonging treatments and late-life decision-making in an era where traditionally accepted boundaries of life and death are being extended and debated.

reflexivity Anthony Giddens's term to refer to the way in which individuals monitor their aspirations and behaviour in response to the ongoing flow of social life; used by some feminists to refer to the ability to interrogate our own actions (that is, critically question our actions) by examining what makes some action logically possible while ruling out alternative action. Feminists thus connect reflexivity to discourse analysis and attempts to make explicit the power relations and the exercise of power in our everyday social practice (see *discourse*).

refugee A legal category of immigration referring to a person outside his or her country of origin who cannot return to a home country due to fear of persecution, imprisonment, punishment, or death due to his or her ethnic, gender, sexual, religious, or other marginalized status.

reintegration The process an individual goes through upon returning to the community after a period of incarceration and attempting to overcome a range of social, economic, and personal challenges that can be obstacles to a crime-free lifestyle. (Also referred to as *resettlement* or *re-entry*.)

reliability Refers to the consistency of a measure, that is, whether under the same conditions a measure will be the same each time it is taken.

retribution Punishment meted out in recompense for wrongdoing.

ritual model of communication A model of communication grounded in an understanding of communication as social; as part of communication processes and practices in culture through which beliefs and ideas are shared.

segmented assimilation A non-linear process of settlement associated with the structuralist perspective. In segmented assimilation, an immigrant may economically integrate (by having a good job that recognizes his or her skills and credentials), but may not socially integrate (by having few friends or acquaintances). It may also refer to the process where at some points in an immigrant's life history, integration is good, but at other points the integration is more problematic.

self-determination The right to free choice over one's own actions without coercion.

self-government A federal policy in Canada that outlines the degree to which Indigenous communities can negotiate semi-autonomous power within their communities while remaining under the jurisdiction of the federal Crown.

situated knowledges Refers to the recognition that all knowledge is situated or contextualized within the context of an agent who produces that knowledge. This term contests the idea that there is a single universal knowledge.

social capital The types of social relationships—often located in families or communities—that help people achieve high educational and occupational goals.

social distance In Bogardus's use, a willingness to admit different (specified) ethnic or racial groups to intimacy with you, your family, friends, or neighbours.

social hierarchy A ranking of members of society dependent upon their social status.

social investment state A modification of the neo-liberal welfare state. The child receives primary emphasis in social investment policies, and the objective of social programs is to ensure

support for the development of future workers and economic innovators.

social media Internet or web-based sites that provide information and content to users and that allow, encourage, or even require that those users interact with that content. In contrast to mass communication, which involves transmitting standardized messages from an organization to a wide audience, social media allows users to respond to content—to express their own views with communicators and with other users.

social justice The pursuit of a just society, in which there is a fair allocation of resources and all are treated equitably. In a just society, there would be no health inequities among groups of people (e.g., between Indigenous and non-Indigenous people).

social welfare net An interlocking network of government, quasi-governmental, and private programs and policies designed to support society's impoverished and marginalized groups. Examples of social welfare programs include government-supported housing, food and housing subsidies, and employment insurance.

society A group of people defined by normative relations and by common interests, goals, meanings, power formations, and so on.

sovereignty The term can have many different meanings, but its most common definition applies to states able to exert independent rule within a given geographic territory. Historically, full sovereignty has only applied to a relatively small number of societies. There are debates currently about the erosion of state sovereignty, although in practice it remains the most common form of political power.

space-biased media As suggested by Harold Innis, a medium that is lightweight and portable and could be transported or communicated over long distances. Societies with space-biased media tended to extend over larger territories because they could easily control information flow through broadcast media, such as radio and TV.

statehood The status of being a state rather than a dependent region or territory.

state-interventionist approach to policing Here, the state takes an active role in providing oversight, standards, operationalization, and funding of services. This is consistent with policing in Canada.

structuration The notion that social systems are created and reproduced through the simultaneous operation of social systems and agency (see *agency*) of individuals, without according primacy to either. In other words, if we want to understand how our social world is reconstituted, we need to study at both the macro-level (of institutions) and micro-level (of everyday activity).

sustainability Refers to the endurance of systems and processes. This term is often used in discussions of the viability of ecological systems to survive human-made changes brought about in the **Anthropocene**.

temporary worker An individual who is temporarily located outside his or her country of origin for the sole purpose of working. This is a legal category of immigrant. Usually, but not always, temporary workers are restricted from remaining permanently in Canada.

The Great Law (*Kainere'ko:wa*) The governing constitution of the Haudenosaunee Confederacy. It outlines the structure, roles, and responsibilities of the Grand Council of the Haudenosaunee, including the Chiefs, Clan Mothers, Faith Keepers, and Warriors. The Great Law functions to maintain peace between nations and among the people.

social theory A conceptual framework that describes, understands, explains, analyzes, or interprets the social world and its meaning horizons.

time-biased media Common to some ancient societies; demonstrate a bias toward time because, as Harold Innis suggested, they are difficult to move yet durable (e.g., stone and clay tablets). Societies with time-biased media tend to grow slowly and develop complex social hierarchies much as in ancient Egypt.

total institutions Coined by Erving Goffman, total institutions are residences where individuals are confined, cut off from broader society, and where their daily activities are highly structured and supervised.

Traditional Ecological Knowledge (TEK) Refers to Indigenous knowledge regarding natural resources, the environment, and sustainability.

transcarceration The cycling of marginalized individuals between the criminal justice, mental health, and social welfare systems.

transmission model of communication The idea that communication can be thought of as the transport of messages as information between a sender and receiver over a distance for the purposes of control.

transnational families Families whose members, living in other countries, are separated by borders.

Two Row Wampum (*Kaswentha*) An international treaty between the Haudenosaunee and the Dutch in 1613, and later adopted by the British Crown. This wampum belt depicts five rows of wampum beads two purple and three white. The purple wampum represents two canoes, travelling down the river of life. One is meant for the Haudenosaunee Confederacy and the other is intended for European nations. The relationship between the two is based on co-existence and non-interference. The three rows of white wampum represent friendship, respect, and peace.

United Nations Declaration on the Rights of Indigenous Peoples (UNDRIP) An international instrument developed by Indigenous peoples from around the world, and adopted by the United Nations in 2007. It contains 46 articles pertaining to the standards and quality of life that Indigenous peoples and their communities have the right to expect. UNDRIP is premised on the idea that Indigenous peoples have the right "to freely determine their political status and freely pursue their economic, social and cultural development."

universalizing The generalization/normalization of social practices, the assumption that the "grand narratives" of modernity apply to all without exception; (positivist sociology was understood as the search for such universal social laws).

validity Refers to a statement that corresponds to the real world, that is, how well a statement measures up to its claims.

victimization The act or process of rendering a person a victim, which typically involves some harm or injury to a party or parties. Research in sociology has repeatedly demonstrated a connection between victimization and future offending. Some groups are overrepresented as victims of crime (i.e., Aboriginal peoples).

welfare state An approach to governing that sees social provision as a responsibility shared among the national population and managed by the state. This process entails market regulation, service provision, and redistribution of income to attain a relative level of income equality and equality of opportunity among citizens.

Woodstock generation The area outside Woodstock, New York, was the site of a large gathering of young people in the summer of 1969 to listen to music and embrace the anti-war and counter-cultural values of the time. Its significance remains because of the constant circulation of musical productions, films, and nostalgia items of the event and the use of the term to signify the hippy movement of the late 1960s, in general.

Young Offenders Act (YOA) Enacted in 1982; governed youthful offenders from 1984 until the Youth Criminal Justice Act (YCJA) was put into place in 2003. The YOA replaced the Juvenile Delinquents Act and ushered in a new era of legal governance for youth.

Youth Criminal Justice Act (YCJA) Came into effect in 2003 and is the contemporary Canadian legislation that regulates youthful offenders between the ages of 12 and 18.

References

Abbott, Andrew. 2000. "Reflections on the Future of Sociology." *Contemporary Sociology* 29 (2): 296.

Adam, Barbara. 2004. "Towards a New Sociology of the Future." Retrieved from http://www.cf.ac.uk/socsi/futures/newsociologyofthefuture.pdf.

Abercrombie, Nicholas, Stephen Hill, and Bryan S. Turner. 1984. *Dictionary of sociology*. London: Penguin.

Aboriginal Affairs and Northern Development Canada. 1995. *The Government of Canada's approach to implementation of the inherent right and the negotiation of Aboriginal self-government.* Retrieved from https://www.aadnc-aandc.gc.ca/eng/1100100031843/1100100031844

Achenbaum, W. Andrew. 1995. *Crossing frontiers: Gerontology emerges as a science.* Cambridge: Cambridge University Press.

Adam, Barry D. 1978. *The survival of domination.* New York: Elsevier/Greenwood.

Adam, Barry D. 1985. "Age, structure and sexuality." *Journal of Homosexuality* 11 (3/4): 19–33.

Adam, Barry D. 1995. *The rise of a gay and lesbian movement.* New York: Twayne.

Adam, Barry D. 1996. "Structural foundations of the gay world." In S. Seidman (Ed.), *Queer theory/sociology.* Cambridge, MA: Blackwell.

Adam, Barry D. 1998. "Theorizing homophobia." *Sexualities* 1 (4): 387–404.

Adam, Barry D. 2004. "Care, intimacy, and same-sex partnership in the 21st century." *Current Sociology* 52 (2): 265–79.

Adam, Barry D. 2006. "Relationship innovation in male relationships." *Sexualities* 9 (1): 5–26.

Adelberg, E., and C. Currie. 1987. *Too few to count: Canadian women in conflict with the law.* Vancouver: Press Gang.

Adkins, Lisa. 2002. *Revisions: Gender and sexuality in late modernity.* Buckingham, UK: Open University Press.

Agger, Ben. 1991. *A critical theory of public life.* London: Falmer Press.

Agyeman, J., P. Cole, R. Haluza-DeLay, and P. O'Riley. 2010. *Speaking for ourselves: Environmental justice in Canada.* Vancouver: University of British Columbia Press.

Akbari, A.H. 1991. "The public finance impact of immigrant population on host nations: Some Canadian evidence." *Social Science Quarterly* 72 (2): 334–46.

Akbari, A.H. 2014. "Human resource deficit in Atlantic Canada: A challenge for regional economic development." *Journal of International Migration and Integration*, 2014: 1–12.

Akyeampong, E.B. 2005. "Business support services." *Perspectives on Labour and Income* 6 (5): 5–9.

Albanese, Patrizia. 2010. "Introduction to Canada's families: Historical and recent variations, definitions, and theories." In D. Cheal (Ed.), *Canadian Families* (pp. 2–26). Toronto: Oxford University Press.

Alberta Solicitor General and Public Security. 2005. Consultation paper: MLA review of private investigators and security guards. Alberta: Alberta Solicitor General and Public Security.

Alfred, Taiaiake, and Jeff Corntassel. 2005. *Being Indigenous: Resurgences against contemporary colonialism.* Blackwell Publishing.

Alfred, Taiaiake. 2005. *Wasáse: Indigenous pathways of action and freedom.* Peterborough, ON: Broadview Press.

Ali, S.H. 2004. "A socio-ecological autopsy of the E. coli O157:H7 outbreak in Walkerton, Ontario, Canada." *Social Science and Medicine* 58 (12): 2601–12.

Amadiume, Ifi. 1980. *Male daughters, female husbands.* Toronto: DEC.

Ambert, Anne-Marie. 2006. *One-parent families: Characteristics, causes, consequences, and issues.* Toronto: Vanier Institute of the Family.

Anderson, Benedict. 1991. *Imagined communities: Reflections on the origin and spread of nationalism.* New York: Verso.

Anderson, Benedict. 1998. *The spectre of comparisons: Nationalism, Southeast Asia and the world.* London: Verso.

Anderson, C. 1999. "Governing Aboriginal justice in Canada: Constructing responsible individuals and communities through tradition." *Crime, Law and Social Change* 31 (2): 303–26.

Anderson, Kim. 2000. *A recognition of being: Reconstructing Native womanhood.* Toronto: Second Story Press.

Andrews, Molly. 2012. "Unexpecting age." *Journal of Aging Studies* 26 (4): 386–93.

Arbour L. 1998. *Report of the Commission of Inquiry into Certain Events at the Prison for Women in Kingston.* Ottawa: Public Works and Government Services.

Arditti, J., and A. Few. 2006. "Mothers' reentry into family life following incarceration." *Criminal Justice Policy Review* 17 (1): 103–23.

Arnst, Catherine. 2006. "Health as a birthright." *Business Week.* Retrieved from http://www.bloomberg.com/bw/stories/2006-05-28/health-as-a-birthright.

Arrigo, B.A. 2001. "Transcarceration: A constitutive ethnography of mentally ill 'offenders.'" *The Prison Journal* 81, 2: 162–86.

Assembly of First Nations. 2005. *Our nations our governments: Choosing our own paths.* Report of the Joint Committee of Chiefs and Advisors on the Recognition and Implementation of First Nation Governments. Ottawa: Assembly of First Nations.

Assembly of First Nations. 2013 (20 May). "Speaking notes": United Nations Permanent Forum on Indigenous Issues, Twelfth Session. UN Headquarters, New York.

Atkinson, J.M. 1971. "Societal reactions to suicide: The role of coroners' definitions." In S. Cohen (Ed.), *Images of deviance.* Harmondsworth, UK: Penguin.

Atkinson, J.M. 1982. *Discovering suicide: Studies in the social organization of sudden death.* London: Macmillan.

Ayling, J., and C. Shearing. 2008. "Taking care of business: Public police as commercial security vendors." *Criminology and Criminal Justice* 8 (1): 27–50.

Babooram, A. (2008). *The changing profile of adults in custody, 2006/2007.* Ottawa: Statistics Canada no.85-002-x. Retrieved from http://www.statcan.gc.ca/pub/85-002-x/2008010/article/10732-eng.htm#a6.

Bagdikian, Ben. 2000. *The media monopoly* (6th ed.). Boston: Beacon Press.

Baines, Donna, and Bonnie Freeman. 2011. "Intergenerational care work: Mothering, grandmothering, and eldercare." In C. Krull and J. Sempruch (Eds), *Demystifying the family/work contradiction* (pp. 67–80). Vancouver: University of British Columbia Press.

Baines, Donna. 2004a. "Caring for nothing: Work organization and unwaged labour in social services." *Work, Employment and Society* 18 (2): 267–95.

Baines, Donna. 2004b. Seven kinds of work— Only one paid: Raced, gendered and restructured care work in the social services sector. *Atlantis: A Women's Studies Journal* 28 (2): 19–28.

Bakan, Abigail, and Audrey Kobayashi. 2000. *Employment equity policy in Canada: An interprovincial comparison.* Ottawa: Status of Women Canada.

Baker, Maureen. 2001. *Families, labour and love: Family diversity in a changing world.* Sydney: Allen and Unwin.

Baker, Maureen. 2010. *Choices and constraints in family life* (2nd ed.). Toronto: Oxford University Press.

Baker, M., and D. Benjamin. 1995. "The receipt of transfer payments by immigrants to Canada." *Journal of Human Resources*, 30: 650–76.

Balfour, G., and E. Comack. 2006. *Criminalizing women.* Halifax: Fernwood.

Barker, J. 2009. *Women in the criminal justice system: A Canadian perspective.* Toronto: Emond Montgomery Publications Ltd.

Barney, Darin. 2000. *Prometheus wired: The hope for democracy in the age of networked technology.* Vancouver: University of British Columbia Press.

Barrett, M.R., K. Allenby, and K. Taylor. 2010. *Twenty years later: Revisiting the Task Force on Federally Sentenced Women.* Research Report R-222. Ottawa: Correctional Service Canada.

Barris, Stephen. 2005. "How long will lesbian, gay, bisexual and transgender rights be ignored at the UN?" *Bulletin of the International Gay and Lesbian Rights Association* 117: 22–5.

Bartholet, Elizabeth. 2005. "Abuse and neglect, foster drift, and the adoption alternative." In S. Haslanger and C. Witt (Eds), *Adoption matters: Philosophical and feminist essays* (pp. 223–33). Ithaca, NY: Cornell University Press.

Bartky, Sandra Lee. 1997. "On psychological oppression." In Mary F. Rogers (Ed.), *Contemporary feminist theory: A text/reader.* Boston: McGraw-Hill.

Bauder, David. 2009. "Study: More Americans think media is biased, inaccurate." *The Huffington Post,* 14 September.

Baudrillard, J. 1997. "The End of the Millennium or the Countdown." *Economy & Society* 26 (4): 447–55.

Baudrillard, Jean. 1983. *Simulations.* New York: Semiotext(e).

Bauman, Zygmunt. 1987. *Legislators and interpreters.* Cambridge, UK: Polity Press.

Bauman, Zygmunt. 1988. *Freedom.* Minneapolis: University of Minnesota Press.

Bauman, Zygmunt. 2001. *Community: Seeking safety in an insecure world.* Cambridge, UK: Polity Press.

Baumrind, Diana. 1966. "Effects of authoritative parental control on child behavior." *Child Development* 37 (4): 887–907.

Beale, Elizabeth. 2008. "As labour markets tighten, will outmigration trends reverse in Atlantic Canada?" Commentary. May. Halifax: Atlantic Provinces Economic Council.

Bean, P. 2008. *Madness and crime.* Portland: Willan Publishing.

Beasley, Chris. 1999. *What is feminism? An introduction to feminist theory.* London: Sage Publications.

Beauchemin, Jacques. 2008. "Le nationalisme québécois entre culture et identité." *Ethique publique* 10 (1), 103–15.

Beaudin, M., and S. Breau. 2001. "Employment, skills and the knowledge economy in Atlantic Canada." *Maritime Series Monographs.* Moncton: Institut canadien de recherche sur le développement regional/The Canadian Institute for Research on Regional Development.

Beck, U. 1992. *Risk society: Towards a new modernity.* New Delhi: Sage.

Becker, D. 2004. "Post-traumatic stress disorder." In P. Caplan and L. Cosgrove (Eds), *Bias in psychiatric diagnosis* (pp. 207–12). Lanham: Jason Aronson.

Becker, Gary. 1993. *Human capital, a theoretical and empirical analysis, with special reference to education* (3rd ed.). Chicago: University of Chicago Press.

Bell, Derrick. 1992. *Faces at the bottom of the well.* New York: Basic Books.

Bell, Wendell. 1996. "The Sociology of the Future and the Future of Sociology." *Sociological Perspectives* 39 (1): 39–57.

Benatar, Solomon R., and Ross Upshur. 2010. "Tuberculosis and poverty: What could (and should) be done?" *International Journal of Tuberculosis and Lung Disease 14* (1): 1215–21.

Bengtson, Vern L. 2001. "The Burgess Award lecture—Beyond the nuclear family: The increasing importance of multigenerational bonds." *Journal of Marriage and Family* 63 (1): 1–16.

Berelson, B. 1959. "The state of communication research." *Public Opinion Quarterly* 23 (1): 16.

Berelson, Bernard, and Gary A. Steiner. 1964. *Human behavior: An inventory of scientific findings.* New York: Harcourt, Brace & World.

Beresford, P. 2005. "Social approaches to madness and distress: User perspectives and user knowledges." In J. Tew (Ed.), *Social perspectives in mental health: Developing social models to understand and work with mental distress* (pp. 32–52). London: Jessica Kingsley Publishers.

Berger, Peter L. 1963. *Invitation to sociology: A humanistic perspective.* New York: Anchor.

Berger, Peter L., and Thomas Luckmann. 1967. *The social construction of reality: A treatise in the sociology of knowledge.* New York: Anchor.

Bertrand, M., and S. Mullainathan. 2003. *Are Emily and Greg more employable than Lakisha and Jamal? A field experiment on labor market discrimination* (No. w9873). Cambridge, MA: National Bureau of Economic Research.

Bezanson, Kate. 2010. "The 'great recession,' families and social reproduction." *Transition* 40 (1): 1–6.

Bibby, Reginald W. 2004. *The future families project: A survey of Canadian hopes and dreams.* Toronto: Vanier Institute of the Family.

Bierly, Margaret. 1985. "Prejudice toward contemporary outgroups as a generalized attitude." *Journal of Applied Social Psychology* 15 (2): 189–99.

Bingham, E., and Sutton, R., 2012. *Cruel, inhuman and degrading? Canada's treatment* of federally-sentenced women with mental health issues. Toronto: International Human Rights Program, University of Toronto Faculty of Law.

Binkley, M. 1994. Voices from offshore: Narratives of risk and danger in the Nova Scotia deep sea fishery. St John's, NF: Iser Books.

Bird, C.E., and M.E. Lang. 2014. "Gender, health, and constrained choice." The Wiley Blackwell Encyclopedia of Health, Illness, Behavior, and Society. John Wiley & Sons, Ltd.

Bittner, Egon. 1990. Aspects of police work. Boston: Northeastern University Press.

Blackstock, C. 2003. "Same country, same land, 78 countries apart." Unpublished paper.

Blanchette, K., and S.L. Brown. 2006. The assessment and treatment of women offenders: An integrative perspective. New York: John Wiley and Sons.

Bloom, B., B. Owen, and S. Covington. 2003. "Gender-responsive strategies research, practice, and guiding principles for women offenders." Washington: National Institute of Justice.

Bloom B., B. Owen, and S. Covington. 2006. "A summary of research, practice, and guiding principles for women offenders: The gender-responsive strategies project: Approach and findings." Washington, DC: National Institute of Corrections. Retrieved from http://nicic.org/Library/020418

Blumer, Herbert, and P.M. Hauser. 1939. Movies, delinquency and crime. New York: MacMillan.

Bogardus, Emory S. 1925. "Measuring social distance." Journal of applied sociology 9 (2): 299–308.

Boily, Frédéric. 2004. "Lionel Groulx et l'esprit du libéralisme." Recherches sociographiques 45: 239–57.

Bolaffi, G. 2003. Dictionary of race, ethnicity and culture. London: Sage.

Bönisch-Brednich, Brigitte, and Catherine Trundle. 2010. Local lives: Migration and the politics of place. Farnham, UK: Ashgate Publishing.

Booker, Loper A., and I. Levitt. 2011. "Mental health needs of female offender." In T. Fagan and R. Lax (Eds), Correctional mental health: From theory to practice. California: Sage.

Borgatta, Edgar F. 1988. The Future of Sociology. Edited by Karen S. Cook. Newbury Park, Calif: Sages.

Boritch, H. 1992. "Gender and criminal court outcomes: An historical analysis." Criminology, 30, 293–325.

Boswell, John. 1994. Same-sex unions in premodern Europe. New York: Villard.

Bouchard, Gérard, and Charles Taylor. 2008. Building the future. A time for reconciliation. Report of the Commission de consultation sur les pratiques d'accommodement reliées aux différences culturelles, Gouvernement du Québec.

Boudarbat, Brahim, and Marie Connolly. 2013. "The gender wage gap among recent post-secondary graduates in Canada: A distributional approach." Canadian Journal of Economics 46 (3): 1037–65. doi:10.1111/caje.12036

Bourdieu, P. 1977. Outline of a theory of practice. Cambridge, UK: Cambridge University Press.

Bourque, Gilles. 2001. "Between nations and society." In Michel Venne (Ed.), Vive Quebec! New thinking and new approaches to the Quebec nation. Toronto: Lorimer.

boyd, danah. 2008. "Why youth ♥ social network sites: The role of networked publics in teenage social life." In David Buckingham (Ed.), Youth, identity, and digital media (Vol. 6, pp. 119–42). Cambridge, MA: MIT Press.

Bradbury, Bettina. 2005. "The social, economic and cultural origins of contemporary families." In M. Baker (Ed.), Families: Changing trends in Canada (5th ed.). Toronto: McGraw-Hill Ryerson.

Bray, Alan. 1982. "Homosexuality and the signs of male friendship in Elizabethan England." History Workshop 29: 1–19.

Bresson, M. 2003. "Le lien entre santé mentale et précarité sociale: Une fausse evidence." Cahiers Internationaux de Sociolgie 115: 311–26.

Brinded, P. M., A.I. Simpson, T.M. Laidlaw, N.A. Fairley, and F. Malcolm. 2001. "Prevalence of psychiatric disorders in New Zealand prisons: A national study." Australian and New Zealand Journal of Psychiatry 35 (2): 166–73.

Britton, Dana. 1990. "Developmental origins of antihomosexual prejudice in heterosexual men and women." Clinical Social Work Journal 19: 163–75.

Brodie, Janine. 1997. "Meso-discourses, state forms and the gendering of liberal-democratic-citizenship." *Citizenship Studies* 1 (2): 223–42.

Brodie, Janine. 2002. "An elusive search for community: Globalization and the Canadian national identities." *Review of Constitutional Studies* 7 (1/2): 155–78.

Brodie, Janine. 2014. "New constitutionalism, neo-liberalism and social policy." In Stephen Gill and Claire A. Cutler (Eds), *New constitutionalism and world order* (pp. 247–60). Cambridge: Cambridge University Press.

Bromaghin, J.F., T.L. McDonald, and S.C. Amstrup. 2013. "Plausible combinations: An improved method to evaluate the covariate structure of Cormack-Jolly-Seber mark-recapture models." *Open Journal of Ecology*, 3: 11–22.

Brommelhoff, J.A., K. Conway, K. Merikangas and B.R. Levy. 2004. "Higher rates of depression in women: Role of gender bias within the family." *Journal of Women's Health* 13 (1): 69–76.

Brookey, R., and K. Cannon. 2009. "Sex lives in second life." *Critical Studies in Media Communication* 26 (2).

Brooks-Gunn, J., and G.J. Duncan. 1997. "The effects of poverty on children." *The Future of Children* 7 (2): 55–71. doi:10.2307/1602387

Brown, Lyn Mikel. 1998. *Raising their voices: The politics of girls' anger.* Cambridge, MA: Harvard University Press.

Brown, M. 2006. "Gender, ethnicity, and offending over the life course: Women's pathways to prison in the Aloha state." *Critical Criminology* 14, 137–58.

Brown, Wendy. 2015. *Undoing the Demos: Neoliberalism's Stealth Revolution.* New York: Zone Books.

Browne, T.K. 2014. "Is premenstrual dysphoric disorder really a disorder?" *Journal of Bioethical Inquiry* 11 (4): 1–18.

Brumberg, Joan Jacobs. 1997. *The body project: An intimate history of American girls.* New York: Vintage.

Bryant, T., D. Raphael, T. Schrecker, and R. Labonte. 2011. "Canada: A land of missed opportunity for addressing the social determinants of health." *Health Policy*, 101(1): 44–58. doi:http://dx.doi.org/10.1016/j.healthpol.2010.08.022

Bryson, B. 2005. *A short history of nearly everything.* New York: Doubleday.

Bryson. M. 2004. "When Jill jacks in: Queer women and the net." *Feminist Media Studies* 4 (3): 239–54.

Buchanan, R. 2000. "1–800 New Brunswick: Economic development strategies, firm restructuring and the local production of 'global' services." In. J. Jenson and B.D.S. Santos (Eds), *Globalizing institutions, case studies in regulation and innovation* (pp. 53–80). Aldershot, UK: Ashgate.

Burawoy, Michael. 2005. "For Public Sociology." *American Sociological Review* 70 (1): 4–28.

Burbidge, S. 2005. "The governance deficit: Reflections on the future of public and private policing in Canada." *Canadian Journal of Criminology and Criminal Justice* 47 (1): 64–85.

Burstow, B. 2004. "Progressive psychotherapists and the psychiatric survivor movement." *Journal of Humanistic Psychology* 44 (2): 141–54.

Burstow, B., and D. Weitz (Eds). 1988. *Shrink resistant: The struggle against psychiatry in Canada.* Vancouver: New Star Books.

Butler, Judith. 1988 (December). "Performative acts and gender constitution: An essay in phenomenology and feminist theory." *Theatre Journal* 40 (4): 519–31.

Butler, Judith. 1990. *Gender trouble: Feminism and the subversion of identity.* London: Routledge.

Butler, Judith. 1993. "Critically queer." *GLQ* 1 (1): 17–32.

Butler, Judith. 1997. *The Psychic Life of Power: Theories in Subjection.* 1 edition. Stanford, f: Stanford University Press.

Butler, Judith. 2005. *Giving an Account of Oneself.* Fourth Edition edition. New York: Fordham University Press.

Butler, Judith. 2006. *Gender Trouble: Feminism and the Subversion of Identity.* First edition. New York: Routledge.

Butler, Peter, and R. Smith. 1983. "The worker, the workplace and the need for unemployment insurance." *Canadian Review of Sociology and Anthropology* 20 (4): 393–412.

Byerly, C. 2012. "The geography of women and media scholarship." In K. Ross (Ed.), *The handbook of gender, sex, and media.* John Wiley & Sons Ltd.

Byrne, Bridget. 2003. "Reciting the self: Narrative representations of the self in qualitative interviews." *Feminist Theory* 4 (1): 29–49.

Cajete, G. 2000. *Native science: Natural laws of interdependence*. Santa Fe, New Mexico: Clear Light Publishers.

Calasanti, Toni M., and Kathleen F. Slevin (Eds). 2006. *Age matters: Realigning feminist thinking*. New York: Routledge.

Calhoun, Craig. 1995. *Critical social theory: Culture, history, and the challenge of difference*. London: Wiley-Blackwell.

Calverley, D. 2010. Adult correctional services in Canada 2008/2009. *Juristat*. Component of Statistics Canada catalogue no. 85-002-X, Vol. 30, no. 3. Ottawa: Statistics Canada.

Campaign 2000. 2014. *Child poverty 25 years later: WE CAN FIX THIS*. Toronto: Author. Retrieved from http://www.campaign2000.ca/anniversaryreport/CanadaRC2014EN.pdf

Campbell, Lara A., Dominique Clement, and Gregory S. Kealey. 2012. *Debating Dissent: Canada and the 1960s*. Toronto: University of Toronto Press.

Camus, Albert. 1991 [1947]. *The plague*. New York: Vintage.

Canada. 1982. *Canadian Charter of Rights and Freedoms*. Ottawa: Government Printer.

Canada Revenue Agency. 2014. *Family tax cut*. Retrieved from http://www.cra-arc.gc.ca/gncy/bdgt/2014/qa10-eng.html

Canadian Broadcasting Corporation (CBC). 2005. *Running off track: The Ben Johnson story*. Video clip. http://archives.cbc.ca/IDD-1-41-1392/sports/ben_johnson.

Canadian Broadcasting Corporation (CBC). 2007, 9 August. "CSIS suspected US would deport Arar to be tortured: Documents." *CBC Online*. Retrieved from http://www.cbc.ca/canada/story/2007/08/09/arar-report.html

Canadian Broadcasting Corporation (CBC). 2009. "Top gun—Dr David Walsh, media in the family." CBC News: *the fifth estate*. Originally aired 6 March 2009. Retrieved from http://www.youtube.com/watch?v=29Ki2IrG0b0.

Canadian Broadcasting Corporation (CBC). 2013. "Selfies: Narcissistic, empowering, or just fun?" *The Current*. Originally aired 30 January 2013. Retrieved from http://www.cbc.ca/thecurrent/episode/2013/01/30/selfies-narcissistic-empowering-or-just-fun/

Canadian Broadcasting Corporation (CBC). 2014a. "Canadian attitudes toward immigrants conflicted, poll says: CBC News survey on discrimination finds attitudes vary notably from region to region." *CBC Online*. Retrieved from http://www.cbc.ca/news/canada/canadian-attitudes-toward-immigrants-conflicted-poll-says-1.2826022

Canadian Broadcasting Corporation (CBC). 2014b (14 October). "Deep racial division exists in Winnipeg poll finds." *CBC Online*. Retrieved from http://www.cbc.ca/news/canada/manitoba/deep-racial-division-exists-in-winnipeg-poll-finds-1.2789954

Canadian Broadcasting Corporation (CBC). 2014c (26 February). "Fukushima radiation hit B.C. earlier than expected." *CBC Online*. Retrieved from http://www.cbc.ca/news/canada/nova-scotia/fukushima-radiation-hit-b-c-earlier-than-expected-1.2552718

Canadian Broadcasting Corporation (CBC). 2015 (1 January). CEO pay increased at twice the rate of average Canadian since 2008. *CBC News/Business Online*. Retrieved from http://www.cbc.ca/news/business/ceo-pay-increased-at-twice-the-rate-of-average-canadian-since-2008-1.2888117

Canadian Centre for Policy Alternatives (CCPA). 2011. "Canada's income gap, the richest 20% vs. the poorest 20%." Retrieved from http://www.policyalternatives.ca/newsroom/updates/you-oughta-know-canadas-income-gap-richest-20–vs-poorest-20.

Canadian Centre for Policy Alternatives (CCPA). 2014. "New study reveals the most and least affordable Canadian cities for child care." Retrieved from https://www.policyalternatives.ca/newsroom/news-releases/new-study-reveals-most-and-least-affordable-canadian-cities-child-care

Canadian Centre on Substance Abuse (CCSA). 2006. "Self-harm among criminalized women." Retrieved from http://www.ccsa.ca/Resource%20Library/ccsa-011338-2006-e.pdf

Canadian Civil Liberties. 2014. *Set up to fail: Bail and the revolving door of pre-trial detention*. Ontario: Canadian Civil Liberties

Association and Education Trust. Retrieved from https://ccla.org/dev/v5/_doc/CCLA_set_up_to_fail.pdf

Canadian Council on Social Development. 2003a. *Campaign 2000: Report card on child poverty in Canada.* Ottawa: Canadian Council on Social Development.

Canadian Council on Social Development. 2003b. *Aboriginal children in poverty in urban communities.* Retrieved from http://www.ccsd.ca/pr/2003/aboriginal.htm

Canadian Council on Social Development. 2004. *Percentage change in welfare benefits in Canada.* Retrieved from http://www.ccsd.ca/factsheets/fs_96wel.htm

Canadian Council on Social Development. 2008. *Family security in insecure times: The case for a poverty reduction strategy for Canada: 2008 report card on child and family poverty in Canada.* Ottawa: Canadian Council on Social Development.

Canadian Council on Social Development. 2010. *Campaign 2000: Report card on child poverty in Canada.* Ottawa: Canadian Council on Social Development.

Canadian Human Rights Commission (CHRC). 2004. *Protecting their rights: A systematic review of human rights in correctional services for federally sentenced women.* Retrieved from http://www.chrc-ccdp.ca/legislation_policies/consultation_report-eng.aspx

Canadian Race Relations Foundation (CRRF) and the Association for Canadian Studies (ACS). 2014. *Information handout on religion, racism, intergroup relations and integration results.* Ottawa and Montreal: CRRF and ACS. Retrieved from http://crr.ca/en/news-a-events/343–media-releases/24974–information-handout-on-religion-racism-intergroup-relations-and-integration-results-from-january-2014–survey

Caplan, P.J. 1995. *They say you're crazy: How the world's most powerful psychiatrists decide who's normal.* Reading, MA: Addison-Wesley.

Carbone-Lopez, Kristin, and Candace Kruttschnitt. 2010. "Risky relationships? Assortative mating and women's experiences of intimate partner violence." *Crime and Delinquency* 56 (3): 358–84.

Cardinal, Linda, and Martin Papillon. 2011. "Quebec and comparative analysis to small countries." *Politique et Societes* 30 (1): 75–93.

Carey, J. 2009. *Communication as culture.* New York: Routledge.

Carlen, P. 2002. "New discourses of justification and reform for women's imprisonment in England." In P. Carlen (Ed.), *Women and punishment: A struggle for justice.* Cullompton, UK: Willan.

Carlton, B., and Seagrave, M. (Eds). 2013. *Women exiting prison: Critical essays on gender, post-release support and survival.* UK: Taylor and Francis.

Carman, T., and D. Meissner. 2014. "Tim Hortons, McDonald's face criticism over foreign worker program." *Vancouver Sun*, October 3. Retrieved from http://www.vancouversun.com/life/Hortons+McDonald+face+criticism+over+foreign+worker+program/9768838/story.html

Carr, Dawn C., and Katrin Komp (Eds). 2011. *Gerontology in the era of the third age.* New York: Springer.

Carr, Nicholas. 2008. "Is Google making us stupid?" *The Atlantic.* Retrieved from http://www.theatlantic.com/doc/200807/google

Carrington, P., and J. Schulenberg. 2004. "Introduction: The Youth Criminal Justice Act: A new era in Canadian juvenile justice?" *Canadian Journal of Criminology and Criminal Justice* 46 (2): 219–23.

Carroll, William K., and R. S. Ratner. 1996. "Master Framing and Cross-Movement Networking in Contemporary Social Movements." *The Sociological Quarterly* 37 (4): 601–25.

Carson, E.A., and D. Golinelli. 2014. "Prisoners in 2012: Trends in admissions and releases, 1991–2012." Washington: Us Bureau of Justice Statistics.

Celinska, K., and J. Siegel. 2010. "Mothers in trouble: Coping with actual or pending separation from children due to incarceration." *The Prison Journal* 1 (90): 447–74.

Chamberlin, J. 1990. "The ex-patients movement: Where we've been and where we're going." *The Journal of Mind and Behavior* 11 (3–4): 323–36.

Chappell, N.L., L. McDonald, and M. Stones. 2008. *Aging in contemporary Canada* (2nd ed.). Toronto: Pearson.

Charland, Maurice. 1986. "Technological nationalism." *Canadian Journal of Political and Social Theory* 10 (1): 196–220.

Charles, Maria. 2011. "A world of difference: International trends in women's economic status." *Annual Review of Sociology* 37 (1): 355–71. doi:10.1146/annurev.soc.012809.102548

Chaundy, David, Fred Bergman, and Ryan MacLeod. 2012. "Meeting the skills challenge: Five key labour market issues facing Atlantic Canada." Halifax: Atlantic Provinces Economic Council.

Chesney-Lind, M. 1977. Judicial paternalism and the female status offender. *Crime and Delinquency* 23: 121–30.

Chesney-Lind, M., and L. Pasko. 2013. *Female offender: Girls, women and crime.* Thousand Oakes, CA: Sage Publications.

Cicero, Hon. J.H., and E.T. DeCostanzo. 2000. *Sentencing women offenders: A training curriculum for judges: A project of the National Association of Women Judges.* Washington DC: National Institute of Corrections, US Department of Justice.

Cicourel, A.V. 1967. "Fertility, family planning and the social organization of family life: Some methodological issues." *Journal of Social Issues* 29 (4): 57–81.

Cicourel, A.V. 1968. *The social organization of juvenile justice.* New York: John Wiley and Sons.

Cicourel, A.V. 1973. *Theory and method in a study of Argentine fertility.* New York: John Wiley and Sons.

Cicourel, A.V., & J.I. Kitsuse. 1963. *The educational decision-makers.* Indianapolis: Bobbs-Merrill.

Citizenship and Immigration Canada. 2014. *Facts and figures 2013, immigration overview.* Ottawa: Citizenship and Immigration Canada.

Clark, N. 2008. "Aboriginal cosmopolitanism." *International Journal of Urban and Regional Research*: 1–8.

Clark, Warren. 2007. "Delayed transitions of young adults." *Canadian Social Trends* 84 (Winter): 14–22.

Clarke, B. 2012. "Communication." In W.J.T. Mitchell and M.B.N. Hansen (Eds), *Critical terms for media studies.* Chicago and London: The University of Chicago Press

Clarke, Laura Hurd. 2011. *Facing age: Women growing older in anti-aging culture.* Lanham, MD: Rowman & Littlefield.

Clio Collective. 1987. *Quebec women: A history.* Toronto: Women's Press.

Coburn, D. 2004. "Beyond the income inequality hypothesis: Class, neo-liberalism and health inequalities." *Social Science & Medicine* 58 (1): 41–56.

Cockerham, W.C. 2003. *Sociology of mental disorder.* New Jersey: Prentice Hall.

Coetzee, J.M. 1991. "The Mind of Apartheid: Geoffrey Cronjé (1907–)." *Social Dynamics: A Journal of African Studies* 17 (1): 1–35.

Cohen, O. 2005. "How do we recover? An analysis of psychiatric survivor oral histories." *Journal of Humanistic Psychology* 45 (3): 333–54.

Cohen, Robin. 1996. "Diasporas and the nation-state: From victims to challengers." *International Affairs* 72 (3): 507–20.

Cohen, S. 1985. *Visions of social control: Crime, punishment and classification.* Cambridge, UK: Polity Press.

Cole, Stephen. 2001. *What's Wrong with Sociology?* NB:Transaction Publishers.

Coleman, James S. 1961. *Adolescent society: The social life of the teenager and its impact on education.* New York: Free Press of Glencoe.

Collins, J.W., and A.G. Butler. 1997. "Racial differences in the prevalence of small-for-dates infants among college-educated women." *Epidemiology* 8 (3): 315–17. Retrieved from http://www.jstor.org/stable/3702260

Collins, Patricia Hill. 1990. *Black feminist thought: Knowledge, consciousness, and the politics of empowerment.* New York: Routledge.

Collins, Patricia Hill. 2000. *Black feminist thought: Knowledge, consciousness, and the politics of empowerment* (Revised 10th anniversary ed.). New York: Routledge.

Collins, Patricia Hill. 2005. *Black sexual politics: African Americans, gender and the new racism.* New York: Routledge.

Comacchio, C. 2014. "Canada's families: Historical and contemporary variations." In D. Cheal and P. Albanese (Eds), *Canadian families today: New perspectives* (pp. 22–42). Don Mills, ON: Oxford University Press.

Comack, E. 1996. *Women in trouble.* Halifax: Fernwood.

"Communication." 1961. *The concise Oxford dictionary of current English* (4th ed., p. 240). Oxford, UK: Oxford University Press.

Comte, Auguste. 1853. *The positive philosophy of Auguste Comte.* Freely translated and condensed by Harriet Martineau. New York: Calvin Blanchard.

Comte, Auguste. 1975 [1838]. *Auguste Comte and positivism: The essential writings.* Gertrude Lenzer, Ed. Chicago: University of Chicago Press.

Comte, A. 2009 [1853]. *The positive philosophy of Auguste Comte* (2 volumes). (H. Martineau, trans.). Cambridge: Cambridge University Press.

Connell, R.W. 1987. *Gender and power.* Palo Alto, CA: Stanford University Press.

Connell, R.W. 2004. "Encounters with structure." *International Journal of Qualitative Studies in Education* 17 (1): 11–28.

Conrad, P. 2007. *The medicalization of society: On the transformation of human conditions into treatable disorders.* Baltimore: Johns Hopkins University Press.

Constatine, M.G. 2006. "Institutional racism against African Americans: Physical and mental health implications." In M.G. Constatine and D.W. Sue (Eds), *Addressing racism: Facilitating cultural competence in mental health and educational settings* (pp. 33–41). Hoboken, NJ: John Wiley and Sons.

Contact Centre Canada. 2009. "Human resource trends in the contact centre sector," Labour Market Study Report.

Cook, J.A., and J.A. Jonikas. 2002. "Self-determination among mental health consumers/survivors: Using lessons from the past to guide the future." *Journal of Disability Policy Studies* 13 (2): 88–96.

Coontz, Stephanie. 2010. "The evolution of American families." In Barbara J. Risman (Ed.) *Families as they really are* (pp. 30–48). New York: W.W. Norton and Company.

Cooper, David (Ed.). *Psychiatry and anti-psychiatry* (Reprint ed.). London: Routledge.

Corbett, Michael. 2007. "All kinds of potential: Women and out-migration in an Atlantic Canadian coastal community." *Journal of Rural Studies,* 23: 430–42.

Cormack, P., J. Cosgrave, and L. Harling Stalker. 2012. "Who counts now? Re-making the Canadian citizen." *Canadian Journal of Sociology 37* (3): 231–52.

Cormier, Jeffrey, and Philippe Couton. 2004. "Civil society, mobilization and communal violence: Quebec and Ireland, 1890–1920." *Sociological Quarterly* 45 (3): 487–508.

Cornell, Stephen E., and Douglas Hartmann. 1998. *Ethnicity and race.* Thousand Oaks, CA: Pine Forge Press.

Correctional Service of Canada (CSC). 1990. *Creating choices: The report of the Task Force on Federally Sentenced Women.* Ottawa: Correctional Service of Canada.

Correctional Service of Canada (CSC). 1998. *Women convicted of homicide serving a federal sentence.* Ottawa, ON: Correctional Service of Canada. Retrieved from http://www.csc_scc.gc.ca/text/prgrm/fsw/homicide/toc_e.shtml

Correctional Service of Canada (CSC). 2007. *Statistical overview 2007 CSC—Women Offender Sector.* Ottawa: Woman Offender Sector. Retrieved from http://www.csc-scc.gc.ca/text/prgrm/fsw/wos33/docs/wos33_stat-ovrvw_2007-eng.pdf

Correctional Service of Canada (CSC). 2010. *Facts, figures, trends and responses.* Ottawa: Statistics Canada.

Correctional Services Program (CSC). 2014. *Adult correctional statistics in Canada, 2013/2014.* Ottawa: Statistics Canada. Retrieved from http://www.statcan.gc.ca/pub/85-002-x/2015001/article/14163-eng.htm#a1

Corrigan, Philip, and Derek Sayer. 1985. *The great arch: English state formation as cultural revolution.* Oxford, UK: Basil Blackwell.

Cossman, Brenda, Shannon Bell, Lise Gotell, and Becki Ross. 1997. *Bad attitudes on trial.* Toronto: University of Toronto Press.

Couldry, Nick. 2009. "Teaching us to fake it. The ritualized norms of television's 'reality' games." In Susan Murray and Laurie Oullette (Eds), *Reality TV: Remaking television culture* (2nd ed.) (pp. 82–99). New York: New York University Press.

Covell, K., and B. Howe. 2001. *The challenge of children's rights for Canada.* Waterloo, ON: Wilfred Laurier University Press.

Craig, R. 2001. "Communication." In T.O. Sloane (Ed.), *Encyclopedia of rhetoric.* New York: Oxford University Press.

Crew, K.B. 1991. "Sex differences in criminal sentencing: Chivalry or patriarchy?" *Justice Quarterly* 8: 59–83.

Cronjé, Geoffrey. 1937. "Die Deterministiese Standpunt in Die Sosiologie." Pretoria.

Cronjé, Geoffrey. 1945. *'N Tuiste Vir Die Nageslag: Die Blywende Oplosing van Suid-Afrika Se Rassevragstuk [A Home for the Future Generations: A Lasting Solution to South Africa's Race Question]*. Stellenbosch: Pro Ecclesia.

Crook, Stephen. 2005. "Change, Uncertainty and the Future of Sociology." Retrieved from http://search.informit.com.au/document-Summary;dn=038774620401479;res=IEL-HSS.

Crossley, M. L., and N. Crossley. 2001. "Patient voices, social movements and the habitus: How psychiatric survivors 'speak out.'" *Social Science and Medicine* 52 (10): 1477–89.

CUPE Ontario. 2008. "Creator of Quebec child care system to be honoured on Child Care Worker Appreciation Day." 20 October. Retrieved from http://www.cupe.on.ca/doc.php?document_id=572&lang=en

Curry, Bill, and Gloria Galloway. 2008. "We are sorry." *Globe and Mail*, 12 June. Retrieved from http://www.theglobeandmail.com/news/national/article690958.ece

Curtis, B. 2001. *The politics of population*. Toronto: University of Toronto Press.

Czyzewski, K. 2011. "Colonialism as a broader social determinant of health." *The International Indigenous Policy Journal*, 2 (1).

Dahrendorf, Ralph. 1973. *Homo sociologicus*. London: Routledge and Kegan Paul.

Dain, N. 1989. "Critics and dissenters: Reflections on 'anti-psychiatry' in the United States." *Journal of the History of the Behavioral Sciences* 25 (1): 3–25.

Daly, Kathleen. 1992. "Women's pathways to felony court: Feminist theories of law breaking and problems of representation." *Review of Law and Women's Studies* 2: 11–52.

Dannefer, Dale. 2003a. "Cumulative advantage/disadvantage and the life course: Cross-fertilizing age and social science theory." *Journal of Gerontology: Social Sciences* 58 (6): S327–37.

Dannefer, Dale. 2003b. "Whose life course is it anyway? Diversity and 'linked lives' in global perspective." In Richard A. Settersen, Jr.

(Ed.), *Invitation to the lifecourse: Toward new understandings of later life* (pp. 259–68). Amityville, NY: Baywood.

Dannefer, Dale, and Jessica A. Kelley-Moore. 2009. "Theorizing the life course: New twists in the paths." In Vern Bengston, Daphna Gans, Norella N. Putney, and Merril Silverstein (Eds), *Handbook of theories of aging* (pp. 389–411). New York: Springer.

Dant, Tim. 2003. *Critical social theory*. London: Sage.

Das Gupta, Tania. 2000. "Families of native people, immigrants, and people of colour." In Nancy Mandell and Ann Duffy (Eds), *Canadian families: diversity, conflict and change* (pp. 146–87). Toronto: Harcourt Brace.

Dauvergne, M. 2012. *Adult correctional statistics in Canada, 2010/2011*. Ottawa: Statistics Canada.

Davidson, A. 2015. *Social determinants of health*. Toronto: Oxford University Press.

Davis, Angela. 2001. "Racism, birth control and reproductive rights." In A. Davis (Ed.), *Women, race and class* (pp. 202–21). London: Women's Press.

Davis, M. 2001. *Planet of slums*. New York: Verso.

Davis, S. 2006. *Community mental health in Canada: Theory, policy, and practice*. Vancouver: University of British Columbia Press.

de Kerckhove, D. 1989. "McLuhan and the 'Toronto School of Communication.'" *Canadian Journal of Communication* 14 (4).

de Vries, Brian. 2010. "Friendship and family: The company we keep." *Transition: Creating Families* 40 (4). Retrieved from http://www.vifamily.ca/media/node/765/attachments/VIF_trans_winter2010E_121010–3.pdf

Deakin, J., and J. Spencer. 2003. "Women behind bars: Explanations and implications." *The Howard Journal* 42 (2), 123–36.

DeHart, D. 2008. "Pathways to prison: Impact of victimization in the lives of incarcerated women." *Violence against Women* 14 (12), 1362–81.

Dell, C.A., C. Fillmore, and J. Kilty. 2009. "Looking back 10 years after the Arbour inquiry: Ideology, policy, practice and the federal female prisoner." *Prison Journal* 89: 286–308.

Della-Mattia, E. 2004. "Martin fingers Liberals for child benefit clawback." *Sault Star* 22 November: A4.

Demerson, V. 2004. *Incorrigible*. Waterloo: Wilfred Laurier University Press.

Denov, M. 2004. "Children's rights, juvenile justice, and the UN Convention on the Child: Implications for Canada." In K. Campbell (Ed.), *Understanding youth justice in Canada*. Toronto: Pearson.

Derkzen, D., L. Booth, A. McConnell, and K. Taylor. 2012. *Mental health needs of federal women offenders*. Research Report R-267. Ottawa, ON: Correctional Service of Canada.

Derrida, Jacques. 2004. *Eyes of the University: Right to Philosophy*. Stanford: Stanford University Press.

Deskaheh. (1925) 2005. "The Last Speech of Deskaheh." in *Akwesasne Notes* 2005: 48.

Dewing, Michael. 2012. "Social media: Who uses them?" Revised. Ottawa: Library of Parliament. Retrieved from http://www.parl.gc.ca/Content/LOP/ResearchPublications/2010-05-e.htm

Diamond, S. 2013. "What makes us a community? Reflections on building solidarity in anti-sanist praxis." In B.A. LeFrançois, R. Menzies, and G. Reaume (Eds), *Mad matters: A critical reader in Canadian mad studies* (pp. 64–78). Toronto: Canadian Scholars' Press.

Dickinson, John A., and Brian Young. 2000. *A short history of Quebec*. Montreal and Kingston: McGill-Queen's University Press.

Donzelot, J. 1984. *L'invention du social*. Paris: Fayard.

Donzelot, J. 1988. "The promotion of the social." *Economy and Society 17* (3): 394–427.

Doob, A., and C. Cesaroni. 2004. *Responding to youth crime in Canada*. Toronto: University of Toronto Press.

Doran, N. 1994. "Risky business: Codifying embodied experience in the Manchester Unity of Oddfellows." *Journal of Historical Sociology* 7 (2): 131–54.

Doran, N. 1996. "From embodied 'health' to official 'accidents': Class, codification and the early British factory legislation, 1831–1844." *Social and Legal Studies* 5 (4): 523–46.

Doran, N. 2001. "Governmentality and class: Some preliminary remarks on cultural incorporation." Paper presented at the "Governmentality and Freedom for Whom and for What?" session of the Canadian Sociological Association annual conference, Quebec City, 30 May.

Doran, N. 2003. "Resisting insurance technology: Some lessons from mid-nineteenth-century England." Paper presented at the "Vital Politics: Health, Politics and Bioeconomics into the 21st Century" Conference (5–7 September). London, UK: London School of Economics. September 5–7.

Doran, N. 2004. "Re-writing the social, re-writing sociology: Donzelot, genealogy and working-class bodies." *Canadian Journal of Sociology* 29 (3): 333–57.

Doran, N. 2008. "Decoding 'encoding' in a cultural studies' classic: Moral panics, media portrayals and Marxist presuppositions." *Theoretical Criminology* 12 (2): 191–221.

Doran, N. Forthcoming. "Beyond phenomenological anti-sociologies: Foucault's care of his self as standpoint sociology." *Canadian Journal of Sociology*.

Doucet, Andrea. 2004. "Fathers and the responsibility for children: A puzzle and a tension." *Atlantis: A Women's Studies Journal: Special Issue on the Politics of Unpaid Work* 28 (2): 103–14.

Doucet, Andrea. 2006a. *Do men mother?* Toronto: University of Toronto Press.

Doucet, Andrea. 2006b. "'Estrogen-filled worlds': Fathers as primary caregivers and embodiment." *Sociological Review* 23 (4): 695–715.

Doucet, Andrea. 2011. "What impedes fathers' participation in care work? Theorizing the community as an institutional arena." In C. Krull and J. Sempruch (Eds), *A life in balance? Reopening the family–work debate* (pp. 115–29). Vancouver: University of British Columbia Press.

Doucet, Andrea. 2014. "Families and work: Connecting households, workplaces, state policies, and communities." In D. Cheal and P. Albanese (Eds), *Canadian families today: New perspectives* (pp. 166–84). Ontario: Oxford University Press.

Douglas, Jack. 1967. *The social meaning of suicide*. Princeton, NJ: Princeton University Press.

Douglas, Jack. 1970a. *Freedom & tyranny: Social problems in a technological society*. New York: Knopf.

Douglas, Jack. 1970b. "Understanding everyday life." In J. Douglas (Ed.), *Understanding everyday life: Toward the reconstruction of sociological knowledge* (pp. 3–44). Chicago: Aldine.

Douglas, Jack, and John Johnson. 1977. *Existential sociology.* New York: Cambridge University Press.

Douglas, M. 2002. "Neediest children feel sting." *Kamloops Daily News* 22 April: A1.

Dover, K.J. 1978. *Greek homosexuality.* New York: Vintage.

Downs, A. 1972. "Up and down with ecology-the issue-attention cycle." *Public Interest* 28: 38–50.

Downes, D., P. Rock, and C. McCormick. 2009. *Understanding deviance: Canadian edition.* Toronto: Oxford University Press.

Doyle, Aaron, and Dawn Moore, eds. 2011. *Critical Criminology in Canada: New Voices, New Directions.* Vancouver: UBC Press.

Doyle, Cathal M. 2014. *Indigenous peoples, title to territory, rights and resources: The transformative role of free prior and informed consent.* New York: Routledge.

Dreby, Joanna. 2006. "Honor and virtue: Mexican parenting in the transnational context." *Gender and Society* 20 (1): 32–59.

Driscoll, Catherine. 2002. *Girls: Feminine adolescence in popular culture and cultural history.* New York: Columbia University Press.

Duffy, Ann, and Norene Pupo. 2011. "Employment in the new economy and the impact on Canadian families." In C. Krull and J. Sempruch (Eds), *Demystifying the family/work contradiction* (pp. 98–114). Vancouver: University of British Columbia Press.

Duggan, Maeve, Lee Rainie, Aaron Smith, Cary Funk, Amanda Lenhart, and Mary Madden. 2014. Online harassment: Summary of findings. Pew Research Center. Retrieved from http://www.pewinternet.org/2014/10/22/online-harassment/

Dumas, Alex, Suzanne Laberge, and Silvia M. Straka. 2005. "Older women's relations to bodily appearance: The embodiment of social and biological conditions of existence." *Ageing and Society* 25 (6), 883–902.

Durkheim, Émile. 1938. *The rules of sociological method.* New York: The Free Press.

Durkheim, Émile. 1952 [1897]. *Suicide: A study in sociology.* London: Routledge and Kegan Paul.

Durkheim, Émile. 1964 [1895]. *The rules of sociological method.* George G. Catlin, Ed.

(Sarah A. Solovay and John H. Mueller, trans.). New York: Free Press.

Durkheim, Émile. 1989 [1893]. *The division of labour in society.* (W.D. Halls, trans.). London: Macmillan.

Edmunds, June, and Bryan S. Turner. 2002. *Generations, culture and society.* Buckingham, UK: Open University Press.

Eisenstein, E.L. 1979. *The printing press as an agent of change: Communications and cultural transformations in early modern Europe.* Cambridge, UK, and New York: Cambridge University Press.

Eitzen, D. Stanley. 1991. "The Prospects for Sociology into the Twenty-First Century." *The American Sociologist* 22 (2): 109–15.

Elder, Jr., Glen H. 1974. *Children of the great depression.* Chicago: Chicago University Press.

Employment and Social Development Canada. 2013. *Imbalances between labour demand and supply.* Ottawa: Employment and Social Development Canada. Retrieved from http://www23.hrsdc.gc.ca/l.3bd.2t.1ilshtml@-eng.jsp?lid=29&fid=1&lang=en

Employment and Social Development Canada. 2014. *Canadian occupational projection system,* Figure 7. Ottawa: Employment and Social Development Canada. Retrieved from http://www23.hrsdc.gc.ca/c.4nt.2nt@-eng.jsp?cid=52&lang=en&preview=1#cn-tphp

Engels, F. 2001 [1883]. *Dialectics of nature.* Transcribed by S. Ryan and jjazz@hwcn.org. Retrieved from https://www.marxists.org/archive/marx/works/1883/don/index.htm

Epel, E.S., E.H. Blackburn, J.J. Lin, F.S. Dhabhar, N.E. Adler, J.D. Morrow, and R.M. Cawthon. 2004. "Accelerated telomere shortening in response to life stress." *Proceedings of the National Academy of Sciences of the United States of America* 101, 49: 17312–15. doi:10.1073/pnas.0407162101

Erikson, E.H. 1968. *Identity: Youth and crisis.* New York: Norton.

Etzioni, Amitai. 1996. "The responsive community: A communitarian perspective." Presidential address, American Sociological Association, 20 August 1995. *American Sociological Review* February: 1–11.

Everett, B. 1994. "Something is happening: The contemporary consumer and psychiatric survivor movement in historical context."

The Journal of Mind and Behavior 15 (1/2): 55–70.

Ewald, F. 1991. "Insurance and risk." In Graham Burchell, Colin Gordon, and Peter Miller (Eds), *The Foucault effect*. Chicago: University of Chicago Press.

Faludi, Susan. 1999. *Stiffed*. New York: Morrow.

Farnsworth, M., and R.H.C. Teske. 1995. "Gender differences in filing court processing: Testing three hypotheses of disparity." *Women and Criminal Justice* 6: 23–44.

Featherstone, Mike. 1988. "In pursuit of the postmodern: An introduction." *Theory, Culture and Society* 5 (2/3): 195–216.

Feld, B. 2000. "Juveniles' waiver of legal rights: Confessions, Miranda, and the right to counsel." In T. Grisso and R.G. Schwartz (Eds), *Youth on trial: A developmental perspective on juvenile justice*. Chicago: University of Chicago Press.

Fillmore, C., C.A. Dell, and The Elizabeth Fry Society of Manitoba. 2000. *Prairie women, violence and self-harm*. Retrieved from http://www.pwhce.ca/pdf/self-harm.pdf

Finnie, R. 2000. *Who moves? A panel logit model analysis of inter-provincial migration in Canada*. Ottawa: Business and Labour Market Analytical Division, Statistics Canada.

Fitzpatrick, Meagan. 2013. "Harper on terror arrests: Not a time for 'sociology'." *CBC News*, 25 April. Retrieved from http://www.cbc.ca/news/politics/harper-on-terror-arrests-not-a-time-for-sociology-1.1413502

Flannery, T. 1994. *The future eaters: An ecological history of the Australian lands and people*. New York: Grove Press.

Fleet, Richard, Patrick Archambault, Jeff Plant, and Julien Poitras. 2013. "Access to emergency care in rural Canada: Should we be concerned?" *Canadian Journal of Emergency Medicine* 15 (4): 191–3.

Flew, T., and R. Smith. 2011. *New media: An introduction* (Canadian ed.). Oxford and New York: Oxford University Press.

Fogg-Davis, Hawley. 2005. "Racial randomization: Imagining non-discrimination in adoption." In Sally Haslanger and Charlotte Witt (Eds), *Adoption matters: philosophical and feminist essays* (pp. 247–64). Ithaca, NY: Cornell University Press.

Fontaine, Louise. 1993. *Un labyrinthe carré comme un cercle; Enquête sur le ministère des communautés culturelles et de l'immigration et sur ses acteurs réels et imaginés*. Montréal: L'Étincelle.

Fontaine, Paul. 2013, 29 November. "Diversity of media ownership literally non-existent in Canada." *J-source.ca*. Retrieved from http://j-source.ca/article/diversity-media-ownership-literally-non-existent-canada

Food Banks Canada. 2010. *Hunger Count 2010: A comprehensive report on hunger and food bank use in Canada, and recommendations for change*. Retrieved from http://www.foodbankscanada.ca/documents/HungerCount2010_web.pdf

Food Banks Canada. 2014. *Hunger Count*. Retrieved from http://www.foodbankscanada.ca/HungerCount

Foster, John Bellamy. 1994. *The vulnerable planet: A short economic history of the environment*. New York: Monthly Review Press.

Foucault, Michel. 1977. *Discipline and punish: The birth of the prison*. (A. Sheridan, trans.) New York: Pantheon.

Foucault, Michel. 1978. *The history of sexuality, Vol. 1: An introduction*. New York: Random House.

Foucault, Michel. 1980a. *Power/knowledge: Selected interviews and other writings, 1972–1977*. New York: Pantheon.

Foucault, Michel. 1980b. *The history of sexuality*. New York: Vintage.

Foucault, Michel. 1982. "The subject and power." In Hubert Dreyfus and Paul Rabinow (Eds), *Michel Foucault: Beyond structuralism and hermeneutics*. Chicago: University of Chicago Press.

Foucault, Michel. 1988 [1964]. *Madness and civilization: A history of insanity in the Age of Reason* (R. Howard, trans). New York: Vintage Books.

Foucault, Michel. 1991. *Remarks on Marx, conversations with Duccio Trombador* (James Goldstein and James Cascaito, trans.). New York: Semiotext(e).

Foucault, Michel. 2005. *The hermeneutics of the subject*. New York: Picador.

Foucault, Michel. 2010. *The government of self and others*. Palgrave: Macmillan.

Foucault, Michel. 2011. *The courage of truth*. Palgrave: Macmillan.

Francis, D., and S. Hester. 2004. *An invitation to ethnomethodology*. London: Sage.

Franklin, A. 2006. "Burning cities: A post-humanist account of Australians and eucalypts." *Environment and Planning D: Society and Space* 24 (4): 555–76.

Friedan, Betty. 1963. *The feminine mystique.* New York: Dell.

Fudge, Judy. 2002. "From segregation to privatization: Equality, the law and women public servants 1908–2001." In Brenda Cossman and Judy Fudge (Eds), *Privatization, law and the challenge to feminism* (pp. 86–127). Toronto: University of Toronto Press.

Gaetz, Stephen, and Bill O'Grady. 2006. *The missing link: Discharge planning, Incarceration and Homelessness.* Ontario: JHS.

Garfinkel, H. 1967. *Studies in ethnomethodology.* Englewood Cliffs, NJ: Prentice Hall.

Garfinkel, H. 1974. "The origins of the term 'ethnomethodology.'" In R. Turner (Ed.), *Ethnomethodology* (pp. 15–18). Harmondsworth, Middlesex: Penguin.

Garfinkel, Harold. 1986. *Ethnomethodological studies of work.* New York: Routledge and Kegan Paul.

Garfinkel, Harold, in collaboration with R. Stoller. 1967. *Studies in ethnomethodology.* Cambridge, UK: Polity Press.

Gartner, R., C. Webster, A. Doob. 2009. Trends in women's imprisonment in Canada. *Canadian Journal of Criminology and Criminal Justice* April: 170–98.

Gee, Ellen M. 1997. "Policy and research on aging: Connections and conundrums." *Canadian Public Policy/Canadian Journal on Aging* (special joint issue) Supplement: i–xviii.

Gee, Ellen M., and Gloria M. Gutman. 2000. *The overselling of population aging: Apocalyptic demography, intergenerational challenges and social policy.* Don Mills, ON: Oxford University Press.

Gee, James Paul. 2000-1. "Identity as an analytic lens for research in education." *Review of Research in Education* 25: 99–125.

Gee, James Paul. 2002. *An introduction to discourse analysis: Theory and methods.* London: Routledge.

Gellner, Ernest. 1997. *Nationalism.* New York: New York University Press.

Gelsthorpe, L., and Morris, A. 2002. Women's imprisonment in England and Wales: A penal paradox. *Criminology and Criminal Justice* 2 (3): 277–30.

George, Daniel, Catherine Whitehouse, and Peter Whitehouse. 2011. "A model of

intergenerativity: How the intergenerational school is bringing the generations closer together to foster collective wisdom and community health." *Journal of Intergenerational Relations* 9: 389–404.

Giddens, Anthony. 1984. *The constitution of society.* Berkeley, CA: University of California Press.

Giddens, Anthony. 1987. *Social theory and modern sociology.* Palo Alto, CA: Stanford University Press.

Gilleard, Chris, and Paul Higgs. 2005. *Contexts of ageing: Class, cohort and community.* Cambridge: Polity.

Gilleard, Chris, and Paul Higgs. 2010. "Ageing without agency: Theorizing the fourth age." *Ageing and Mental Health* 14 (2): 121–8.

Gleeson, Kate, and Hannah Frith. 2004. "Pretty in pink: Young women presenting mature sexual identities." In Anita Harris (Ed.), *All about the girl: Culture, power and identity.* New York: Routledge.

Goffman, Erving. 1961. *Asylums.* London: Penguin.

Goffman, Erving. 1971. *The presentation of self in everyday life.* Harmondsworth, UK: Penguin.

Goffman, Erving. 1976. *Gender advertisements.* London: Macmillan.

Goldthorpe, J., D. Lockwood, F. Bechhofer, and J. Platt. 1968a. *The affluent worker: Industrial attitudes and behaviour.* Cambridge: Cambridge University Press.

Goldthorpe, J, D. Lockwood, F. Bechhofer, and J. Platt. 1968b. *The affluent worker: Political attitudes and behaviour.* Cambridge: Cambridge University Press.

Goldthorpe, J, D. Lockwood, F. Bechhofer, and J. Platt. 1969. *The affluent worker in the class structure.* Cambridge: Cambridge University Press.

Gordon, Avery. 1997. *Ghostly matters.* Minneapolis, MN: University of Minnesota Press.

Gosine, A., and C. Teelucksingh. 2008. *Environmental justice and racism in Canada: An introduction.* Toronto: Emond Montgomery Publications Ltd.

Gouldner, A. 1970. *The coming crisis of Western sociology.* New York: Basic Books.

Government of Canada. 2015. *Job market trends and news.* Ottawa: Government of Canada. Retrieved from http://www.jobbank.gc.ca/LMI_bulletin.do

Gramsci, Antonio. 1992. *Prison notebooks.* Joseph A. Buttigieg, Ed. New York: Columbia University Press.

Green, Joyce. 2007. "Balancing strategies: Aboriginal women and constitutional rights in Canada." In Joyce Green (Ed.), *Making spaces for Indigenous feminisms* (pp. 140–57). Winnipeg, MB: Fernwood Publishing.

Greenberg, David. 1988. *The construction of homosexuality.* Chicago: University of Chicago Press.

Greenberg, G. 2013. *The Book of Woe: The DSM and the Unmaking of Psychiatry.* New York: Blue Rider Press.

Grenier, Amanda, and Jill Hanley. 2007. "Older women and 'frailty': Aged, gendered and embodied resistance." *Current Sociology* 55 (1): 211–28.

Grenier, Amanda. 2012. *Transitions and the lifecourse: Challenging the constructions of "growing old."* Bristol: The Policy Press.

Haan, M. 2012. "Counting and contemporary governance: Introduction to the special issue." *Canadian Journal of Sociology* 37 (3): 223–30.

Habermas, Jürgen. 1971. *Towards a rational society: Student protest, science and politics.* Boston: Beacon.

Habermas, Jürgen. 1975. *Legitimation crisis.* (T. McCarthy, trans.). Boston: Beacon.

Hacking, I. 1982. "Biopower and the avalanche of printed numbers." *Humanities in Society* 5 (1): 279–95.

Haggerty, K. 2001. *Making crime count.* Toronto: University of Toronto Press.

Hall, G. Stanley. 1904. *Adolescence.* New York: D. Appleton & Co.

Hall, G. Stanley. 1922. *Senescence: The last half of life.* New York: D. Appleton.

Halperin, David. 1990. *One hundred years of homosexuality.* New York: Routledge.

Halperin, David. 1995. *Saint Foucault.* New York: Oxford University Press.

Halperin, David. 2002. *How to do the history of homosexuality.* Chicago: University of Chicago Press.

Hameed, Syed Morad, Nadine Schuurman, Tarek Razek, Darrell Boone, Rardi Van Heest, Tracey Taulu, Nasira Lakha, et al. 2010. "Access to trauma systems in Canada." *The Journal of Trauma: Injury, Infection, and Critical Care* 69 (6): 1350–61. doi:10.1097/TA.0b013e3181e751f7

Hamilton, S.N. 2009. *Law's expression: Communication, law and media in Canada.* Markham, ON: LexisNexis.

Hamilton, S.N. 2014. "Considering critical communication studies in Canada." In L. Shade (Ed.), *Mediascapes: New patterns in Canadian communication.* Toronto: Nelson Education Ltd.

Hammarberg, T. 1990. "The UN Convention on the Rights of the Child—And how to make it work." *Human Rights Quarterly* 12 (1): 97–105.

Hancock, T. 1986. "Lalonde and beyond: Looking back at 'A new perspective on the health of Canadians.'" *Health Promotion International* 1 (1): 93–100.

Hannah-Moffat, K. 2001. *Punishment in disguise: Penal governance and federal imprisonment of women in Canada.* Toronto, ON: University of Toronto Press.

Hannah-Moffat, K. 2004. "Losing ground: Gender, responsibility and parole risk." *Social Politics* 11: 363–85.

Hannah-Moffat, K. 2010. "Sacrosanct or flawed: Risk, accountability and gender-responsive penal politics." *Current Issues in Criminal Justice* 22 (2): 193–216.

Hannah-Moffat, K., and M. Shaw. 2000. *Ideal prison: Critical essays on women's imprisonment in Canada.* Halifax: Fernwood.

Hannah-Moffat, K., and M. Shaw. 2001. *Taking risks: Incorporating gender and culture into the assessment and classification of federally sentenced women in Canada.* Ottawa, ON: Status of Women.

Hansen, Karen V. 2005. *Not-so-nuclear families: Class, gender and networks of care.* New Brunswick, NJ: Rutgers University Press.

Hansen, M.B.N. 2009. "New media." In W.J.T. Mitchell and Mark B. N. Hansen (Eds), *Critical terms for media studies* (pp. 172–185). Chicago: University of Chicago Press.

Hansen, M.B.N. 2010. "New media." In W.J.T. Mitchell and M.B.N. Hansen (Eds), *Critical terms for media studies.* Chicago and London: The University of Chicago Press.

Haraway, Donna. 1988. "Situated knowledges: The science question in feminism and the privilege of partial perspective." *Feminist Studies* 14 (3): 575–99.

Harder, L. 2011. *After the nuclear age? Some contemporary developments in families and family law in Canada*. Ottawa: The Vanier Institute of the Family.

Hardin, Herschel. 1985. *Closed circuits. The sellout of Canadian television*. Toronto: Douglas & McIntyre.

Harding, S. 1986. *The science question in feminism*. Ithaca, NY: Cornell University Press.

Hardoon, Deborah. 2015. "Wealth: Having it all and wanting more." OXFAM International.

Harris Ali, S. 2004. "A socio-ecological autopsy of the E. coli O157:H7 outbreak in Walkerton, Ontario, Canada." *Social Science and Medicine*, 58: 2601–12.

Harrison, D., and L. Laliberté. 1994. *No life like it*. Toronto: Lorimer.

Hartsock, N. 1987. "Rethinking modernism: Minority vs. majority theories." *Cultural Critique* 7: 187–206.

Haslanger, Sally, and Charlotte Witt (Eds). 2005. *Adoption matters: Philosophical and feminist essays*. Ithaca, NY: Cornell University Press.

Hayman S. 2006. *Imprisoning our sisters: The new federal women's prisons in Canada*. Kingston, ON: McGill-Queens University Press.

Hearn, Alison. 2009. "Hoaxing the 'real.' On the metanarrative of reality television." Susan Murray and Laurie Oullette (Eds), *Reality TV. Remaking television culture* (2nd ed.) (pp. 165–78). New York: New York University Press.

Hebdige, Dick. 1979. *Subculture: The meaning of style*. London: Methuen.

Heimer, Karen, and Candace Kruttschnitt. 2006. *Gender and crime: Patterns in victimization and offending*. New York: New York University Press.

Henley, Nancy, and Fred Pincus. 1978. "Interrelationship of sexist, racist and antihomosexual attitudes." *Psychological Reports* 42 (1): 83–90.

Hennessy, Rosemary. 1995. "Queer visibility in commodity culture." In L. Nicholson and S. Seidman (Eds), *Social postmodernism: Beyond identity politics*. Cambridge, UK: Cambridge University Press.

Henri, D. 2012. "Managing nature, producing cultures: Inuit participation, science and policy in wildlife governance in the Nunavut Territory, Canada." D. Phil Thesis, Oxford University.

Herdt, Gilbert. 1984. *Ritualized homosexuality in Melanesia*. Berkeley: University of California Press.

Herek, Gregory. 1988. "Heterosexuals' attitudes toward lesbians and gay men." *Journal of Sex Research* 25 (4): 451–77.

Herman, Edward, and Noam Chomsky. 1988. *Manufacturing consent: The political economy of the mass media*. New York: Pantheon.

Hermer, Joe, and Janet Mosher. 2002. *Disorderly people: Law and the politics of exclusion in Ontario*. Halifax: Fernwood.

Hilbert, Richard. 1992. *The classical roots of ethnomethodology: Durkheim, Weber and Garfinkel*. Chapel Hill: University of North Carolina Press.

Hird, M.J., and A. Zahara. Forthcoming. "The Arctic wastes." In R. Grusin (Ed.), *Anthropocene feminism*. Minneapolis, MN: University of Minnesota Press.

Hird, M.J., S. Lougheed, K. Rowe, and C. Kuyvenhoven. 2014. "Making waste management public (or falling back to sleep)." *Social Studies of Science* 44 (3): 441–65.

Hobbes, Thomas. 1989 [1651]. *The leviathan*. Belmont, CA: Wadsworth.

Hobsbawm, Eric J. 1992. *Nations and nationalism since 1780: Programme, myth, reality*. Cambridge, UK: Cambridge University Press.

Hogeveen, B. 1999. "An intrusive and corrective government: Political rationalities and the governance of Plains Aboriginals 1870–1890." In R. Smandych (Ed.), *Governable places: Readings on governmentality and crime control*. Aldershot, UK: Dartmouth.

Hogeveen, B. 2005. "'If we are tough on crime, if we punish crime, then people get the message': Constructing and governing the punishable young offender in Canada during the late 1990s." *Punishment and Society* 7 (1): 73–89.

Hogeveen, Bryan, and Andrew Woolford. 2006. "Critical Criminololgy and Possibility in the Neo-Liberal Ethos." *Canadian Journal of Criminology and Criminal Justice* 48 (5): 681–701. Inglis, Christine. 2005. "Comments on Michael Burawoy's ASA Presidential Address." *British Journal of Sociology* 56 (3): 383–86.

Hogle, Linda F. 2007. "Emerging medical technologies." In Edward J. Hackett, Olga Amsterdamska, Michael Lynch, and Judy Wajcman (Eds), *The handbook of science and technology studies* (3rd ed.) (pp. 841–73). Cambridge, MA: The MIT Press.

Hollingshead, A.B. 1949. *Elmtown's youth: The impact of social classes on adolescents.* New York: John Wiley and Sons.

Holmshaw, J., and S. Hillier. 2000. "Gender and culture: A sociological perspective to mental health problems in women." In D. Kohen (Ed.), *Women and mental health.* London: Routledge.

Homans, George. *The human group.* 1950. New York: Harcourt, Brace and Company.

Home office. N.d. *Reducing re-offending: National Action Plan.* Retrieved from http://noms.justice.gov.uk/news-publications-events/publications/strategy/reducing-reoffending-action-plan?view=Binary

Hondagneu-Sotelo, P. 2007. *Domestica: Immigrant workers cleaning and caring in the shadows of affluence* (2nd ed.). Berkeley, CA: University of California Press.

Horton, Khim. 2006. "Gender and the risk of falling: A sociological approach." *Journal of Advanced Nursing* 57 (1): 69–76.

Horton, Khim, and Sara Arber. 2004. "Gender and the negotiation between older people and their carers in the prevention of falls." *Ageing & Society* 24 (1): 75–94.

House of Commons, Standing Committee on Canadian Heritage. 2011. *Impact of private television ownership changes and the move towards new viewing platforms.* Report. Ottawa: Publishing and Depository Services Public Works and Government Services Canada.

Howard, Albert, and Frances Widdowson. 2008. *Disrobing the Aboriginal industry: The deception behind Indigenous cultural preservation.* Montreal and Kingston: McGill-Queen's Press. Retrieved from https://www.oxfam.org/en/pressroom/pressreleases/2015-01-19/richest-1-will-own-more-all-rest-2016. Accessed 30 April, 2015.

Hunt, Alan, and Gary Wickham. 1994. *Foucault and the law: Towards a sociology of law as governance.* London: Pluto.

Iacovetta, Franca. 1999. "Gossip, contest and power in the making of suburban bad girls: Toronto, 1945–60." *Canadian Historical Review* 80 (4): 585–623.

Iacovetta, Franca. 2006. "Recipes for democracy? Gender, family, and making female citizens in Cold War Canada." In A. Glasbeek (Ed.), *Moral regulation and governance in Canada* (pp. 169–87). Toronto: Canadian Scholars' Press.

Innis, H.A. 1951. *The bias of communication.* Toronto: University of Toronto Press.

Institut de la Statistique du Québec. 2010. "Immigrants selon la connaissance du français et de l'anglais, Québec, 1980–2009." Québec: Gouvernement du Québec. Retrieved from http://www.stat.gouv.qc.ca/donstat/societe/demographie/migrt_poplt_imigr/607.htm

Ireland, Patrick. 2013. "A macro-level analysis of the scope, causes, and consequences of homophobia in Africa." *African Studies Review* 56 (2): 47–66.

Irwin, A. 2001. *Sociology and the environment: A critical introduction to society nature and knowledge.* Cambridge: Polity Press.

Ivison, Duncan. 1997. *The self at liberty: Political liberty and the arts of government.* Ithaca, NY: Cornell University Press.

Jackson, C. 2000. "Waste and whiteness: Zora Neale Hurston and the politics of eugenics." *African American Review* 34 (Winter): 639–60.

Jackson, John D., Greg M. Nielsen, and Yon Hsu. 2011. *Mediated sociology: A critical sociology of media.* Toronto: Oxford University Press.

Jackson, M. 1989. "Locking up Natives in Canada." *University of British Columbia Law Review* 23 (special issue): 213–40.

Jacobs, Sue Ellen, Wesley Thomas, and Sabine Lang. 1997. *Two-spirit people.* Urbana, IL: University of Illinois Press.

Jaggar, Alison M., and Paula S. Rothenberg. (Eds) 1993. *Feminist frameworks: Alternative theoretical accounts of the relations between women and men* (3rd ed.). New York: McGraw-Hill.

Jaggar, Alison M., and Iris Marion Young, eds. 2000. *A Companion to Feminist Philosophy.* Malden, Mass.: Wiley-Blackwell.

Jarman, J., Butler, P., and D. Clairmont. 1997. "Sweatshops and teleprofessionalism: An investigation of life and work in the tele-service industry." In Paul J. Jackson and Jos M. Van der Wielen (Eds), *Building actions on ideas, Amsterdam: Second International Telework Conference Proceedings.*

Javdani, M., and K. Pendakur. 2014. "Fiscal effects of immigrants in Canada." *Journal of International Migration and Integration* 15 (4): 777–97.

Jenkins, Henry, Sam Ford, and Joshua Green. 2013. *Spreadable media: Creating value and meaning in a networked culture.* New York: New York University Press.

Jenson, J., and D. Saint-Martin. 2003. "New routes to social cohesion? Citizenship and the social investment state." *Canadian Journal of Sociology* 28 (1): 77–99.

Jenson, J., and M. Sineau. 2001. *Who cares? Women's work, childcare and welfare state redesign.* Toronto: University of Toronto Press.

Johansen, Bruce E. 1995 (Fall). "Dating the Iroquois Confederacy." *Akwesasne Notes New Series* 3–4: 62–3.

Johnson, H. 2006. "Concurrent drug and alcohol dependency and mental health problems among incarcerated women." *The Australian and New Zealand Journal of Criminology* 39 (2): 190–217.

Johnson, Steven. 2005. *Everything bad is good for you.* New York: Riverhead.

Johnsrude, L. 1999. "Budget restraints hurt children." *Edmonton Journal,* 7 August: A3.

Johnston, John. 2008. *The allure of machinic life: Cybernetics, artificial life, and the new AI.* Cambridge, MA, and London, UK: The MIT Press.

Johnston, Les, and Clifford Shearing. 2003. *Governing security: Explorations in policing and justice.* London: Routledge.

Jones, Alison. 1993. "Becoming a 'girl': Post-structuralist suggestions for educational research." *Gender and Education* 5 (2): 157–67.

Jones, T. 2003. "The governance and accountability of policing." In Tim Newburn (Ed.), *Handbook of policing.* Collompton, UK: Willan.

Jones, T., and T. Newburn. 1998. *Private security and public policing.* Oxford, UK: Police Studies Institute, Clarendon.

Jordan, Mark. 1997. *The invention of sodomy in Christian theology.* Chicago: University of Chicago Press.

Jordison, S., and D. Kieran (Eds). 2004. *Crap towns II.* London: Boxtree.

Katz, Stephen. 1996. *Disciplining old age: The making of gerontological knowledge.* Charlottesville: University of Virginia Press.

Katz, Stephen. 2013. "Active and successful aging: Lifestyle as a gerontological idea." *Recherches sociologiques et anthropologiques* 44 (1): 33–49.

Katz, Stephen. 2014. "Music, performance, and generation: The making of boomer rock and roll identities." In C. Lee Harrington,

Denise D. Bielby, and Anthony R. Bardo (Eds), *Aging, media, and culture* (pp. 93–106). Landham, MD: Lexington Books.

Katz, Stephen, and Jessica Gish. 2015. "Aging in the biosocial order: Repairing time and cosmetic rejuvenation in a medical-spa clinic." *The Sociological Quarterly* 56 (1): 40–61.

Kaufman, Sharon R. 2010a. "Time, clinic technologies, and the making of reflexive longevity: The cultural work of time left in an ageing society." *Sociology of Health & Illness* 322: 225–37.

Kaufman, Sharon R. 2010b. "The age of reflexive longevity: How the clinic and changing expectations of the life course are reshaping old age." In Thomas R. Cole, Ruth E. Ray, and Robert Kastenbaum (Eds), *A guide to humanistic studies in aging: What does it mean to grow old?* (pp. 225–43). Baltimore: Johns Hopkins University Press.

Kazemipur, A., and S. Halli. 2000. *The "new" poverty in Canada: Ethnic groups and ghetto neighbourhoods.* Toronto: Thompson.

Keane, T.M., A.K. Silberbogen, and M.R. Weirerich. 2008. "Post-traumatic stress disorder." In J. Hunsley and E.J. Mash (Eds), *Assessments that work* (pp. 293–316). Oxford: Oxford University Press.

Keating, Michael. 2004. "European integration and the nationalities question." *Politics and Society* 32: 367–88.

Keen, Andrew. 2007. *The cult of the amateur: How today's internet is killing our culture.* New York: Doubleday.

Kellough, Gail, and Scot Wortley. 2002. Remand for plea: Bail decisions and plea bargaining as commensurate decisions. *British Journal of Criminology* 42: 186–210.

Kelly, Deirdre M., Shauna Pomerantz, and Dawn H. Currie. 2005. "Skater girlhood and emphasized femininity: 'You can't land an ollie properly in heels.'" *Gender and Education* 17 (3): 129–48.

Kemp, Candace L. 2005. "Dimensions of grandparent-adult grandchild relationships: From family ties to intergenerational friendships." *Canadian Journal on Aging* 24 (2): 161–78.

Kidder, Tracy. 2003. *Mountains beyond mountains: The quest of Dr. Paul Farmer, a man who would cure the world.* New York: Random House

Kinsman, Gary. 1996. *The regulation of desire.* Montreal: Black Rose.

Kinsman, Gary, and Patrizia Gentile. 2010. *The Canadian war on queers*. University of British Columbia Press.

Klein, Naomi. 2000. *No logo*. Toronto: Knopf.

Klein, Naomi. 2014. *This changes everything: Capitalism vs the climate*. Toronto: Knopf Canada.

Kleinman, Zoe. 2009. "Children who use technology are 'better writers.'" *BBC News*, 3 December. Retrieved from http://news.bbc.co.uk/go/pr/fr/-/2/hi/technology/8392653.stm

Kong, R., and K. AuCoin. 2008. Female offenders in Canada. *Juristat*. Statistics Canada Catalogue no. 85-002-XIE, Vol. 28, no. 1. Ottawa, ON: Statistics Canada.

Kontos, Pia. 2011. "Rethinking sociability in long-term care: An embodied dimension of selfhood." *Dementia: An International Journal of Social Research and Practice* (11) 3: 324–46.

Kontos, Pia, and Wendy Martin. 2013. "Embodiment and dementia: Exploring critical narratives of selfhood, surveillance, and dementia care." *Dementia: The International Journal of Social Research and Practice* (12) 3: 288–302.

Koons, B., J. Burrow, M. Morash, and T. Bynum. 1997. "Expert and offender perceptions of program elements linked to successful outcomes for incarcerated women." *Crime & Delinquency* 43 (4): 512–32

Krekula, Clary. 2007. "The intersection of age and gender: Reworking gender theory and social gerontology." *Current Sociology* 55 (2): 155–71.

Krull, Catherine. 2006. "Historical and cross-cultural perspectives on family life." In Anne-Marie Ambert (Ed.), *One-parent families: Characteristics, causes, consequences, and issues* (pp. 31–57). Toronto: Vanier Institute of the Family.

Krull, Catherine. 2010. "Investing in families and children: Family policies in Canada." In D. Cheal (Ed.), *Canadian families* (pp. 254–73). Toronto: Oxford University Press.

Krull, Catherine. 2011. "Destabilizing the nuclear family ideal: Thinking beyond essentialisms, universalisms and binaries." In C. Krull and J. Sempruch (Eds), *Demystifying the family/work contradiction* (pp. 1–29). Vancouver: University of British Columbia Press.

Krull, Catherine, 2014. "Investing in families and children: Family policies in Canada." In D.

Cheal and P. Albanese (Eds), *Canadian families today: New perspectives* (pp. 292–317). Don Mills, ON: Oxford University Press.

Kruttschnitt, C., and J. Hussemann. 2008. Female violent offenders: Moral panic or more serious offenders? *The Australian and New Zealand Journal of Criminology* 41 (1): 9–35.

Kuhn, T.S. 1970. *The structure of scientific revolutions* (2nd ed.). Chicago: University of Chicago Press.

Kunz, W.A. 2006. *Culture conglomerates: Consolidation in the motion picture and television Industries*. Lanham, MD: Rowan and Littlefield.

Kurlansky, Mark. 2005. *1968: The Year That Rocked the World*. Reprint edition. New York: Random House Trade Paperbacks.

Kutchins, H., and S.A. Kirk. 1997. *Making us crazy—DSM: The psychiatric bible and the creation of mental disorders*. New York: The Free Press.

Kymlicka, Will. 1995. *Multicultural citizenship: A liberal theory of minority rights*. Don Mills, ON: Oxford University Press.

Kymlicka, Will. 1998. *Finding our way: Rethinking ethnocultural relations in Canada*. Toronto: Oxford University Press.

Kymlicka, Will. 2000. "Nation-building and minority rights: Comparing west and east." *Journal of Ethnic and Migration Studies* 26: 183–212.

Labonté, R. 2015. "Globalization and health." In J. D. Wright (Ed.), *International encyclopedia of the social & behavioral sciences* (2nd ed.) (pp. 198–205). Oxford: Elsevier.

Laczko, Leslie S. 2000. "Canada's linguistic and ethnic dynamics in an evolving world-system." In Thomas D. Hall (Ed.), *A world-systems reader: New perspectives on gender, urbanism, cultures, indigenous peoples, and ecology* (pp. 131–42). Lanham, MD: Rowman and Littlefield.

Laforest, Guy. 2001. "The true nature of sovereignty: Reply to my critics concerning Trudeau and the end of a Canadian dream." In Ronald Beiner and Wayne Norman (Eds), *Canadian political philosophy*. Don Mills, ON: Oxford University Press.

Laing, R.D. 1971. *The politics of the family and other essays*. New York: Pantheon Books.

Laishes, J. 2002. *The 2002 mental health strategy for women offenders*. Ottawa, ON: Mental Health, Health Services, Correctional Services.

Laitin, David D. 1998. *Identity in formation: The Russian-speaking populations in the near abroad.* Ithaca, NY: Cornell University Press.

Lan, Pei-Chia. 2003. "Maid or madam? Filipina migrant workers and the continuity of domestic labor." *Gender and Society* 17 (2): 187–208.

Lang, Sabine. 1998. *Men as women, women as men.* Austin: University of Texas Press.

Langton, M. 1999. "The fire is the centre of each family: Landscapes of the ancients." In A. Hamblin (Ed.), *Visions of future landscapes.* Tenner Conference on the Environment 2.5. Canberra: Proceedings of the Australian Academy of Science.

Larsen, Knud, Rodney Cate, and Michael Reed. 1983. "Antiblack attitudes, religious orthodoxy, permissiveness and sexual information." *Journal of Sex Research* 19: 105–18.

Laslett, Peter. 1987. "The emergence of the third age." *Ageing and Society* 7: 133–60.

Latour B. 2007. "Turning around politics: A note on Gerard de Vries' paper." *Social Studies of Science* 37(5): 811–20.

Laurin, A., and J.R. Kesselman. 2014. *Income splitting for two-parent families: Who gains, who doesn't, and at what cost?* Toronto: CD Howe Institute.

Lazarsfeld, P., B. Berelson, and H. Gaudet. 1944. *The peoples' choice.* New York: Duell, Sloan, and Pearce.

Le Bourdais, Céline, and Évelyne Lapierre-Adamcyk. 2004. "Changes in conjugal life in Canada: Is cohabitation progressively replacing marriage?" *Journal of Marriage and Family* 66: 929–42.

Levinson, Paul. 2013. *New new media* (2nd ed.). Boston: Pearson.

Levitas, Ruth. 2010. "Back to the Future: Wells, Sociology, Utopia and Method." *Sociological Review* 58 (4): 530–47.

Lewis, J. 2001. "Legitimizing care work and the issue of gender equality." In M. Daly (Ed.), *Care work: The quest for security.* Geneva: International Labour Office.

Li, P.S. 2003. *Destination Canada: Immigration controversies and debates.* Don Mills, ON: Oxford University Press.

Little, Margaret Hillyard. 2011. "The increasing invisibility of mothering." In C. Krull and J. Sempruch (Eds), *A life in balance? Reopening the family–work debate* (pp. 194–205).

Vancouver: University of British Columbia Press.

Loader, I. 2000. "Plural policing and democratic governance." *Social and Legal Studies* 9 (3): 323–45.

Loader, I, and N. Walker. 2001. "Policing as a public good: Reconstituting the connection between policing and the state." *Theoretical Criminology* 5 (1): 9–35.

Lodge, Tom. 2011. *Sharpeville: An Apartheid Massacre and Its Consequences.* Oxford; New York: Oxford University Press, USA.

Lorber, Judith. 2005. *Gender inequality: Feminist theories and politics* (3rd ed.). Los Angeles: Roxbury.

Louw, P. Eric. 2004. *The Rise, Fall and Legacy of Apartheid.* Westport, Connecticut: Praeger.

Lowe, Elaine. 2006. "What a difference 50 years makes: Coming of age, then and now" (issue title). *Transition Magazine* 36 (1).

Lowman, J., R.J. Menzies, and T.S. Palys. 1987. *Transcarceration: Essays in the sociology of social control.* Aldershot: Gower Publishing Company.

Lum, Z.-A. 2014, 23 December. "A Canadian city once eliminated poverty and nearly everyone forgot about it." *The Huffington Post.* Retrieved from http://www.huffingtonpost.ca/2014/12/23/mincome-in-dauphin-manitoba_n_6335682.html.

Luxton, Meg, and June Corman. 2001. *Getting by in hard times: Gendered labour at home and on the job.* Toronto: University of Toronto Press.

Lyotard, J.F. 1984. *The postmodern condition: A report on knowledge.* Manchester, UK: Manchester University Press.

Lyotard, J.F. 1988. "An interview." *Theory, Culture and Society* 5 (2–3): 277–309.

MacBride, S. 2011. *Recycling reconsidered: The present failure and future promise of environmental action in the United States.* Cambridge, MA: The MIT Press.

MacDonald, A.P., Jr, J. Huggins, S. Young, and R.A. Swanson. 1973. "Attitudes toward homosexuality." *Journal of Consulting and Clinical Psychology* 40 (1): 161.

MacDonald, H. 2010. "Who counts? Nuns, work, and the census of Canada." *Histoire sociale/Social History* 86 (November): 369–91.

MacKay, R. 1974. "Standardised tests: Objective/objectified measures of 'competence.'"

In A.V. Cicourel, K.H. Jennings, S.H. Jennings, K.C. Leiter, R. MacKay, H. Mehan, and D.R. Roth (Eds), *Language use and school performance* (pp. 218–47). New York: Academic Press.

Mackenzie, D., and J. Wajcman. 1999. "Introductory essay: The social shaping of technology." In D. Mackenzie and J. Wajcman (Eds), *The social shaping of technology*. Buckingham: Open University Press.

Maclean's. 2008. Special issue on internet porn. Retrieved from http://www.macleans.ca/culture/lifestyle/article.jsp?content=20080618_9719_9719

Maclean's. 2013. "Should Canada make it easier for immigrants to send money home?" 19 February. Retrieved from http://www.macleans.ca/news/canada/homeward-bound-2/

Maclure, Jocelyn. 2003. *Quebec identity: The challenge of pluralism*. Montreal and Kingston: McGill-Queen's University Press.

Magder, Ted. 2009. "Television 2.0. The business of American television in transition." In Susan Murray and Laurie Oullette (Eds), *Reality TV. Remaking television culture* (2nd ed.) (pp. 141–64). New York: New York University Press.

Mahony, Tina Hotton. 2015. "Women and the criminal justice system." In *Women in Canada: A gender-based statistical report* (89-503-X). Ottawa: Statistics Canada. Retrieved from http://www.statcan.gc.ca/pub/89-503-x/2010001/article/11416/tbl/tbl010-eng.htm

Mandell, Nancy (Ed.). 2005. *Feminist issues: Race, class and sexuality* (4th ed.). Toronto: Prentice Hall of Canada.

Mandell, Nancy, and Sue Wilson. 2011. "Intergenerational care work: Mothering, grandmothering, and eldercare." In C. Krull and J. Sempruch (Eds), *A life in balance? Reopening the family–work debate* (pp. 30–46). Vancouver: University of British Columbia Press.

Mannheim, Karl. 1998 [1952]. "The problem of generations." In P. Kecskemeti (Ed.), *Essays on the sociology of knowledge*. New York: Routledge and Kegan Paul.

Mantilla, Karla. 2013. "Gendertrolling: Misogyny adapts to new media." *Feminist Studies*, 39 (2): 563–70.

Manuel, Frank E. 1962. *The Prophets of Paris— Turgot, Condorcet, Saint-Simon, Fourier, Comte* New York: Harper Torchbooks.

Marcus, A. "Shelterization revisited: Some methodological dangers of institutional studies of the homeless." *Human Organization* 62 (2): 134–42.

Marcuse, Herbert. 2007. *The Essential Marcuse: Selected Writings of Philosopher and Social Critic Herbert Marcuse*. Edited by Andrew Feenberg and William Leiss. Boston: Beacon Press.

Marks, Pauline. 1976. "Femininity in the classroom." In Juliet Mitchell and Ann Oakley (Eds), *The rights and wrongs of women* (pp. 176–98). Harmondsworth, England: Penguin Books.

Markusoff, J. 2007. "Albertans losing at track, Grits say: Wagers up only slightly despite $190M in aid." *Edmonton Journal*, 18 January: A1.

Marsh, J. 2008. "Ben Johnson." *Canadian Encyclopedia*. Retrieved from http://www.thecanadianencyclopedia.ca/en/article/ben-johnson/

Marshall, T. 1996. "The evolution of restorative justice in Britain." *European Journal on Criminal Policy and Research* 4 (4): 21–43.

Marshall, Victor. 2009. "Theory informing public policy: The life course perspective as a policy tool." In Vern Bengston, Daphna Gans, Norella N. Putney, and Merril Silverstein (Eds), *Handbook of theories of aging* (pp. 573–93). New York: Springer.

Martin, R.E., D. Hanson, C. Hemingway, V. Ramsden, J. Buxton, A. Granger-Brown, L.L. Condello, A. Macaulay, P. Janssen, and T.G. Hislop. 2012. "Homelessness as viewed by incarcerated women: Participatory research." *International Journal of Prisoner Health* 8 (3/4): 108–16.

Martineau, Harriet. 1983 [1869]. *Autobiography*. London: Virago.

Marx, Karl. 1970 [1859]. *A contribution to the critique of political economy*. M. Dobb, Ed. (S.W. Ryazanskaya, trans.). Moscow: Progress Publishers.

Marx, Karl. 1973 [1939]. *Grundrisse*. (M. Nicolaus, trans.). Harmondsworth, UK: Penguin.

Marx, K. 1998 [1848]. *The Communist manifesto*. New York: Penguin Books.

Marx, K. 1998 [1894]. *Capital. Volume III: Critique of political economy*. New York: Penguin Classics.

Marx, Karl, and Friedrich Engels. 1947 [1846]. *The German ideology*. New York: International Publishers.

Marx, Karl, and Friedrich Engels. 1948 [1848]. *Manifesto of the Communist Party*. New York: International Publishers.

Marx, Karl, and Friedrich Engels. 1976. *Collected works, vol. 5*. London: Lawrence and Wishart.

Massey, D. 2005. *For space*. London: Sage.

Mathews, H. 2001. "Citizenship, youth councils and young people's participation." *Journal of Youth Studies* 4 (3): 299–318.

Mauer, Marc. 2013. *Changing racial dynamics of women's imprisonment*. Washington: The Sentencing Project.

Maupin, A. 2007. *Michael Tolliver lives*. San Francisco, CA: HarperCollins.

McClelland, David. 1971. *The thought of Karl Marx: An introduction*. London: Macmillan Press.

McConnell, A., S. Rubenfeld, J. Thompson, and R. Gobeil. 2014. *A profile of women under community supervision* (Research Report R-287). Ottawa, ON: Correctional Service of Canada.

McDaniel, S., and H. MacDonald H. 2012. "To know ourselves—not." *Canadian Journal of Sociology* 37 (3): 253–71.

McDaniel, Susan A. 1997. "Intergenerational transfers, social solidarity, and social policy: Unanswered questions and policy challenges." *Canadian Public Policy/Canadian Journal on Aging* (joint issue) 23 (Supplement 1): 1–21.

McDaniel, Susan A. 2001. "'Born at the right time?' Gendered generation and webs of entitlement and responsibility." *Canadian Journal of Sociology* 26 (2): 193–214.

McDaniel, Susan A. 2002. "Women's changing relations to the state and citizenship." *Canadian Review of Sociology and Anthropology* 9 (2): 125–49.

McDaniel, Susan A. 2003. "Pensions, privilege and poverty: Another "take" on intergenerational equity." In Jacques Veron, Sophie Pennec, and Jacques Legare (Eds), *Ages, générations et contrat social: L'état providence face aux changements démographiques* (pp. 259–78). Paris: Institut national de la recherche scientifiques.

McDaniel, Susan A. 2008. "The 'growing legs' of generation as a policy construct: Reviving its family meaning." *Journal of Comparative Family Studies* 40 (2): 243–53.

McDiarmid. Jessica. 2006. "The Asper-ization of Canadian news: Media concentration

continues despite Senate warning." *King's Journalism Review* 12: 1–6.

McIntyer, M. 2009, 2 July. "Deportation decision debated: Immigration officials fear sex offender's safety if he is deported to Iran." *Winnipeg Free Press Online*. Retrieved from http://www.winnipegfreepress.com/local/deportation-decision-debated-49682852.html

McKenzie, K., and K. Bhui. 2007. "Institutional racism in mental health care: Services have some way to go before they meet the challenges of a multicultural society." *British Medical Journal* 334: 649–50.

McLaughlin, Neil. 2006. "Whither the Future of Canadian Sociology? Thoughts on Moving Forward." *Canadian Journal of Sociology/Cahiers Canadiens de Sociologie* 31 (1): 107.

McLean, A. 1995. "Empowerment and the psychiatric consumer/ex-patient movement in the United States: Contradictions, crisis and change." *Social Science & Medicine* 40 (8): 1053–71.

McLean, Archie. 2006. "Morton stakes out far right in leadership race: Clarity on issues hallmark of professor turned politician." *Edmonton Journal*, 14 October. Retrieved from http://www2.canada.com/edmontonjournal/features/passingthetorch/story.html?id=188c1580–a6cd–4ff1–8cc6–a227603f3b9f.

McLean, Archie. 2010. "Who is Ted Morton, Alberta's new finance minister?" *Edmonton Journal*, 17 January. Retrieved from http://communities.canada.com/edmontonjournal/blogs/electionnotebook/archive/2010/01/17/who-is-ted-morton-alberta-s-new-finance-minister.aspx.

McLuhan, M. 1994. *Understanding media: The extensions of man*. Cambridge, MA, and London, UK: MIT Press.

McNay, Lois. 1993. *Foucault and feminism: Power, gender and the self*. Boston: Northeastern University Press.

McNay, Lois. 1994. *Foucault: A critical introduction*. New York: Continuum Publishers.

McPhail, Thomas L., and Brenda M. McPhail. 1990. *Communication: The Canadian experience*. Toronto: Copp Clark Pitman.

McRobbie, A. 1980. "Settling accounts with subcultures: A feminist critique." *Screen Education* 34: 37–49.

Meltzer, H., Lader, D., T. Corbin, N. Singleton, R. Jenkins, and T. Brugha. 2002. *Non-fatal suicidal behaviour among adults aged 16 to 74 in Great Britain*. UK: Stationery Office.

Mental Health Commission of Canada (MHCC). 2009. *Towards recovery and well-being: A framework for a mental health strategy for Canada*. Ottawa: Mental Health Commission of Canada. Retrieved from http://www.mentalhealthcommission.ca/SiteCollectionDocuments/boarddocs/15507_MHCC_EN_final.pdf.

Merton, Robert K. 1938. "Social structure and anomie." *American Sociological Review* 3 (5): 672–82.

Meyer, M.D.E., A.M. Fallah, and M.M. Wood. 2011. "Gender, media, and madness: Reading a rhetoric of women in crisis through Foucauldian theory." *Review of Communication* 11 (3): 216–28.

Michel, S., R. Gobeil, and A. McConnell. 2012. *Older incarcerated women offenders: Social support and health needs*. Research report R275.Ottawa, ON: Correctional Service of Canada.

Mikkonen, J., and D. Raphael. 2010. *Social determinants of health: The Canadian facts*. Toronto: York University School of Health Policy and Management. Retrieved from http://www.thecanadianfacts.org/

Milan, Anne. 2000. "One hundred years of families." *Canadian Social Trends*, Statistics Canada Catalogue no. 11–008 (Spring): 2–13.

Milan, Anne. 2013. "Fertility: Overview, 2011." Report on the Demographic Situation in Canada, Statistics Canada. Catalogue no. 91–209-X.

Milanovic, Branko. 2013. "Global income inequality in numbers: In history and now." *Global Policy* 4 (2): 198–208. doi:10.1111/1758-5899.12032

Miller, David. 1991. *Liberty*. Oxford, UK: Oxford University Press.

Milloy, John S. 1999. *A national crime: The Canadian government and the residential schools system*. Winnipeg, MB: University of Manitoba Press.

Mills, C. Wright. 1959. *The sociological imagination*. Oxford, UK: Oxford University Press.

Mills, C. Wright. 1963. *Power, politics and people: The collected essays of C. Wright Mills*. Introduction by Irving Louis Horowitz (Ed.). New York: Oxford University Press.

Mills, C. Wright. 2004. "The promise of sociology." In John J. Macionis, Nijole V. Benokraitis, and Bruce Ravelli (Eds), *Seeing ourselves: Classic, contemporary, and cross-cultural readings in sociology* (Canadian ed.) (pp. 1–4). Toronto: Pearson.

Mills, D. 2002. "Children will be protected despite cutbacks." *National Post*: 3 October.

Milner, Murray, Jr. 2004. *Freaks, geeks, and cool kids: American teenagers, schools, and the culture of consumption*. London: Routledge.

Moodie, T. Dunbar. 1975. *The Rise of Afrikanerdom: Power, Apartheid, and the Afrikaner Civil Religion*. Berkeley: University of California Press.

Moretti, Marlene M., Candice L. Odgers, and Margaret A. Jackson. 2004. *Girls and aggression: Contributing factors and intervention principles*, vol. 19. New York: Kluwer Academic/Plenum.

Morrison, T. 1992. *Playing in the dark: Whiteness and the literary imagination*. New York: Vintage.

Morrow, Raymond A. 2009. "Rethinking Burawoy's Public Sociology: A Post-Empiricist Critique." In *The Handbook of Public Sociology*, edited by Vincent Jeffries, 47–70. Lantham, MD: Rowman & Littlefield.

Morton, Ted. 1998. "Why family matters." *Calgary Sun*, 1 November. Retrieved from http://fathersforlife.org/families/morton.htm

Mosco, V. 1983. "Critical research and the role of labor." *Journal of Communication*. Summer.

Mosco, Vincent. 2009. *The political economy of communication* (2nd ed.). Seven Oaks, CA: Sage.

Moyers, Bill. 2007. "Society on steroids: A Bill Moyers essay." Retrieved from http://www.pbs.org/moyers/journal/blog/2007/12/society_on_steroids_a_bill_moy.html.

MRSB Consulting Services. 2003. "PEI urban call centre labour market profile." Charlottetown, PE: PEI Labour Market Development Agreement, Human Resources Development Canada and PEI Department of Development and Technology.

Murphy, C. 1998. "Policing postmodern Canada." *Canadian Journal of Law and Society* 13 (2): 1–28.

Murphy, C., and C. Clarke. 2005. "Policing communities and communities of policing:

A comparative study of policing and security in two Canadian communities." In Dennis Cooley (Ed.), *Re-imagining policing in Canada*. Toronto: University of Toronto Press.

Murray, Janet H. 1998. *Hamlet on the holodeck. The future of narrative in cyberspace*. Cambridge, MA: MIT Press.

Murray, Stephen. 2000. *Homosexualities*. Chicago: University of Chicago Press.

Nakamura, L. 2009. "Don't hate the player, hate the game: The racialization of labour in World of Warcraft." *Critical Studies in Media Communication* 26 (2): 128–44.

Nancy, Jean-Luc. 2000. *Being Singular Plural*. Meridian, Crossing Aesthetics. Stanford, Calif.: Stanford University Press.

National Council on Welfare. 2005. *Welfare incomes, 2005*. Ottawa: Ministry of Public Works and Government Services.

National Council of Welfare. 2006. *Welfare incomes, 2005*. Ottawa: National Council of Welfare.

Neborak, J. 2013. *Family reunification? A critical analysis of Citizenship and Immigration Canada's 2013 reforms to the family class*. Toronto: Ryerson Centre for Immigration & Settlement.

Nelson, Joyce. 1988. *The colonized eye: Rethinking the Grierson legend*. Toronto: Between the Lines.

Nelson, Lise. 1999. "Bodies (and spaces) do matter: The limits of performativity." *Gender, Place and Culture* 6 (4): 331–53.

Nelson, Margaret K. 2006. "Families in not-so-free fall: A response to comments." *Journal of Marriage and Family* 68 (4): 817–23.

Neugarten, Bernice L. 1974. "Age groups in American society and the rise of the young-old." *Annals of the American Academy of Political and Social Science* 415 (1): 187–98.

Newfoundland and Labrador Government. 2001. "Budget: Industry profile: Customer contact centres." Retrieved from http://www.budget.gov.nl.ca/budget2001/economy/contactCont.htm

Ng, C.F., H.C. Northcott, B. Abu-Laban, and S. McIrvin. 2007. "Housing and living arrangements of South Asian immigrant seniors in Edmonton, Alberta." *Canadian Journal on Aging* 26 (3): 189–94.

Nguyen, Mai. 2011. "Closing the education gap: A case for Aboriginal early childhood education in Canada, a look at the Aboriginal Headstart Program." *Canadian Journal of Education/Revue Canadienne de L'éducation* 34 (3): 229–48.

Nichols, Lawrence T. 2011. *Public Sociology: The Contemporary Debate*. Transaction Publishers.

Nicholson, Judith A. 2010. "The third screen as cultural form in North America." In Barbara Crow, Michael Longford, and Kim Sawchuk (Eds), *The wireless spectrum: The politics, practices, and poetics of mobile media* (pp.77–94). Toronto: University of Toronto Press.

O'Connor, Julia, Ann Shola Orloff, and Sheila Shaver. 1999. *States, markets, families: Gender, liberalism and social policy in Australia, Canada, Great Britain and the United States*. Cambridge, UK: Cambridge University Press.

O'Hara, K. 1998. *Comparative family policy: Eight countries' stories*. Ottawa: Canadian Policy Research Network.

O'Malley, Pat. 1999. "'Social Justice' After the 'Death of the Social.'" *Social Justice* 26 (2 (76)): 92–100.

O'Malley, Pat, and Alan Hunt. 2003. "Does Sociology Need to Be Disciplined?" *Society/Société* 1: 7–13.

Öberg, Peter, and Lars Tornstam. 2003. "Attitudes toward embodied old age among Swedes." *International Journal of Aging and Human Development* 56 (2):133–53.

Offe, Claus. 1984. *Contradictions of the Welfare State*. MIT Press edition. Cambridge, Mass: The MIT Press.

Office of the Correctional Investigator (OCI). 2008. *Annual report of the Correction Investigator, 2008-2009*. Ottawa: Minister of Public Works and Government Services.

Office of the Correctional Investigator (OCI). 2013. *Risky business: An investigation into the treatment and management of chronic self-injury among federally sentenced women*. Ottawa, ON: Office of the Correctional Investigator Canada.

Office of the Correctional Investigator Canada (OCI). 2014. *Annual report of the Office of the Correctional Investigator 2013-2014*. Ottawa, ON: Office of the Correctional Investigator Canada.

Ontario. 2003. *Private Investigators and Security Guards Act: Discussion paper*. Toronto:

Ontario Ministry of Public Safety and Security. June.

Ontario. 2004. *Bill 88: An Act to Amend the Private Investigators and Public Security Guards Act.* Toronto: Legislative Assembly of Ontario. June.

Oprea, M.G. 2015. "How France grew its own terrorists." *The Federalist.* 15 January. Retrieved from http://thefederalist.com/2015/01/16/how-france-grew-its-own-terrorists/

Organisation for Economic Co-operation and Development (OECD). 2008. *Growing up unequal? Income distribution and poverty in OECD countries.* Retrieved from http://www.oecd.org/document/53/0,3746,en_2649_33933_41460917_1_1_1_1,00.html.

Osennontion (Marilyn Kane) and Skonaganleh:ra (Sylvia Maracle). 1989. "Our world: According to Osennontion and Skonaganleh:ra." *Canadian Woman Studies/Les Cahiers de la Femme* 10 (23): 7–19.

Oxfam International. 2015. "Richest 1% will own more than all the rest by 2016." *News.* Retrieved from from https://www.oxfam.org/en/pressroom/pressreleases/2015-01-19/richest-1-will-own-more-all-rest-2016

Padva, G. 2008. "Educating *The Simpsons*: Teaching queer representations in contemporary visual media." *Journal of LGBT Youth* 5 (3).

Pahl, Ray, and Liz Spencer. 2004. "Personal communities: Not simply families of 'fate' or 'choice.'" *Current Sociology* 52: 199–221.

Parkes, D., and K. Pate. 2006. "Time for accountability: Effective oversight of women's prisons." *Canadian Journal of Criminology and Criminal Justice* April: 251–85.

Parsons, Talcott, and Robert Bales (Eds). 1955. *Family, socialization and interaction process.* Glencoe, IL: Free Press.

Patten, Christopher. 1999. *The Report of the Independent Commission on Policing in Northern Ireland.* London: HMSO.

Pavlich, George C. 2000. *Critique and radical discourses on crime.* Aldershot, UK: Ashgate.

Pavlich, George C. 2005. "Experiencing critique." *Law and critique* 16: 95–112.

Pavlich, George C. 2013. "Dissociative grammar and constitutional critique?" In Karin van Marle and Stewart Motha (Eds), *Genres of critique: Law, aesthetics and liminality* (pp.

31–48). Stellenbosch, South Africa: Sun Press.

Pavlich, George. 2014. "Administrative Sociology and Apartheid." *Acta Academica* 46 (3): 153–76.

Peck, Jamie. 2001. *Workfare states.* New York: Guilford.

Perreault, S. 2011. *Self-reported Internet victimization in Canada, 2009. Juristat.* Ottawa: Component of Statistics Canada Catalogue no. 85-002-X.

Perreault, S. 2013. *Correctional services key indicators, 2012/2013.* Ottawa, ON: Statistics Canada. Retrieved from http://www.statcan.gc.ca/pub/85-002-x/2014001/article/14007-eng.htm

Perrault, S., and S. Brennan. 2010. *Criminal victimization in Canada, 2009.* Ottawa: Statistics Canada. Retrieved from http://www.statcan.gc.ca/pub/85-002-x/2010002/article/11340-eng.htm

Peters, J. 1999. *Speaking into the air.* Chicago and London: The University of Chicago Press.

Peterson-Badali, M., and R. Abramovich. 1992. "Children's knowledge of the legal system: Are they competent to instruct legal counsel?" *Canadian Journal of Criminology* 34 (2): 139–60.

Pfohl, S. 1994. *Images of deviance and social control: A sociological history* (2nd ed.). New York: McGraw-Hill.

Phillipson, Chris. 2006. "Ageing and globalisation." In John A. Vincent, Chris R. Phillipson, and Murna Downs (Eds), *The futures of old age* (pp. 201–7). London: Sage Publications.

Phillipson, Chris. 2009. "Reconstructing theories of ageing: The impact of globalization on critical gerontology." In Vern Bengston, Daphna Gans, Norella N. Putney, and Merril Silverstein (Eds), *Handbook of theories of aging* (pp. 615–28). New York: Springer.

Phillipson, Chris. 2013. "Ageing and class in a globalised world." In Marvin Formosa, and Paul Higgs (Eds), *Social class in later life: Power, identity and lifestyle* (pp. 53–72). Bristol: Policy Press.

Phoenix, Ann, Stephen Frosh, and Rob Pattman. 2003. "Producing contradictory masculine subject positions." *Journal of Social Issues* 59 (1): 179–95.

PIH (Partners in Health). 2014. "Paul Farmer discusses the end of TB." Retrieved from http://www.pih.org/blog/dr.-paul-farmer-discusses-the-end-of-tb-deaths-in-the-huffington-post. Accessed December 12 2015

Pipher, Mary. 1994. *Reviving Ophelia: Saving the selves of adolescent girls*. New York: Ballantine.

Police Futures Group. 2005. "Private policing." Retrieved from http://www.policefutures.org/docs/PFG_Private_Policing

Pollack, S. 2005. "Taming the shrew: Regulating prisoners through women-centered mental health programming." *Critical Criminology* 13 (1): 71–87.

Pollack, S. 2009. "'You can't have it both ways': Punishment and treatment of imprisoned women." *Journal of Progressive Human Services* 20 (2): 112–28.

Pomerantz, Shauna, Dawn H. Currie, and Deirdre M. Kelly. 2004. "Sk8er girls: Skateboarders, girlhood and feminism in motion." *Women's Studies International Forum* 27 (5/6): 547–57.

Porter, John. 1965. *The Vertical Mosaic: An Analysis of Social Class and Power in Canada*. Reprint Edition. Toronto: University of Toronto Press.

Porter, Lindsay, and Donna Calverley. 2011. "Trends in the use of remand in Canada." *Juristat*. Ottawa: Component of Statistics Canada Catalogue no. 85-002-X.

Poster, Mark. 1995. *The second media age*. Chicago: Polity Press.

Postman, Neil. 1985. *Amusing ourselves to death. Public discourse in the age of show business*. New York: Penguin

Postman, Neil. 1992. *Technopoly: The surrender of culture to technology*. New York: Vintage.

Pratte, André (Ed.). 2008. *Reconquering Canada: Quebec federalists speak up for change*. Toronto: Douglas & McIntyre.

Prentice, A., P. Bourne, G. Cuthbert Brandt, B. Light, W. Mitchinson, and N. Black. 1988. *Canadian women: A history*. Toronto: Harcourt, Brace and Jovanovich.

Private Investigators and Security Guards Act. 2010. Alberta: Alberta Queen's Printer.

Public Safety Canada (PSC). 2013. *Corrections and conditional release statistical overview: Annual report 2013*. Ottawa, ON: Public Safety Canada.

Pyne, S. 2001. *Fire: A brief history*. Seattle: University of Washington Press.

Raboy, Marc. 1990. *Missed opportunities. The story of Canadian broadcast policy*. Montreal and Kingston: McGill-Queen's Press.

Rae, Heather. 2002. *State identities and the homogenisation of peoples*. Cambridge, UK: Cambridge University Press.

Raffles, H. 2002. "The dreamlife of ecology: South Pará, 1999." In *Amazonia: A natural history* (pp. 150–79). Princeton: Princeton University Press.

Rahman, Momin. 2014. "Queer rights and the triangulation of Western exceptionalism." *Journal of Human Rights* 13: 274–89.

Ramp W., and T. Harrison. 2012. "Libertarian populism, neoliberal rationality, and the mandatory long-form census: Implications for sociology." *Canadian Journal of Sociology* 37 (3): 273–94.

Ramsay, Richard, and Pierre Tremblay. 2005. "Bisexual, gay, queer male suicidality." University of Calgary. Retrieved from http://www.fsw.ucalgary.ca/ramsay/homosexualitysuicide.

Raphael, D. 2009. *Social determinants of health: Canadian perspectives* (2nd ed.). Toronto: Canadian Scholars' Press.

Raphael, D. 2011. "Poverty in childhood and adverse health outcomes in adulthood." *Maturitas* 69: 22–6.

Ratner, R. S. 2006. "Pioneering Critical Criminology in Canada." *Journal of Criminology and Criminal Justice*, 48 (5): 647–62.

Ray, Regan. 2008. "CBC-commissioned report says public broadcaster's election coverage 'fair and balanced.'" 23 October. Retrieved from http://j-source.ca/article/cbc-commisioned-report-says-public-broadcasters-election-coverage-fair-and-balanced

RCMP (Royal Canadian Mounted Police). 2014 (May). "Missing and murdered Aboriginal women: A national operational overview." Retrieved from http://www.rcmp-grc.gc.ca/pubs/mmaw-faapd-eng.htm

Reading, C., and F. Wien. 2009. *Health inequalities and the social determinants of Aboriginal peoples' health*. Prince George, BC: National Collaborating Centre for Aboriginal Health.

Readings, Bill. 1997. *The University in Ruins*. Cambridge: Harvard University Press. Reiman, J. 1979. *The rich get richer and the poor get prison: Ideology, class and criminal justice*. New York: John Wiley and Sons.

Reiner, Robert. 1993. *The politics of the police.* Oxford: Oxford University Press.

Reitsma-Street, M. 1999. "Justice for Canadian girls: A 1990s update." *Canadian Journal of Criminology* 41 (3): 335–58.

Rich, Adrienne. 1989. "Compulsory heterosexuality and lesbian existence." In L. Richardson and V. Taylor (Eds), *Feminist frontiers II.* New York: Random House.

Richie, B. 1996. *Compelled to crime: The gender entrapment of battered black women.* New York: Routledge.

Richie, B. 2001. "Challenges incarcerated women face as they return to their communities: Findings from life history interviews." *Crime and Delinquency* 47, 368–89.

Richie B., and C. Johnsen. 1996. "Abuse histories among newly incarcerated women in a New York City jail." *Journal of the American Medical Women's Association* 51 (3): 111–14.

Ridout, Vanda. 2003. *The continentalization of Canadian telecommunications: The politics of regulatory reform.* Montreal and Kingston: McGill-Queen's University Press.

Ringrose, Jessica. 2008. "'Every time she bends over, she pulls up her thong': Teen girls negotiating discourses of competitive, heterosexualized aggression." *Girlhood Studies: An Interdisciplinary Journal* 1 (1): 33–59.

Rissmiller, D.J., and J.H. Rissmiller. 2006. "Evolution of the anti-psychiatry movement into mental health consumerism." *Psychiatric Services* 57: 863–66.

Roberts, Dorothy. 2005. "Feminism, race and adoption policy." In S. Haslanger and Charlotte Witt (Eds), *Adoption matters: Philosophical and feminist essays* (pp. 234–56). Ithaca, NY: Cornell University Press.

Roberts, J., and R. Melchers. 2003. "The incarceration of Aboriginal offenders." *Canadian Journal of Criminology* 45 (2): 170–89.

Robertson, Roland. 1990. "After nostalgia? Willful nostalgia and the phases of globalization." In Bryan S. Turner (Ed.), *Theories of modernity and postmodernity.* London: Sage.

Rodriguez, S.F., T.R. Curry, and G. Lee. 2006. "Gender differences in criminal sentencing: Do effects vary across violent, property, and drug offences?" *Social Science Quarterly* 87 (2): 318–39.

Roediger, D. 1991. *Wages of whiteness: Race and the making of the American working class.* New York: Verso.

Rogers, A., and D. Pilgrim. 2010. *A sociology of mental health and illness* (4th ed.). Buckingham, UK: Open University Press.

Rose, N. 1991. "Governing by numbers: Figuring out democracy." *Accounting, Organizations and Society,* 16 (7): 673–92.

Rose, N. 1996. "The Death of the Social— Re-Figuring the Territory of Government." *Economy & Society* 25 (3): 327–56.

Rose, Tricia. 1994. *Black noise: Rap music and black culture in contemporary America.* Middletown, CT: Wesleyan University Press.

Roseneil, Sasha, and Shelley Budgeon. 2004. "Cultures of intimacy and care beyond 'the family': Personal life and social change in the early 21st century." *Current Sociology* 52 (2): 135–59.

Rosenhan, D.L. 1973. "On being sane in insane places." *Science* 179 (4070): 250–8.

Rosenthal, Robert, and Lenore Jacobson. 1968. *Pygmalion in the classroom.* New York: Holt, Rinehart and Winston.

Rousseau, Jean-Jacques. 1983 [1762]. *The social contract and discourses.* London: J.M. Dent and Sons.

Royal Commission on Aboriginal Peoples. 1993. *Aboriginal peoples and the justice system.* Ottawa: Minister of Supply and Services.

Royal Commission on Aboriginal Peoples. 1996. *Bridging the cultural divide: A report on Aboriginal peoples and criminal justice in Canada.* Ottawa: Minister of Supply and Services.

Rozanova, Julia, Herbert C. Northcott, and Susan A. McDaniel. 2006. "Seniors and portrayals of intra-generational and inter-generational inequality in the *Globe and Mail.*" *Canadian Journal on Aging* 25 (4): 373–86.

Rubin, Beth A., and Charles J. Brody. 2005. "Contradictions of commitment in the new economy: Insecurity, time, and technology." *Social Science Research* 34: 843–61.

Rubin, Gayle. 1975. "The traffic in women." In R. Reiter (Ed.), *Toward an anthropology of women.* New York: Monthly Review.

Rusnock, A. 2002. *Vital accounts.* Cambridge, UK: Cambridge University Press.

Russell, D. 1995. *Women, madness & medicine.* Cambridge, UK: Polity Press.

Saccoccio, Sabrina. 2007. "Revenge of the only children." *CBC News in Depth,* 3 July.

Retrieved from http://www.cbc.ca/news/background/family/only-children.html

Saetnan, A.R., H.M. Lomell, and S. Hammer. 2011. *The mutual construction of statistics and society*. New York: Routledge.

Saint-Martin, Denis. 2007. "From the welfare state to the social investment state: A new paradigm for Canadian social policy?" In Michael Orsini and Miriam Smith (Eds), *Critical Policy Studies* (pp. 279–98). Vancouver: University of British Columbia Press.

Saint-Simon, Henri de. 1814. "The reorganization of Europe." In F.M.H. Markham (Ed.), *Henri Comte de Saint-Simon: Selected writings*. Oxford: Basil Blackwell.

Salazar Parreñas, Rhacel. 2005. *Children of global migration: Transnational families and gendered woes*. Palo Alto, CA: Stanford University Press.

Salazar Parreñas, Rhacel. 2008. *The force of domesticity: Filipina migrants and globalization*. New York: New York University Press.

Sandberg, Linn. 2011. *Getting intimate: A feminist analysis of old age, masculinity and sexuality*. Linkoping: Sweden: Linkoping University.

Sapolsky, R.M. 2004. *Why zebras don't get ulcers* (3rd ed.). New York: Holt Paperbacks.

Sartre, Jean-Paul. 1964 [1938]. *Nausea*. (L. Alexander, trans.). New York: Penguin.

Sartre, Jean-Paul. 1970. "An existentialist's view of freedom." In R. Dewey and J. Gould (Eds), *Freedom, its history, nature and varieties*. London: Macmillan.

Satz, Debra. 2007. "Remaking families: A review essay." *Signs* 32 (2): 523–38.

Savage, S., and S. Charman. 1996. "Managing change." In F. Leishman, B. Loveday, and S. Savage (Eds), *Core issues in policing*. London: Longman.

Savage, M., and R. Burrows. 2007. "The Coming Crisis of Empirical Sociology." *Sociology* 41 (5): 885–99.

Sawchuk, K. 2014. "Beyond the F-word: A constellation of feminist concepts for media researchers." In L. Shade (Ed.), *Mediascapes: New patterns in Canadian communication*. Toronto: Nelson Education Ltd.

Schneck, Stephen Frederick. 1987. "Michel Foucault on Power/Discourse, Theory and Practice." *Human Studies* 10 (1): 15–33.

Schudson, Michael. 1991. "The sociology of news production revisited." In James Curran and Michael Gurevitch (Eds), *Mass media and society* (pp. 141–59). London: Arnold.

Schutz, Alfred. 1962. *Collected papers, volume 1*. The Hague: Martinus Nijhoff.

Scott, Wilbur, and Sandra Stanley. 1994. *Gays and lesbians in the military*. Hawthorne, NY: Aldine de Gruyter.

Sealy, P., and P.C. Whitehead. 2004. "Forty years of deinstitutionalization of psychiatric services in Canada: An empirical assessment." *Canadian Journal of Psychiatry* 49 (4): 249–57.

Sedgwick, Eve. 1990. *Epistemology of the closet*. Berkeley: University of California.

Seeman, Melvin. 1959. "On the meaning of alienation." *American Sociological Review* 24 (6): 783–91.

Segre, Sandro. 2012. *Talcott Parsons: An Introduction*. Lanham, MD: UPA.

Seidman, Steven. 1991. "Postmodern anxiety: The politics of epistemology." *Sociological Theory* 9 (2): 180–90.

Seidman, Steven. 2013. *Contested knowledge: Social theory today* (5th ed.). Chichester: John Wiley & Sons.

Seltzer, Richard. 1992. "The social location of those holding antihomosexual attitudes." *Sex Roles* 26 (9/10): 391–8.

Sennett, Richard. 1992. *The fall of public man*. New York: Norton.

Service Canada. 2014. "Sectoral outlook, Nova Scotia." Her Majesty the Queen in Right of Canada as represented by Employment and Social Development. Retrieved from http://www.esdc.gc.ca/.../sectoral-outlooks/2013–15/ns-winter2014.pdf

Settersten Jr., Richard A., and Barbara E. Ray. 2010. *Not quite adults*. New York: Bantam Books.

Shade, L., and M. Lithgow. 2014. "Media ownership, public participation, and democracy in the Canadian mediascape." In Leslie Regan Shade (Ed.), *Mediascapes: New patterns in Canadian communication*. Toronto: Nelson Education Ltd.

Shanahan, Suzanne. 2007. "Lost and found: The sociological ambivalence toward childhood." *Annual Review of Sociology* 33: 407–28.

Shankardass, R.D. 2001. "Where the mind is without fear and the head is held high: Mental health and care of women and children in prison." In *Andhra Pradesh—A thematic review. Report of the PRAJA Project "Mental Health and Care of Women and Children in Prisons in Andhra Pradesh, 2000-2001."* Hyderabad, India: Andhra Pradesh: Penal Reform and Justice Association (PRAJA), Penal Reform International (PRI) and Andhra Pradesh Prisons Department.

Shannon, C., and W. Weaver. 1949. *The mathematical theory of communication.* Urbana, IL: University of Illinois Press.

Shapin, S. 2010. *Never pure: Historical studies of science as if it was produced by people with bodies, situated in time, space, culture, and society, and struggling for credibility and authority.* Baltimore: The Johns Hopkins University Press.

Sharp, F. 2014. *Mean lives.* New York: Rutgers University Press.

Sharrock, W., and B. Anderson. 1986. *The ethnomethodologists.* London: Tavistock.

Shaw, A. 2009. "Putting the gay in games: Cultural production and GLBT content in video game." *Games and Culture* 4 (3): 228–53.

Shaw, M., and S. Hargreaves. 1994. *Ontario women in conflict with the law: A survey of women in institutions and under community supervision in Ontario.* Toronto: Ministry of the Solicitor General and Correctional Services.

Shearing, C., and Jennifer Wood. 2003. "Nodal governance, democracy and new denizens." *Journal of Law and Society* 30 (3): 400–19.

Shearing, C., and P. Stenning. 1982. *Private security and private justice: The challenge of the eighties.* Montreal: Institute for Research on Public Policy.

Shiva, V. 1988. *Staying alive: Women, ecology and development.* London: Zed Books.

Siltanen, Janet, and Andrea Doucet. 2008. *Gender relations in Canada: Intersectionality and beyond.* Toronto: Oxford University Press.

Simmel, Georg. 1990 [1900]. *The philosophy of money.* David Frisby (Ed.). (Tom Bottomore and David Frisby, trans.). London and New York: Routledge.

Simpson, Audra, and Andrea Smith, eds. 2014. *Theorizing Native Studies.* Durham: Duke University Press.

Simpson, Mark. 1994. *Male impersonators.* London: Cassell.

Simpson, S., J.L. Yahner, and L. Dugan. 2008. "Understanding women's pathways to jail: Analysing the lives of incarcerated women." *The Australian and New Zealand Journal of Criminology* 41 (1): 84–108.

Sinha, M. 2013. "Portrait of caregivers, 2012. Spotlight on Canadians: Results from the General Social Survey." Catalogue no. 89–652-X.

Slack, J. 2012. "Beyond transmission, modes, and media." In J. Packer and S. Wiley (Eds), *Communication matters: Materialist approaches to media, mobility, and networks.* London and New York: Routledge.

Smart, B. 1985. *Michel Foucault.* London: Tavistock.

Smart, Carol. 1976. *Women, crime and criminology.* London: Routledge and Kegan Paul.

Smart, Carol. 1989. *Feminism and the power of law.* London: Routledge.

Smart, Carol, and Bren Neale. 1999. *Family fragments.* Cambridge, UK: Polity Press.

Smith, Adam. 2010 [1759]. *The theory of moral sentiments.* London: Penguin

Smith, Andrea. 2005. *Conquest: Sexual violence and American Indian genocide.* Cambridge, MA: South End Press.

Smith, D. 1974a. "The ideological practice of sociology." *Catalyst* 2: 39–54.

Smith, D. 1974b. "The social construction of documentary reality." *Sociological Inquiry* 44 (4): 257–68.

Smith, D. 1975. "The statistics on mental illness: What they will not tell us about women and why." In D. Smith and S. David (Eds), *Women look at psychiatry* (pp. 73–119). Vancouver: Press Gang Publishers.

Smith, D. 1978. "'K is mentally ill': The anatomy of a factual account." *Sociology* 12 (1): 25–53.

Smith, D. 1987. *The everyday world as problematic: A feminist sociology.* Toronto: University of Toronto Press.

Smith, D. 1990a. "The statistics on women and mental illness: The relations of ruling they conceal." In *The conceptual practices of power* (pp. 107–38). Toronto: University of Toronto Press.

Smith, D. 1990b. "No one commits suicide: Textual analyses of ideological practices." In *The Conceptual Practices of Power* (pp. 140–73). Toronto: University of Toronto Press.

Smith, D. 1992. "Sociology from women's experience: A reaffirmation." *Sociological Theory* 10: 88–98.

Smith, D. 1999. *Writing the social: Critique, theory and investigations*. Toronto: University of Toronto Press.

Smith, Dorothy E. 1991. *The Conceptual Practices of Power: A Feminist Sociology of Knowledge*. Boston: Northeastern University Press.

Smith, Dorothy E. 2005. *Institutional Ethnography: A Sociology for People*. 1 edition. Walnut Creek, CA: AltaMira Press.

Snider, L. 2003. "Constituting the punishable woman: Atavistic man incarcerates postmodern woman." *British Journal of Sociology* 43 (2): 354–78.

Snider, L. 2004. "Female punishment: From punishment to backlash." In C. Sumner (Ed.), *The Blackwell companion to criminology*. Malden, MA: Blackwell.

Snow, D.A., S.G. Baker, A. Leon, and M. Martin. 1986. "The myth of pervasive mental illness among the homeless." *Social Problems* 33 (5): 407–23.

Sokoloff, Natalie. 2005. "Women prisoners at the dawn of the 21st century." *Women and Criminal Justice* 16 (1–2): 127–37.

Sokolovsky, Jay (Ed.). 2009. *The cultural context of aging: Worldwide perspectives* (3rd ed.). Westport, CT: Praeger.

Soroka, Stuart. 2007. *Canadian perceptions of the health care system: A report to the health council of Canada*. Toronto: Health Council of Canada.

Sorokin, Pitirim A. 1950. *Altruistic love: A study of American "good neighbors" and Christian saints*. Boston: Beacon Press.

Spencer, Emily. 2006. "Lipstick and high heels: War and the feminization of women in *Chatelaine* magazine, 1928–1956." PhD dissertation, Royal Military College of Canada, Kingston, Ontario.

Spohn, C. 1999. "Gender and sentencing of drug offenders: Is chivalry dead?" *Criminal Justice Policy Review* 9: 365–99.

Stacey, Judith. 1996. *In the name of the family: Rethinking family values in the postmodern age*. Boston: Beacon Press.

Stacey, Judith. 2004. "Cruising to familyland: Gay hypergamy and rainbow kinship." *Current Sociology* 52: 181–97.

Standing, G. 2008. "How cash transfers promote the case for basic income." *Basic Income Studies* 3 (1).

Starr, Paul. 2004. *The creation of the media. Political origins of modern communication*. New York: Basic Books.

Statistics Canada. 2000. *Youth in custody and community services in Canada, 1998–9*. Ottawa: Centre for Justice Statistics.

Statistics Canada. 2006a. "Average hourly wages of employees by selected characteristics and profession, unadjusted data, by province." *Labour force survey, April 2005*. Retrieved from http://www40.statcan.ca/101/cst01/labour69a.htm

Statistics Canada. 2006b. *Violence against Aboriginal women: Statistical trends*. Ottawa: Statistics Canada.

Statistics Canada. 2007. *Quarterly demographic estimates: January to March 2007, preliminary*. Ottawa: Statistics Canada.

Statistics Canada. 2008a. *Canadian demographics at a glance*. Catalogue no. 91–003–X. Ottawa: Ministry of Industry. Retrieved from http://www.statscan.gc.ca/

Statistics Canada. 2008b. "Census snapshot—Immigration in Canada: A portrait of the foreign-born population, 2006 census." *Canadian Social Trends* (April).

Statistics Canada. 2009. "Employment insurance coverage survey." *The Daily*. June 2009.

Statistics Canada. 2010. *Aboriginal statistics at a glance*. Ottawa: Statistics Canada. Retrieved from: www5.statcan.gc.ca/olc-cel/olc.action?ObjId=89–645–X&ObjType=2&lang=en&limit=0:

Statistics Canada. 2011a. *Aboriginal peoples in Canada: First Nations people, Métis and Inuit*. Catalogue no. 99–011–X2011001.

Statistics Canada. 2011b. *Life expectancy at birth, by sex and by province*. Ottawa: Statistics Canada.

Statistics Canada. 2012a. *Portrait of families and living arrangements in Canada: 2011 Census of population families, households and marital status*. Catalogue no. 98–312–X2011001. Ottawa: Statistics Canada.

Statistics Canada. 2012b. *Immigration and ethnocultural diversity in Canada*. Catalogue no. 99–010–X2011001. Ottawa: Statistics Canada.

Statistics Canada. 2013a. *Education in Canada: Attainment, field of study and location of study.* Catalogue no. 99–012–X2011001. Ottawa: Statistics Canada.

Statistics Canada. 2013b. *Immigration and ethnocultural diversity in Canada.* Catalogue no. 99–010–X2011001. Ottawa: Statistics Canada.

Statistics Canada. 2013c. "2011 National Household Survey: Immigration, place of birth, citizenship, ethnic origin, visible minorities, language and religion." *The Daily.* Ottawa: Statistics Canada. Retrieved from http://www.statcan.gc.ca/daily-quotidien/130508/dq130508b-eng.htm

Statistics Canada. 2014. "Population projections: Canada, the provinces and territories, 2013 to 2063." *The Daily.* Ottawa: Statistics Canada. Retrieved from http://www.statcan.gc.ca/daily-quotidien/140917/dq140917a-eng.htm

Statistics Canada. 2015. "Labour force characteristics, seasonally adjusted, by province (monthly) (Newfoundland and Labrador, Prince Edward Island, Nova Scotia, New Brunswick), population 15 and over." CANSIM, table 282–0087 and Catalogue no. 71–001–XIE.

Steeves, Valerie. 2014. *Young Canadians in a wired world, phase III: Encountering racist and sexist content online.* Ottawa: MediaSmarts.

Steffensmeier, D., and E. Allan. 1998. "The nature of female offending: Patterns and explanations." In R.T. Zaplin (Ed.), *The female offender: Critical perspectives and effective treatment intervention* (pp. 5–29). Gaithersburg, MD: Aspen Publishers.

Stenfert Kroese, B., and G. Holmes. 2001. "'I've never said "no" to anything in my life': Helping people with learning disabilities who experience psychological problems." In C. Newnes, G. Holmes, and C. Dunn (Eds), *This is madness too: Critical perspectives on mental health services* (pp. 71–80). Ross-on-Wye: PCCS Books.

Stenning, Philip. 2009. "Governance and accountability in a plural policing environment—The story so far." *Policing* 8 February.

Sterne, J. 2005. "C. Wright Mills, the Bureau for Applied Social Research, and the meaning of critical scholarship." *Cultural Studies ↔ Critical Methodologies* 5 (1): 65–94.

Stinchcombe, Arthur L. 1994. "Disintegrated Disciplines and the Future of Sociology." *Sociological Forum* 9 (2): 279.

Stoddart, M., and H. Ramos, H. 2015. "Communications breakdown: To move the masses, speak boldly and carry a big schtick." *Alternatives Journal* 41 (1): 71–2.

Straubhaar, J., and R. LaRose. 2000. *Media now: Communications media in the information age.* Belmont, CA: Wadsworth.

Strohschein, Lisa. 2007. "Challenging the presumption of diminished capacity to parent: Does divorce really change parenting practices?" *Family Relations* 56: 358–68.

Stroman, D.F. 2003. *The disability rights movement: From deinstitutionalization to self-determination.* Lanham: University Press of America.

Stubbs, Julie. 2015. "Downsizing prisons in an age of austerity? Justice reinvestment and women's imprisonment." *Oñati Socio-Legal Series* 6 (1), 2016. Retrieved from SSRN: http://ssrn.com/abstract=2636756

Stychin, Carl. 1998. *A nation by rights.* Philadelphia: Temple University Press.

Sudnow, D. 1967. *Passing on: The social organization of dying.* Englewood Cliffs, NJ: Prentice Hall.

Sydie, R.A. 1987. *Natural Women, Cultured Men: Feminist Perspective on Sociological Theory.* New York: New York University Press.

Sydie, R.A. 2005. "Response to Neil McLaughlin's 'Canada's Impossible Science: Historical and Institutional Origins of the Coming Crisis in Anglo-Canadian Sociology,' Canadian Journal of Sociology, 30(1), 2005, Pp. 1–40." *The Canadian Journal of Sociology,* no. 4: 533.

Szasz, T. 1989. *Law, liberty, and psychiatry: An inquiry into the social uses of mental health practices.* Syracuse, NY: Syracuse University Press.

Szreter, S. 1988. "The importance of social intervention in Britain's mortality decline c.1850–1914: A re-interpretation of the role of public health." *Social History of Medicine* 1 (1): 1.

Tanner, J. 1996. *Teenage troubles: Youth and deviance in Canada.* Scarborough, ON: Nelson.

Taras, David. 2001. *Power and betrayal in the Canadian media.* Peterborough: Broadview Press.

Taylor, Catherine, and Tracey Peter. 2011. "We are not aliens, we're people, and we have rights." *Canadian Review of Sociology* 48 (2): in press.

Teeter, Brad. 2005. "Court slams BC bullying." *Xtra!* 534: 22.

Tew, J. 2005. "Core themes of social perspectives." In J. Tew (Ed.), *Social perspectives in mental health: Developing social models to understand and work with mental distress* (pp. 13–31). London: Jessica Kingsley Publishers.

Theckedath, Dillan, and Terrence J. Thomas. 2012. *Media ownership and convergence in Canada.* Ottawa: Library of Parliament.

Theriault, Joseph-Yvon. 2002. *Critique de l'américanité.* Montréal: Éditions Québec-Amérique.

Thiessen, V., and J. Blasius. 2002. "The social distribution of youth's images to work." *Canadian Review of Sociology and Anthropology* 39, 1: 49–78.

Thompson, Kenneth, ed. 1976. *Auguste Comte: The Foundation of Sociology.* London: Thomas Nelson & Sons Ltd.

Throsby, Karen, and Rosalind Gill. 2004. "'It's different for men': Masculinity and in vitro fertilization (IVF)." *Men and Masculinities* 6 (4): 330–48.

Tipper, Jenni, and Roger Sauvé. 2010. "The risks and realities of recovery." *Transition* 40 (1): 1–6.

Torjman, Sherri. 2015. "Cut the tax cut." Caledon Commentary, Caledon Institute of Social Policy. Retrieved from http://www.caledoninst.org/Publications/PDF/1060ENG.pdf

Trafzer, C., W. Gilbert, and A. Madrigal. 2008. "Integrating native science into a tribal Environmental Protection Agency (EPA)." *American Behavioral Scientist* 51 (12): 1844–66.

Treasury Board of Canada (TBC). 2012. *Secretariat Correctional Service Canada, report on plans and priorities, 2010–2011.* Retrieved from http://www.tbs-sct.gc.ca/rpp/2011-2012/inst/pen/pen-eng.pdf

Trend, David. 2007. *The myth of media violence. A critical introduction.* Oxford: Blackwell.

Tuchman, Gay. 1980. *Making news: A study in the construction of reality.* New York: Free Press.

Tulle, Emmanuelle. 2008. *Ageing, the body and social change.* London: Palgrave Macmillan.

Turcotte, Martin. 2006. "Parents with adult children living at home." *Canadian Social Trends* 80 (Spring): 2–10.

Turcotte, Martin. 2013. "Family caregiving: What are the consequences?" Retrieved from http://www.statcan.gc.ca/pub/75-006-x/2013001/article/11858-eng.pdf

Turner, Bryan S. 1990. "Periodization and politics in the postmodern." In Bryan S. Turner (Ed.), *Theories of modernity and postmodernity.* London: Sage.

Turner, Bryan S. 2009. *Can we live forever? A sociological and moral inquiry.* London: Anthem Press.

Turner, R. 1974. "Words, utterances and activities." In R. Turner (Ed.), *Ethnomethodology* (pp. 197–215). Harmondsworth, UK: Penguin.

Twigg, Julia. 2013. *Fashion and age: Dress, the body and later life.* London: Bloomsbury Academic.

Uleman, J. 2010. *An introduction to Kant's moral philosophy.* Cambridge: Cambridge University Press.

UNESCO. 2015 (25 October). "Sustainable development goal for education cannot advance without more teachers." *UIS fact sheet, No. 33.* UNESCO Institute for Statistics. Retrieved from http://unesdoc.unesco.org/images/0023/002347/234710e.pdf

United Nations (UN). 2008. *Draft United Nations rules for the treatment of women prisoners and non-custodial measures for women offenders.* Vienna, Austria: Commission on Crime Prevention and Criminal Justice, Eighteenth Session. Retrieved from http://zh.unrol.org/files/ECN152009_CRP8.pdf

United Nations (UN). 2014. "Handbook on women and imprisonment: 2nd edition, with reference to the United Nations rules for the treatment of women prisoners and non-custodial measures for women offenders (The Bangkok Rules)". In *Criminal justice handbook series.* New York: UN.

Usher, Alex. 2015. "The Canada apprentice loan: Adventures in federalism." *Higher Education Strategy Associates Blog.* 9 January. Retrieved from http://higheredstrategy.com/blog/

Ussher, J.M. 1991. *Women's madness: Misogyny or mental illness?* New York: Harvester Wheatsheaf.

Valverde, M. 1991. *The age of light, soap, and water: Moral reform in English Canada, 1885–1925.* Toronto: McClelland & Stewart.

Valverde, M. 1999. "Democracy in governance: Socio-legal framework." Report for the Law Commission of Canada. Toronto: University of Toronto.

van Loon. 2008. *Media technology: Critical perspectives*. New York: Open University Press.

van Wormer, K., and L. Kaplan. 2006. "Results of a national survey of wardens in women's prisons: The case for gender-specific treatment." *Women & Therapy* 29 (1/2): 133–51.

Vanier Institute of the Family. 2010a. "Two incomes the norm... and the necessity." *Fascinating Families* 25 (February). Retrieved from http://www.vifamily.ca/sites/default/files/ff25.pdf

Vanier Institute of the Family. 2010b. "Children growing up in stepfamilies." *Fascinating Families* 31 (October). Retrieved from http://www.vifamily.ca/media/node/513/attachments/stepfamilies.pdf

Vanier Institute of the Family. 2010c. "Families count IV: Family diversity." *Transition* 40 (2): 5–14.

Vanier Institute of the Family. 2010d. "Families count IV: Family economic security and caring." *Transition* 40 (3): 4–11.

Vanier Institute of the Family. 2010e. "Families working shift." *Fascinating Families* 26 (March). Retrieved from http://www.vifamily.ca/media/node/79/attachments/ff26.pdf

Vanier Institute of the Family. 2011. "Changing families, new understandings." *Contemporary Family Trends* (June): 1–46. Retrieved from http://www.vanierinstitute.ca/include/get.php?nodeid=164

Vanier Institute of the Family. 2013. "In it together: Multigenerational living in Canada." *Transition* 43 (3): 11–13.

Venne, Michel. 2001. *Vive Quebec! New thinking and new approaches to the Quebec nation*. Toronto: James Lorimer & Company.

Vicinus, Martha. 1992. "They wonder to which sex I belong." *Feminist Studies* 18 (3): 467–97.

Vincent, Richard, and L. McKeown. 2008. "Trends in the telephone call centre industry." Catalogue No. 63F0002–XIE. Ottawa: Statistics Canada.

Vipond, Mary. 1992. *Mass media in Canada* (Revised ed.). Toronto: James Lorimer & Company.

Wacquant, L. 1999. "Urban marginality in the coming millennium." *Urban Studies* 36 (10): 1639–47.

Wacquant, L. 2001. "Deadly symbiosis: When ghetto and prison mesh." *Punishment and Society* 3 (1): 95–134.

Wainright, Steven, and Bryan S. Turner. 2003. "Aging and the dancing body." In Christopher A. Faircloth (Ed.), *Aging bodies: Images and everyday experience* (pp. 259–92). Walnut Creek, CA: Altamira Press.

Wainright, Steven, and Bryan S. Turner. 2006. "'Just crumbling to bits'? An exploration of the body, ageing, injury and career in classical ballet dancers." *Sociology*, 40 (2): 237–55.

Walker, J. 2003. "Radiating messages: An international perspective." *Family Relations* 52: 406–17.

Walker J. 2008. "Family life in the twenty-first century: The implications for parenting policy in the UK." *Journal of Children's Services* 3 (4): 17–29.

Wallace, Paul A.W. 1990. *White roots of peace: Iroquois book of life*. Clear Light Publishing.

Walmsley, R. 2006. *World female imprisonment list*. London: King's College, International Centre for Prison Studies.

Waters, Johanna L. 2002. "Flexible families? Astronaut households and the experiences of mothers in Vancouver, British Columbia." *Social and Cultural Geography* 3: 117–34.

Watts, Vanessa. 2006. Thesis: *Towards Anishnaabe governance and accountability: Reawakening our relationships and sacred bimaadiziwin*. Victoria, BC: University of Victoria.

Weber, Max. 1904–5. *The Protestant ethic and the spirit of capitalism*. (Talcott Parsons, trans.). New York: Charles Scribner's Sons.

Weber, Max (Ed.). 1947. *The theory of social and economic organization*. New York: Free Press.

Weber, Max. 1948. *From Max Weber: Essays in sociology*. H. Gerth and C. Wright Mills (Eds). London: Routledge and Kegan Paul.

Weber, Max. 1980. *Basic concepts in sociology*. New York: Citadel.

Weber, Max. 1991. From *Max Weber: Essays in sociology*. London: Routledge.

Webster, Edward. 2004. "Sociology in South Africa: Its Past, Present and Future." *Society in Transition* 35 (1): 27–41.

Weedon, Chris. 1996. *Feminist practice and poststructuralist theory* (2nd ed.). Cambridge, MA: Wiley-Blackwell.

Weeks, Jeffrey, Brian Heathy, and Catherine Donovan. 2001. *Same sex intimacies.* London: Routledge.

Weissman, Aerlyn. 2002. *Little sisters vs. big brother.* Video.

Whitaker, R. 2010. *Anatomy of an epidemic: Magic bullets, psychiatric drugs and the astonishing rise of mental illness.* New York: Broadway Paperbacks.

White, Emily. 2002. *Fast girls: Teenage tribes and the myth of slut.* New York: Scribner.

Webster, Edward. 2004. "Sociology in South Africa: Its Past, Present and Future." *Society in Transition* 35 (1): 27–41.

Wiegers, Wanda. 2007. "Child-centred advocacy and the invisibility of women in poverty discourse and social policy." In Dorothy Chunn, Susan Boyd, and Hester Lessard (Eds), *Reaction and resistance: Feminism, law, and social change* (pp. 229–61). Vancouver: University of British Columbia Press.

Wiggershaus, R., and M. Robertson. 1995. *The Frankfurt School: Its history, theories, and political significance.* Cambridge, Mass: MIT Press.

Wilkinson, Cai. 2014. "Putting 'traditional values' into practice." *Journal of Human Rights* 13: 363–79.

Wilkinson, L., J. Bucklaschuk, Y. Shen, I.A. Chowdhury, P. Bhattacharyya, and T. Edkins. 2015, Forthcoming. *What do we know about the settlement experiences of immigrants to Canada's west?* Final Report Submitted to Citizenship and Immigration Canada. Ottawa: Citizenship and Immigration Canada, Research and Evaluation Branch.

Wilkinson, R., and M.E. Marmot. 2003. *The social determinants of health: The solid facts* (2nd ed.). Copenhagen: World Health Organization.

Wilkinson, R., and K. Pickett. 2009. *The spirit level: Why more equal societies almost always do better.* London: Penguin Books.

Wilson, S. 1996. "Consumer empowerment in the mental health field." *Canadian Journal of Community Mental Health* 15 (2): 69–85.

Winseck, D. 2008. "The state of media ownership and media markets: Competition or concentration and why should we care?" *Sociology Compass* 2 (1): 34–47.

Winseck, Dwayne. 2015. "David wins against Goliath: CRTC bolsters 'net neutrality,' limits 'zero-rating' and strengthens local TV." *Mediamorphis Blog.* Retrieved from https://dwmw.wordpress.com/2015/01/29/david-wins-against-goliath-crtc-decisions-strengthen-network-neutrality-limit-zero-rating-strengthens-local-tv/

Wister, Andrew, and Barry D. McPherson. 2014. *Aging as a social process: Canadian perspectives* (6th ed.) Don Mills, ON: Oxford University Press.

Wittgenstein, L. 1953. *Philosophical investigations.* Oxford, UK: Blackwell.

World Commission on Environment and Development. 1987. *Our common future: Report of the World Commission on Environment and Development.* Oxford: Oxford University Press.

World Health Organization Commission on the Social Determinants of Health. 2008. *Closing the gap in a generation: Health equity through action on the social determinants of health.* Geneva: World Health Organization.

Wright, E.M., P. Van Voorhis, E.J. Salisbury, and A. Bauman. 2012. "Gender-responsive lessons learned and policy implications for women in prison: A review." *Criminal Justice and Behavior* 39 (12): 1612–32.

Wrong, Dennis. 1988. *Power: Its forms, bases and uses.* Oxford, UK: Blackwell.

Wynne B. 2006. "Public engagement as a means of restoring public trust in science—Hitting the notes, but missing the music?" *Community Genetics* 9: 211–20.

Yeo, M. 2012. "The politics of science and the rights of politics: Lessons from the long-form census controversy." *Canadian Journal of Sociology* 37 (3): 295–317.

Yibarbuk, D. 1998. "Notes on traditional use of fire in Upper Codell River." In M. Langton (Ed.), *Peoples in Northern Australia.* Northern Territories, Darwin: Centre for Indigenous, Natural and Cultural Resource Management.

Youdell, Deborah. 2005. "Sex-gender-sexuality: How sex, gender and sexuality constellations are constituted in secondary schools." *Gender and Education* 17 (3), 249–70.

Young, Brigitte. 2001. "The 'mistress' and the 'maid' in the globalized economy." *Socialist Register* 37: 287–327.

Young, T., B. Revich, L. Soininen. 2015. "Suicide in circumpolar regions: An introduction and overview." *International Journal of Circumpolar Health*, 74. doi:http://dx.doi.org/10.3402/ijch.v74.27349

Zahara, A., and M.J. Hird. Forthcoming. "Inhuman colonialism: Learning how to inherit in colonized and ecologically challenged lifeworlds." Special issue of *Environmental Humanities* (forthcoming).

Zhou, M., and C.L. Bankston. 1998. *Growing up American: How Vietnamese children adapt to life in the United States.* New York: Russell Sage Foundation.

Zickuhr, Katherine. 2010. "Generations 2010." Retrieved from http://www.pewinternet.org/2010/12/16/generations-2010/

Zittrain, Jonathan. 2008. *The future of the Internet and how to stop it.* New Haven: Yale University Press.

Zucker, K.J., and R.L. Spitzer. 2005. "Was the gender identity disorder of childhood diagnosis introduced into *DSM-III* as a backdoor maneuver to replace homosexuality? A historical note." *Journal of Sex and Marital Therapy* 31 (1): 31–42.

Index